REVOLUTIONS
IN WRITING

Indiana
Masterpiece
Editions

MARK MUSA   EDITOR

REVOLUTIONS
IN WRITING

◆

READINGS IN NINETEENTH-CENTURY
FRENCH PROSE

Selected and Translated by

Rosemary Lloyd

INDIANA UNIVERSITY PRESS   BLOOMINGTON & INDIANAPOLIS

Rosemary Lloyd's translation of Stéphane Mallarmé's "Richard Wagner" was previously published in Bojan Bujic, ed., Music in European Thought, 1851–1912 (New York: Cambridge University Press, 1988) and appears here by permission of the publisher. Selections from Rosemary Lloyd, trans., Baudelaire's Short Prose Poems and La Fanfarlo (New York: Oxford University Press, 1991) have been included by permission of the publisher.

The paper used in this publication meets the minimum requirements of American National Standard for Information Sciences—Permanence of Paper for Printed Library Materials, ANSI Z39.48-1984.

Manufactured in the United States of America

Library of Congress Cataloging-in-Publication Data

Revolutions in writing : readings in nineteenth-century French prose / selected and translated by Rosemary Lloyd.
    p.   cm. — (Indiana masterpiece editions)
    ISBN 0-253-33054-8 (cloth : alk. paper). — ISBN 0-253-21069-0
        (pbk. : alk. paper)
    1 French prose literature—19th century—Translations into English.   I. Lloyd, Rosemary.   II. Series.
            PQ1113.R48   1996
        848'.70808—DC20   96-3372

        1 2 3 4 5 01 00 99 98 97 96

CONTENTS

◆ PROSE POETRY

◆ IMAGES OF CHILDHOOD

The "long" nineteenth century, running from the outbreak of the Revolution in 1789 to the beginning of the war of 1914–1918, was a time of extraordinary social change in France. A time of political rebellion, social transformation, and industrial revolution, it was also a time of rapid developments in art and literature. Romanticism's doomed, melancholy heroes and heroines gave way to the stolid, instantly recognizable figures of realism, and drifted from the wild exotic spaces of Africa and America to the dance halls, streets, and domestic interiors of impressionism. As the country moved, by fits and starts, toward democracy, and as the political and social spotlight turned from the iconic leaders to typical middle-class and working-class individuals, art and literature were also undergoing significant changes. Reading became increasingly a means not just of information, but of entertainment, enlightenment, escape, while writing became ever more manipulative, provocative, experimental. In an age marked by the most wonderful flowering of French poetry since the sixteenth century, the novel, that "lawless" genre as Gide calls it in *The Counterfeiters*, also prospered, and with it, all manner of prose writing. In this anthology, I have sought to provide a reflection of the enormous variety and vigor of the prose works of the day, guided partly by a desire to show experimentations, partly by the need to indicate the extraordinary flexibility of nineteenth-century prose, and partly—inevitably—by personal preferences.

This was an age marked by the revolutions of 1789, 1830, and 1848, by the Commune of 1870–1871, and by the Napoleonic and Franco-Prussian wars, an age that saw, partly as a direct result of those revolutions and wars, enormous changes in social and physical mobility. Travelers sought to convey their excitement and wonderment as they discovered new places, whether those travelers were well-off young men visiting Egypt or itinerant workers seeing their country's capital for the first time. Chateaubriand writes lyrically of the Mississippi, Fromentin evokes the extraordinary light and vegetation of North Africa, while Banville sings the praises of the Mediterranean.

With improvements in transport, the transformation of work through the industrial revolution, and the long series of educational reforms that marked the century, literacy became less the privilege of the rich and the church, and far more an increasingly vital necessity for all social levels. As the century progressed, the emphasis among many intellectuals gradually turned away from a concept of government by an enlightened elite toward the belief in the value of mass access to the advantages of education. Such a conviction had inevitable consequences for what was being written and published.

From 1836, the use of advertisements to cover a large percentage of production costs allowed newspapers to enjoy spectacular successes, even though censorship laws frequently threatened to hamstring them. Young writers increasingly turned to journalism as a way of earning a living from their pens, while successive governments, facing the fear of violent overthrow, attempted to stem the power of newspapers by financial and political means. Overcoming or sidestepping such laws was, inevitably, seen by many writers as a flexing of the rhetorical muscles, a game that in turn led to increasing sophistication among writers and readers alike.

Those perhaps most eager to seize on the possibilities of prose in an increasingly literate society were writers of political polemics and of popular science. Both genres profess a desire to inform which is also and perhaps primarily an urge to convince and persuade. For that reason, such writing demands a particular use of language, a manipulation of rhetorical devices that is as clearly in evidence in the monarchist Chateaubriand's virulent attack on Napoleon, as it is in Michelet's evocations of natural history, where the anthropocentric images frequently carry a puritanical political message.

As newspapers increased in number and circulation, two particular prose types, the critical review and the short story, both flourished. The desire to convey to those living in the provinces the delights of contemporary Parisian theater or ballet, or the latest developments in painting and sculpture, also posed particular challenges. For a Banville or a Mallarmé there seems to have been a special pleasure in using prose to evoke the movement and excitement of ballet and mime, while the need to convey color and texture in the days before color photography inspired the rhetorical skills of several critics who were also poets or novelists, from Baudelaire to Huysmans. Writing about art exhibitions provided the young Baudelaire, for instance, with a means of demonstrating his rhetorical prowess, sharpening skills he would later use in *The Flowers of Evil*, while the eccentric novelist Joris-Karl Huysmans combines his sinewy, idiosyncratic prose style with his extensive knowledge of art to explore the notion of pornographic art. Literary criticism, especially the kind of criticism that normally enjoys only the briefest of lives and that is called on to respond to new works and current trends, also demanded particular prose skills. There is a special art, exemplified by Baudelaire's and Sainte-Beuve's articles, in holding a newspaper reader's attention while exploring works that may be of considerable sophistication, or that may be alien to the writer's own interests and convictions—or while analyzing trends that the writer may detest.

The tradition of adding to more conventional news stories a *feuilleton*, a section devoted to reviews of artistic or social life, developed into an attempt to entice readers with fictional pieces, either serialized novels or short stories which continued through several installments: the demands imposed by such external restrictions honed and refined storytelling techniques, sometimes introducing a certain homogeneity but also leaving room for the remarkable variety of writers such as Mérimée and Maupassant. Infinitely adaptable, the short story reflects changing fashions and varying political situations. Balzac's *Girl with the Golden Eyes*, for instance, captures a society of rich and idle young men, a society on the point of disintegration as the monarchy collapsed after the 1848 revolution, but the story also reflects a fascination (shared by writers such as Baudelaire, and by a series of painters from Ingres to Courbet) with lesbian relationships. The exoticism Balzac attaches to his lesbian tale (an exoticism no doubt intended to make the main theme more acceptable to a French bourgeois audience) disappears, however, in the story Maupassant wrote some four decades later, replaced by a sense of banality typical of the general atmosphere of the naturalist school with which he was loosely associated. Similarly, while Gautier and Mérimée, writing in the days of Romanticism, appealed to current interest in exotic places and in the fantastic, Maupassant's *Ball of Lard* caught a later public's taste by exploring a France in the grip of the disastrous Franco-Prussian war.

Just as some of Maupassant's short stories exploit a prose verging on the poetic, other writers explored more directly the newly released possibilities of prose poetry. Although Aloysius Bertrand, writing in the 1830s, remains much closer to the traditional notion of poetry, and particularly of balladic forms and rhythms, later prose poets transformed the genre into something radically different. For Baudelaire, these brief, evocative pieces were ideally suited for conveying the complexity of modern urban existence, its unpredictable mingling of banalities and epiphanies, and its constantly changing mixture of linguistic registers. For Mallarmé, prose poetry shared with verse poetry the inestimable power of transforming the hackneyed and insipid nature of everyday experience. As a result, the spectator of a trivial animal show, for instance, is suddenly granted insight into profound truths of the human condition. Moved by rather different needs and convictions, Rimbaud makes his prose poetry the perfect vehicle for the *voyant*'s rapid notation of experiences, transforming them into lyrical or mystical moments by his unexpected images and rhythms.

That sense of rapid change, which many of the prose poets strive to capture in their works, also underlay other developments in prose at the time. This is the age in which the joint thrust of Romanticism's emphasis on the individual and growing notions about the development of the human psyche resulted in the proliferation of autobiographical writing, often as experimental in theme and technique as creative writing itself. Such writing was influenced not only by individual works such as Rousseau's *Confessions*, but also by the urgent desire to capture ways of life and traditions that were being lost through industrialization and the rapid changes in social life. While some writers, such as Judith Gautier, followed novelistic conventions, others (and especially Jules Vallès) attempted to convey the child's view of a chaotic, illogical society through a language rich in the onomatopoeas, puns, and verbal misunderstandings of childhood.

Throughout the century, prose writers experimented with the apparently boundless possibilities of their medium, drawing inspiration from artistic movements, historical events, musical developments, social change, travel and, of course, their own fertile imaginations. This anthology aims to offer a representative sample of at least some of those wonderfully seductive experiments.

NOTE ON THE TEXTS USED IN THIS TRANSLATION

In general, the earliest edition available was used for the basic translation, which was then checked against the most recent editions. Some minor alterations were introduced when necessary.

1789	**French Revolution**
1790–1869	Alphonse de Lamartine
1792	Abolition of the Monarchy
1793	Execution of Louis XVI
1793–1794	**Reign of Terror**
1795–1799	**Directory**
1798–1874	Jules Michelet
1799–1850	Honoré de Balzac
1799–1804	**Consulate**
1802–1885	Victor Hugo
1803–1869	Hector Berlioz
1803–1870	Prosper Mérimée
1804–1814	**First Empire** (reign of Napoleon I)
1804–1869	Charles-Auguste Sainte-Beuve
1804–1876	George Sand
1807–1841	Aloysius Bertrand
1808–1855	Gérard de Nerval
1811–1872	Théophile Gautier
1814–1830	**Restoration** (reigns of Louis XVIII and Charles X)
1817	Death of Madame de Staël
1820–1876	Eugène Fromentin
1821–1867	Charles Baudelaire
1823–1891	Théodore de Banville
1823–1892	Ernest Renan

1830–1848	**July Monarchy** (reign of Louis-Philippe)
1832–1885	Jules Vallès
1842	Death of Stendhal
1842–1898	Stéphane Mallarmé
1845–1917	Judith Gautier
1848–1852	**Second Republic**
1848	Death of René de Chateaubriand
1848–1907	Joris-Karl Huysmans
1850–1893	Guy de Maupassant
1850–1923	Pierre Loti
1852–1870	**Second Empire** (reign of Napoleon III)
1854–1891	Arthur Rimbaud
1859	Death of Marceline Desbordes-Valmore
1870–1914	**Third Republic**

PERSUASIVE PROSE

Madame de Staël

◆

Anne Louise Germaine Necker (1766–1817), who married the Swedish ambassador to Paris, Baron Staël-Holstein, in 1785, was a highly intelligent, deeply passionate, and exhaustingly energetic woman. Madame de Staël wrote innovative studies of literature, stressing the importance of its social context (see, for instance, her De la littérature considérée dans ses rapports avec les institutions sociales*). Her novels include* Delphine *and* Corinne, *both of which celebrate the creative power of woman but also lament the limitations society placed on her. Her political tracts revealed a profound scorn for Napoleon.* De l'Allemagne (On Germany), *which privileges feeling over form, imagination over reason, and northern mysticism over southern paganism, revealed to French readers the great writers of the German tradition, and was to have a profound influence on French Romanticism. Her salons, both before and after Napoleon sent her into exile (in 1803), attracted a range of brilliant thinkers and writers, including Benjamin Constant. Napoleon exiled Mme de Staël again in 1806 and then in 1810, when he ordered the pulping of* De l'Allemagne, *which had just been published. She republished it in 1813, and revised it several times.*

FURTHER READING: *Ten Years of Exile*, tr. Doris Beik (New York: Saturday Review Press, 1972); *An Extraordinary Woman*, tr. Vivian Folkerflik (New York: Columbia University Press, 1987); *Corinne*, tr. Avriel Goldberger (Rutgers, 1987).
BIOGRAPHY: Renee Winegarten, *Madame de Staël* (Leamington Spa, UK: Berg, 1985).
TEXT USED: *De l'Allemagne* (Paris: Charpentier, 1852).

ON POETRY

FROM DE L'ALLEMAGNE (1810)

That which is truly divine in the human heart is beyond definition. If we have words for some of its aspects, we have none that expresses the whole, and no words can convey the full mystery of true beauty in all the different forms of art. It is hard to say what is not poetry; but if we wish to understand what it is, we are obliged to summon to our aid the impressions aroused by beautiful countryside, harmonious music, the sight of an object we love, and above all the sacred emotion that leads us to experience within ourselves the presence of the Divinity. Poetry is the language natural to all cults. The Bible is full of poetry; Homer is full of religion. It is not that there are fictions in the Bible or dogma in Homer, but enthusiasm draws diverse emotions together in the same focus; enthusiasm is the incense that flies from earth to heaven and links the two together.

The gift of revealing in words what one feels in the depths of one's heart is rare. Nevertheless, poetry exists in all those capable of affections that are lively and deep; the gift of expressing themselves is lacking in those who are not trained to use it. All the poet does, so to speak, is set emotions free from their imprisonment deep within our souls. Poetic genius is an inner quality, identical in nature to the genius of generous self-sacrifice. Poets dream of heroism when they compose a fine ode. If talent were mobile, it would inspire fine actions as frequently as it inspires touching words, for both derive equally from the awareness of beauty that makes itself felt within us.

A man of superior intellect used to say that *prose was artificial and poetry natural*. Indeed, those nations that are not highly civilized always begin with poetry, and as soon as a strong passion moves the soul, the most commonplace men use, all unbeknownst to them, images and metaphors. They summon external nature to their aid to express the inexpressible things they are experiencing. The common people are much closer to being poets than are those of the elite, for decorum and banter are suited only to imposing boundaries, and can inspire nothing.

In this world there is an endless tussle between poetry and prose, and jesting always has to take the side of prose, for to jest is to lower oneself. The society mentality is nonetheless very favorable to a poetry of grace and gaiety, of which Ariosto, La Fontaine, Voltaire[1] are the most brilliant models. Our leading writers produce admirable dramatic poetry; descriptive poetry, and especially didactic poetry, have been brought by the French to a very high degree of perfection. But it seems that the French have not so far been summoned to distinguish themselves in lyric or epic poetry, such as the ancients, and other nations, conceive it.

Lyric poetry is expressed in the name of the author; writers no longer transform themselves into a character, but find within themselves their

---

1. Ludovico Ariosto (1474–1533), Italian poet whose fame rests on his long poem *Orlando furioso*, one of the greatest works of the Italian renaissance; Jean de La Fontaine (1621–1695), best known for his verse fables; François-Marie Arouet (1694–1778), who took the pen name Voltaire, was one of the greatest geniuses of the eighteenth century, a dramatist, philosopher, essayist, poet, novelist, scientist, historian, and polemicist. Voltaire epitomizes the Enlightenment.

different driving forces. J. B. Rousseau[2] in his religious *Odes*, Racine[3] in *Athalie*, revealed themselves to be lyric poets. They were nourished on psalms and steeped in an intense faith; nevertheless, the difficulties of the French language and of French versification almost always thwart attempts to abandon oneself to emotion. It is possible to quote admirable stanzas in a few of our odes; but is there a single one in all of those stanzas where the god has not abandoned the poet? Fine lines are not poetry; inspiration, in the arts, is an inexhaustible source that invigorates the poet from the first word to the last. Love, fatherland, faith, everything must be rendered divine in an ode, for the ode is the apotheosis of sentiment. To conceive of the true grandeur of lyric poetry, one must wander in dream through ethereal regions, forget the noise of the earth as one listens to the harmonies of the spheres, and consider the entire universe as a symbol of the soul's emotions.

The enigma of human destiny plays no great role for the majority of men; poets have it constantly in their imaginations. The idea of death, which discourages the common folk, makes the genius more audacious, the combination of nature's beauty and the terrors of destruction arouses some ineffable frenzy of happiness and dread, without which no one can understand or describe the marvels of this world. Lyric poetry tells no stories, binds itself in no way to the succession of time or the limits of place. It floats over countries and ages, it lends a certain permanence to that sublime moment in which the individual rises above the pain and pleasure of life. In the midst of the world's marvels, the individual feels at once creator and creature, mortal, yet incapable of ceasing to exist, and his heart, at once trembling and strong, takes pride in itself and throws itself at God's feet.

The Germans, who have the rare gift of bringing together imagination and contemplative meditation, are more capable than the mass of other nations of creating lyric poetry. Modern Germans cannot do without a certain profundity in their ideas. Such thinking has become a habit with them because they possess a degree of spiritualist religion. Yet if this depth were not clad in images, it would not be poetry. Nature must therefore grow in men's eyes if they are to be able to make use of it as an emblem of their thoughts. The groves, flowers, and streams were enough for the poets of paganism; the solitude of the forests, the limitless Ocean, the starry sky, can barely express the eternal and the infinite with which the Christian soul is imbued.

The Germans, just like us, have no epic poetry. That admirable genre does not seem to have been granted to modern people, and perhaps

---

2. Jean-Baptiste Rousseau (1671–1741), French lyric poet whose odes exemplify rigid French classicism at its most arid.

3. Jean Racine (1639–1699), French dramatist and tragic poet. In *Athalie*, which he wrote in 1691, a pagan queen fights the God of the Jews, defies him, then admits his power over her.

there is no work other than the *Iliad* that fully conforms to our conception of the epic. An epic poem requires a curious combination of circumstances, a combination encountered only with the Greeks, who united the imagination of heroic times with the linguistic perfection of civilized times. In the middle ages, imagination was strong, but language was imperfect; whereas now our language is pure, but we lack imagination. The Germans are very bold in their ideas and their style, but they lack invention in getting to the heart of their subject, and their attempts at epic almost always resemble lyric poetry. The attempts made by French writers belong more to drama, and offer more interest than they do grandeur. When it is necessary to please in a theater, the art of containing oneself within a given framework, of predicting the tastes of the audience and of accommodating them skillfully, plays a large part in the success of the work, whereas nothing should depend on external and fleeting circumstances when it comes to the creation of an epic poem. That demands absolute beauty, beauty that seizes a solitary reader, when his sentiments are more natural, and his imagination more intrepid. Anyone who tries to go too far in an epic poem could well encounter stern criticism from French good taste, but anyone who does not go far enough will be disdained in like measure.

Boileau,[4] while perfecting taste and language, gave the French mind—and no one would deny this—a caste that is very unfavorable to poetry. He spoke only of what should be avoided, and insisted only on the precepts of reason and wisdom, thus introducing into literature a kind of pedantry that is very harmful to the sublime impetus of the arts. We possess masterpieces of versification in French, but how can one call versification poetry! Translating into verse something that ought to have stayed in prose—using ten syllables, like Pope,[5] to express card games in all their tiny details, or, like the most recent poems that have appeared here, describing backgammon, chess, or chemistry—that is just a conjuring trick performed with words. That is merely composing with words, as a musician does with musical notes, sonatas that are given the name of poems.

Yet one needs a deep knowledge of poetic language to describe with this nobility the objects that give least scope to the imagination, and we are right to admire a few isolated fragments from these art galleries; but the links between them are perforce prosaic, being what goes through the writer's mind. He has said to himself: "I'll write some po-

---

4. Nicholas Boileau (1636–1711), French poet and critic. His *L'Art poétique* (1674), though satirical and topical in intention, came to be regarded as prescriptive and is widely considered to have been highly detrimental to the development of French verse in the following century.

5. Alexander Pope (1688–1744), English poet, best known for his masterly use of the heroic couplet in such poems as "An Essay on Criticism" and the mock epic "Rape of the Lock." The third canto of "The Rape of the Lock" describes in considerable detail the card game *ombre*, depicting the play as though it were a battle.

etry on that subject, then on another, and then on that other subject." And without realizing it, he lets us in on the secrets of his way of working. True poets conceive, so to speak, their entire poem instantly in the depths of their souls; were it not for the difficulties of language, they would improvise, like the sibyl and the prophets, holy hymns of genius. They are shaken by the images they conceive as they would be by an event in their own lives; a new world opens up to them; the sublime image of each situation, each character, each beauty of nature, strikes their gaze, and their hearts beat in a heavenly happiness that surges through the darkness of fate like a lightning bolt. Poetry is a fleeting possession of all our soul longs for; talent blots out the limits of our existence and transforms the vague hopes of mortals into brilliant images.

It would be easier to describe the symptoms of talent, than to provide any precepts for it; genius can be detected like love through the very depth of the emotion with which it penetrates the person who is granted it. But if I dared to advise a genius, I would say that nature should be the sole guide, so the advice one should give would not be purely literary in nature. One would need to talk to poets as one does to citizens or heroes; one would have to say: "Be virtuous, believe, be free, respect what you love, seek out immortality in love, and Divinity in nature; finally, make your soul as holy as you would a temple, and the angel of noble thoughts will not disdain to visit you."

Chateaubriand

◆
───────

*Vicomte François René de Chateaubriand (1768–1848) is often seen, with
Mme de Staël and Rousseau, as central to the birth of French Romanticism.
His fascination with the medieval and the gothic, his attraction to the wild
forces of nature, particularly after he visited America in 1791, and the powerful
rhetoric of his mellifluous prose all made him a focus for the symbols of Romantic melancholy, yearning, and dissatisfaction. His short novel* René *created a hero who was to see many avatars in the course of the century. His
argument in favor of Christianity,* The Genius of Christianity, *published
in 1802, led to his being appointed by Bonaparte to the embassy in Rome, a
position he relinquished on hearing of the execution of the Duc d'Enghien.
From then until the fall of Napoleon he was vocal in his opposition to the
emperor, using his persuasive rhetoric to argue his case at every opportunity.
Louis XVIII, who came to power after the collapse of the empire, described the
pamphlet translated here as having been of more aid to him than an army.
The pamphlet's powerful rhetoric depends partly on its appeal to former glories, partly on its insistence on Bonaparte as foreigner (underscored by the use
of the original form of Napoleon's name, "Buonaparte"), partly on the range
of its references, and the way in which it builds up its myth of deadening, but
ultimately defeatable, tyranny. As a political figure, Chateaubriand was more
inflammatory than successful, but when he used similar rhetorical devices in
his defense of Christianity he provided a powerful impetus to the revival of
Catholicism.*

FURTHER READING: *Memoirs*, tr. Robert Baldick (New York: Knopf, 1961), *Travels
in America*, tr. Richard Switzer (Lexington: University of Kentucky Press, 1969).
BIOGRAPHY: George D. Painter, *Chateaubriand: A Biography* (New York: Knopf,
1979).
TEXT USED: *De Buonaparte et des Bourbons* (Paris: Mame, 1814).

BUONAPARTE AND THE BOURBONS (1814)

No! I will never believe that I am writing on the tomb of France: I cannot persuade myself that after the day of vengeance we are not about to see the day of mercy. The ancient heritage of the most Christian kings cannot be divided up: the realm to which Rome gave birth as she lay dying, the realm she produced in the midst of her ruins, as a final trial of her grandeur, that realm will never die. It is not mankind alone that has guided the events we have witnessed: the hand of Providence can be seen in all this. God Himself marches openly at the head of armies and sits at the councils of kings. How can one, without recourse to divine intervention, explain both the prodigious rise and the even more prodigious fall of him who so recently trampled the world beneath his feet?[1] Only fifteen months ago he was in Moscow, and now the Russians are in Paris; all trembled under his laws, from the Pillars of Hercules[2] to the Caucasus, and now he is a fugitive, a wanderer, seeking asylum: his power surged in like the tide and has now ebbed back like the tide.

How can one explain the faults of such a madman? We are not yet talking of his crimes.

A revolution, prepared by the corruption of our morals and the errors of our intellects, has exploded in our midst. In the name of the laws, both religion and morality have been turned on their heads; the experience and customs of our fathers have been set aside; we have broken up the ancestral tombs, the sole solid base of any government, and founded on an uncertain cause a society with neither past nor future. Wandering in our own follies, having lost any clear idea of justice and injustice, good and evil, we went through the various forms of republican government. We summoned the populace to deliberate in the streets of Paris, on great matters that the Roman people used to debate in the Forum, after they had set down their arms and bathed in the waters of the Tiber. Then all those half-naked kings, grimy and brutalized by poverty, mutilated and made ugly by their labors, treating virtue with nothing but the insolence of their poverty and the pride of their rags, all these kings came out of their lairs. The country fell into hands such as these and was soon covered in wounds. What remains of our rages and our illusions? Crimes and chains!

But at least the byword that seemed to guide us in those days was *noble.* Liberty cannot be accused of the crimes committed in its name. True philosophy is not the mother of the poisoned doctrines peddled

---

1. *him who so recently:* The allusion here is to Napoleon.
2. *Pillars of Hercules:* Two promontories at the entrance to the Mediterranean Sea (at the east end of the Strait of Gibraltar).

by false wise men. Enlightened by our experiences, we at last realized that government by a monarchy was the only government that could suit our country.

It would have been natural to call on the legitimate princes, but we believed our faults too great to be pardoned. We did not realize that the heart of a son of Saint Louis[3] was a bottomless treasure of mercy. Some feared for their lives, others for their fortunes. Above all, it was too harsh a blow to human pride to admit that we had been wrong. Could all those massacres, those upheavals, those misfortunes, have succeeded merely in returning us to the point from which we set out? Passions that remained high, pretensions of all kinds, could not abandon that illusory equality, the principal cause of all our ills. Great reasons drove us on, little reasons held us back; public happiness was sacrificed to personal interest, justice to vanity.

So it was necessary to think of establishing a supreme leader who would be a child of the revolution, a leader in whom the law, polluted at its very source, protected corruption and became its ally. Magistrates of integrity, firm and courageous, captains famed for their probity as much as for their talents, had arisen in the midst of our discord, but they were not offered power that their principles would in any case have forbidden them to accept. We lost hope of finding among Frenchmen a brow that would dare to wear the crown of Louis XVI.[4] A foreigner stepped forward and was chosen.[5]

Buonaparte did not announce his intentions openly; it was only little by little that his character evolved. Under the modest title of consul, he first accustomed independent minds not to fear the power that they had bestowed. He conciliated the true French people by proclaiming himself the restorer of order, law, and religion. The wisest were caught in the trap, the most clear-sighted were blinded. The republicans considered Napoleon their own creation, and thought of him as the popular head of a free state. Royalists thought he was playing the role of a Monk,[6] and rushed to serve him. Everyone put their hopes in him. Striking victories, due to the bravery of the French, surrounded him with glory. Then success went to his head, and his tendency to evil began to reveal itself. Future generations will wonder whether that man was more guilty for the evil he committed or for the good he could have done but did not do. Never has a usurper had a role that was eas-

---

3. *Saint Louis:* Louis IX (1214–1270) was regarded as the model of a medieval Christian king. He was canonized in 1297.

4. Louis XVI (1754–1793): An economic crisis forced him to convene the Estates General and precipitated the revolution of 1789. Louis was guillotined in 1793.

5. *a foreigner:* Chateaubriand was roundly denounced for his description of the Corsican Napoleon as a foreigner.

6. George Monk (1608–1670) was an English general who, according to Chateaubriand's study of the Stuarts, ruled Scotland and who, while appearing to be a republican, worked for the return of the Stuarts.

ier to fulfill and more brilliant to perform. With a little moderation he could establish himself and all his race on the leading throne of the universe. No one was disputing his right to that throne: the generations born after the revolution did not know our former masters, and had seen nothing but trouble and tragedy. France and Europe were weary and longed only for rest. They would have bought peace at any price. But God was unwilling for so dangerous an example to be given to the world, for an adventurer to trouble the order of royal succession, make himself the heir of heroes, and profit in a single day from the spoils of genius, glory, and time. When he does not have the rights granted by birth, a usurper can legitimate his claims to the throne only by his virtue. Given that fact, Buonaparte had nothing in his favor, apart from his military talent, which was equalled if not outstripped by that of several of our generals. All Providence had to do to bring about his downfall was to abandon him and leave him to his own madness.

A French king used to say that if good faith were banished from the general run of humanity, it would have to be found again in the hearts of kings: this essential quality of a royal soul was fundamentally absent in Buonaparte. The first known victim of his tyranny was one of Normandy's royalist leaders. Monsieur de Frotté[7] had the noble imprudence to go to a meeting, which he attended on the strength of a promise; he was arrested and shot. Shortly afterwards, Toussaint L'Ouverture[8] was similarly taken through treachery from America and strangled in the European castle in which he had been imprisoned.

Soon a more famous murder caused consternation in the civilized world. People feared they were seeing a rebirth of that barbarity that marked the middle ages, those scenes that are now to be found only in novels, those catastrophes that the civil war in Italy and Machiavelli's policies had made familiar sights beyond the Alps. The foreigner who was not yet the king wanted the bloody corpse of a Frenchman to serve as his stepping-stool to the French throne. And great God, what a Frenchman! Everything was violated to commit this crime: human rights, justice, religion, humanity. The duke of Enghien[9] was arrested in peace time on foreign soil and forcibly removed from the Château d'Offemburg. At the time he left France, he was too young to know it well. It was from the seat of a mail coach, placed between two police-

7. *Frotté:* Louis, Count of Frotté (1755–1800) attempted on several occasions to inspire royalist uprisings in Normandy. Captured in February 1800, he was court-martialed and executed.

8. *Toussaint L'Ouverture:* François-Dominique Toussaint L'Ouverture (c.1753–1803) was a Haitian slave who led a slave uprising in Haiti, achieving self-government under French protection. The French forcibly retired him from the governor generalship in 1802. Subsequently arrested and imprisoned in the Jura, he died in miserable conditions.

9. *Enghien:* Louis-Antoine de Bourbon-Condé, duc d'Enghien (1772–1804) led the royalist campaign of 1792. In 1801, he abandoned his arms and took up residence at Ettenheim. Napoleon was convinced that the duke was the man most likely to foment a counter-revolution, and had him seized on March 15, 1804. Enghien was condemned and shot at the château of Vincennes.

men, that he first saw his fatherland, and it was on the way to his death that he crossed fields made famous by his ancestors. He reached the keep at Vincennes in the dead of night. In the light of torches, under the vaults of a prison, the grandson of the Great Condé[10] was declared guilty of having appeared on the field of battle: convicted of this hereditary crime he was immediately condemned. He demanded in vain to speak to Buonaparte (oh, what touching and heroic simplicity!) for this brave young man was one of his murderer's greatest admirers. He could not believe that a captain could want to assassinate a soldier. Still weak from hunger and fatigue, he was sent into the ravines around the keep and there found a freshly dug grave. He was stripped of his coat, and they hung a lantern on his breast, the better to see him in the darkness, or rather the better to aim their bullets at his heart. He attempted to give his watch to his executioners and begged them to convey his last possessions to his friends: they insulted him with foul oaths. The order to fire was given and the duke fell. Without witnesses, unconsoled, in his own country, a short distance from Chantilly,[11] and a few paces from those old trees under which Saint Louis dispensed justice to his subjects, in the prison in which Monsieur le Prince had been incarcerated, the young, handsome, brave last descendent of the victor of Rocroi[12] died as the Great Condé would have died, and as his assassin will not die. His body was buried secretly, and no Bossuet[13] returned to life to speak over his ashes.

All that remains for the man who has set himself below the human race by committing a crime, is to feign to set himself above humanity by virtue of his projects, to give as a pretext for a felony reasons beyond the reach of the crowd, and to make an abyss of iniquity pass for the deep thinking of a genius. Buonaparte had recourse to this pitiable expedient that deceives no one and which lacks the merit of even a single feeling of remorse. Unable to hide what he had done, he advertised it.

When Condé's death was publicized in Paris, there was a movement of horror that no one dissimulated. People asked what right a Corsican had to shed the finest and the purest blood of France. Did he believe his part-African family could replace the French family he had just snuffed out? The military in particular trembled: Condé seemed their particular property, and in their eyes he represented the honor of the French army. Several times in the course of the melee, our grenadiers had encountered the three generations of heroes: the Prince de Condé, the Duc de Bourbon, and the Duc d'Enghien.[14] They had even wounded the Duc

---

10. *Great Condé:* Louis II, prince of Condé (1621–1686), was an outstanding general.

11. *Chantilly:* Ancestral home of the Condé family.

12. *Rocroi:* The site of one of Great Condé's victories against the Spanish.

13. Jacques Bénigne Bossuet (1627–1704) was famous for his funeral orations in honor of prominent persons.

de Bourbon, but a Frenchman's sword could not deplete that noble blood—only a foreigner could drain it dry.

Each nation has its own vices. Those of the French are not treachery, malevolence, and ingratitude. The murder of the Duc d'Enghien, the torture and assassination of Pichegru,[15] the Spanish war and the incarceration of the Pope all revealed in Buonaparte a nature foreign to that of the French. Despite the weight of the chains burdening us, we remained as sensitive to misfortune as to glory, we wept for the Duc d'Enghien, Pichegru, Georges[16] and Moreau,[17] we admired Saragossa,[18] and covered with homages a pontiff in chains.[19] The man who overthrew that venerable priest, although that very priest had placed the crown on his own head, the man who at Fontainebleau dared to strike the sovereign pontiff with his own hand and drag the father of the faithful by the hair, that man may have thought he was carrying off a further victory—he did not know that the heir of Jesus Christ still retained that reed scepter and that crown of thorns that sooner or later triumph over the power of the wicked.

The time will come, I hope, when the French, free again, will declare by a solemn act that they took no part in these tyrannous acts, that the murder of the Duc d'Enghien, the incarceration of the Pope and the Spanish war are impious, sacrilegious, odious, and above all anti-French, and the shame of those acts must fall on the head of the *foreigner*.

Buonaparte took advantage of the horror aroused in us by the assassination at Vincennes to take the final step and sit on the throne.

Then began the great Saturnalia of royalty: crimes, oppression, and slavery walked arm in arm with madness. All freedom dies, all honorable feelings, all generous thoughts become plots against the state. Anyone who mentions virtue is suspect; anyone who praises a fine action harms a prince. Words change their meanings. A nation that fights for

14. *three generations:* Louis Joseph de Bourbon (1736–1818) organized an army that Chateaubriand and his brother joined in 1792. Louis-Henri Joseph Bourbon (1756–1830) was the son of the prince de Condé and father of the duc d'Enghien.

15. Jean-Charles Pichegru (1761–1804) was a general in the French revolution and then switched allegiance to the royalist cause. He was arrested for his participation in a royalist plot, and was found strangled in his cell, but there is no proof that Napoleon ordered his murder.

16. *Georges:* The reference is to the great royalist general Cadoudal, executed in 1804 for plotting to abduct Napoleon.

17. Jean Victor Moreau (1763–1813), Napoleon's rival who was exiled as a result of the Cadouard plot. In 1813 he joined the coalition army formed to oppose Napoleon and died in the battle of Dresden.

18. Saragossa, in northeastern Spain, long resisted the French army during Napoleon's Peninsular Wars.

19. *pontiff:* Pius VII (1742–1843), who was Pope from 1800 to 1823, crowned Napoleon emperor but was eventually relieved of his duties and taken prisoner in 1809, after the French conquest of Rome.

its legitimate sovereigns is a rebellious nation; a traitor is a faithful subject; the whole of France becomes the empire of lies; newspapers, pamphlets, speeches, prose and poetry, everything disguises truth. If it has rained, we are assured that the sun has shone. If the tyrant strolled among a silent crowd, he is said to have marched amid the acclamations of the masses. The sole aim is the Prince: morality consists in devoting oneself to his whims, duty consists in praising him. Above all it is necessary to cry out in admiration whenever he commits an error or a crime. Men of letters are forced, with threats, to celebrate the despot. They compose, capitulating on the degree of praise, happy when, through a few clichés on the glory of war, they have bought the right to shed a few tears, to denounce a few crimes, to recall a few forbidden truths! No book could appear without bearing some praise of Buonaparte, like the brand set on a slave. In new editions of classic authors, censorship withdrew every statement against conquerors, servitude, and tyranny, as the Directory[20] had planned to correct in the same authors everything that spoke of the monarchy and of kings. Almanacs were all meticulously examined; conscription was an article of faith in the catechism. In the arts the same servitude could be observed. Buonaparte poisons the plague victims of Jaffa; an artist makes a painting that depicts him touching, through excessive courage and humanity, those very plague victims.[21] It was not in such a manner that Saint Louis healed the ill—who presented themselves to his royal hands—with touching and religious faith. And do not even mention public opinion: as the maxim says, the sovereign has to engage it every morning. In Buonaparte's perfectly formed police force there was a committee charged with guiding minds, and at the head of this committee there was a director of public opinion. Deception and silence were the two great means for keeping the people misinformed. If your children die on the field of battle, do you think anyone has a high enough opinion of you to tell you what has become of them? No one will inform you of events that are of the highest importance to the country, to Europe, to the entire world. If the enemy is at Meaux, you will hear of it only through the flight of the local people. You who will be wrapped in darkness, your anxieties will be made fun of, your pain will be a source of jest, what you might think or feel is a matter of scorn. You want to raise your voice, a spy gives you away, a policeman arrests you, a military tribunal judges you; they bash you on the head, and you are forgotten.

Enchaining the fathers was not enough for them: they also had to get rid of the children. Mothers could be seen running from the far

---

20. *Directory:* The government of France between 1795 and 1799.

21. *Jaffa:* Chateaubriand is conjoining two separate events, one in which Napoleon visited the hospital at Jaffa where plague-stricken members of his army were housed, and did indeed touch their wounds; and another episode in which, obliged to abandon the city, he gave opium to the worst sufferers.

corners of the empire begging, tears in their eyes, for the return of sons whom the government had taken from them. Those children were sent to schools where irreligion, debauchery, scorn for domestic values, and blind obedience to the sovereign were drummed into them. Paternal authority, which the most frightful tyrants of antiquity had respected, was treated by Buonaparte as abuse and prejudice. He wanted to turn our sons into Mamelukes,[22] without God, without family, without country. It seems that this universal enemy was determined to destroy France, down to its very foundations. He corrupted men more deeply, and did more evil to the human race in the short space of ten years, than all the tyrants of Rome put together, from Nero to the last persecutor of the Christians. The principles on which his administration was based moved from his government into the various social classes, for a perverse government introduces vice to the nation just as a virtuous government makes virtue flourish. Irreligion, the taste of pleasure, spending more than you own, scorn for moral bonds, the spirit of adventure, violence, and domination trickled from the throne down to families. Had such a reign lasted a little longer, France would have been nothing but a nest of brigands.

The crimes of our republican revolution were the work of passions, which always leave resources; society was disordered but not destroyed. Morality was hurt, but not annihilated. Consciences suffered remorse, a destructive indifference did not confound the innocent and the guilty. Thus the misfortunes of that time could have been swiftly repaired. But how can one cure a wound caused by a government that made despotism into a principle? A government that, while it spoke only of morality and religion, constantly destroyed morality and religion through its institutions and its scorn. A government that made no attempt to found order on duty and law, but on might and police spies. A government that took the stupor of slavery for the peace of a well-ordered society, a society faithful to the customs of its fathers, a society advancing in silence along the path of ancient virtues. The most terrible revolutions are preferable to such a state. If civil wars produced public crimes, they at least give birth to private virtues, talents, and great men. It is in despotism that empires disappear. Through its abuse of all the means at its disposal, through killing souls as well as bodies, despotism leads sooner or later to dissolution and defeat. There is no example of a free nation that has perished as the result of civil war: a State bent down under its own storms has always arisen more flourishing than before.

---

22. *Mamelukes:* The slaves brought from the Caucasus to Egypt to form an army. In 1254 they raised one of their number to supreme power and reigned over Egypt until 1517.

Baudelaire

◆

Charles Baudelaire (1821–1867), although best known as the author of The
Flowers of Evil *and his* Short Prose Poems, *was also a brilliant art and
literary critic. In his evaluation of the Salon of 1846 (a national competitive
art exhibition), a twenty-five-year-old Baudelaire seizes on the opportunity
to explore the nature and effect of color. This analysis is itself a virtuoso stylistic
exercise. An essay on the Romantic poet Marceline Desbordes-Valmore reveals
Baudelaire's ability to enter the imaginative universe of his subject, skillfully
conveying both the nature of her work and suggesting how he might have
treated her techniques and themes himself. That gift for projecting himself into
other people's minds which is clearly revealed in Baudelaire's poetry is also very
much a part of his artistic and literary criticism. Through his passionate and
intelligent involvement in the challenges each artist or writer had taken up,
and his refusal to judge on any but aesthetic grounds, he played a central role
in the development of critical thinking. These articles are remarkable for the
subtlety and variety of their prose, as well as for Baudelaire's ability to weave
into his own discourse that of the person he is discussing.*

FURTHER READING: *Flowers of Evil,* tr. Richard Howard (Boston: D. R. Gadine,
1982), *The Mirror of Art,* tr. Jonathan Mayne (New York: Phaidon, 1955), *Selected
Letters,* tr. Rosemary Lloyd (Chicago: University of Chicago Press, 1986), *Short
Prose Poems,* tr. Rosemary Lloyd (Oxford: Oxford University Press, 1992).
BIOGRAPHY: Claude Pichois, *Baudelaire,* tr. Graham Robb (London: Hamilton,
1989).
TEXT USED FOR "CONCERNING COLOR": *Curiosités esthétiques* (Paris: Michel Lévy,
1868).
TEXT USED FOR "MARCELINE DESBORDES-VALMORE": *Les Poètes français, IV*
(Paris: 1862).

CONCERNING COLOR

FROM THE *SALON OF 1846*

Imagine a fine natural space in which everything glows green, shines red, is dusty or shimmering, everything enjoys complete freedom, and everything, diversely colored in accordance with its molecular constitution, changes from instant to instant as the shadows and light move over it. A space where everything quivers under the action of its own internal heat and is thus permanently vibrating, making the lines tremble and fulfilling the law of eternal and universal movement. —An immense space, sometimes blue and often green, extends to the rim of the sky: that's the sea. The trees are green, the grass is green, the mosses are green; green snakes its way through the trunks, the twigs that are not yet mature are green; green is nature's background color, for green combines so well with all the other hues. What strikes me first and foremost is that everywhere—through poppies in the grass, ragged robin, parrots, etc.—red proclaims the glory of green; black—when it exists—acts as a solitary and insignificant zero or comes to the assistance of blue or red. The blue, which is to say the sky, is broken up with light white flecks or grey masses so that its gloomy crudeness is, fortunately, reduced— and, as the seasonal mist—winter or summer—washes over, tones down or swallows up the contours, nature resembles a rapidly spinning top which appears gray to our eyes, although it contains within it all the colors of the rainbow.

The sap rises and, since it is a mixture of elements, it flourishes in mixed tones; trees, rocks, and granite are mirrored in water, leaving their reflections; all the transparent objects attract light and color from near and far as they pass by. As the day star moves, the tones change their values, but they always respect each other's natural sympathies and antipathies, and thus, by making concessions each to the other, they continue to live in harmony. The shadows move slowly, setting the colors fleeing before them, or stifling them as the light, itself in motion, seeks to make them resound anew. These shades send back their reflections, and modify their qualities by *glazing* them with transparent and borrowed qualities, thus multiplying their melodious marriages an infinite number of times, and facilitating them. When the great fire drops into the waters, fanfares of red leap up from all sides, a blood-stained harmony bursts out along the horizon, and green grows richly crimson. But soon vast blue shadows rhythmically chase before them the crowd of oranges and tender pinks which are like a far-off and muted echo of the light. This great symphony of the day, which is the eternal variation of yesterday's symphony, this succession of melodies in which variety arises constantly from the infinite, this complex hymn is what we call color.

In color we find harmony, melody, and counterpoint.

If you will take the time to examine a detail within a detail, on an object of modest dimensions, for instance a woman's hand, a hand that is rather slender and with very fine skin through which the blood can be detected, you will see that there exists a perfect harmony between the green in the tracery of strong veins, and the blood-colored tones that mark the joints: the pink nails stand out against the first finger-joint with its grey and brown tones. As for the palm, the life-lines, pinker and more wine-colored, are separated from each other by the system of green or blue veins that run through it. If you study the same object through a magnifying glass, you will find in every part of it, no matter how tiny, a perfect harmony of grays, blues, browns, greens, oranges, and whites, warmed by a little yellow. This harmony, combined with shadows, produces the colorists' shading, which is different in essence from that of those who specialize in the line and for whom the main difficulty lies more or less in the copying of a plaster cast.[1]

Color, therefore, results from the concordance of two tones. Warm tones and cool tones (and all theory consists merely in opposing these two) cannot define themselves in any definitive fashion, since they exist only in relation to each other.

The magnifying glass is the colorist's eye. I do not mean to imply by this that the colorist has to proceed through a minute study of the tones blended together in a very limited space. For if we were to admit that each molecule possesses a particular tone, we would have to assume that matter is infinitely divisible. Moreover, since art is abstraction and involves the sacrifice of the detail in favor of the whole, it is important that the artist's attention should be focused above all on the large groups. But I wanted to prove that, if the case were possible, the tones, however numerous they might be, will, provided they are juxtaposed logically, naturally melt into each other according to the rule that governs them.

Chemical affinities are the reason nature cannot commit errors in arranging tones, since for nature, shape and color are one and the same.

The true colorists cannot make errors either, and can do whatever they please, because they know from birth the full range of tones, the strength of a particular shade, the results of combinations, and all the science of counterpoint, and thus they can create a harmony of twenty different reds.

This is so true that if an anticolorist who owned a property took it into his head to repaint his land in an absurd way, following a discor-

---

1. At the time Baudelaire was writing, one of the great artistic debates concerned the relative values of line and color: the kind of painting that gives preference to the purity of line is represented by Ingres, while that which values color more is represented by Delacroix. Throughout his adult life, Baudelaire championed the works of Delacroix.

dant color system, the thick and transparent varnish provided by our atmosphere and the knowing eye of a Veronese would rescue everything and produce on his canvas a satisfying whole, conventional no doubt, but at least logical.

This explains how a colorist can appear paradoxical in expressing color and how the study of nature often leads to a result which is entirely different from that of nature.

Air plays so great a role in the theory of color, that if a landscape artist painted the leaves of trees as we really see them, the tones would be false, for there is far less space between the spectator and the painting, than between the spectator and nature.

Lies are constantly necessary even to create trompe-l'œil.

Harmony is the basis of any theory of color.

Melody is the basic unit of a color or of color in general.

Melody seeks a conclusion; it is the ensemble in which all the effects conspire to create the general impression.

Thus melody leaves in the mind a profound memory.

Most young colorists lack melody.

The best way of knowing whether a painting is melodious is to look at it long enough for the subjects and the lines to lose meaning. If it is melodious, it already has a meaning, and it will already have established itself in the repertory of your memories.

Style and sentiment in color come from selection, and selection comes from temperament. There are colors that are gay and frolicsome, colors that are frolicsome and sad, rich and gay, rich and sad, common and original.

The color of Veronese, for instance, is calm and gay. Delacroix's color is often plaintive, and M. Catlin's color is frequently terrible.

For a long time my window looked out on an inn that was painted partly in crude green and partly in shocking red, and inflicted delicious pain on my eyes. I do not know if some analogist has solidly established a complete scale of colors and emotions, but I remember a passage from Hoffmann[2] that perfectly expresses my idea and will please all those who truly love nature: "It's not merely when I dream or in that light delirium that precedes sleep but also when I'm awake, when I hear music, that I find an intimate analogy between colors, sounds, and perfumes. It seems to me that all these things have been engendered by the same ray of light, and that they cannot help blending into a wonderful concert. The odor of red and brown marigolds in particular produces a magical effect on me. It makes me fall into a profound reverie,

2. Ernst Theodore Amadeus Hoffmann (1776–1822), German novelist and composer whom the young Baudelaire, like many of his compatriots, admired. The passage in question is part of Hoffmann's meditations on music, *Kreisleriana*.

and then I seem to hear in the distance the deep and serious sounds of the oboe."

One often wonders whether the same man can be at once a great colorist and a great draftsman. Yes and no; for there are different sorts of line drawings.

The quality of a pure draftsman consists above all in finesse, and such finesse excludes personal style. Well, there are fortunate styles, and the colorist whose duty it is to express nature through color would often lose more in suppressing fortunate mannerisms than in seeking out a greater austerity of line.

Color certainly does not exclude the great line, that of Veronese for instance, which arises above all from the ensemble and the blocks; but it does exclude the depiction of detail, the contours of the small segment, in which a personal style would always devour the line.

The love of air, and therefore the choice of subjects in motion, demands the use of floating and fading lines.

Those who are exclusively draftsmen act according to an inverse and yet analogous procedure. Careful to follow and surprise the line in its most secret undulations, they do not have time to see air and light, by which I mean the effects of air and light, and even deliberately blind themselves to such effects, in order not to do violence to the principle of their school.

So it is possible to be both colorist and draftsman, but only in a certain sense. Just as a draftsman can be a colorist where large blocks are concerned, so a colorist can be a draftsman through a complete logic of the general appearance of the lines; but one of these qualities totally absorbs the details of the other. The colorists draw as nature draws; their shapes are naturally limited and outlined by the harmonious struggle of the colored blocks.

Pure draftsmen are philosophers and abstracters of the quintessentials.

Colorists are epic poets.

MARCELINE DESBORDES-VALMORE (1861)

Have you, like me, noticed that on several occasions, when you have confided in a friend one of your tastes or passions, you have heard him exclaim: "But how strange! That is in complete opposition to all your passions and to your doctrines"? And haven't you answered: "That may be so, but that is how it is. I like it, I really do, probably precisely because of the violent contradiction I find between it and my entire being"?

That is the case with me and Mme Desbordes-Valmore. If the cry, if the natural sigh of an elite soul, if the heart's despairing ambition, if sudden, unpremeditated faculties, if all that is free and comes from the good Lord, are enough to make a great poet, then Marceline Desbordes-Valmore is and always will be a great poet. It is true that if you take the time to notice all the things she lacks, things that could be acquired by work, her greatness would be singularly diminished, but at the very moment when you feel most impatient and disappointed at the negligence, at the jolt, at the disorder, all of which you, as a thoughtful man, a highly responsible man, take to be the deliberate counsel of laziness, a sudden, unexpected, and unparalleled beauty arises and lifts you irresistibly to the summit of poetry's heaven. Never has a poet been more natural; never has a poet been less artificial. No one has been able to imitate her charm, because it is entirely original and innate.

If ever a man were to desire for his wife or daughter the gifts and honors of the muse, he could not want them to be any other than those granted to Mme Valmore. Among the fairly large group of women who have recently thrown themselves into literary work, there are very few whose works have not been, if not a desolation for their families and even for their lovers (for the least modest men like modesty in those they love), at least stained with one of those masculine follies that in women assume the dimensions of monstrosity. We have known the female philanthropic author, the systematic priestess of love, the republican poetess, the poetess of the future, be it Fourierist or Saint-Simonian.[3] And our eyes, enraptured by beauty, have never been able to grow accustomed to all that stiffly formal ugliness, all that criminal impiety (there are even poetesses of impiety), all these sacrilegious pastiches of the male mind.

Mme Desbordes-Valmore was a woman, was always a woman, and was never anything but a woman. But she was to an extraordinary degree the poetic expression of all those beauties which are natural to women. Whether she sings of the languid desires in the maiden, the dreary desolation of an abandoned Ariadne,[4] or the warm enthusiasm of maternal love, her song retains forever the delicious accents of the woman. She has borrowed nothing, uses no artificial ornaments, nothing but the *eternal feminine*, as the German poet puts it.[5] It is in her very sincerity that Mme Valmore has found her reward, that is, a glory we believe to be as solid as those of perfect artists. The torch that she brandishes in our eyes to illuminate the mysterious groves of sentiment,

---

3. *Fourierist or Saint-Simonian:* Charles-François-Marie Fourier (1772–1837) and Claude-Henri de Rouvroy, Comte de Saint-Simon (1760–1825), were French socialist writers who sought to reorganize society in the wake of the chaos of the Revolution of 1789 and the wars of the Napoleonic era.

4. In Greek legend, Ariadne was the daughter of Minos and Pasiphaë. She helped Theseus kill the Minotaur and escape from the Cretan labyrinth. He abandoned her on the island of Naxos, where she was found by Dionysus.

5. *German poet:* The reference is to Johann Wolfgang von Goethe (1749–1832), who coins the expression *the eternal feminine* in his play *Faust*.

or that she places, to set it blazing afresh, on our most intimate memories as sons or lovers, that torch has been lit in the very depths of her own heart. Victor Hugo[6] has expressed magnificently, like everything he expresses, the beauties and enchantments of family life; but only in the poetry of the ardent Marceline will you find that warmth a mother gives her brood, and of which some of us, among the sons of women, less ungrateful than others, still retain a delicious memory. If I were not afraid that a simile drawn too closely from the animal world would be taken as a lack of respect toward that adorable woman, I would say that I find in her the grace, the watchfulness, the suppleness, and the violence of the female cat or lioness, loving her offspring.

It has been said that Mme Valmore, whose first poems were written some time ago (1818)[7] has been rapidly forgotten by modern readers. Forgotten by whom, may I ask? By those who, feeling nothing, can remember nothing. She reveals great and vigorous qualities that brand themselves on the memory, deep incisions made unexpectedly into the heart, magic explosions of passion. No author can pluck more easily the unique formula of sentiment, that which is sublime but unaware of itself. As the most simple and easy carefulness is an invincible obstacle to that wild and unconscious pen, what for anyone else would be the object of laborious research falls naturally into her lap; her work is a perpetual windfall. She traces wonderful patterns with the unreflecting ease you find in notes destined for the mailbox. A charitable and passionate soul as she defines herself so well, but always involuntarily, in these lines:

While one can still give, one cannot die!

A soul too sensitive, on which the rough edges of life left an ineradicable imprint, she had the right to exclaim, especially in her longing for oblivion:

But if we have no cure for memory,
What is the use, my soul, of death?

Certainly no one had more right than she to write at the opening of her recent volume:

Imprisoned in this book my soul lies fettered.

At the point when death came to take her from this world in which she had known so well how to suffer, when death carried her to a heaven whose peaceful joys she so ardently desired, Mme Desbordes-Valmore, that indefatigable priestess of the muse, who had never known how to be silent, because she was always full of cries and songs which longed to burst from her, was preparing another volume, the proofs of

---

6. Victor Hugo (1802–1885) writes of family relationships in his collection of poems *Les Feuilles d'automne* (1830).

7. The volume in question here, *Elégies*, is the first collection of French verse that can truly be considered Romantic.

which fell one by one on the bed of pain she had not left for two years. Those who piously aided her in preparing her farewells have told me that we will find in that volume all the fire of a vitality that never felt so much alive as when it was in pain. Alas! The book will be a posthumous crown to add to all those, already so brilliant, that will adorn one of our most flower-strewn tombs.

I have always taken pleasure in seeking in external and visible nature examples and metaphors that can help me characterize delights and impressions that are by nature spiritual. I dream of the effect created on me by Mme Valmore's poetry when I ran through it with the eyes of adolescence, eyes which are, in high-strung souls, at once so ardent and so clear-sighted. This poetry struck me as a garden; but it is not the solemnity of Versailles, nor yet the vast and theatrical picturesqueness of erudite gardens of the Italians, who know so well the art of *garden building (aedificat hortos)*; not even, no, not even the Valley of Flutes or the Tenare of our old Jean-Paul.[8] It is a simple English garden, full of romance and romanticism. Flower beds represent her work's abundant expressions of feelings. Ponds, limpid and motionless, reflecting everything so that it leans upside down against the overturned vault of the sky, embody profound resignation richly bedecked with memories. There is nothing missing in this charming garden of an age gone by, neither the gothic ruins hiding in a rustic spot, nor the nameless mausoleum which at a bend of a path surprises your soul and urges it to think of eternity. Sinuous and shady avenues end in sudden horizons. Thus the poet's thought, after having followed capricious meanders, suddenly opens onto vast perspectives of the future or the past; but those skies are too vast to be completely cloudless, and the temperature in these climes is too warm not to build up storms. The walker, in contemplating these vast vistas veiled in mourning feels his or her eyes fill with those hysterical tears. The flowers bend down, defeated, and the birds speak only in hushed tones. After a warning lightning flash, a thunder clap growls; this is the lyrical explosion, and finally an inevitable deluge of tears confers on everything prostrate, suffering and discouraged, the freshness and the solidity of a new youth!

---

8. *Jean-Paul:* Johann Paul Friedrich Richter (1763–1825) was a German novelist who published under the pen name of Jean-Paul.

Sainte-Beuve

———◆———

Charles-Auguste Sainte-Beuve (1804–1869), a poet and novelist whose works exercised a degree of influence on such writers as Baudelaire and Gautier, is best remembered as a literary critic. His Monday newspaper columns did much not only to shape the taste of the reading public, but also to form a school of criticism in which a writer's life and works are seen as intimately connected. His long studies of French renaissance literature played an important role in the reassessment of that period. While Sainte-Beuve failed to perceive the genius of either Chateaubriand or Baudelaire, his rejection of dogmatism, his boundless curiosity, and his anger at the increasing commercialism of both literature and literary criticism make him an entertaining and often sympathetic figure. His novel Volupté *(1834), loosely based on his love affair with Adèle Hugo, is in many ways a compendium of early romantic sensibility, while his* Joseph Delorme *(1829), purported to be the thoughts and verse of a poet who died young, also reflect the themes and tone of the young Romantics who gathered around Victor Hugo.*

FURTHER READING: *Literary Criticism of Sainte-Beuve*, tr. Emerson A. Marks (Lincoln: University of Nebraska Press, 1971), *Selected Essays*, tr. Francis Steegmuller and Norbert Guturnan (Garden City, N.Y.: Doubleday, 1963).
TEXT USED: *Portraits contemporains* (Paris: Didier, 1855), II.

INDUSTRIAL LITERATURE (1839)

From a distance, we see the literature of a particular age as something very simple and homogenous. From close up, however, it unfolds successively in all manner of diversity and difference. It is moving forward with nothing accomplished as yet. It has its progress, its moments of side-tracking, of hesitation or of enthusiasm. The distress and disasters of the book trade in France over the last few years is an undeniable fact. Literary matters seem to have been more and more compromised, and through the fault of literature itself. About ten years ago,[1] a sudden revolution broke the series of studies and ideas which were rapidly developing, and provoked an immediate and prolonged period of anarchy. In this inevitable confusion, new talents did at least arise; the old talents had not died, and there was hope for a renascent order which would foster a development of literature along lines likely to satisfy the heart and bring glory. But now we have a situation where, in literature as in politics, as the external causes of agitation have faded, the internal symptoms of profound disorder have appeared all the more clearly.

There is no doubt that under the Restoration,[2] much was written, and in all kinds of styles. Next to one or two real monuments, a mass of works was produced that were all more or less secondary, predominantly political or historical. The imagination had barely awakened yet, except in truly outstanding talents. A moral idea, an appearance of patriotism, a banner, lent this mass of occasional writings and propaganda a certain nobility and in the eyes of public, indeed in the eyes of authors and compilers themselves, covered over the less obvious motivation. At the time of the restoration of the monarchy, and at the moment when that monarchy collapsed, those moral and political ideas were, in large part, suddenly abandoned. The flag ceased to fly over a whole cargo of works it had honored and whose merchandise, as the saying goes, it had guaranteed. The great mass of literature, all those free-floating resources which are designated somewhat vaguely under the name of literature, no longer felt internally, and no longer revealed externally, anything other than its real motives, which is to say an unbridled display of egotism and a pressing need to live. Industrial literature thus increasingly showed its true face.

Industrial literature has always been with us. Especially since the invention of printing, people have written to earn a living, and the majority of printed books are no doubt due to this very respectable motive. Combined with a person's passions and beliefs, and with natural talent, poverty has created a part of even the most noble works and those that appear the most disinterested. *Paupertas impulit audax*, as Horace[3] tells us, and Lesage wrote *Gil Blas*[4] for the bookseller. Yet in general, and especially in France, during the seventeenth and eighteenth centuries, ideas of open-handedness and unselfishness were, and with good reason, linked to fine works. Boileau[5] made a present of his poems to

---

1. *about ten years ago:* The reference is to the Revolution of 1830, as a result of which Louis-Philippe came to power.
2. *the restoration:* The period between the fall of Napoleon in 1815 and the revolution of 1830; comprises the reigns of Louis XVIII and Charles X.
3. *paupertas impulit audax:* Poverty drives one to rash deeds.
4. *Gil Blas:* Alain-René Lesage (1668–1747) is best known for this picaresque novel.
5. Nicholas Boileau (1636–1711), a French poet and critic, became a legend in his own lifetime.

Barbin[6] and did not sell them. In all the majestic works and variously extended careers of the Bossuets,[7] the Fénelons,[8] the La Bruyères,[9] in those of Montesquieu[10] or Buffon,[11] you cannot see a door leading to a bookseller's small back room. Voltaire[12] grew far richer with the aid of his foreign investments than through his books, although he did not neglect them, either. Diderot,[13] in need though he was, gave his work away more willingly than he sold it. Bernardin de Saint-Pierre[14] was one of the first to offer the sorry spectacle of a lofty, ideal, poetical spirit quibbling with the booksellers. Beaumarchais,[15] the great corruptor, began speculating brilliantly on publishing and combining the thinking of Law[16] with the talent of a writer. But in general, the dignity of literature survived, papering over all that material and secondary aspect, and maintaining the honorable convictions that are being so violently shaken today. Under the Empire there was relatively little writing. Under the Restoration, people wrote a great deal, but, as I have said, kept up the noble trappings. Thus it came about that as we left behind the habits, both the heartfelt and the insincere, adopted under the Restoration, and brought with us a supply of prejudices which were somewhat delicate where this question is concerned, we have reached the point where today our purely industrial literature declares itself crudely, and the whole thing strikes us as far newer than it really is. It is true that pretentions have never been made more manifest nor invasion

6. Claude Barbin, bookseller and publisher (1629?–1698?), published Boileau's *Satires* and is mentioned by the poet in *Le Lutrin*, canto V.

7. Jacques Bénigne Bossuet (1627–1704), the greatest of French orators.

8. *Fénelon:* François de Salignac de la Mothe Fénelon (1651–1715), a French churchman and man of letters, best known, perhaps, for his Homeric imitation *Télémaque*.

9. Jean de La Bruyère (1645–1696) was a French satirist, best known for his extremely successful study of human nature, *Les Caractères*.

10. *Montesquieu:* Charles-Louis de Secondat Baron de la Brède et de Montesquieu (1689–1755) was a French social and political thinker and a satirist.

11. *Buffon:* Georges-Louis Leclerc, comte de Buffon (1707–1788), was a French scientist, known both for a study of style and for his forty-four volumes of scientific studies.

12. Voltaire (François-Marie Arouet [1694–1778]), one of the great geniuses of the eighteenth century.

13. Denis Diderot (1713–1784) was a French philosopher, novelist, and man of letters. He played a central role in the creation of the *Encyclopédie*.

14. *Bernardin de Saint-Pierre.* Jacques-Henri Bernardin de Saint-Pierre (1737–1814) was a French naturalist and novelist, best known for his tale of youthful innocence in the exotic landscape of Mauritius, *Paul et Virginie*.

15. *Beaumarchais.* Pierre-Augustin Caron de Beaumarchais (1732–1799), French dramatist and publicist best known for *The Barber of Seville* and *The Marriage of Figaro*. His works were sometimes banned, since they suggested that servants might be superior to their aristocratic masters.

16. John Law (1671–1729), Scottish financier who became Controller General of the French royal bank and created the French Company of the Indies. During the Regency of Philippe, duc d'Orléans, Law's Mississippi scheme seemed to promise a way out of the severe financial difficulty in which the French government found itself, but the boom was followed by a sudden collapse. Law's scheme forms an introduction to modern speculative finance.

made more menacing. What characterizes this literature is the naivety and often the boldness of the requests it makes, the way it is so needy, and exceeds in its demands all the limits of what is necessary, mingling frantic passion with glory, or rather celebrity, and intimately mingling with the pride of literature, both offering itself as model and taking itself for model.

Every age has its own brand of folly and ridicule; in literature, we have already witnessed (and perhaps given too much aid to) many manias. The demon of elegy and despair had its day; pure art had its own cult, its mysticity, but now the mask has changed. Industry has penetrated the dream and formed it in its own image, while at the same time becoming fantastic, as a dream is fantastic. *The demon of literary property* excites people and seems to constitute in certain individuals a real Pindaric[17] illness, a Saint Vitus dance it would be interesting to describe. They all exaggerate their own importance and set about evaluating their own genius in round figures. The fountain that spurts up from every act of conceit falls back in a rain of gold. It easily goes into the millions; people are not ashamed of making a show of their riches or of begging for them. With more than one famous name the conversation goes no further. It is a cry of suffering in the style of a high bank official and accompanied by the clink of coins. Marot,[18] stretching out his hand to "The King, for a hundred crowns" in an attractive ten-line verse was less pretentious and more graceful about the whole business:

May the King not refuse—
May anyone feel free to give—
Marot a hundred crowns exactly,
And he promises that he will not
Sew them into his vest to keep them safe.

In this regard, as in almost all matters concerning literature, one hears not a word of criticism, no loud and unabashed laughter: the external policing system no longer operates. Industrial literature has succeeded in suppressing criticism and taking over the place more or less unopposed, as if it alone existed. No doubt there are other literatures, for instance those of the Academy, of the university. But the entire literary glory of a nation does not reside there: a certain form of life, free and bold, has always sought its adventures outside those precincts. It is in the outside world that imagination has the best chance of unfurling. Well, do you know what has become of it, that outside world, which up to now has formed the principal glory of France? The very fact that

---

17. *Pindaric:* The Greek poet Pindar (518–438 B.C.) lent his name to loose, irregular verses similar to those he used in his odes.

18. Clément Marot (1496–1544) was a French poet who served in the households of Marguerite de Navarre and her brother Francis II.

it was common and open to all no doubt left it at all periods vulnerable to all intellectual chances. The different forms of bad taste, the gaudy fashions, the noisy schools have all passed through it. False colors have streamed into it. This field, in a word, has always been infested by gangs, but never has it been invaded, exploited, proclaimed as their own by so large a gang, a gang as disparate and almost organized as the one we see today, and with only this motto written on their flag: "Live by writing!" Through disdain or intimidation we hold our peace, and they gain by our silence; serious minds that honor the age, minds enclosed within their special vocations, say nothing about these excesses, which they would find difficult to describe. Nevertheless, great and lofty talents, obsessed or blinded, yield to the torrent and grow there, imitating or encouraging behavior from which they believe they can withdraw without dishonor. A few wise pens here and there protest, in muted tones, but nowhere does anyone throw up a protective dike. Complicity stifles all cries of warning.

In the provinces, indeed in Paris itself, unless you are more or less involved with it, you do not really know what the press is, that noisy meeting place, that dusty boulevard of contemporary literature, which nevertheless possesses along each avenue its secret passages. In talking of the press, I know that a few exceptions should be made; in terms of politics above all I could mention some, but in literature there are very few. The slight importance attached to a branch which is considered subordinate has meant that, where literature is concerned, things have been allowed to develop as they will. The result has been that in the majority of newspapers, even among those that would willingly pass themselves off as Puritan, there is a mass of abuse, and a purely mercantile organization has arisen, fomenting the literary wreck around it and depending on that wreck.

You simply have to resign yourself to new customs, to the invasion of a literary democracy, as you have to accept the arrival of all the other democracies. It matters little that it seems so much more obvious in literature. The fact that one writes and publishes will be less and less a distinction. With our electoral and industrial customs, everyone, at least once in their life, will have their page, their speech, their prospectus, their toast, everyone will be an *author*. From that to writing a review column is only a step. *Why not me too?*, everyone will say. There are respectable incentives in all this. You have a family, you married for love, your wife will write too, under a pseudonym. What could be more honorable, more worthy of interest than the hard work (even if it is a bit hasty and rushed?) of a writer who is poor and depends on his writing to support his family? Such situations are far from rare. I would feel uneasy devaluing them. And after all, in our days, who can honestly say that their writing is not in part for survival (*pro victu*), from the most famous down? Such a motive goes hand in hand with even the most legitimate fame. Pascal,[19] Montaigne,[20] speaking of philosophers who write against fame, show them to be in contradiction with themselves and reveal that what they desired all along was fame. *"And I who am writing this,"* adds Pascal . . . *And I who am writing this*, is what one should say whenever one writes about those who write to earn a living.

The current state of the daily press, where literature is concerned, is, not to put too fine a point on it, disastrous. Since no moral idea is in question, it has come to pass that a series of material circumstances has gradually changed thought and has altered its expression. The advertisement was born[21] and rapidly performed wonders. The consequences of the advertisement were swift and boundless. It was in vain that people tried to separate what was conscientious and free in the newspaper from what had become public and venal: the boundaries of the paragraph were very quickly invaded. The advert served as a bridge. How can you condemn something you are two inches away from? How can you call detestable and baleful something proclaimed and paraded two inches further down as the wonder of the age? The attraction of the increasing number of capital letters in the advertisement carried the day. They were a mountain of magnets that made the compass lie. In order to have in the cash box the profits the adverts brought in, a great deal of complacency was shown in regard to the books advertised, and thus criticism lost its credibility. So what! Were the adverts not the most productive and obvious part of the enterprise? Newspapers were set up, founded uniquely on the gains it was presumed that the ads would bring in. And in those cases in particular, blind eyes were turned, and all independence and reserve came to an end.

The ill-starred system of advertisements had a no less deadly influence on the book trade. Indeed, it played a good part in destroying the trade. How so? Well, once the book has been printed, the advertisement constitutes a further hundred percent of the costs that have to come out of the first sale before you can make any profit at all. It costs a thousand francs to advertise a new book. Given that fact, the presses have been pitiless in their demands that authors produce two volumes instead of one, and in-octavo volumes instead of a smaller format.[22] For it costs no more to advertise a book of that size and, as the advertisement costs stay the same, the sales are at least doubled and make up for the costs.

The situation of newspapers has clearly deteriorated. They have increasingly become tributaries of advertisements and have lost any shred

---

19. Blaise Pascal (1623–1662), French mathematician, physicist, and theologian.

20. Michel de Montaigne (1533–1592), French essayist.

21. *advertisement:* It was in 1836 that French newspapers began using advertisements as their major source of revenue.

22. The English novelist George Gissing makes a similar complaint in his novel *New Grub Street.*

of shame they may have possessed. Now when one reads, in a quality paper, a glowing review of a book, one is never very sure that the book-seller or even the author may not have had a role in formulating that praise. The literary morality of the press has dropped. If these morals were to be described in detail, it would not be believed. M. de Balzac brought together a great number of these vile acts in *Un grand homme de province*[23] but wrapped them up in his usual fantastic vision; and as a final characteristic that he had omitted, all these curious revelations in no way put him in bad odor with the people in question, as soon as they once again had pecuniary interests in common.

In the theater, the same wounds would be found; the blatantly industrial morals occupy an even more obvious place. It has always been thus but, in a history of the theater over the last ten years, the reader would follow the growing and disorderly after-effects of this bad literary regime. The demands of fashionable writers increase and often come close to resembling voraciousness. To keep them loyal, for instance, there is the attraction of "bonuses": as soon as a play by one of them has been received and read, a sum is given, 5,000 francs, I believe, for a five-act play. When the play succeeds, when the writer performs fairly faithfully, all goes well, but normally this is not the case. The theaters however get out of it better than the rest. What really cripples them has always been the rareness of good plays, good subjects, and good actors. One single piece of good luck of this type makes up for many a loss.

It is printed literature—especially that of the imagination, books hitherto liable to become fashionable, and, in varying degrees, all the new books—that this disease is fiercely attacking. Over the last two years in particular, books are no longer being sold; it is killing the book trade. The public has been abused to such a degree, so many blank pages have been included in volumes that are swollen and pumped up, so much old stuff has been reprinted and passed off as new, there has above all been so much praise for what is insipid and flat, that the public has literally become corpse-like. Besides, what can one expect from a book when all it does is group together pages which have been written in order to provide the maximum of columns with the minimum of ideas? Empty words, pointless descriptions, redundant epithets all have been redoubled. The style is drawn out in all its fibers like material that has been stretched too much. There are writers who now write their serialized novels only in dialogue, because that way at every sentence and almost at every word they can introduce a blank space and thus wangle an extra line. Well, do you know what a line means? A line without any idea, when it recurs often, is a noteworthy saving of brain cells;

---

23. Balzac's novel, which is the central part of *Illusions perdues*, charts the rise and fall of a provincial poet who loses his literary illusions in the greedy reality of Paris.

an extra line in the accounting is often a goodly sum. Thus everyone has forged ahead in their own best interests, cutting the tree down by the roots. Each, in passing through, has trampled the ground under their feet: who cares about those who will come after? After us, the floods can come! The writer has divided his brain up into regular doses, and this has led to some errors. Swings and roundabouts, as the saying goes; it has not always been possible for books bought and paid for in advance to be delivered. Scandalous trials have only too often revealed these trifles. Why should anyone be surprised, then, that the book trade, perched like this among all the causes of ruin, between its own charlatanism, the demands of writers, the extortion of newspapers, and finally foreign counterfeits,[24] has succumbed? For the only book trade that exists now is that of the university, in law, medicine, religion, precisely because in these special branches the trade keeps more or less free from these various attacks.

---

24. *counterfeits:* Balzac also complains about the lack of regulations concerning copyright. His novels were frequently published in pirated versions in Belgium and then sold in France, with no royalties for him.

Huysmans

◆
─────

Georges Charles (known as Joris-Karl) Huysmans (1848–1907) came to epito-
mize the decadent movement in late-nineteenth-century France. His early
novels adopt a profoundly pessimistic but often wittily realistic view of lower-
middle-class existence and particularly the grim truths of day-to-day married
life. Marthe, *his portrait of a prostitute, established his reputation as one of*
the naturalists, although his idiosyncratic and imaginative use of language is
entirely his own. His novel Against Nature (À Rebours) *is an inventive,*
highly original, and deeply ironic compendium of decadent taste. His later
*novels (*Là-bas, En Route, *and* La Cathédrale) *chart his hero's conversion*
to Catholicism, and reveal Huysmans's powers as a descriptive writer. He was
also an influential art critic, one of the first to appreciate the Impressionists.
His study Modern Art *(1883) displays many of his finest gifts: the sharpness*
of perception, the linguistic exuberance and precision, the refusal to bow to con-
vention, and the untiring curiosity that lead him to question and explore a
range of works and artists far beyond the normal centers of interest. The ex-
tract translated here shows his idiosyncratic style at work in an exploration
of both the contemporary artist Gustave Moreau and the simultaneous attrac-
tion and repulsion Huysmans felt for pornographic art. In his highly descrip-
tive prose style, Huysmans shuns the hackneyed and the familiar, seeking out
precise and often surprising formulations. His predilection for Latinate con-
structions and vocabulary is slightly less in evidence here than in his novels,
but the same analysis of sexual drives and the same misogyny are very much
to the fore.

FURTHER READING: *Down There,* tr. Keene Wallis (New Hyde Park, NY: University Books, 1958); *Against Nature,* tr. Robert Baldick (Baltimore: Penguin,
1959).
TEXT USED: *L'Art moderne* (Paris: Plon, 1911).

MODERN ART (1883)

Monsieur Gustave Moreau[1] is an extraordinary artist. He's unique. He's a mystic who lives locked away, in the heart of Paris, in a cell which is no longer even penetrated by the noise of contemporary life, even though it beats furiously against the doors of his cloister. Sunk in ecstasy, he sees the glory of enchanted visions, of the bloody apotheoses of other ages.

Having been haunted by Mantegna,[2] and by the da Vinci[3] whose disturbing princesses wander in mysterious landscapes of black and of blue, M. Moreau has given his heart to the hieratic art of India and the double stream of Italian art and Hindu art. Spurred on, too, by the feverish colors of Delacroix,[4] he has carved out an art which is truly his own, created a personal and new form of art, whose disquieting taste is at first disconcerting.

The reason is that these paintings no longer seem to belong to painting in the strict sense of the term. In addition to the extreme importance Gustave Moreau places on archeology in his work, the methods he uses to make his dreams visible seem to have been borrowed from the techniques used by German engravers from the past, from ceramics and from jewelry. There is a bit of everything in it: mosaic, inlaid enamel work, Alençon lace, the patient embroidery of the distant past, and there is a hint, too, of the illuminations of old missals and barbaric watercolors from the Orient of antiquity.

It is even more complex, even more beyond description. The only analogy one could make between these works and those created hitherto would really exist only in literature. Indeed, when one looks at these paintings, one feels a sensation which is almost equal to that experienced on reading certain bizarre and charming poems, like the Dream in *The Flowers of Evil*, which Charles Baudelaire dedicates to Constantin Guys.[5]

---

1. Gustave Moreau (1826–1898), French symbolist painter best known for his mythological and biblical fantasies, especially, perhaps, his series of depictions of Salomé.

2. Andrea Mantegna (c.1431–1506), Italian painter, strongly influenced by Donatello. He is considered one of the instigators of the Italian renaissance and his paintings reveal a particular purity of line and inspiration.

3. Leonardo da Vinci (1452–1519), the great Italian renaissance genius.

4. Eugène Delacroix (1798–1863), French romantic painter, famous for such works as "Liberty Leading the People," "The Women of Algiers," and a series of animal paintings inspired by trips to Morocco. He was greatly admired by the poet Charles Baudelaire, who devoted several brilliant pages of art criticism to his work.

5. Constantin Guys (1802–1892), best known for his drawings and water colors of soldiers, horses, and contemporary fashions. His ability to seize the transient and thus to represent modern life in both its heroism and its banality inspired Baudelaire to write a long study of his works in *The Painter of Modern Life*. The poem in question is "Rêve parisien" in the "Tableaux Parisiens" section of Baudelaire's *Flowers of Evil*.

And yet, Moreau's style would be even closer to the highly wrought language of the Goncourt brothers.[6] If it were possible to imagine the admirable and definitive *Temptation* of Gustave Flaubert[7] written by the authors of *Manette Salomon*,[8] perhaps one would have the exact equivalent of M. Moreau's so deliciously refined art.

The *Salomé* he exhibited in 1878 possessed a strange, superhuman life; the paintings he has shown us this year are no less original and no less exquisite. One depicts Helen, standing upright, highlighted against a terrible horizon splattered with phosphorescence and streaked with blood. She is clad in a dress encrusted with precious stones, like a reliquary; in her hand she holds, like the Queen of Spades in a deck of cards, a huge flower; walking with her eyes wide open, staring, in a cataleptic pose. At her feet lie piles of corpses pierced with arrows and in her august blonde beauty she dominates the carnage, as majestic and superb as Salammbô[9] appearing before the mercenaries, like a malignant deity who poisons, without even being conscious of doing so, all that draws near or all that she looks at and touches.

The other canvas shows us Galatea, naked, in a grotto, watched over by the enormous face of Polyphemus.[10] It's above all in this painting that the magic touches of this visionary's brush burst forth.

The grotto is a vast jewel box, in which, under the light that falls from a lapis-colored sky, a strange mineral flora produces its fantastic growths and mingles the delicate lacework of its improbable leaves. Branches of coral, foliage of silver, star fish, filigreed and colored grayish brown, burst forth at the same time as green twigs supporting imaginary or real flowers, in this lair illuminated by precious stones as if it were a tabernacle, and containing the inimitable and radiant jewel, the white body, tinged with pink at the breasts and the lips, of Galatea asleep in her long pale hair!

Whether or not one likes these magic scenes which have flowered in an opium-eater's brain, one is forced to admit that M. Moreau is a great artist and that today he stands head and shoulders above the trite throng of genre painters.

And yet they are all great artists, if I am to believe the clichés that pour out every year at this time; the painter of the *Honorius* is a great artist, with his dark-hued urchin, wearing a red disguise and crowned

---

6. *Goncourt brothers:* Edmond (1822–1896) and Jules (1830–1870), French writers who formed a unique partnership, producing works of art criticism, novels, and their famous diary as joint productions.

7. *Temptation:* The reference is to Flaubert's imaginative interpretation of the temptation of Saint Anthony, published in 1874.

8. *Manette Salomon* is a novel written by the Goncourt brothers.

9. Salammbô is the eponymous heroine of Flaubert's historical novel, published in 1868.

10. *Polyphemus:* In Greek mythology, a one-eyed giant, the unrequited lover of the nymph Galatea, who, for her part, loved the shepherd Acis. When the giant pinned Acis to the ground with a boulder, Galatea turned her lover into a river.

with a diadem, the kind of hooligan we've seen wandering through the streets of Paris, playing hopscotch in the street, or dragging himself along on his knees on café terraces to pick up cigar butts and pipe dottles from between the legs of the drinkers. And Puvis de Chavannes[11] is a great artist, too. Obviously he is superior but he draws out a joke that has perhaps lasted rather too long. He for his part specializes in the "sublime": that's a specialty like the one adopted by M. Dubuffe,[12] who concentrates on the "pretty." M. Puvis de Chavannes forces spiky postures onto people he has clumsily clumped in groups. He exempts himself from the need to seek out the perfect tone, giving his people, and the settings in which their heavy ossifications sprawl out, no appearance of truth or life, and for critics all this becomes the naivety of the primitive artist, a fresco, or a decorative machine, great art, sublime, reminiscent of Bornier,[13] of God knows what! . . .

Cézanne[14]

Steeped in light, ranged in porcelain fruit dishes, or on white table cloths, brutal apples and pears, unpolished, built up with a trowel, napped with lurching thumb blows. Close by, a furious rubble work of yellow and vermillion, green and blue; to the side, perfectly ripe, are fruit destined for the windows of Chevet brothers, a plethora of tempting, tasty fruit.

And truths which up until then had been left unstated can be seen in the strange real tones, those strokes of bizarre authenticity, the shades in the linen, the vessels of shadows spread out around the curve of the fruit, and thickly placed in the possible and charming blue shades which make of these canvasses works of initiation, when one thinks of the usual still life set out against bituminous surroundings on incomprehensible backgrounds.

Then sketches of landscapes done out of doors, attempts which have never fully come out of limbo, experiments in which the freshness has been spoilt by touching up, infantile and barbaric drafts, finally, with staggering imbalances. Houses leaning over to one side, like tipplers; fruit all awry in drunken bowls; naked bathers, surrounded by lines that are unhealthy but spurt off, for the glory of the eyes, with the speed of a Delacroix, lacking refinement of vision and fine fingers, whipped up by a fever of spoiled colors, howling, standing out in high relief, on the canvas which is so weighed down it bulges!

---

11. *Puvis de Chavannes:* Pierre Cécile Puvis de Chavannes (1824–1898) was a French painter, particularly well known for his murals.

12. Edouard-Louis Dubuffe (1820–1883), painter of portraits and genre paintings.

13. Nicolas Bornier (1762–1826), French sculptor.

14. Paul Cézanne (1839–1906), the great painter associated primarily with his still lifes and his landscapes inspired by the area around Mont Sainte Victoire.

In a word, a revealing colorist, who contributed more than the late Manet to the Impressionist movement, an artist with sick retinas, who, in the exasperated perception of his vision, discovered the base of a new art: that seems to be one possible way of summing up this painter who has been too much forgotten, M. Cézanne.

Félicien Rops[15]

The sight of an erotic work of art, created by an artist who has a real talent, leads me to strange descents into the depths of souls. Far from the nudities that, at the outset, gave me a melancholy pleasure when I contemplated them, I dream about their creators and I wonder what impulses, what feelings drove them to carry out such works.

Setting venal considerations aside, if we're speaking of an artist whom I know to be respectable, I must also reject the suspicion of despicable morals, drive away the thought that his paintings reproduce episodes of his intimate life, for, from the moment that real debauchery proves its presence, art, starved of sustenance, falls asleep in the coma of an old profligate, and dies. Moreover, anyone who gives in to lewd temptations is hardly in any state to translate them onto paper or canvas. I would add that in general those who celebrate virtue, proclaim decency, and exalt love, hide, beneath the appearance of frozen bigotry that they give to their work, the studious turpitudes they give rein to in the costly silence of secure hiding places.

The hypocrisy which throws so deliberate a veil over the ordures of old England as it falls prey to the infantile passion for rape, easily explains the behavior of such people, in their private existence and in their works.

Fundamentally, when you think about it, only the opposite is true, for the only really obscene people are those who are chaste. Indeed, everyone knows that abstinence engenders horrible lewd thoughts, that anyone who is not a Christian and who is therefore pure against his will, whips himself up, particularly in solitude, inflames his imagination and rambles. And then he proceeds in imagination, in his waking dreams, right to the summits of orgiastic delirium.

It's possible, therefore, that the artist who treats those questions of the flesh in a violent manner, is, for one reason or another, someone who is chaste.

But such a statement doesn't seem sufficient, for, if you examine it yourself, you discover that even if you don't abstain completely, even if

---

15. *Rops:* Félicien Joseph Vidon Rops (1833–1898), painter, lithographer, etcher, engraver, and writer who produced an enormous number of lithographs, many signed under false (and sometimes ludicrous) names.

you are satisfied, even if you feel a sincere disgust at sensual joy, you're still troubled by lascivious thoughts.

It's at that point that there appears the bizarre phenomenon of a soul that suggests lewd visions to itself, even though it has no physical desires.

Impure or not, artists whose nerves are taut to the point of snapping have, more than anyone else, constantly suffered from the unbearable torment of Lewdness. I am not speaking here of the act caused by lewdness, the act of fornication, which is merely unclean and which simply bears witness to a more or less excitable nature, nerves that are more or less vibrant, a body that is more or less strong. I am not even talking of the covetousness that precedes these venerian travails and longs for them, for that merely reveals an easy arousal of the senses, or reserves that are docile and that have long been reined in. I am talking exclusively of the Spirit of Lewdness, of isolated erotic ideas, with no material correspondence, which has no need of an animal outcome to calm them.

And almost always the scene perceived in dreams is identical: images arise, naked bodies offer themselves; but, with a leap, the natural act disappears, as if stripped of interest, as if too brief, as if it provoked merely a foreseeable commotion, a banal cry. And at once there is a surge toward preternatural beastliness, a postulation toward crises which have escaped from the limits of the flesh and have bounded beyond the possibility of spasms. The soul's infamy grows worse, if you will, but it also becomes more refined, ennobled by the thought that is mingled with all this, the thought of an ideal of superhuman vices, sins that one would like to be new.

When filth is thus spiritualized, a real discharge of phosphorous takes place in the brain and if, during this disquieting state the soul suggested to itself and for itself alone, it should happen that reality becomes mingled with these heated visions of the senses, that a woman, a flesh and blood woman, arrives on the scene, then the man, overtaxed by dream, feels embarrassed, becomes almost frigid, experiences, in all cases, after a real pollution, atrocious disillusionment and sorrow.

This strange attraction to the complications of the flesh, this obsession with filth for filth's sake, this rutting which takes place entirely in the soul and without any intervention from the consulted body, this livid and limited impulse which, in brief, has merely remote links with the reproductive instinct, remains strangely mysterious, if you think about it. Erethism of the brain, science calls it: and if this state persists or grows worse, creating certain disorders in the organism, science speaks of "mental hysteria," recommends counter-irritants, lupuline and camphor, bromide of potassium, and cold showers.

As for the causes behind these disturbances, science is obliged to remain hesitant. It does not know, as is the case for terrible nervous illnesses, the motives underlying the disturbances and crises. All it does is watch over the development of the episodes, averting or delaying them, but in no case can science in its present state explain the turbulent nature of those unhealthy thoughts.

As for the Church, it's in its element here. It recognizes the sinuous actions of old sin. This mental hysteria is what the Church calls morose delight and what it defines as "the acceptance of something evil offered by the imagination as if it were really present, although there is no real desire to carry out the act." From the point of view of one's responsibilities, the Church judges such hysteria as being as dangerous as the act itself, and classes it, without any hesitation, in the series of mortal sins.

In this mental masturbation it sees the insidious appeals of the Most Low. As a remedy, it can offer only curses and prayers. If necessary, it could also have recourse to relics and brandish the rusty weapon of exorcism: but, believing in the virtue of the Sacraments, the church's great soul doctors are content merely to force people afflicted with this illness to take communion, and await the deliverance of the patient through his approaches to the Holy Table.

In brief, this phenomenon is straightforward as far as Catholics are concerned, but profoundly obscure for materialists, who are not used to discovering in the brain the mechanism of that soul that they consider merely as a function of a self-contained nervous system.

In art, this mental hysteria or this morose delight had inevitably to express itself in the artist's work and give permanent form to the images it had itself created. There, indeed, it found its spiritual outlet, and the only possible outlet, for a physical outlet is, as I have already reported, the most certain destroyer of art.

It is therefore to this special state of the soul that can be attributed true artists' carnal whinnyings, written or painted.

Manipulated by lesser men or by parasites enamored of fame, this dry erethism, if I may term it so, has produced abject and stupid works of art. Controlled, commanded by masters, it has been the foundation of those great erotic works that sleep in the Arcana of libraries, in hidden boxes and closed files.

It is these last works alone that I wish to discuss. Some of the most famous, the secret museums of Antiquity, the libertine works of Giulio Romano,[16] Marco Antonio,[17] Carpaccio,[18] for instance, are, it must be

---

16. Giulio Romano (1499–1542), who also signed works as Jules Romains, was a painter and architect, one of the founders of Mannerism. His fresco *The Fall of the Giants* is created in such a way as to give the spectator the impression of standing in the midst of carnage and destruction.

17. Marco Antonio, seventeenth-century Neapolitan painter.

18. Vittore Carpaccio (1460/65–1523/26), best known for his cycle of large pictures known as *The Legend of Saint Ursula*, showing the martyrdom of the saint and her 1,000 associates.

admitted, extremely mediocre. And even if we allow that the Dutch sixteenth-century painter Torrentius[19] was endowed with genius, how can we prove it, since all his paintings were burned in the Place du Grève, while he himself, after having undergone torture, was exiled as an Adamite?

On the other hand, the engravings of Rembrandt[20] are heavy, lacking that sharp savor that certain priapisms exude, and therefore I won't linger over them. I will also make no mention of last century's blemished prettinesses. At bottom, that age eroticized furniture in a charming way, aphrodisiacked the industry of tapestry makers and carpenters, triumphed in the boundaries of art, but where painting itself is concerned it shows merely an interloping smirk, the refinement of a dressing room, an irritating decor of a bidet impregnated with amber. Leaving aside the rummagings painted by the Fragonards[21] and the Bouchers,[22] we'd arrive, if we were to follow that slope, at the senile frivolities of the Baudoüins[23] and the Carêmes[24] who create things at once licentious and pretty, that dishonor through the baseness of their suggestions and the pettiness of their vision, the great Biblical vice of Lewdness.

Likewise neglecting Gavarni's[25] ridiculous scenes of intimate life, Devéria's[26] libertinages, and the skinny vignettes of gentle Tassaert,[27] I shall pause as I come to Rowlandson[28] and the Japanese, before stopping definitively at M. Rops, whose production I should like to try to define.

Rowlandson treated those subjects with ferocious humor, exaggerated banter, and mad gaiety. The vast majority of his heroes are trouserless hussars who whip the wind, and unceremoniously rape girls who are astonished at such good fortune and writhe about in paroxysms of joy. In one of his color plates, there is an amazing uproar of rutting

---

19. Jan Simonsz Torrentius (1589–1644), Dutch painter who was condemned as a leader of the Rosicrucians, tortured, and imprisoned. Later released, he was again captured and tortured, dying as a result of his treatment.

20. Rembrandt van Ryn (1606–1669), although better known for his paintings and particularly his long series of self-portraits, also produced a large number of etchings that reflect the general tendencies of his work.

21. Jean-Honoré Fragonard (1732–1806), a French rococo painter, best known for his delicately erotic paintings.

22. François Boucher (1703–1770), a French rococo painter whose paintings are mainly nudes, and pastoral or mythological scenes.

23. Paul Baudoüin (1844–1931), a well-known fresco painter, famous for his decoration of the Petit Palais and for his frescos in his native Rouen.

24. Claude-François Carême (1709–1796), French artist.

25. *Gavarni:* Sulpice Guillaume Chevalier, known as Paul Gavarni (1804–1866), was a watercolor specialist who also produced lithographs and sketches, particularly of the urban poor.

26. Achille Devéria (1800–1857), French painter and engraver. He illustrated the works of several of the romantic writers.

27. Octave Tassaert (1800–1874), painter whose main subject was the poor. He committed suicide by inhaling coal gas.

28. Thomas Rowlandson (1756–1827) was a British caricaturist and book illustrator. Two of his comic satires of social types were *Dr Syntax* and *The English Dance of Death.*

crowds: on a public square, a female acrobat, naked, with a stomach like a pumpkin, does the splits, upside down, in a cradle, to the sound of an organ. Windows fly open; a thunderstruck Turk, sitting cross legged, smokes his pipe, belly in the air; an old marquis, his sword aloft, preceded by scarlet spindle-shaped figures, while a hussar in action is killing himself, and a doctor from the Sorbonne is struck motionless and dumb with amazement. There's a woman squatting on the head of a man who is blowing a trumpet, while she clambers, skirts over her thighs, up to the windows. Amidst this incoherent realism there is the unbuttoned gaiety of a big naval wedding, a bawdy laugh whipped up by the comic speed of the old savant, stripped of glory, and recognizing that fact with a furious sneer and scornful eyes that beg for patient help.

This big-bellied and massive joy takes on a finer and more willowy aspect, however, in certain works of Rowlandson, where it often focuses, as in the reticent plates of Hogarth,[29] on some scene closely observed in its rich episodes, in its comic corners. So it is in another of his colored plates, *The Miser.*

In a closed room, an old skinflint, wearing a pink bonnet, sits near a safe box. There are two girls present. One is sitting on the side of the bed with her shirt rucked up, her legs splayed open; the other is doing her utmost to resuscitate this old man, whose trousers are down around his ankles. In one hand he holds a sack of gold coins, with the other he scratches his forehead, working out, in a groaning smile, the price demanded by these two prostitutes, torn between the demands of penny-pinching, and the appeals of his lust.

The man's hesitation and the bantering and sly gaze of the women—who, fascinated by the bulges and the jingling sounds of the sack, almost forget to keep an eye on the libertine stew they're preparing for the old man—are truly conveyed with good-natured scorn, with a knowledge of what is funny, with such understanding and verve that the obscene aspects fade away, leaving only the study of behavior with its physiognomical details lit by the ardent reflections of vices that meet there.

The fat, pretty woman, with her rustic temptation of healthy flesh, the woman with her simultaneously serious and cunning face, her joyful flesh, the woman Rowlandson carries off with such deliberation, appears in these engravings as in others of the same sort, in which hussars are deep in debauchery, where monks are flinging themselves on nuns, where half-naked musicians, their bows in the wind, beat out like a metronome the orgiastical measure and blow, red-faced, into instruments with mouths of brass.

But, it has to be said, however desirable she may be, the Rowlandson

---

29. William Hogarth (1697–1764), English painter and engraver who excelled in social satires such as *A Rake's Progress* and *Gin Lane.*

woman is entirely animal, without any interesting complications of the senses. He has made of her, in a word, more of an instrument for fornicating, a solid and sanitary beast, than the terrible she-faun of Lewdness. His men are fools, with the muscles of porters, his prostitutes are canteen keepers with the buttocks of draft horses. Sometimes these are creatures who have stepped out of a Rubens painting, and who, at Nature's call, relieve themselves. That's all.

With the Japanese, the point of view changes; that somewhat virile understanding of hilarious, abundant flesh, that preposterous gaiety which in my view diminishes the libertine work of Rowlandson, has disappeared and the opposite is revealed. What is evident in their albums is suffering.

For them, carnal dealings seek to break the nervous system, as they pass through erect members, stretched to breaking point, flashing fiery sparks. It tortures the couples, stiffens their fists, and, like an electric charge, pulls legs up and turns toes twisted inside out.

Their women, with their indolent flesh, as white as that of emphysemiacs, die, lying upside down, eyes closed, teeth gritted in the blood from their lips; the belly, horribly slit, gapes open under a little powder puff, looking like a wound with wattles. Their men gasp prostrate, sprouting inconceivable phalluses, topped with parasols, with swollen tubes and striped with veins. Intermingled in impossible poses they all lie there like corpses whose bones have been broken as a result of terrible punishments.

The finest etching of this sort I know is terrifying. It's of a Japanese woman covered by a squid; with his tentacles the horrible beast pumps her nipples and pries into her mouth, while the head itself drinks the lower parts. The almost superhuman expression of anguish and pain that convulses that long Pierrot face with its hooked nose, and the hysterical joy that simultaneously filters from the brow and from the closed eyes of that dead woman, are quite admirable!

The Japanese, then, have rehabilitated through suffering that Lust that hobnobs so enthusiastically in the galloping, rutting scenes of the English painter; but there, too, we merely have anecdotes, and not works that are elevated by a general concept that lifts them up and provides them with a spiritual support.

In these engravings, there is no concept that pulls together and condenses even that Licentiousness we find in the Bible, a licentiousness that arises from its very first pages under the Tree of Eden, and surfaces again at the end of the Book, when, summoned forth by the angel with its seven phials, there arises, clad in metal and purple, the sovereign whore seen by Saint John.

Deified by the pagans who adored it in the diverse incarnations of its Venuses and its Priaps, Licentiousness, which later became a Christian sin, was symbolized in the carnivorous dances of the Herodiades.

Then Licentiousness handed over, like so many arable fields, to the old Harrower of sins, the horrified soul of saints, tortured in their hermitages the solitary, corrupted for century after century the resolute chastity of the cloister.

She, too, it was who provoked the tribal migrations, the crushing of populations, who piled up a stumbling history on pillars of phalluses. Now it is She who controls the world, and who can struggle all alone against the other power of the age, against money, which in the most avaricious hands trembles and fails when the flesh burns!

It was nevertheless worth revealing the mechanism of this lever of carnal weights, this pulley of souls, it was worth showing its causes and summing it up in orthodox fashion, so to speak, in ardent and sad images, and where plastic images are concerned it was worth putting in the place of the allegorical deities of paganism, a new Demon, a new Sataness. Held back in infancy from all the different poses that reveal what worldly prudery forbids one to see, badly and stupidly delighted by ingenious and low details, painting did not realize that it had to gravitate, like humanity which had given it birth, like the very earth that bears it, between these two poles: purity and Licentiousness, between the hell and heaven of art. Painting did not realize that if a work is to be exceptionally acute, it has to be satanical or mystical, that beyond those two extremes there is nothing but temperate works, purgatorial works, works stemming from human concerns that are more or less feeble.

Purity for its part has inspired paintings beyond compare; it has sublimated the talent of great Christian painters, the Fra Angelicos[30] and Grünewalds,[31] the Roger van der Weydens[32] and the Memlings.[33]

Purity died with the Middle Ages. Just like the divine feeling from which it emanated, it is now no longer accessible in art to generations bereft of faith.

As for licentiousness, it has not produced a single work that is really powerful. And we have had to wait until our own day to find an artist who has thought of really exploring those Antarctic regions unknown to art. Adopting the old medieval concept of man floating between Good and Evil, being debated between God and the Devil, between Purity which is the divine essence and Licentiousness which is the Devil himself, M. Félicien Rops, who has the soul of a primitive in reverse, has been able to achieve an inverted version of Memling's great

---

30. Fra Angelico (c.1387/1400–1455), Italian Dominican friar who painted religious subjects.

31. Mathias Grünewald (c. 1470/1480–1528), German painter who made use of renaissance techniques to heighten the impact of his late Gothic religious imagery.

32. Roger Van der Weyden (1399/1400–1464), major Flemish painter specializing in religious and historical subjects.

33. Hans Memlinc or Memling (1430/1440–1494), a pupil of van der Weyden. Painted devotional pictures, full of a calm joy.

work; he has penetrated Satanism and summed it up in admirable etchings which are like inventions, or symbols, or an incisive and sinewy art, an art which is ferocious and distraught, and they are truly unique.

But, it has to be said that M. Rops did not attain this synthesis of Evil at one stroke. In the agile frontispieces that he engraved in the past for those libertine works which were reprinted by Poulet-Malassis,[34] in Brussels, he merely reveals a mocking and impious verve, a bizarre and swift imagination.

With sometimes pointed wit, he overdoes his engravings, sometimes as elegant and beribboned as those of the eighteenth century—like the etching that precedes the *Théâtre gaillard* or the *Point de lendemain*, by Vivant Denon[35]—sometimes summed up in entirely personal allegories, with a complete liberty of behavior. Among the latter one could cite those etchings of the *Parnasse satyrique*:[36] one of them in which flights of minuscule women and little bacchantes clamber after the rigid joystick of a pagan statue whose goat's beard spreads out in delight while with his fatherly eyes he contemplates one of the women who ride, wildly, on the crest of his formidable member and stretches out her arms, swooning and crying for mercy while her companions hang, screaming, to the globes of his weighty balls; the other represents the reverse of this scene: a troop of little aegypans mounting an assault on an armless female faun, crowned with vine leaves, her ears pricked and her breasts heavy. She too is in a state of delight, smiling, maternally and lasciviously, at these little goatfooted fauns who seize her breasts, clamber over her large belly, forage in the depths of her navel, slide as if through a cat door into the gaping pod of her sex. But one of the most ingenious works, one of the most vehement of this series, is the one that precedes the little volume of *Joyeusetés du vidame de la braguette*, by poor old Glatigny.[37]

Imagine a good Flanders joker sitting down, potbelly in the air, holding the folded bottom of a pair of full-fall trousers. He's roaring so much with laughter he has tears in his eyes, so exuberant that he's almost choking, while a swarm of sweet little creatures pours out over his prodigious nudity which rises up like a light house whose base sinks into a thick scrub.

And they are quite exceptional, those tiny nymphomaniacs! Never

---

34. *Poulet-Malassis:* This editor, best known as Baudelaire's publisher, was also involved in the illegal publication of erotic and pornographic works.

35. *Denon:* Dominique Vivant Baron Denon (1747–1825) was a diplomat and art critic, and became director of the central museum of arts in 1802. A great art collector, he was also an etcher in his own right.

36. *Le Parnasse satyrique:* This parody of the poetry anthology *Le Parnasse contemporain* contains several scatological and semi-pornographic engravings of the kind described here.

37. Albert Glatigny (1839–1873), French poet. His adventurous life, bohemianism, and duels make him a Don Quixote of nineteenth-century French poetry. His early death prevented him from fulfilling the promise his work displays.

before has any painter rendered with such a sense of warm flesh, with such ardor, that madness of rutting cats! Taut, they cling with all the force of their wrists to the clumps of hair, ascend the mast, wend their way around the sacks, clamber over each other, devouring each other and turning head over heels in dying clusters . . .

Berlioz

♦

Hector Berlioz (1803–1869), the French Romantic composer, perhaps best known for La Symphonie fantastique _and his opera_ The Trojans, _was also the author of a famous treatise on orchestration, and of lively, entertaining, and unbuttoned memoirs. The following extracts are not only evocative of the musical scene in the heyday of Romanticism, but also reveal the ease with which Berlioz was able to convey the joy, excitement, and occasionally rage that music could inspire in him. Berlioz's prose is fast moving, moderately colloquial, witty, and unselfconsciously egocentric._

FURTHER READING: _Memoirs_, tr. David Cairns (New York: Norton, 1975).
BIOGRAPHY: D. Kern Holoman, _Berlioz_ (Cambridge, Mass.: Harvard University Press, 1989); David Cairns, _Berlioz 1803–1832_ (London: Deutsch, 1989).
TEXT USED: _Mémoires_ (Paris: Calmann-Levy, 1881).

MUSICAL APPRECIATION (1881)

Most opera performances were solemn occasions for which I used to prepare myself by reading and meditating on the works that were to be performed. The fanatical admiration that I and a few habitués of the orchestra stalls used to profess for our favorite authors could be compared only to our intense hatred for the others. The Jupiter of our Olympus was Gluck,[1] and the cult we paid him bears no comparison with whatever the most exaggerated dilettantism of today could conceive. But if some of my friends were faithful sectarians of this musical religion, I can say without a trace of vanity that I was its pope. When-

---

1. Christoph Willibald Gluck (1714–1787), a German composer. In Paris, between 1774 and 1780, a rivalry pitted the supporters of Gluck against those of Piccini; Gluck was much favored by Marie-Antoinette. Berlioz's enthusiasm seems to owe less to this old quarrel than to a dislike for the French tradition.

ever I saw their fervor was fading, I would rekindle it with sermons worthy of the Saint Simonians.[2] I would take them to the opera house willy nilly, often giving them tickets I'd bought at the ticket office with my own money, and that I'd claim to have received from an employee of the house. As soon as this ruse had enabled me to drag my companions to a performance of one of Gluck's masterpieces, I would establish them on a bench in the stalls, advising them strongly not to change it for any other, for not all seats provided equally good possibilities of hearing the music, and there was not a single spot whose drawbacks and advantages I had not already tested. Here you were too close to the horns, there you couldn't hear them at all; on the right, the sound of the trombones was too dominant; on the left, that sound was bounced off the ground-floor boxes and produced a disagreeable effect; down there, you were too close to the orchestra, and up here you were too far from the stage to make out the words or the facial expressions of the actors; the instrumentation of this work should be heard from a certain place, while the choruses of another work were best from another spot; in such and such an act, in which the scenery represented a sacred wood, the stage was enormous and the sound drifted off into the theater and was lost, and so you had to get closer; another, on the contrary, took place inside a palace, the scenery being what the machine operators call a "closed salon," so that the power of the voices was doubled by a circumstance that might strike you as very indifferent, but it meant that you had to go a little further back in the stalls, so that the orchestra and the voices, heard from a slight distance, seemed more intimately linked, combined in a more harmonious ensemble.

Once these instructions have been given, I would ask my neophytes if they were familiar with the opera they were about to hear. If they had not read the words, I would take the libretto from my pocket, and taking advantage of the time that remained before the curtain rose, I would make them read it, adding to the main passages all the observations I thought appropriate to help them understand the composer's intentions, for we always came very early, partly to get the best seats, partly to avoid missing the first notes of the overture, and partly to delight in that singular charm of waiting before a great joy one is sure to obtain. Moreover, we used to take great pleasure in watching the orchestra pit, at first empty and containing nothing but an unstrung piano, gradually fill with music and musicians. The orchestra boy would come in first, to put the parts on the music stands. That moment was not without its mixture of fear for us; since the moment when we'd arrived, some accident might have taken place; they might have changed the show and put in the place of a monumental work of Gluck some

---

2. *Saint-Simonians:* Utopian sect inspired by the writings of Count Henri de Saint-Simon (1760–1825), who called for a communist reorganization of society.

Nightingale, or a few *False Heroes*, or a *Caravan from Cairo*, a *Panurge*, or a *Village Sorcerer*, a *Lasthénie*, all of which were more or less pale and skimpy productions, more or less flat and false, for which we professed an equal and supreme scorn. The name of the piece inscribed in large letters on the parts for the double basses, which were those placed nearest to the stalls, rescued us from our uneasiness or confirmed our worst fears. In the latter case, we would rush from the theater swearing like marauding troopers unable to find anything but water in what they had taken to be barrels of brandy, and directing our curses at the author of the work that had been substituted, the director who inflicted it on the public, and the government who allowed it to be performed. Poor Rousseau,[3] who attached as much importance to his score for the *Village Sorcerer* as to those masterpieces of eloquence that have immortalized his name, he who believed firmly that he had completely eclipsed Rameau,[4] including the trio from *The Fates*, together with the little songs, the little refrains, the little rondeaux, the little solos, the little pastorals, the little comic pieces of all kinds of which that little interlude is composed; he who was so tormented; he whom the Holbach[5] sect so envied for his musical work; he who was accused of not being its author; he who was acclaimed throughout the length and breadth of France, from Jéliotte and Mlle Fel[6] right to King Louis XV, who never grew tired of repeating "I have lost my servant" in the worst voice in the entire realm; he, finally, whose favorite work obtained all kinds of success when it first came out; poor Rousseau! What would he have said of our curses if he had been able to hear them? And could he have foreseen that his beloved opera, which had aroused so much applause, would one day fall, never to rise again, under the blow of an enormous wig all powdered white, thrown at Colette's[7] feet by an insolent joker? By sheer chance I was present at that final performance of the *Sorcerer*; many people, as a result, accused me of orchestrating the wig trick, but I swear I'm completely innocent. I even believe I was quite as indignant as I was amused by this grotesque piece of irreverence, with the result that I cannot really tell whether or not I would have been capable of doing such a thing. But can anyone imagine that fifty years ago Gluck, yes Gluck himself, in reference to that paltry *Sorcerer* pushed the irony even further and dared to write and publish in the most serious letter possible addressed to Queen Marie-Antoinette that "France, poorly fa-

---

3. Jean-Jacques Rousseau (1712–1778), better known for such literary masterpieces as *Julie, or The New Heloise* and his *Reveries*, was also a composer.

4. Jean-Philippe Rameau (1683–1764), French composer renowned for his opera-ballets and his operas.

5. *Holbach:* Paul Henri Dietrich, baron d'Holbach (1723–1789), French philosopher.

6. Marie Fel (1713–1794), opera singer who created the role of Colette in Rousseau's *Devin du village (Village Sorcerer)*.

7. *Colette:* Character in Rousseau's opera, *The Village Sorcerer*.

vored where music is concerned, nevertheless possessed a few remarkable works, among which must be cited *The Village Sorcerer*, by M. Rousseau"? Who would ever have taken it into their heads to think that Gluck could be so witty? This single blow from a German is enough to strip the Italians of the palms for perfidious jokes.

But to get back to my story. When the title on the orchestral parts announced to us that nothing in the performance had been changed, I would continue my sermon, singing the most striking passages, explaining the techniques of instrumentation that allowed the main effects, and, by my words, obtaining in advance the enthusiasm of all the members of our little club. Such agitation greatly astonished our neighbors in the stalls, good provincials for the most part, who, hearing me hold forth on the wonders of the score that was going to be played, expected to lose their minds in the emotion and so found in it more anxiety than pleasure. And then I never failed to point out by name each of the musicians as they came into the pit, adding a few comments on their habits and talents.

"Here's Baillot! He doesn't behave like other violin soloists and reserve himself exclusively for ballet; he doesn't think it's a stain on his honor to accompany a Gluck opera. In a moment you will hear a tune he performs on the fourth string; you can hear it above the entire orchestra."

"Oh! That fat redhead, over there! That's the first double bass, old Chénié. He's a lively old stick, despite his age. On his own he's worth four ordinary double basses. You can be sure he'll perform the score as the composer wrote it. He doesn't belong to the school of simplifiers."

"The conductor ought to pay some attention to M. Guillou, the first flute, the one coming in now. He takes extraordinary liberties with Gluck. In the religious march for *Alceste*, for instance, the composer wrote the flute parts in the lower register just so he could obtain the special effect of the deeper sounds of that instrument, but M. Guillou doesn't like his part set out like that; he has to dominate, he has to be heard, and for that reason he plays the flute's song an octave higher, thus destroying the result the composer had promised himself, and turning an ingenious idea into something puerile and vulgar."

The three knocks announcing that the performance was about to begin would interrupt us in the midst of our severe examination of the main members of the orchestra. We would immediately fall silent, waiting with muffled heartbeats for Kreutzer's or Valentino's baton to give the beat. Once the overture had started, it was imperative that none of our neighbors take it into their heads to talk, hum, or beat time; we had adopted for our own use in such circumstances this well known phrase from a music lover: "Curses on those musicians who deprive me of the pleasure of hearing what the gentleman has to say!"

Since we had such intimate knowledge of the score that was being performed, it wasn't a very good idea to make any changes in it either. I would have preferred to be killed rather than let any such familiarity taken with the great masters pass by unchallenged. I wasn't going to wait to protest coldly in writing against such a crime of sacrilege, oh no! It was in full sight of the public and at the top of my voice that I would chastise the sinners. And I can assure you that no criticism carries such weight as that. Thus, one day, they were performing *Iphegenia en Tauride* and I'd noticed that at the preceding performance cymbals had been added to the Scythians' dance tune in G minor where Gluck used only string instruments, and that in Orestes' great recitative in the third act, the trombone parts so wonderfully motivated by the scene on stage and written into the score, had not been performed. I was determined, if the same errors recurred, to draw attention to them. So when the Scythians' ballet began, I waited for the cymbals in that particular passage: they could be heard just as the previous time in the music I have indicated. Boiling with wrath, I nevertheless controlled myself until the end of the piece, and immediately, taking advantage of the brief moment of silence that separates that piece from the next, I shouted at the top of my voice: "There are no cymbals in that tune! Who has taken it on himself to correct Gluck?"

You can imagine the uproar! The audience, which doesn't have too clear an idea of all these questions of art, and who couldn't give a damn whether the composer's instrumentation was changed or not, couldn't understand why on earth the young madman in the stalls was so enraged. But it was far worse when in the third act the suppression of the trombones in Orestes' monologue took place as I had feared it would, and the same voice could be heard shouting these words: "The trombones didn't play! This is unbearable!"

The astonishment in the pit and the audience can be compared only with the rage (entirely natural, I confess) of Valentino, who was conducting on that evening. I later learned that those wretched trombonists had merely submitted to an order not to play at that point; for the copied parts were in perfect accord with the original.

As for the cymbals that Gluck had so felicitously placed in the first of the Scythians' choruses, someone or other had taken it into his head to introduce them likewise in to the dance tune, thus distorting the color and disturbing the sinister silence of the ballet. But I know full well that in the following performances, everything returned to the accustomed order, the cymbals were silent and the trombones played, and I was content to mutter: "Well, that's fortunate!"

Shortly afterwards, de Pons, who was at least as fanatical as I, judged it unsuitable that, for the first act of *Œdipus*, we were given dance tunes other than those written by Sacchini,[8] and he came to me to propose

8. Antonio Sacchini (1730–1786), Italian opera composer.

that we force justice to be done to the interminable horn and cello solos with which they'd been replaced. How could I fail to support such a praiseworthy intention? The means employed for *Iphigenia* served us just as well for *Œdipus*; and after the two of us alone had launched a few comments from the stalls one evening the new dance tunes disappeared for ever afterwards.

Only once did we succeed in whipping up the audience. The poster had announced that the violin solo for the ballet *Nina* would be performed by Baillot. The virtuoso fell ill, or there was some other problem, so that he couldn't be heard, and the administration thought it sufficient to forewarn the audience with a minute piece of paper stuck on the poster on the doors of the Opera, where no one ever looks. The vast majority of the audience was thus expecting to hear the famous violinist.

At the moment when Ninon, in the arms of her father and her lover, is restored to her right mind, Mlle Bigottini's very touching pantomime could not move us enough to make us forget Baillot. The performance was nearing its end. "Hey! Hey! the solo violin part, where is it?" I said, loudly enough to be heard. "That's right," a member of the audience responded, "it looks like they want us to do without it." "Baillot! Baillot! The solo violin part!" At that moment the stalls exploded and something took place that was never seen before in the opera house: the entire audience loudly demanded that the promises made in the poster be honored. The curtain fell in the midst of a great uproar. The noise redoubled. The musicians, seeing how furious the stalls were, took flight. In a rage, everyone leapt into the pit, the musicians' chairs were thrown left, right, and center, stands were overturned. The head of the kettledrums was cracked, and it was in vain that I shouted: "Gentlemen, gentlemen, what are you doing? You mustn't break the instruments! . . . What barbaric behavior. Can't you see that that's old Chénié's bass? An admirable instrument which sounds as if it came from hell!" They were no longer listening to me, and the mutineers withdrew only after they'd turned the whole orchestra topsy-turvy and broken goodness knows how many benches and instruments.

That was the down side of the active criticism that we used to indulge in so despotically at the Opera; the good side was our enthusiasm when everything succeeded.

Then you should have seen just how frantically we applauded those passages no one in the audience paid attention to, such as a beautiful bass, a successful modulation, a note of truth in a recitative, expressive playing from the oboe, and so forth. The audience took us for the claque, hoping to outnumber our rivals, whereas the head of the official claque—who knew quite well how far from the truth that was, and whose carefully orchestrated moves were thrown out of kilter by our untimely applause—would from time to time glare at us with a look worthy of Neptune pronouncing the *quos ego*.[9] Then in the lovely moments of Mme Branchu's performance there were exclamations and stampings of feet such as are no longer encountered today, not even at the Conservatorium, the only place in France where true musical enthusiasm still appears from time to time.

The strangest scene of this type that I remember is the following. *Œdipus* was being performed. Although far removed from Gluck in our estimation, Sacchini did not fail to find in us sincere admirers. That evening I had dragged along to the Opera one of my friends, a student who was completely unmoved by all arts other than that of petty theft, yet I was determined to turn him into a musical enthusiast. The sufferings of Antigone and her father had only a mediocre effect on him. So after the first act, despairing of making anything of him, I left him behind me, moving forward to a bench where I would not be troubled by his coolness. As if to underline his passivity even more, chance had placed at his right a spectator as impressionable as he was unmoved. I soon became aware of this. Dérivis had just produced a beautiful effect in his famous recitative:

My son! You are no longer my son!
Go! My hatred is too strong!

However absorbed I was by this scene, which is so beautiful in its naturalness and in the way it conveys the sense of antiquity, it was impossible for me not to hear the dialog taking place behind me, between my young man, who was peeling an orange, and the unknown spectator sitting next to him, who was suffering from the most intense emotion.

"Good God, sir, calm yourself!"

"No! This is irresistible! It's overwhelming! It's killing me!"

"Sir, you really shouldn't carry on like that. You'll make yourself ill."

"No, let me go! Oh!"

"Come on, sir, chin up! After all, it's only a play. . . . Would you like a nice piece of orange?"

"Oh! It's sublime!"

"It's from Malta!"

"What heavenly art!"

"Do take one."

"Oh, sir, what music!"

"Yes, it is pretty, isn't it."

During this clashing conversation, the opera had reached the fine trio that follows the reconciliation scene: "O sweet moments!" The penetrating sweetness of this simple melody seized me in my turn; I began to weep, my head plunged in my hands, like a man sunk in deep affliction. Scarcely had the trio ended than two robust arms picked me up

---

9. *quos ego:* These words from Virgil's *Aeneid* (I.135) were uttered by Neptune to the disobedient winds.

from my bench and hugged me so tightly around the chest that I thought it would burst asunder. These were the arms of the unknown spectator, who—unable to master his emotions any more, and having noticed that of all those around him I alone seemed to share them—embraced me with intensity, shouting in a convulsed voice, "Motherrrr of God, sir, that was beautiful!" Without feeling the slightest amazement, I asked him, my face quite stained with tears, "Are you a musician?"

"No, but I feel music as intensely as anyone alive."

"Of course it's all one and the same, give me your hand; gracious me, sir, you're a fine man!"

On that, utterly deaf to the snickers of the spectators who had gathered around us, and untouched by the amazement of my orange-eating tyro, we exchanged a few words softly: I gave him my name, and he entrusted to me his own and his profession. He was an engineer! A mathematician!!! Isn't it amazing where sensitivity chooses to hide away?

Mallarmé

◆

*Stéphane Mallarmé (1842–1898), best known for his finely wrought, demand-
ing, and very beautiful poetry, also produced translations, journalism, and
prose poetry. His subtle, enigmatic style derives in part from his refusal of
cliché, his rejection of any form of banality, and his determination to give his
readers the joy of discovering little by little the meaning of what he wrote. His
prose poems are frequently self-reflective meditations on the function and possibilities of writing, but they also show him striving to create a blend of creative and critical writing that would elevate the prose of the daily papers to
the level of imaginative writing.*

FURTHER READING: *Poetry*, tr. Henry Weinfield (Berkeley: University of Califor-
nia Press, 1994).
BIOGRAPHY: Gordon Millan, *A Throw of the Dice* (New York: Farrar, Straus, and
Giroux, 1994).
TEXT USED: *Pages* (Brussels: Edmond Deman, 1891).

RICHARD WAGNER: A FRENCH POET'S REVERIE
(1891)

A modern French poet, who, for a variety of reasons, is excluded from
any participation in official displays of beauty, takes pleasure, as an outcome of a task undertaken—the mysterious refinement of poetry for
solitary Celebrations—in reflecting on the sovereign pageantry of poetry, such as cannot exist alongside the flood of banality borne along by
the arts in our counterfeit civilization.—A Ceremony of a day which
lies in the heart of the crowd, unknown to it: almost a Cult!

The certainty that neither he nor any of his contemporaries is involved in any such enterprise frees him from any constraints that might
be imposed on his dream by a feeling of incompetence and the remote-
ness of the facts.

His gaze, untroubled in its integrity, penetrates the far distance.

It is easy for him, and the least he can do, to accept the heroic and solitary task of considering, in the proud coil of the consequences, the Monster-Which-Cannot-Exist! Leaving on its side the wound of a pure, affirmative gaze.

Leaving aside his glimpses of the extraordinary but currently incomplete splendor of plastic figuration, among which Dance is outstanding at least in the perfection of its representation, for its elliptical writing can alone transform the fleeting and sudden into the Idea—such a vision includes entirely, absolutely entirely, the Dream of the future. If this art-lover considers what Music has brought to the Theater, a marvel that music is best able to set in motion, he does not long remain immersed in his own thoughts. Already, with whatever bounds his mind leaps, it senses the colossal approach of an Initiation. Or rather, see if your wish has not already been realized.

What a unique challenge for poets, whose task he has usurped with the most candid and splendid bravura, this Richard Wagner!

The emotions inspired by this foreigner are complex, exaltation and veneration, but also a feeling of unease that everything should be done by other means than directly shining forth from the literary principle itself.

To reach a judgment one has to face the doubts and imperative of perceiving what circumstances surrounded the master's first attempts. He sprang up in the days of the only form of theater which can be described as decrepit, so coarse are the elements of which its Fiction is formed: since that Fiction imposes itself directly and instantaneously, demanding that one believe in the existence of the character and the adventure—believe, simply, nothing more. As if that act of faith demanded from the spectator should not be the very result he extracts from the conjunction of all the arts giving birth to the miracle of the stage, which otherwise remains inert and void! You have to fall under a spell, to achieve which no means of enchantment implied by the magic of music is superfluous, in order to empower your reason grappling with a simulacrum, and from the outset it is proclaimed: "Let us suppose that all this really happened and you are right in the middle of it!"

Modern man scorns all demands to use his imagination, but since he is a past master at exploiting the arts, he expects every art to transport him to the point where a special power of illusion bursts forth and then he gives his consent.

Before the use of Music, Theater was obliged to make its starting-point a concept which was authoritarian and naive, at the time when this new source of evocation was not available to its masterpieces, which, alas!, lay entombed in the pious leaves of a book, and none of which had any hope of surging forth from it at our celebrations. Theater's mechanism remains attached to the past, such that a popular representation would repudiate it because of that intellectual tyranny—for the crowd wants to remain master of its own belief, following the suggestions the arts provide. The simple addition of an orchestra changes the old theater completely, annulling its very principle, and it is a purely allegorical way that the current theatrical act, which is in itself empty and abstract, impersonal, must, if it is to move forward with any semblance of certainty, make use of the invigorating effluvia of Music.

The mere presence of Music is a triumph, provided it does not attempt to retain the old conditions, even with the aim of extending them sublimely, but bursts forth as the generator of all vitality. The audience will have the impression that if the orchestra stopped exerting its influence, the mime would instantly become a statue.

Was it possible for the Musician, the close confidant of his Art's secret, to confine its function to this simple initial aim? Such a metamorphosis demands the impartiality of a critic who does not have behind him, ready to rear up with impatience and joy, the abyss of musical performance, which in this case is the most tumultuous a man has ever restrained with his clear will.

This is what he achieved.

Going at once to what was most urgent, he reconciled an entire tradition, intact but on the point of falling into disuse, with what he divined to be welling up, pure and undetected, in his scores. Excluding perspicacity, that form of sterile suicide, the strange gift of assimilation existed in such lasting abundance in this creator in spite of everything, that between two elements of beauty, mutually exclusive or at least unaware of each other, personal drama and ideal music, he was able to bring about a marriage. Yes, through a harmonious compromise, generating a precise theatrical phase which corresponds, as if by surprise, to the temperament of his race!

Although from a philosophical viewpoint it merely places itself alongside Drama, Music (I insist that someone intimate where it stems from, what its primary meaning is, and its destiny) penetrates and envelops Drama through the composer's dazzling willpower, and thereby links up with it. There is no candor or depth which, with an enthusiastic awakening, it does not pour forth to bring about that fusion, except that Music's own principle escapes.

What amazing sureness of touch to be able to fuse these diverse forms of pleasure on the stage and in the symphony without totally transforming either of them.

Now, indeed, a form of music which, apart from the observance of very complex laws, at first retains of that art only what is innate and elusive, blends the colors and outlines of the hero with the timbres and themes, in an atmosphere richer in Reverie than any earthly song, a deity clad in the indivisible folds of a fabric of chords, or will carry the hero away on a wave of Passion, whose unleashing is too vast when directed at a single being, will hurl him and twist him and withdraw him from his notion, swept aside before that superhuman flood, only to make him seize it afresh when he dominates everything through song, a song which bursts forth, as it rends asunder the thought that inspired it. The hero, who treads not so much on our earth as on mist, will always be revealed in a distant prospect filled with the haze of laments, glories and joy emerging from the instrumentation, cast back by this means to the beginnings of time. He is effective only when surrounded in the Grecian way, by that blend of stupor and intimacy an audience experiences when it is faced with myths which seem barely to have existed, so completely does their instinctive past melt away! But at the same time he constantly benefits from having the familiar outer forms of the human individual. Some forms even satisfy the intellect because they seem not entirely unconnected with random symbols.

Behold, enthroned on the stage, Legend.

With a prior piety, an audience on the second occasion since time began, the first being Greek, the second German, considers the theatrical representation of the secret of our origins. Some remarkable happiness, new and barbaric, establishes it: in front of that moving veil, the subtle orchestration magnificently decorates its genesis.

Everything is steeped anew in the primal stream, but without completely reaching the source.

If the French mind, which is strictly imaginative and abstract, and thus poetic, blazes forth, it will not be like this. In accordance with Art in all its integrity, for Art is inventive, the French mind is repelled by Legend. See how, from the days forever gone they retain no anecdote, enormous and rough hewn, as if they foresaw what Legend would bring, anachronistically, to a theatrical representation, the enthronement of one of the acts of Civilization.* That is, unless the Fable, devoid of any known place, time, and character, appears, a product of the meaning latent in the concourse of all, the Fable inscribed on the page of the Heavens and of which History itself is merely a shadowy interpretation, namely a POEM, the Ode, could it be that the age, or our country, which exalts it, have dissolved Myths through thought, only to forge new ones! These are what the Theater calls for, not myths which are fixed, or venerable, or famed, but one, stripped of all personality, for it combines our manifold facets: and it is this myth that Art evokes from the magic corresponding to our national behavior, in order to reflect that behavior in us. A Type without any preliminary name, so as to liberate a sense of surprise: his gestures draw together toward him our dreams of sites or edens, which the theater of the past engulfs, in the vain pretension of containing or depicting them. Do not think of

---

*Exhibition, Handing over of Powers etc. Do I see you there Brünhilde, or what would you do there, Siegfried! [Mallarmé's note]

the actor as an individual, or of the stage as having any precise location! (the double error, a fixed set and a real actor, in Theater lacking music): does a spiritual fact, the flowering of symbols, or their preparation, demand a place in which to develop other than the fictional focus of the crowd's gaze? Holy of holies, but all in the mind . . . then, in some supreme burst of light, which arouses the Figure that is No One, there converges every mimic gesture that Figure seizes from a rhythm provided in the symphony, and setting it free! Then there come to breathe their last, as if at the feet of the incarnation, but an incarnation revealing a definite link between them and its humanity, those quintessences and natural summits which Music recreates, that ultimate vibrant prolongation of all things, like life itself,

Man, and his true earthly abode, exchange reciprocal proofs.

Thus the Mystery is accomplished.

The City which provided a Theater for the sacred experience sets on the earth the universal seal.

As for its people, it was the very least they could do to testify to the august fact—I call as witness Justice which cannot but reign there— since that orchestration, which a moment since revealed the presence of the god, never produces anything other than the synthesis of those moments of delicacy and magnificence, immortal and innate, which are present unknown to all whenever a silent audience assembles.

That is why, Genius!, I, who in my humility remain the servant of an eternal logic, o Wagner, I am filled with suffering and self-reproaches, in those minutes marked by lassitude, because I cannot count myself among those who, wearying of everything in their search for definitive salvation, go straight to the edifice of your Art, which for them is the end of the journey. That undeniable portico offers, in these days which are not times of jubilation for any people, welcome shelter from our own insufficiencies and the mediocrity of our homelands; it exalts some fervent devotees to the point of certainty; for them this is not the greatest distance toward the goal ever ordained by a human gesture, which they run with you as guide, but the completion of Humanity's voyage toward an Ideal. At least, for I want my share of the ecstasy, you will allow me to enjoy a moment of rest in your Temple, half-way up the holy mountain, whose sunrise of truths, the most comprehensive yet, fills the dome with its fanfare and invites, as far as the eye can see from the parvis, lawns where the feet of your chosen brothers tread. It is as if the mind were set apart from our harrying incoherence, and sheltered from the too lucid obsession with that menacing pinnacle of the absolute, whose outline can be divined in the parting of the clouds on high, fulgurating, bare, and alone: which looms above and beyond and which, it seems, no one is to scale. No one! The words do not strike remorse into the heart of the passer-by drinking at your convivial fountain.

Banville

◆

*Théodore de Banville (1823–1891) was a virtuoso poet, known for his extraor-
dinary skill in manipulating rhyme and rhythm. He wrote many volumes of
poetry, including his* Stalactites *of 1843, his* Blood of the Cup *in 1857, and
his playful* Odes Funambulesques *(*Tightrope Odes*) also of 1857. In addition he was a master of prose style, writing short stories, a travelogue, and
a delicately nostalgic autobiography. While his autobiography focuses primarily
on the writers and artists he had known, he does devote several witty, bittersweet chapters to his early childhood. The limpidity and sensitivity of his prose
style confer on what might otherwise be banal incidents a symbolic dimension
of timeless power. Like many of his contemporaries, notably Nerval, Gautier,
Baudelaire, and Mallarmé, Banville was fascinated with performing artists,
particularly those street artists whose use of their bodies to entertain and whose
precarious existence offered parallels with the concept of the modern poet. One
of Banville's finest poems depicts a clown leaping so high from his trampoline
that he bounds through the tent roof and into the stars. In this study from his*
Parisian Sketches *of 1859, he exercises all his verbal sorcery to transform the
apparent banality of the artiste's act into a symbol not merely of the performing arts, but more generally of human aspirations and human frailty.*

TEXT USED: *Esquisses parisiennes* (Paris: Poulet-Malassis, 1859).

THE OLD TIGHTROPE WALKER: HÉBÉ CARISTI
(1859)

She was the sister of comets and stars; her hair whipped the vast
azure. Like the gods, she walked through the skies, tearing the clouds
with her Olympian brow. Her fame lasted a quarter of a century, and
during that time, which was long enough to see the making and breaking of so many realms, so many duchies, so many empires, she saw at

her feet the crowns of kings and the snows of mountain peaks. She could have held in her hands the fowl of the air. For days on end, intoxicated with pride, this artiste balanced on her rope, lost in the welkin, with the faint sound of the people's applause floating up to meet her like the murmur of a conquered and trembling sea. Hébé Caristi recently died in her 73rd year, for her birth certificate bears the fabulous date of July 22, 1781. She died unknown, forgotten, neglected. Nothing shows so clearly the vanity of artistic fame, a fame pursued at so great a cost.

Her name, which today summons up no image in our minds, was, only a short time ago, acclaimed with transports of wild admiration, and the woman who bore it was applauded by hands that shaped the destiny of empires. The implacable laws that bind us to the earth probably did not exist for this drinker of space and the infinite, held up as she was by invisible wings. Her serenity and her intrepid bravery made her superhuman. She was a rival (what's more, a successful rival) of Mme Saqui, that poetic figure whom she instantly relegated to the second rank. Hébé Caristi single-handedly, without teachers, without precursors, without any inspiration apart from that of her own lofty spirit, created an entire art, an art that was unprecedented, exceptional, and sometimes grandiose, the tightrope mime, a prodigious effort of organization and intelligence that no one had taught her and that she was unable to teach to any one else. But can I succeed in conveying to my reader this kind of drama, in which there can be no doubt that the abstract was presented in a more rarified form than in the tragedy *Bérénice* or in the most perfect symphonies?[1]

The great tightrope walker—who, even in our history's epic days, was able to become one of Paris's exemplary figures—was born in Serbia, in a gypsy band, all of whom were professional tightrope walkers and wandering performers. Before turning ten, as her father and mother were dead, she took over the leadership of their wandering company, and all these itinerant gentlefolk, subjugated by her wonderful dance, obeyed her without question. Moreover, a witch who was greatly feared in Belgrade had made a prediction about Hébé Caristi, that exercised an immense effect on her companions. She and all her family were to accomplish prodigies of boldness and rapidly make their fortune. She would be complimented by the greatest king in the whole world and would help to celebrate his victories. "And lastly," the gypsy went on, "you will have eyes of glowing coals and a heart of ice, and thus you will succeed in everything you set your hand to, but only until the day when you walk in blood."

The little dancer had high hopes that she would never walk in blood,

---

1. *Bérénice*: This tragedy by Jean Racine (1639–1699) is used here to represent the purest form of dramatic art.

and confidently rejoiced in the prophecy, blinded, moreover, about the future, like all those marked for a disastrous fate. If she encountered a single drop of blood on the highways, her companions rivaled each other to carry her in their arms, believing that they were thus sidestepping the restriction that blotted her rich horoscope. When four years had passed, the girl had worked so well for the company entrusted to her care that all of those gypsies, whom she had made rich, could appear luxuriously dressed and equipped when they appeared at the Beaucaire fair in 1795.

It was the first time since the Revolution that this famous fair had taken place, a fair at which merchants from Astrakhan, Baghdad, and Mosul gathered with pearl fishers from the Coromandel coast and garlic merchants from Marseille. The little narrow streets, lined with houses with high Gothic gables, created a most appropriate and picturesque framework for this fair. Hébé Caristi was not the least of its wonders. She had an olive complexion with eyes of jet, long brown eyelashes, and straight eyebrows. Her narrow nose, her thick and deeply curved lips, her curly hair, her long straight neck, her bust and hips, already clear despite her exceptional slimness, all made her appear like those Egyptian figures enclosed in a sheath of squared muslin, holding a lotus flower. In her hair she wore Venetian glass necklaces bound into a mass of bizarrely arranged braids, and she was dressed in barbaric style with striped silk in bright colors.

She climbed up the bell tower on a tight rope, but she did it with such courage and grace that her performances whipped her audience into a real delirium. Before the fair was over, her name was already popular throughout France. In 1800, Hébé, about to turn twenty, had not gone abroad again a single time, and had acquired a fortune large enough for her to construct on the corner of the rue d'Angoulême a theater for which she obtained the license and which she called the Theater of Military Exploits.

Indeed, the only shows performed there were mimes representing Buonaparte's battles and recent victories: Monetnotte, Millesimo, Lodi, Castiglione, Arcole, Rivoli, the Pyramids, Marengo; the first consul went on winning, and Hébé went on writing. But these military plays, which resembled those that are performed everywhere, were the least interesting part of her performance. Her glory and her real triumph were the tragedy she played out on her own, on the tightrope.

Through all this time when we were victorious and our domination was transforming the universe, there was no rejoicing, no celebration, without Hébé Caristi. The sound of cannon and brass bands, the joyous cries of an idolatrous nation, the lights of illuminations and fireworks always accompanied her, as, a hundred feet above a Seine decked with flags and set ablaze with a thousand fires, in the azure amid trembling stars, she walked clad in crimson and gold, waving tricolor flags in her hands, a goddess of the sky and the air, who seemed the very soul of the city celebrating the intoxication of Power and Sovereignty.

All of Paris was at Hébé Caristi's feet—but don't speak to her of adoration, don't speak to her of love. Her love was the wild and haughty struggles she waged with the infinite and with vertigo. It was that remarkable duel with death during which she gazed into the very eyes of the stars and kissed the moist brow of Night. As the Belgrade witch had told her, Hébé bore within her lovely breast a heart of ice. Her passions, her deliriums, were the extravaganzas in the midst of which she declaimed, from a height where eagles fly, the news of our latest battles. At the national celebration where the consular guard, having marched all the way from Marengo, arrived covered with dust and with their uniforms in rags, at the celebrations given to celebrate peace, at the celebration of the flags of Austerlitz, I can see her again, young and slender in the scarlet flames. At the Emperor's wedding and at the birth of the King of Rome,[2] it was still she whose airborne silhouette floated above a Champs Elysées driven wild with crowds and lights.

Just think how the dandies of the time must have despaired over the invincible coldness of that Galatea who had covered herself in glory! Yes, covered herself in glory, including that of having been compared to a full meal, in an ingenious and interminable metaphor! She had performed in the Gymnastic Games in an interlude from *The Queen at Persepolis*, and she had offset the exceptional success of the *Ruins of Babylon*! For an entire week, the Corneille of the Gaiety Theater[3] had been envious of the tightrope walker's success. All the theaters were abandoned when, radiant in her fantastic costume as a Persepolite, she appeared on her tightrope, caring nothing for difficulties, astonished at her own grace! And, despite her purity, or perhaps even because of that inexplicable and fierce purity, how much luxury was set at her feet, how much pomp gathered around her eccentric existence! For her the pumpkin-yellow cabriolet and the linen-grey *briska*. She would have lace made by Madame Colliau, porcelain by Degotty, and trinkets by Garnesson. It was for her bedroom in the rue du Mont-Blanc that a cabinet maker, driven wild by this Pallas, invented furniture in olive wood. If only you could have seen her in that little temple of Taste, scarcely penetrated by a voluptuous half-light. Her shoulders covered by a light shawl in Berlin knit, her hair arranged by Palette (the inventor of the *tousled braids*, so rightly named the Lycophron of hairstylists), she would receive her guests as she lay on her daybed, beside which arose a broken column. A young dandy would appear in his meticu-

---

2. *King of Rome:* Napoleon's son, who died in exile.
3. *Gaiety Theater:* The leading popular theater of Paris. The name Corneille here is being used to imply the leading dramatist.

lously casual outfit: witch's hat, hare-ears shirt, cravat *à l'artiste*, American trousers, sailoress's waistcoat.

"Divine Hébé," he would exclaim, "you're making the stag, Coco de Franconi, and the entire company of the Fabulists' Theater wilt."

With a smile, Hébé would call for her essential oils, which she bought at Riban's boutique in the rue Helvétius, and play absent-mindedly with her Mellerio motto rings, piled up on her dresser. Then she would go out in a barouche with a Pauly umbrella, to try on a coat inspired by the Empress Eugénie or a toque in the fashion of la Cortey! . . . Oh yes, glory came to her in all its forms.

But would you believe that these madrigals, no matter from how high they came, scarcely touched the woman who had only to stretch out her hands to pluck her bouquets of roses at the gates of paradise. What incense would have satisfied someone who could fly to the delights of her own apotheosis? You can still read in the *Mercure de France* the enthusiastic review of a mime danced by Hébé at the Theater of Military Exploits. This is her famous siege of Saragossa,[4] the masterpiece of the genre which was destined to die with the woman who was both its poet and its interpreter.

Her stage set was even less realistic than those of Shakespeare, for it consisted of a simple rope on which the spectators would see in turn Suchet's camp, Junot's tent, the public places of Saragossa with their gallows raised by Palafox and his fanatical monks, the bridge over the Huerba, Saint Engracia Street, site of a horrible killing, and the Portillo Gate through which the Spanish garrison departed, laying down its arms. As for Hébé, dressed as Bellona in armor of scales, she represented all the characters one after another. Here the Marquis de Lassan aroused the besieged, there Marshal Lannes harangued the French army, there women, townsfolk, captains, and that fierce, heroic mother who fought on the ramparts clutching to her breast a child she protected with her wild blade. When necessary she could also present characters who were pure abstractions: sometimes Horror and Fury, or the Charge that drags the trembling legions to assault the breach. Without words, with nothing but her gestures and poses, she expressed a town ravaged by an epidemic, the cruelties of a frenzied populace, the assaults on convents, war waged within houses, struggles, skirmishes, the noisy exchanges of artillery, the intoxication of the final struggles, with their countless episodes, then the capitulation, the sad and grandiose procession of conquered enemies, then at last in all its symbolic magnificence, Victory herself filling the trumpets with sound and waving in the breeze the conquered flags, burned by the sun! If you consider that the

---

4. In 1809, during the Peninsular Wars, Saragossa (in northeastern Spain) held out heroically against the besieging Napoleonic troops. Suchet and Junot were French generals, Palafox the defending Spanish commander.

face, that wonderful keyboard of passion, played no role in this pantomime seen, in the theater, at fifteen feet above the ground and on the
public square at a hundred feet above the heads of the crowd, and that
all this epic recital was imagined, expressed, and understood by means
of gestures, poses, and movements on the rope, you will understand the
admiration it aroused. In vain did Madame Saqui seek to fight back in
giving her *Monk of Mount Saint Bernard*, a mime on the rope in which
she attempted to represent the elegy of a traveler lost under avalanches,
and his rescue by kind monks helped by their devoted dogs. Popular
enthusiasm was on the side of Hébé Caristi, and it stayed with her.

But not forever. A very young colonel of hussars, as handsome and
as proud as a lion, with his boyish head decorated by a large scar received at Austerlitz, fell madly in love with the artiste. He resolutely
offered her his hand, but in vain. It was one of those blazing passions
that destroy their victims. This man realized he was lost, and as nothing
was able to alter his mistress's coldness, he sought to end it all at once,
and blew his brains out in the middle of the Theater of Military Exploits.

Returning home, Hébé stepped in the blood that had inundated the
threshold of the theater when they carried off the victim's body. This
tragic event caused such emotion that, from that day on, Hébé was detested and hated as deeply as she had been adored. In vain did she leave
France, the murder's curse pursued her relentlessly. Her brilliant fortune
disappeared as if by magic, everywhere she encountered hatred, scorn,
and poverty. Paris, where all memories fade so quickly, had completely
forgotten her for thirty years, when an unexpected circumstance again
put in the spotlight not merely the name but also the person of that
tightrope walker, whose death was to bring an end to this lamentable
story.

This moving tale, drawn from the inmost parts of Parisian life, was
told in my presence at the end of a supper by a strange woman called
Martirio, who had chosen to remain a horseback rider at the Circus
after having signed some fine musical compositions. She had a very
sympathetic kind of beauty, with her brown eyes, her tanned face, and
her wavy dark hair, so fine and soft, to which a few silver threads lent
an air of melancholy. Pure moreover as the goddess Vesta,[5] in a theater
of horses and clowns, the Spanish Martirio is one of those eccentric
and attractive figures that Paris adores.

"You remember," she said, "the extraordinary exhibition put on by
Mme Saqui last year at the Hippodrome. The director of the Circus
didn't want to be outdone, and sought an even greater attraction. Well,
he found it. M. Arnault had conjured up Mme Saqui and her climb up

---

5. *Vesta:* Roman goddess of the hearth. Her cult was performed by the Vestal virgins, whose
purity Banville seems to have in mind here.

Mount Saint Bernard, so M. Dejean resuscitated the *Siege of Saragossa* with Hébé Caristi, at the age of 73.

"The very announcement of her arrival surprised us greatly, for we thought she'd been dead these hundred years. But how can I convey the hateful impression I felt when she appeared? I saw a crabbed Fairy Carabossa,[6] so bent over and wizened with age you'd have wanted to put her back in her box! On her skin, which was so shriveled up it looked like parchment, the wrinkles formed a series of sketches and inescapable labyrinths. Her eyes were still lively, but they'd lost their sparkle and their lashes, and they were hidden by a wild forest of eyebrows, white under their pretentious dye. But her outfit! Oh! Who could describe the effect of her false hair, so black and smooth, or her false teeth, white as snow! She was dressed in the most irritating height of fashion. Over a dress of pompadour taffeta in white with designs of flowers, fruit, and birds, she wore a tulle mantelet, striped with velvet, with two great flounces in Chantilly lace. Her twisted feet were strangled in narrow ankle boots of black silk, and her old hands in corn-colored gloves which were exquisitely clean. Her elegant rice-straw hat was adorned with a bunch of pink camellias, and she fiddled with a white parasol covered with lace. The whole way she was decked out indicated a clear intention to please, and it gave you goose bumps. She looked like some witch setting out for Cythera[7] and loading onto Watteau's barque a cargo of toads and hissing snakes!

"But when the old tightrope walker rehearsed before us her eternal *Siege of Saragossa*, on a rope set a little above the floor, the disgust that her funereal coquettery had inspired in us rapidly disappeared, for on that day as on the day of the show she was sublime. Yet, it wasn't long before I fell back into that hateful nightmare. It was my fate to see in all its abjectness a spectacle that went beyond the horrors of *Macbeth*, where the witches at least get calmly on with their cooking and don't deck themselves out in pink ribbons. But watching a delirious mummy breathing in the perfumes of Essbouquet, while you're suffocating from the stench of bitumen and sulphur, and listening to the tortured souls howling idle chatter amidst the instruments and machines of torture in the seventh level of hell, isn't that a degree of monstrosity that's just too unbearable and that could move stones to tears?

"At the circus there is a beautiful girl called Emma Fleurdelix, who, for a brief time, delighted the Parisians on Sundays in a scene entitled *Joan of Arc*, which she performed standing up on a free-moving horse, the archetypal performance of a Circus equestrienne. Like many of her sort, Emma loved a ne'er-do-well, an admirable youth decked out like

---

6. *Carabossa:* The evil fairy in *The Sleeping Beauty*.

7. *Cythera:* Mythical island of love, celebrated in Watteau's famous painting "Embarkation for Cythera." Watteau is known for his rendering of shimmering pastel fabrics

a Malek-Adel on a pendulum, who stole from her, beat her, and cheated on her. One day he went beyond his ordinary tricks, for he set out for London in the company of some little actress or other. Well, that morning, Emma had found her diamonds missing and thought it was merely a slip on her chambermaid's part. She understood the full truth when, as she was dressing to appear on horseback, she received at the Circus itself a hypocritically tender farewell letter. Seeing herself so hatefully abandoned and scorned, she couldn't refrain from an outburst of grief and burst into sobs and tears.

"Already dressed in her poetic rags as the Maid of Vaucouleurs, but with her hair in disarray and covered with bruises, for she had driven her nails into her flesh, she screamed in desolation while five or six flibbertigibbets, dressed in satin and tinsel, were consoling her, chattering like magpies, making her smell salts. Hébé Caristi entered the dressing room in the midst of this fine disorder and was quickly informed of its cause. 'Oh, you poor thing,' she said, in her marionette's voice, 'it's your lover who's causing us all that suffering! Listen, I know all about that, mine has done exactly the same. If I were to tell you! Well, it's true that my Raphaël, to whom I sacrificed everything, cheats on me with plain Janes. Well, my poor darling,' she went on with a sigh, 'our suffering isn't over yet.'

"Of course the dancers who were there were astonished, terrified, and shocked when they heard these sweet words pronounced by a walking ruin who offered the very picture of decrepitude. But on Emma Fleurdelix, ill and worn out with her despair, the effect of this phantasmagoria was to unleash real violence. With bulging eyes, she stared at Hébé Caristi, and burst out laughing. She laughed, she laughed inordinately, and this wild, unending, tyrannical laugh just grew and grew in intensity. Her mouth foamed, you saw the whites of her eyes, her limbs were twisted, and she still laughed. The crisis came to an end with dreadful spasms and a long nervous attack, at the end of which Emma had to be taken home and handed over to the care of a doctor.

"As for me, I avoided the end of the scene by going into the Circus, for I was performing dressage on my lovely Arab horse and was no longer aware of anything else. I thought I'd been taken to a witches' Sabbath by some ironic Mephistopheles, and I gazed stupidly at the ringmaster with his long whip and his buttoned coat, expecting to see a scarlet moth leap from his mouth at any moment. As I carried out the exercises in a mechanical fashion, I stared at the gas lights with the idea that they would turn into bleeding comets. The applause that rang in my ears seemed to me the rumble of hell's thunderstorms. The spectators all seemed to me to have green faces. Raphaël, Raphaël, Raphaël! I repeated in spite of myself to the point of going mad. This name had become for me more extraordinary than those of all the antediluvian monsters exterminated in the fabulous past by heroic birds. O heavens!

who could this Raphaël be who was the lover of Hébé Caristi, and who made her suffer the martyrdom of unhappy love? I closed my eyes and tried to imagine him, but I could not picture him as having a human face!

"Meanwhile, this ill-starred old woman continued to display her touching madness. Sometimes she came with bouquets she planned to give as gifts when we left the rehearsal, or she consulted us on men's cravats and jewels. She showed us flat rings with the motto: "God be with you," or wedding rings recently bought at Palais-Royal and bearing the two names of Hébé and Raphaël. Each time I was present at these infernal jokes, I felt that unspeakable nausea that seizes you on the edge of a thousand-foot abyss when you suddenly lose your footing and you feel you're about to tumble into the dreadful void. I avoided, indeed I fled, the confessions of the old tightrope walker by all the means at my disposal. But how could I flee them when she attached herself to me and spoke to me with the openness of a child, convinced that nothing was more interesting for the world at large than to hear her cooing her love songs.

"O rage! O delirium! What revenge love was taking on that hideous prey! I could not repeat those conversations and yet they pursued me, they knitted themselves into my dreams, they took the place of sentences I wanted to say, they obsessed me as the lines of a mindless song sometimes do, so that despite yourself you repeat them over and over to yourself for days on end. I had forgotten them and they devoured me, they assassinated me by summoning up within me a lasting impression like what one feels in a dark and dank tunnel, where you see spiders' eyes glowing and the eyes of toads, and where you are aware of the scuttling movements of ice-cold reptiles. Not only Raphaël, who fortunately stayed in the wings, but Hébé herself no longer seemed real to me. At every moment I thought I would see her break into pieces or evaporate in smoke, and believed that once the black spell had dissipated, calm would return immediately to my spirit and to the heavens. But no, it did all happen. Hébé Caristi really did live, for I saw her die.

"Sometimes she arrived, clad in apple green or pale lilac. She would try to smile in the fashion of Mme de Pompadour. Her wig was curled into a cloud, and she radiated joy. 'Ah, my dear!' she would say, 'I was wrong, he loves me, he's faithful to me. If only you knew how happy I am, he bought me a delightful bouquet! And as for that Florestine I thought was his mistress! Oh how wrong I was to get into a state. She's just a friend of his sister. But you're not taking much pleasure in my happiness. O Martirio, how cold you are! Really, you have no heart.'

"Hébé's face and outfits were the thermometer of her horrible happiness, and told you exactly what her current relations with Raphaël were. With that inexplicable eagerness that drives us to all that is perverse, I sometimes felt a lively curiosity to set eyes on this nameless being whose nickname forever dishonors the most handsome of men. And yet I knew that if he happened to be standing behind me atop the towers of Notre Dame I would have leapt over the edge rather than look. Luckily, what I feared never came to pass, and I never had to find out exactly how much horror we could bear. I have read the romantic poet's *Inferno*, with its ingenious equipment of pincers and saws, its men made of red-hot iron and the ovens in which human flesh is cooked. It's a fine book, but it has its lacunae; the author, who can dream up such fine tortures, forgot to invent for his hell a torment worthy of Raphaël.

"It was clear that this perfect Dorante[8] was quickly running through the full gamut of his tricks, and with fatal speed Hébé Caristi's outfits began to turn somber, black invaded and conquered her, and what black! One after the other, as if by magic, the velvets and silks, the dresses with the pretty pink bouquets, the engraved jewelry, the carefully curled wigs, the little shawls, all disappeared. Pale, green, shabby, forgetting her rouge, the old tightrope walker, drowning in tears, stupefied by grief, walked abroad in the rags of poverty. This was her period of madness, when, like Shakespeare's Ophelia, she could be heard murmuring snatches of songs, reciting fragments of poems, perfumed with roses and violets. Destiny seemed to have chosen this unfortunate specter for all manner of parodies and profanations. Like the victims pursued by the savage gods of Leda and Pasiphae, victims branded for the embraces of a monster, she writhed in the depths of her void, condemned to laughable suffering, ridiculous torture, torments which struck the eye as grotesque. Truly that woman drove back the limits of human suffering!

"Then, in those dreadful moments when she was watching her last, stupid hopes fly away, Hébé Caristi still clung to me, madly begging me, 'Oh tell me, do tell me, Martirio, do you really think there are philters that make men love us, that can keep an unfaithful lover? I've heard tales of a witch and of bleeding hearts, but there's no truth in it, is there? Moreover, I've tried and it didn't work for me. But there has to be something! It can't be true that it's just not possible. It's just too painful to be consumed with love like this and not to be loved. Martirio, Martirio, tell me how to make him love again!'

"That was the sort of thing Hébé would say in her delirium. And of course I didn't say anything. What was there to reply to these outpourings of madness? Then her old face, which was already wrinkled more than you can imagine, would crinkle even more in an outburst of furious irony. 'Oh yes!' she would say, with an expression of hatred and scorn, 'I was forgetting you don't know anything about all that! When I was young, I too was proud and happy not to feel anything moving in my

---

8. *Dorante:* Archetype of the young lover.

veins, but you will grow old, never fear!' And while she made this terrible prophecy I could see before my eyes a crowd of pale figures bearing the marks of vice, and I would stare at these hideous faces that my imagination attached one after the other to the legendary Raphaël.

"Soon the old tightrope walker bore the true livery of poverty. Her last dresses and her last shoes had been devoured and, horrible to say, Hébé in order to find something to wear took out of their cases, hidden below the dust of fifty years, dresses from the First Empire, tunics, sky-blue satin sheaths, bound under the breast with hair belts, and hats with brims the size of houses, clothes we wouldn't believe existed if the fashion plates hadn't been kept to prove their existence. . . . Her startled eyes were bloodshot, a dry cough wore her down, she was becoming tuberculous at an age when illness itself spurns our company, and she was dying like the heroine of a novel. Devoted, like the model for Marguerite Gautier,[9] to white camellias and willowy poses, she too spoke feverishly of the future and smiled in a melancholy way as the leaves began to fall. But at that moment she was no longer ridiculous, she seemed dreadful, like all those transformed by a violent passion, for she expended in seeking money the frenzied rage of a lion seeking its prey in the gorges of the Atlas Mountains. She felt that her last moments of illusion had to be bought at this price, and she roared as she defended her life. Then the former mistress of the Theater of Military Exploits revealed herself. You should have heard her discussing matters of salary with M. Dejean. She was clever, violent, eloquent, secretive, imperious, insinuating, unstoppable. She would speak for two hours without any sign of weariness, holding to her lips a handkerchief steeped in blood.

"But she became too ill to continue her performances, and she expended all her energy in borrowing money from us, performing on brute natures unspeakable miracles of seduction. From a hundred francs down to the tiniest sums, she used it all; nothing exhausted her patience, she drank shame as if from a beloved chalice. Finally we would flee her presence, escaping when we saw her coming, and when her victim decamped in such a way she would stop dead, hurling a final curse to heaven, looking at the clouds to see if they would break asunder, or the earth to see if it would open to throw her some last help.

"I myself had done for her all that was possible and all that was impossible. Determined to fill the abyss that yawned under her feet, I had gone badly into debt, and I could see the moment coming when I would have to become insensitive, cost what it might. Hébé came to my place and entered despite my chambermaid. She dared not ask me for anything, but her eyes looked as if they sought to tear down the

---

9. Marguerite Gautier is the heroine of Alexandre Dumas's novel *La Dame aux camélias*.

wallpaper. She trembled mechanically, repeating to me: 'It's over, I don't have anything left, not a thing. Raphaël will leave me.' As I turned my head away, painfully moved, I saw out of the corner of my eye a reddish glow. Hébé had thrown herself on a ruby pin which had been sitting on a corner of the mantelpiece and had hidden it under her shawl. However swift my glance had been, it had met that of Hébé. She saw that I had seen. She stayed calm but as if thunderstruck. As for me, I thought it would take me a thousand years to turn my head and talk to her, and I felt I needed to make an effort more difficult than that needed to lift the earth. I would have liked that second of anxiety to be eternal. At last I succeeded in breaking the silence and murmured, 'If you like that bauble, Hébé, I'd be only too pleased to give it to you.' 'Very well,' she said, 'I'll take it!'

"She'd raised her eyes with an expression of absolute distress. Wildly, she showed she'd offered everything to the holocaust! But when she saw me shed a tear, she was moved. Before she left she took my hand and kissed it with a sob. As for me, I was persecuted by the idea of Raphaël and said to myself, 'What's he doing at this moment?' And I could still hear in the stairwell the heart-rending cough of Hébé Caristi.

A week later, I saw her again in M. Dejean's office, although he had refused in vain to see her. She was absolutely determined to give one final performance for which she was asking five hundred francs. Seeing that she was dying, the director refused, out of sheer humanity. But she was victorious in this terrible bargaining, and the day was set. The announcement of this last appearance of the old artiste had attracted many people to the Circus. Paris, which knows everything, knew her story, and people were curious to see just how far desperate heroism could go. When I saw Hébé wearing a golden helmet, armor of scales, glinting with enamel, silver, and scarlet, dolled up in her dear costume as Pallas, she looked ten years younger. Her face was aglow; she was thinking of the five hundred franc note that she'd feel crackling in her hand when she came down from the tight rope!

"But she was excessively weary, she was coughing, spitting blood. She fainted three times in the fifteen minutes before her performance. These swoons were unlike anything I had ever seen. Usually, when a person faints, you feel their life is suspended but only for a while. With Hébé, it was a true death, complete, absolute. It was as if she'd been a corpse for many years, and a magician's art had given her an appearance of life, but, once the charm ended, she became again death's legitimate prey. Her heart no longer beat in any discernible way, her breath did not leave any trace on a mirror held against her lips, she was white, frozen, rigid.

" 'Madame,' said the theater doctor, when she came to herself the last time, 'you can't go on the tightrope today, and I above all cannot permit it. You must understand that I cannot undertake such a serious responsibility.'

"Old Hébé leapt wildly as if she'd been bitten by a tarantula.

" 'Wretch!' she cried, 'you're the one that wants me dead!' Then she added with a funereal smile, 'Come, dear doctor, you're too kind to want to go against a lady's wishes!'

"At last, quite beside herself, she drew a little dagger from her pocket and went on wildly, 'I swear on the bones of my mother that if you prevent my performance, I'll kill myself with this.'

"The circus doctor was a tough man who had seen many dramas like this one and many others as well, over the thirty years he'd spent patching up the bitter wounds made by Parisian passions. So he wasn't shaken by the artiste's little dagger. Unfortunately he was urgently summoned to help a famous person who had just suffered a stroke in the theater itself. Hébé took advantage of this to enter the circus, and, trembling, she climbed the ladder that led to her tightrope, thirty feet away from all human help.

"At the first steps she took on the rope, there was a great cry of admiration, for, on her imaginary stage, this goddess of mime recovered her suppleness, her extraordinary ardor, her panther-like agility, her exceptional ability to make of herself a multi-layered show and a complex symbol. Yes, to the sound of trumpets, to the proud sound of fanfares, that woman, that Pallas, that female warrior with her red plumes, was the French army itself forgetting sufferings that had lasted six months and advancing to the harsh intoxication of conquest. Now she's a general restraining his troops' ardor, her eye dominating and her mouth immobile and severe. Now she's a soldier happy to gamble on his life. Now she's a drummer boy beating the advance as he sees his first battle appear in the intense crimson of dawn. You could follow on Hébé Caristi's face the changing fortunes of military tragedy. Suddenly the tightrope walker stopped, stiffened, motionless as if frozen or transformed into a pillar of salt. With a gesture of despair she raised both arms to the sky and at the same time blood rushed to her face. Even from the back of the amphitheater, you could see her go completely red.

"A vast sigh arose from six thousand chests; everyone closed their eyes; everyone was convinced she'd fall from that terrible height where Willpower kept her, down to the sand of the arena, where her bones would be broken. But after that moment of horror, when we raised our eyes again, we saw her living and still on her feet. With a superhuman effort, of which she herself was not even conscious, she had been able to keep her balance at the moment when life abandoned her, a greater miracle than all the tricks she'd used to astonish emperors in the time of her wild youth. Yes, she was still on her feet, but like a soldier shot

in the heart who continues to march for a few steps in the very swoon
of death. At last, her limbs relaxed, her back bent, and she fell back,
but on the rope where she collapsed, still gracefully, and clung on with
one hand, as she used to do in playing the episode of the wounded
trumpeter. But her strength was utterly gone. To return to the ladder,
she had to crawl, drag herself on her knees, clamber along the rope on
her knees, the rope that a moment before she had trod with an inso-
lently scornful and arrogant foot.

"For the audience, that final effort was a thousand times more moving even than the minute when they had believed her dead, for now
she resembled a bird sweeping the ground with its mudstained belly
and its shattered wings. She made it, but she no longer looked human, her bones were ice cold, and she was wrapped in a black shroud
of horror.

"Scarcely had she come down the ladder than people rushed to help
her, to console her, to hear of the unspeakable terrors she must have
suffered. She didn't have time for that! Hébé Caristi was already at the
cashier's desk, demanding her 500 francs as a desert tigress demands
her cubs, with a gaze that would have melted the Bank of France's gold
bars.

" 'But' said the cashier, 'M. Raphaël came and collected them just
now, with a letter from you; he even had your receipt, which I've registered, as you can see.'

" 'Oh!' was all the old artiste cried out. Although that syllable might
have been taken by the cashier for a sign of approval, hell knows how
much utter misery and fury it contained.

"Hébé left. An hour later, just as I was getting ready to eat, there
arrived an old shrew decked out in squalid rags. This was the door-
keeper of the building where Hébé Caristi lived. She told me that the
unhappy woman was dying and had asked to see me one final time.

"When I arrived at a foul dump in the Rue de Venise, I went upstairs,
following the directions of the old drunk cobbler who presided over that
lair. When I reached the top of the circular stone stairway, and had
dropped the greasy rope that served as a bannister, I went into a little
hallway, which was completely empty of furniture. This hallway, whose
walls were covered with torn paper, led to the garret in which the tightrope walker was breathing her last.

"There I stopped, despite myself, for I heard a lively conversation between two voices. One was low and hypocritical, the other violent, energetic, imperious, although broken with suffering. This second voice
was that of Hébé. I listened for a long time, truly believing I was having
a nightmare, for I no longer felt I was leading my own life.

" 'Listen,' the low voice was saying, 'here are the four hundred-franc
notes and that really is my last word. Will you sign?'

"I heard the sound of a pen on paper; I could imagine the gesture with which Hébé sunk her claws into the banknotes.

" 'Now,' she cried, 'leave me alone, you torturer!' And I saw walk by me a young man, almost bald, his brow pensive and ravaged.

"I had just witnessed the final torments of Hébé Caristi, the bargain in which she sold her corpse to a young but already famous surgeon, whose soul was as greedy and implacable as Science itself.

"I turned the doorhandle and went in. I sat down by the truckle bed on which lay dying the woman who had felt snaking round her shoulders the cashmir shawl of Princess Borghèse.[10]

" 'You heard,' she murmured feebly.

"And as I replied that I heard, turning my eyes away, she went on, 'You'll agree it's not an act of sacrilege, won't you? I'm not guilty, you see that, don't you? Besides, he himself said to me that everything is permitted in the interests of science! But Martirio, listen, I don't need anything either now or (and she gave a harsh laugh) after my death. One day I stupidly threatened you with an old age like mine. For the last hour I've been begging the good Lord to spare you that cup. I want to bless you. Will you forgive me?'

"I pressed a pious kiss on the brow of that poor victim who had had the good fortune to suffer such expiations, and I went out in search of the spiritual and material help she would need for her final moments. Night had almost fallen. On the stairs I heard, a few steps below me, a hoarse voice humming Nadaud's[11] latest song, embroidering it with disgusting ornaments.

"I shut my eyes, but it was too late: in the last glow of dusk, I'd caught sight of a blue velvet beret, a red cravat, a face as pale as the death mask of Boswell. There could be no doubt that this vision was Raphaël. I shrunk against the wall to let him pass, holding my breath, and only opened my eyes again when I heard Hébé Caristi's door shut again.

"I returned within thirty minutes. The priest and doctor went upstairs, and I waited for them in the cab. A few minutes later, the doctor returned by himself. Hébé Caristi was dead. Doctor Crestié is an old friend of mine. I asked him to undertake all the necessary arrangements and, if it was still possible, to annul the horrible bargain signed at the edge of the open grave, but I did not have the strength to go back into that room where the blood pact had taken place. Many times since then I have seen in my dreams the pale face I caught sight of on that day in the stairwell of the Rue de Venise, and that is why I am invulnerable, for, if some particularly attractive danger tempts me, I always think of that ignoble face which for me embodied the infamous demon of Perversity."

---

10. *Borghèse:* Napoleon's sister, Pauline.
11. Gustave Nadaud (1820–1893), French song writer, author of some three hundred songs.

When Martirio had told the story of the woman who, along with Madame Saqui, had been the goddess of the tightrope, we remained plunged in a kind of stupor. Rosier in particular seemed greatly shaken. "Well," he said to Martirio, "I can really understand why this gutter drama left so deep a mark on you, for, after all, we know you have a remarkable gift for never getting your feet dirty as you walk through the mud of the theater! Well, however absurd Hébé Caristi's prediction may be, the parallel between her youth and yours must give you pause for thought."

"Yes," replied Martirio dreamily. "But I am Spanish and have noble blood in my veins. . . . I would kill myself."

Renan

♦

Ernest Renan (1823–1892) was an orientalist and moralist whose writings, particularly before the German defeat of France in 1870, reveal an enlightened but elitist vision of society and a distrust of materialism. Famous for his study of Christ, The Life of Jesus, *which focuses attention away from Christ's divinity and onto the poetic beauty of the Bible, Renan is also celebrated for his study entitled* The Future of Science, *which proclaims his belief that humanity will find liberation through scientific knowledge and under the leadership of an intellectual élite. In addition, he wrote a study of semitic languages and various volumes of essays on morality, as well as a history of the origins of Christianity.*

FURTHER READING: *Life of Jesus*, no translator mentioned (Buffalo, N.Y.: Prometheus Books, 1991).
TEXT USED: *L'Avenir de la science* (Paris: Calmann-Lévy, 1890).

THE FUTURE OF SCIENCE (1890)

There is only one thing we really need! I accept, with all its philosophical implications, this precept handed down by the Grand Master of morality. I consider it to be the principle of all noble lives, the formula that, for all the dangers of its conciseness, best expresses human nature, from the point of view of morality and duty. The first step that must be taken by anyone who wants to acquire wisdom, as principled antiquity used to say, is to divide life into two parts: the first commonplace and having nothing of the sacred about it, containing nothing but needs and pleasures of a lower order (material life, pleasure, riches, etc.); the other, which one could call the ideal, celestial, divine, disinterested, has as its goals the pure forms of truth, beauty, moral goodness, that is, to use the term that is most comprehensive and most consecrated by the respect of the past, God Himself, touched, perceived, and felt in his thousands of forms by the understanding of all that is true, and the love of all that is beautiful. This is the great conflict between *body* and *soul*, recognized by all religions and all noble philosophies. It is a very superficial conflict if you claim to find in it a duality of substance in the human individual, but it remains perfectly true if, by suitably elaborating the meaning of those two words, and applying them to two kinds of phenomena, you understand them to apply to the two kinds of life that are open to the individual. When we recognize the distinction between these two worlds, we realize that the higher world, the ideal world, is all-important, and that the lesser one, the world of interests and pleasures, is nothing. This lesser world fades away before the first as the finite does before the infinite, and if practical wisdom commands us to bear the lesser world in mind, it is merely in view of, and as a condition of, that higher world.

In beginning with such weighty truths, I have, I realize, put on my dunce's cap. But where such questions are concerned I have no false shame; I've long put myself among the simple and cumbersome minds who take matters at face value. I'm weak enough to consider as very easily imitated bad taste that self-proclaimed delicacy that cannot bring itself to take life as something serious and holy; and if there were no other choices to make, I would prefer, at least where morals are concerned, formulas of the strictest dogmatism to such levity. That levity is overly honored by the name of skepticism and ought rather to be called idiotic and empty. If it were true that human life were merely a succession of commonplace facts, bereft of any value which went beyond the evidence of the senses, then as soon as one had a thought which was the slightest bit serious, one would have to commit suicide; there would be no middle path between intoxication, a tyrannical occupation of every single moment, and suicide. To live the life of the mind, to breathe in the infinite through every pore, to achieve beauty and attain perfection, each of us according to our gifts, that is all that is necessary. All the rest is vanity and spiritual affliction.

Christian asceticism, when it proclaimed its great simplification of life, showed such a strict understanding of the sole thing that was necessary, that its teaching gradually became an intolerable chain for human minds. Not only did it totally neglect truth and beauty—for philosophy, science, and poetry were regarded as mere vanity—but its exclusive attachment to good made it conceive of that good in the narrowest possible terms: for Christian asceticism, good was the realization of a superior being's will, a kind of humiliating enslavement for human dignity: for the realization of moral good lies no more in obedience to laws imposed than the realization of beauty in a work of art lies in carrying out certain rules. Thus the loftiest aspects of human nature were mutilated. Among intellectual matters, which are all equally holy, a difference was made between the sacred and the profane. The profane, thanks to natural instincts which are stronger than the principles of an artificial asceticism, was not entirely banned; it was tolerated, although regarded as mere vanity. Sometimes the ascetics relented to the point of calling it the least vain of vanities, but if they had been consistent, they would have proscribed it pitilessly. It was a weakness that the perfect ascetics renounced. This was a fatal distinction, which poisoned the lives of so many fine and free spirits who were born to savor the ideal in all its infinity and whose lives drained away in sadness and oppression under the grip of a fatal vice. How many struggles it cost me! The first philosophical victory of my youth was to proclaim from the depths of my conscience: all that is of the soul is sacred.

So I am not seeking to impose any strict limit on human nature when I argue that only one single activity is worthy of it, for that single activity includes the infinite. All it excludes is the commonplace, which has value only insofar as it is experienced, and that lower sphere is itself far less extensive than one might believe. There are very few things in human life that are utterly profane. The progress of morality and intelligence will yield new insights that will give an elevated value to acts that appear extremely gross. Christianity, aided by the instincts of the Celtic and Germanic races, did after all raise to the dignity of an aesthetic and moral sentiment a fact which all antiquity, with the exception of Plato, saw as mere pleasure. Is it not true that the most material act of life, that of eating, received from the first Christians a wondrous mystic meaning? Physical work, which today is merely an exhausting task for those condemned to it, was quite different in the Middle Ages, for those workers who built the cathedrals and sang as they worked. Who can tell whether one day the sight of the general good of humanity for which one builds may not sweeten and sanctify the sweat of the workers? For from the human point of view, the most humble tasks have an ideal value, since they are what at least makes intellectual conquests possible. The sanctification of the inferior world by outer practices and ceremonies is a characteristic common to all religions. The progress brought about by rationalism has succeeded in being the first—there's no great merit in this—to declare such ceremonies pure superstitions. What was the result of that? Stripped of idealization, life became something profane, commonplace, prosaic, to such an extent that for certain acts, where the need for a religious meaning was most keenly felt, such as birth, marriage, and death, ancient ceremonies have been preserved, even though people no longer believe in their effectiveness. Later on, progress, I believe, will reconcile these two tendencies by supplementing sacramental acts whose value can lie only in their meaning, and which when envisaged from the point of view of their material execution are completely ineffectual, mere unadulterated moral sentiment.

Thus, everything that's connected to humankind's superior existence, that existence which distinguishes us from animals, is sacred and worthy of a passionate response from fine souls. Fine sentiments are the equivalent of fine thoughts, and a fine thought is worth as much as a fine act. A system of philosophy is worth as much as a poem, while a poem is just as valuable as a scientific discovery, and a life of learning is as valuable as a life of virtue. The perfect human being would be the one who was simultaneously poet and philosopher, sage and saint, and not just from time to time and at special moments (for then that person would be all those things only in a mediocre fashion), but through an intimate penetration of all moments of life, the poet would also be a philosopher, the philosopher would at the same time be a sage, so that, to put it in a nutshell, all human aspects would find themselves united in a superior harmony, as they are in humanity as a whole. Our analytical age is flawed in that it does not permit this high unity; life becomes a trade, a profession; one has to proclaim oneself a poet, an artist, or a sage, create a little world in which one lives in isolation without understanding all the rest and often denying all those other aspects. No one can really consider denying that this is made necessary by the current state of the human mind; yet it has to be recognized that such a way of life, although it is excused by its necessity, runs counter to human dignity and to the perfection that can be found in an individual. If you consider him as a man, a Newton,[1] a Cuvier,[2] a Heyne strikes a less magnificent chord than a sage of antiquity, a Solomon or a Pythagoras for instance. Man's purpose is not to know, to feel, to imagine, but to be perfect, that is, to be a human being in the full meaning of the term. Such perfection can be found in an individual who provides the abbreviated tableau of humanity in all its fullness and shows, combined in a powerful union, all the facets of life that humanity has sketched out through all the ages and all the places in which it has existed. All too often people imagine that in morality alone lies perfection, that the pursuit of the true and the beautiful constitutes mere pleasure, that the perfect man is the man of honor, the Moravian friar for instance. The model of perfection is given to us by humanity itself; the most perfect life is that which best represents all humanity. And cultured humanity is not merely moral; it is also knowledgeable, inquisitive, poetic, and impassioned.

Doubtless it would be pushing our trust in the future of humanity far beyond the bounds respected by the boldest utopians, to think that an individual could one day embrace the entire field of intellectual endeavor. But there are, in the different branches of the sciences and the arts, two elements that are completely separate and yet equally neces-

---

1. *Newton:* The reference here is to Sir Isaac Newton (1642–1727), the English physicist and mathematician who formulated the law of gravity and invented calculus.

2. Georges, Baron Cuvier (1769–1832), the French zoologist and founder of the sciences of comparative anatomy and palaeontology.

sary for scientific or artistic works to be produced, two elements whose contribution to the perfection of the individual is very unequal: on the one hand there are the procedures, the practical skills, which are indispensable for the discovery of truth and the creation of beauty; on the other, the intellect that creates and animates, the soul that brings to life the work of art, the great law that gives a meaning and value to a scientific discovery. It will always be quite impossible for the same individual to employ with equal skill the painter's brush, the musician's instrument, the chemist's apparatus. These things require a special education and a practical skill that, if it is to become an ingrained and spontaneous habit, demands an entire lifetime of use. But what could become possible in a more advanced form of intellectual culture is that the feeling that gives life to an artist's or a poet's composition, the penetration of a sage or a philosopher, the moral sense of an outstanding individual, could unite to form a single soul, open to all that is beautiful, good, and true, and constitute a moral template for all humanity, an ideal that may not be realized in particular individuals but that will be in the future what Christ has been these eighteen centuries,—a Christ who would no longer merely represent the moral side at its highest point, but also the aesthetic and scientific side of humanity.

When it comes down to it, all these categories of pure forms that the intellect perceives are no more than different aspects of a single unity. Divergence begins only at a lower level. There is a great central focus in which poetry, science, and morality are identical, where knowing, admiring, loving are one and the same thing, and where all oppositions disappear, where human nature rediscovers in the identity of the object the lofty harmony of all our faculties and that great act of adoration that sums up the way in which our entire being strives toward the eternal infinite. The saint is the person who is utterly devoted to that great ideal and declares everything else useless.

Pascal has shown in masterly fashion the vicious circle made necessary by practical life. One works in order to obtain rest, and then rest is unbearable. We do not live, but merely hope to live. The fact is that worldly people never have, at least as far as I can see, a clearly determined system of living. They cannot say with any precision what is essential, what is secondary, what is an end, and what is merely a means. Riches cannot be a final goal, since money has value only insofar as it can provide pleasure. And yet all the serious part of life is used up in connection with acquiring riches, and pleasure is considered only an amusement for our free moments and our useless years. Only philosophers and the devout can rest fully at any moment; they alone can embrace the passing moment without putting anything aside for the future.

Someone remarked one day to a philosopher of antiquity that he didn't believe he had been born for philosophy. "Wretch," replied the philosopher, "why then were you born?" Certainly if philosophy were a specialty or a profession like any other, if being a philosopher meant studying, or seeking to solve, a certain number of more or less important questions, the sage's reply would be a strange contradiction. And yet, if one is able to understand the true sense of philosophy, that person is indeed wretched who is not a philosopher, that is, who has not succeeded in understanding the lofty meaning of life. Many people renounce just as willingly the title of poet. If being a poet means being used to a certain linguistic mechanism, then that could be excused. But if one means by poetry the soul's ability to be touched in a particular way, to give forth a sound of a particular and undefinable nature when faced with the beauty of things, those who are not poets are not human beings, and renouncing that title is a voluntary abdication of the dignity of one's nature.

Famous examples would prove, if proof were needed, that this high harmony of the powers of human nature is no figment of the imagination. The life of the genius always offers the delightful spectacle of a vast intellectual capacity combined with a very elevated poetic sense and a charming kindness of soul, with the result that their life, in its calm and smooth placidity is almost always their finest production, and forms an essential element of their complete works. To tell the truth, the words "poetry," "philosophy," "art," "science," designate not so much the different objects proposed for mankind's intellectual activity, but different ways of considering the same object, which is existence in all its manifestations. These are merely different forms, which, like those of literature, are capable of expressing everything. Béranger[3] was able to say everything in the form of songs, another writer in the form of novels, someone else as history. All these geniuses are universal as far as the object of their work is concerned, and, just as the minor spirits are unbearable when they seek to establish the exclusive pre-eminence of their particular art form, so the great minds are right when they proclaim that their art is humanity in its entirety, since it does indeed enable them to express that which is uniquely indivisible, the soul, and God.

Yet it must be recognized that the secret of blending together these diverse elements has yet to be discovered. In the current state of human intelligence, too rich a nature is a source of torment. Someone born with an outstanding gift that absorbs all the other gifts is far happier than someone who constantly discovers new needs that cannot be satisfied. Such a person would need a whole life for knowledge, another for feeling and loving, another for acting, or rather, he or she would want to be able to juggle a series of parallel existences, while blending into a

---

3. Pierre-Jean de Béranger (1780–1857), French song writer and poet who achieved immense fame in his lifetime, when he was considered the poet of the people.

higher union the simultaneous awareness of each of them. Limited by time and external needs, such concentrated activity would inwardly devour the individual. Such people have so much living to do for themselves that they have no time to live for the external world. They do not want to lose anything of this burning, multiple life that escapes their grasp and that they devour with haste and avidity. They swing from one sphere to another, or rather, poorly harmonized spheres collide in their breast. They envy in turn, for they can understand in turn, the simple soul that lives on faith and love, the virile soul that seizes life like a muscular athlete, the penetrating and critical mind that savors at leisure the delight of handling an exact and reliable instrument. Then, when they find themselves unable to realize this multiple ideal, when they see how short life is, how divided, how fatally incomplete, when they consider that entire aspects of their rich and fertile nature will remain forever buried in shadow, they are overwhelmed by an unparalleled bitterness. They curse that superabundance of life, which leads to nothing but merely consumes itself fruitlessly, or, if they pour their activity into some external work, they suffer there, too, from being unable to pour into it more than a portion of themselves. Scarcely have they fulfilled one aspect of their life than a thousand others no less lovely reveal themselves, deceptively dragging them away in their turn, until the day comes when they must put an end to it and when, glancing behind them, they can at last say consolingly, "I have led a full life." That is the first day on which they receive their reward.

Michelet

Jules Michelet (1798–1874) was primarily a historian whose studies of French history and particularly the French revolution of 1789 reveal a powerful blend of erudition and romanticism, expressed in terms of unabashed nationalism. When Napoleon III declared himself emperor in 1852, Michelet retired from public life and concentrated on works of natural history, remarkable for their highly imaginative presentation of scientific facts. Although undoubtedly anthropocentric to modern eyes, these studies played an important part in drawing his contemporaries' attention to the natural world around them. Works such as The Insect *and* The Bird *repay close reading for the wonderful richness of Michelet's style, his rhythmic prose, and his powerfully imaginative metaphors. His attempts to enter the mentality of the animal world reveal the originality of his mind, at a time when the vast majority of writers were still locked into the French Romantic projection of the human onto the external world.*

FURTHER READING: *History of the French Revolution*, tr. Charles Cooks (Chicago: University of Chicago Press, 1967), *Joan of Arc*, tr. Albert Guerard (Ann Arbor: University of Michigan Press, 1957), *Michelet*, ed. Roland Barthes, tr. Richard Howard (New York: Hill and Wang, 1987).
BIOGRAPHY: Arthur Mitzman, *Michelet, historian* (New Haven: Yale University Press, 1990).
TEXT USED FOR "FIRST FLIGHTS": *L'Oiseau* (Paris: Hachette, 1856).
TEXT USED FOR "THE INSECT": *L'Insecte* (Paris: Hachette, 1856).

FIRST FLIGHTS (1856)

There is no one, however illiterate or ignorant, however sated or unfeeling, who can fail to feel a sense of respect, I would almost say of terror, as they step into the rooms of our Museum of Natural History.

No foreign collection, to my knowledge, produces such an impression.

Others, no doubt, like that of the splendid museum of Leyden, are richer in certain types; but none is more complete or more harmoniously balanced. This grandiose harmony can be felt instinctively, compelling recognition and seizing the mind. Casual visitors, chance visitors, are gripped without expecting to be. They stop and ponder. Faced with this vast riddle, this immense hieroglyph which rises before them for the first time, they would consider themselves happy could they but read a single character, spell out a single letter. How often have the common people, surprised and tormented by some bizarre shape, asked me to explain its meaning! A single word would put them on the right path, a simple indication charmed them; they left happy and promising themselves they would return. How different were those who sailed across this ocean of objects they neither knew nor understood, and who went away weary and sad.

Let me express the wish that so enlightened and knowledgeable an administration will return to the early constitution of the Museum, which created *instructor custodians* and admitted as guardians of this treasure only those who were capable of understanding it and, when necessary, explaining it.

Another wish I dare to formulate is that beside the pictures of the great naturalists, images be placed of the brave sailors, undaunted travelers, who, through the work they performed and the perils they encountered, risking their lives a hundred times over, brought these treasures back to us. However worthy they are in themselves, these treasures are perhaps even more worthy through the heroism and the greatness of heart of those who won them for us. Are you aware that this charming hummingbird, Madame, this winged sapphire in which you are tempted to see a trivial object of adornment, was brought back for you by an Azara or a Lesson, from deadly forests in which all one can breathe is death? You should know that for this magnificent tiger, whose fur you admire, to be placed here it had to be sought out in the jungles, met face to face, aimed at, and shot in the brow by the bold Levaillant. These illustrious travelers, these ardent lovers of nature, often without means or help, followed nature through the deserts, observed and surprised her in her mysterious retreats, suffered thirst and hunger and unbelievable weariness, never complaining, believing themselves but too richly rewarded, full of love and thankfulness at every discovery. They regretted nothing they gained at that price, not even the death of La Pérouse or Mungo Park,[1] death in shipwrecks, death among the Barbarians.

---

1. *La Pérouse and Mungo Park:* Jean-François de Galaup, comte de La Pérouse (1741–1788), a French explorer, set out (at the command of Louis XVI) on a voyage of discovery from which he never returned. He is believed to have been murdered by the inhabitants of Vanikoro. Mungo Park (1771–c.1806) was a Scottish surgeon and explorer who made two explorations of the River Niger. He died when his expedition was attacked.

May they come back and live among us! Since their solitary existence unfolded far from Europe, yet in Europe's service, let their portraits be placed in the midst of the grateful crowds, with a brief indication of their fortunate discoveries, their suffering and their great courage. More than one young person will feel moved at having seen these heroes and will be tempted to dream of imitating them.

That is what makes this place doubly great. Heroes sent these objects, and they were gathered in, classified, made sense of by great men to whom everything poured in as if to a legitimate center and who through their position as much as through their genius were enabled to carry out here the centralization of nature.

In the previous century the great movement of the sciences converged around a man of genius whose rank, situation, and fortune all made him an important person: Count Buffon.[2] All the gifts of the knowledgeable, of travelers, of kings, came to him and were classified by him in this Museum. In our days, a yet greater spectacle attracted to this sight the passionate attention of all the nations of the world when two immense men (more than two men, they were two methods), Cuvier and Geoffroy, fought for supremacy here.[3] Everyone took sides with either one or the other, everyone became involved, sent proof to the Museum either for or against a particular method, proof such as books, animals, or unknown facts. As a result, these collections you might presume dead are very much alive. They still palpitate with that struggle, animated by the great minds that called on all these creatures as witnesses in their fertile combat.

This is no haphazard collection. Here you can find very complete series, series formed and created systematically by deep thinkers. The species that form the strangest transitions between genera are richly represented here. It is here that you can see far better than elsewhere what Linnaeus[4] and Lamarck[5] proclaimed: that as our museums grow richer and more complete, with fewer and fewer gaps, people will be forced to concede that nature does nothing abruptly but proceeds by smooth and imperceptible transitions. Whenever we think we have found in her work a leap or a vacuum, an abrupt and unharmonious passage, we

---

2. *Buffon:* Georges Louis Leclerc, comte de Buffon (1707–1788) was a French naturalist who intuited the evolution of species.

3. *Cuvier and Geoffroy:* Georges, Baron Cuvier (1769–1832), a French zoologist, was considered the father of the sciences of comparative anatomy and palaeontology. Etienne Geoffroy Saint-Hilaire (1772–1844), a French naturalist, argued that all animals conformed to the same basic structural plan. Unlike Cuvier, he argued that modern species were unchanging but derived from ancestral species through the appearance of successful "monstrosities."

4. Carl von Linnaeus (1707–1788). Swedish naturalist who created the system of binomial nomenclature that is still used today.

5. *Lamarck:* Jean-Baptiste de Monet, chevalier de Lamarck (1744–1829), French naturalist. His work on spontaneous generation and on transformism prepared the way for Darwin's theory of evolution.

should call ourselves into question: that gap is the product of our own ignorance.

Let us stop for a few moments at the solemn passages where life seems uncertain and appears to waver still, where nature seems to ask herself questions and test her own desires. The creature asks, "*Shall I be fish or flesh?*" It hesitates and remains a warm-blooded fish: it belongs to the good and gentle tribe of seals. "*Shall I be bird or beast?*" A great question, a perplexing question, leading to a long and varied combat. All the twists and turns of that evolution have been told, the different solutions to these naively posed problems have been given form by strange beings like the platypus, which has nothing of the bird but its beak, or like the poor bat, that innocent and tender creature when it is in the bosom of its family but whose uncertain shape creates its ugliness and its ill fortune. In the bat, nature can be seen in search of the wing, but finds only a hairy hideous membrane which nevertheless performs the function of the wing:

I am a bird, see my wings.

But the wing in itself does not make the bird.

Stand in the center of the museum, right next to the clock. There you will see on your left the early rudiments of a wing in the penguin of the southern pole and in its brother the northern auk, where it is slightly more developed. Scaly pinions whose gleaming pennae recall the fish much more than the bird. On land, it is a cripple: the earth is difficult for it, and the air is impossible. Do not pity it too much. The penguin's farseeing mother has destined it for the polar seas, where it will have little call to walk. She clothes it carefully in a fine sheath of blubber and a waterproof skin. She wants it to be warm in the ice. What is the best way of achieving that end? It seems she hesitated and felt her way: beside the penguin can be seen a surprisingly different attempt, but recalling maternal forethought just as clearly. This is the very rare gorfou, which I have not seen in any other museum and which is clad in the rough fur of the quadruped, rather like the skin of a goat, but probably more shiny than that of the land animal and certainly impermeable to water.

To group together the birds that do not fly we would have to add to these that navigator of the desert, the camel-bird, the ostrich, which recalls the camel by its internal structure. At least if its half-formed wing cannot raise it from the earth, it acts as a powerful aid in walking and gives it extreme speed. This is its sail, allowing it to cross the arid ocean of Africa.

Let us return to the penguin, the true starting point for this series, the penguin whose rudimentary wing does not act as a sail, does not assist the bird to walk, is a mere hint, a kind of memory on the part of Nature.

Nature breaks away, lifts herself up with difficulty in an early attempt at flight through these two strange figures which seem to us grotesque and pretentious. The penguin is neither of those things: an honest and simple creature, it is clear that it never had ambitions to fly. But here is one who breaks free and who seems to seek the adornments or the grace of movement. The gorfou seems to be a penguin determined to change its status; it takes a coquettish coxcomb which heightens its ugliness. The shapeless puffin, which seems the caricature of a caricature, the parrot, which it recalls through its heavy beak, poorly hewn and without sharpness of strength, tailless and unbalanced, it can always be tipped over by the weight of its great head. It risks flight, however, despite the likelihood of spills. It soars nobly close to the ground and may well fill penguins and seals with envy. Sometimes it risks the sea; an ill-starred vessel, the slightest wind shipwrecks it.

But it cannot be denied that it has become airborne. Birds of diverse types continue in more happy vein. The species which is so rich in divers in all their great diversity, links those that fly to those that swim; some, whose wings are better formed and whose flight is bold and sure, undertake immense journeys; others, still clad in the shiny scales of the penguin, wriggle and play in the depths of the seas; all that stops them being perfect fish is the lack of fins and gills; they alternate and are the masters now of one element and now of the other.

THE INSECT (1856)

Even in its hours of deep silence, the forest sometimes has voices, noises, murmurs that remind you of life. Sometimes the hardworking woodpecker, in its strenuous task of hollowing oaks, encourages itself with a strange cry. Often the heavy hammer of the quarrier falling again and again on the sandstone sends its muffled sound far into the distance. Finally, if you listen hard, you manage to seize a revealing rustling sound, and at your feet you can see, running through the crushed leaves, those infinite populations, those true inhabitants of the place, the legions of ants.

Each one is an image of persevering work that blends with the fantastic a solemn gravity. They dig, each in its own way. You, too, pursue your work, you dig in your thoughts.

It is an admirable place to heal the great illness of our day: our mobility and meaningless agitation. Our age is unaware of its evil; people say they are satisfied when they have barely started on something. They set out from the very false idea that in all things the best is the surface, the top that you need only touch with your lips. What is on top is often foam. It is lower down, it is within that you will find the drink of life.

You need to go deeper in, mingle more with things through willpower and habit, to find their harmony, in which lies happiness and strength. Unhappiness and moral poverty are what disperse the mind.

I love those places that concentrate and restrict the field of thought. Here, in this narrow circle of hills, changes are all on the surface, and all are mere effects of our vision. With so much shelter, the winds naturally vary little. The fixed atmosphere creates a state of mind. I do not know if thoughts that awaken there are stronger than others, but anyone who comes with an awakened thought can keep it for a long time, caress his or her dream free of distractions, seize and taste all its external accidents and all its internal mysteries. Your soul will set down roots here and find that the true meaning, the exquisite meaning of life, is not to run over the surfaces but to study, to seek, to enjoy in depth.

This place carries a warning for your soul. Fixed and unchangeable sandstone under the moving leaves speaks loudly enough in the silence. It was set down there, how long ago? Long, long ago, since, despite the hardness of the stone, rain has succeeded in hollowing it out. No other power has any strength over it. It was like that, and it is like that. The sight of it sends a message to the heart: "Persevere."

It seems to want to exclude vegetable life. But the heroic oaks are not put off. Condemned to live there, they have prevailed. With their twisted roots, with their powerful claws that grip the rocks, they too in their own way say eloquently: "Persevere." The unconquerable tree, growing all the more obstinate the more its task is made difficult, has plunged all the more deeply into the earth where it is free to do so, and has drawn from it incalculable strength. One of them, a poor old giant called Charlemagne, worn away, hollowed out, struck by lightning, after so many centuries and so many accidents is still so strong on its haunches that in a single one of its branches it seems to carry in its outstretched arms a great oak.

Between the sandstone and the oaks there is much from which to profit. And if you come across a man working there, he is not too weak for the job. The valiant quarrymen that I used to meet struggling with the rock, with those monstrous hammers which do not seem designed for the hand of a man, I would willingly have believed them to possess the power of resistance one finds in sandstone and the steely heart of the oak. And that no doubt also holds true for their souls and their willpower. But the body puts up less resistance. The majority of them die at the age of forty, and the first ones to be carried off are precisely the best, those who work hardest.

The quarrymen and the ants sum up the forest's entire life. In the past one would also have talked of the bees. They used to be very numerous, and you can still encounter them, especially in the area around Franchart. Their numbers must have dropped after people started planting so many pines and Northern trees which allow nothing to grow in their shadow, and which have, in many places, killed off the heather and the flowers. In recompense, the wild ants, which prefer to use the needles and cones of pines, appear to prosper. There may well be no forest richer in ant species.

Those are the true inhabitants of the desert, and they are the desert's very soul. The ants working the sand, the quarrymen working the sandstone, are both members of the same work-force, the men being ants above ground, and the ants almost men below ground.

I used to marvel at how closely their destinies resembled each other, how alike they were in their hard-working patience and their admirable perseverance. The sandstone, which is a very refractory and rebellious material, often breaks badly, greatly disappointing these poor workers over and over. It is particularly hard on those whom a lingering winter forces to return to the quarry before the end of the bad weather, for they find those blocks (so hard and yet so permeable) full of moisture and half-frozen. Consequently, numerous slabs cannot be used and must be rejected. They do not lose heart, but begin their hard work again without a murmur.

The same lesson in patience is given by the ants. Constantly those who raise birds, those who fatten pheasants, upset and overturn immense constructions which have cost the ants an entire season. Constantly they begin again with heroic zeal.

I used to go and see them frequently and sympathized with them more and more. Their patient acts, their active and thoughtful lives, recall more closely, in truth, the life of a worker than the winged life of the birds that had been occupying me up until that time. That free owner of the light, that darling of nature, floats so high above man! . . . To what could I compare my long, hard-working life? I have certainly seen the sky from time to time, and sometimes I have heard songs from on high; but for my entire existence, the unwearying toil that binds me to my work makes of me something far closer to the modest corporations of the bee and the ant.

The toil of their comrades, the quarrymen, is at first glance not very pleasant to watch. So many stones are spoiled and badly quarried, so many fragments, so much dust and sand, there is little that is attractive in that. You would think you were looking at a field of ruins. But what does Nature think of it? To judge by the eagerness with which the plants seize hold of that sand, mix it together and make of it a soil they can use, Nature seems happy to see all that substance which has been held in the sandstone for thousands of years, and kept out of circulation, now returning to the mobility of universal existence. That productive struggle of man against rock finally frees the captive element from its long enchantment. The grass commandeers it; the tree commandeers it; the animals commandeer it. All that sand, which is what the rock will eventually become in the course of ages, becomes accessible to the activity of a vast underground world.

Nothing gave me more pause for thought, no spectacle brought me back more forcefully to myself. I, too, have long been, as a result of some unknown poverty or slowness, like that recalcitrant sandstone, into which, often enough, nothing can enter, or which, splitting badly, yields only shapeless fragments, irregular and suitable only to be discarded. History, with its heavy iron hammer, was obliged to split me from myself, separate me from my obstacles, break me and set me free.

It was a harsh liberation. For the few stones I gave to the great masonry of the future, how many did I lose myself? Sometimes, struck both by the present and the past, I felt myself fall into pieces. Into pieces? Say rather into powder and dust. And from time to time I saw myself, as I see the bottom of this quarry, all sand and rubble.

And yet it is from these elements that all-powerful Nature, through some sap hidden in the heart of the pebble, allowed me to renew myself. With a little grass and a little heather, linking what History and the world had crushed, she said with a smile: "The rest of you, you are time. I am eternal Nature."

So, there is the rough quarry, bristling with the rubble of ages, which turns green, goes on producing, is covered with leaves far more numerous than was the case before the iron went to work on it. "Wild winter vegetation? Black firs? Sad birches? . . . " But no, for among this melancholy there mingles the flowering hawthorn.

What I so greatly requested, and desired, in my long years of silence, when I was like an arid block and a man of stone, was the fluidity of sap, its power to flow forth. My youth, which came to me late, yearns to pour out my delayed soul. Yesterday, I published *The Bird*, the upward surge of my heart toward the light. Today, the same force leads me, on the contrary, under the earth, to embark with you on the great living sea of metamorphosis. A world of mysteries and shadows. Yet it is in that world that can be found the lights that penetrate most deeply into the two dear treasures of the soul: Immortality and Love.

Fontainebleau, September 8, 1856

TRAVEL

Chateaubriand

◆

When the Revolution broke out, Chateaubriand, his political career in tatters, traveled to America, discovering sights, vegetation, and traditions that were to have a powerful influence on his future writing and thinking.

TEXT USED: *Atala* (Paris: Lefèvre et Ladvocat, 1830).

THE MISSISSIPPI (1801)

In days gone by, France possessed in North America a vast empire stretching from Labrador to Florida, from the shores of the Atlantic up the farthest lakes in the top of Canada.

Four great rivers, each having its source in the same mountains, divided these immense regions: the Saint Lawrence, which flows off to the east into the Gulf that bears its name, the Western River that takes its waters into unknown seas, the Bourbon River which rushes from the south to the north into Hudson Bay, and the Mississippi, which drops from the north to the south, into the Gulf of Mexico.[1]

This last river, which flows for more than a thousand leagues, waters a delightful country that the inhabitants of the United States call New Eden, and to which the French gave the sweet name of Louisiana. A thousand other rivers, tributaries of the Mississippi, the Missouri, the Illinois, the Arkansas, the Ohio, the Wabash, and the Tennessee, enrich it with their silt and fertilize it with their waters. When all these rivers are swollen with the winter floods, when storms have flattened entire swaths of forests, uprooted trees gather on the waters. Soon mud cements them, vines lash them together, and plants take root in them at every point, binding the debris together. Carried along by the foaming

---

1. The "Western" river is the Oregon river.

waves, they go down the Mississippi. The river takes hold of them, drives them on to the Bay of Mexico, throws them up on sand banks and thus succeeds in increasing the number of its mouths. Here and there it raises its voice, as it passes under mountains, and spreads its overflowing waters around the columns of forests or the pyramids of Indian tombs. It is the Nile of the wilderness. But grace and magnificence always go hand-in-hand in scenes from nature. While the central current rushes the corpses of pines and oaks to the sea, on the two side currents flowing by the banks you can see floating islands of water lettuce and water lilies, whose yellow roses rise up like little flags. Green snakes, blue herons, pink flamingos, and young crocodiles embark, passengers on these ships of flowers, and the colony opens its golden sails to the wind, to come ashore at some bay away from the main stream.

The two banks of the Mississippi offer the most extrordinary sight. On the western side savannahs extend as far as the eye can see. As they move away, their green waves seem to mount up into the azure of the sky and disappear. In these boundless prairies you can see wandering at random herds of three or four thousand wild bison. Sometimes a bison weighed down with years swims across the water and rests in the high grass on an island in the Mississippi. From its brow, which is adorned with two crescent horns, and its ancient, silt-covered beard, you might take it for a river god gazing in satisfaction at the grandeur of its waves and the wild luxuriance of its banks.

That is the scene on the western bank, but on the opposite bank it changes and offers a sharp contrast. Hanging over the current, clustered on the cliffs and mountains, scattered through the valleys, trees of all kinds, trees of all colors, trees of all scents, mingle and grow together, climbing up into the skies to heights that weary the gaze. The wild vines, the bignonias, the colocynths intertwine at the feet of these trees, climb up the branches, clamber to the tips of twigs and leap from maple to tulip tree, from tulip tree to alcea, forming myriad grottoes, vaults, and porticos. These lianas, which often wander from tree to tree, cross branches of the rivers over which they throw bridges of flowers. From the depths of these clumps the magnolia raises its motionless cone; topped by its large white roses, it dominates the entire forest and has no rival other than the palm tree which gently sways its green fans beside the magnolia.

A multitude of animals, set down in these wildernesses by the hand of the Creator, lend enchantment and life to the scene. From the end of avenues you can see bears intoxicated on grapes, stumbling along under elm branches; caribou bathe in a lake; black squirrels play in the thick foliage; mocking birds, Virginia doves the size of a sparrow, drop down onto grass turned red with strawberries; green parrots with yellow heads, scarlet woodpeckers, fire-colored cardinals clamber around the summits of cypresses; hummingbirds sparkle on the Florida jasmine, and bird-catching snakes hiss as they hang from the domes of the woods, swinging like lianas.

If all is silence and repose in the savannahs on the other side of the river, here on the contrary, is movement and murmurs. Beaks hammer on oak trunks, you hear the rustle of animals moving, browsing, or cracking fruit pits between their teeth; faint moans, soft lowing, gentle cooing fill these wildernesses with a wild and tender harmony. But when a breeze arouses these solitudes, setting the floating bodies swaying, blending these masses of white, blue, green, and pink, mingling all these colors, combining all these murmurs, then there issue from the depths of the forests such noises, such sights pass before the eyes, that I could never succeed in describing them to those who have never traveled through these primitive fields of nature.

Fromentin

◆

Eugène Fromentin (1820–1876) was a novelist, art critic, and artist. In addition to his travel journals, he wrote a wonderfully atmospheric novel, Dominique, *and a superb study of the Dutch masters,* Maîtres d'autrefois (Past Masters), *often and justly considered the finest piece of writing about art to be produced in the nineteenth century. Like many artists of his time, he traveled to Africa in search of subjects and in order to experience the vitality and intensity of the local cultures. In the following extract, he writes to a friend describing his first sight of the Sahara. Just as his paintings are marked by a strong awareness of the light and space of North Africa, so his prose reflects the intensity of his response to all that was new in what he saw and heard in his travels.*

FURTHER READING: *Masters of Past Time*, tr. H. Gerson (New York: Phaidon, 1948); *Dominique* (London: New English Library, 1962).
TEXT USED: *Un été dans le Sahara* (Paris: M. Lévy Frères, 1857).

A SUMMER IN THE SAHARA (1857)

Reduced as I am to whipping up my weakening enthusiasm by all kinds of reveries, dreams of the future or memories of the past, I warmly welcomed a moment ago a memory that will have to serve here, for I have no better. It could, moreover, serve as the preface to my notes where I plan to take my revenge later on by telling you of the feasts of the Sun.

You surely know a little etching by Rembrandt, cross-hatched, impetuous, of an incomparable color like all the fantasies of that singular genius, half-nocturnal, half-radiant, who seems to have known the light only at that doubtful moment of twilight, or at the violent moment of lightning bolts. It's very simple in its composition: there are three bristling trees, gruff in both shape and foliage; on the left a plain spreads as far as the eye can see; a vast sky in which descends an immense storm cloud, and, on the plain, two barely visible travelers who walk quickly and hastily, backs to the wind. This etching evokes all the fears of a traveling life, together with something mysterious and pathetic, which has always given me much food for thought. Sometimes even I thought I'd discovered in this etching a meaning applying to me alone: it was in a rainstorm that I was to meet for the first time some five years ago the land of never-ending summer; it was by fleeing wildly from that rain that at last I encountered the sun free of fogs.

It was in 1848, in February. That season there had been no break between the November rains and the great winter downpours, which had lasted for three and a half months almost without a single day's respite. I had fled from Blidah to Algiers, from Algiers to Constantine, without finding a spot on the coast that was spared this horrible winter; I had to seek out an area it could not reach, and that's when I thought of the desert. The road that leads there stretched out under the *Coudiat-Aty* drenched in water, and from time to time I saw long lines of people coming down it, their faces marked by an eternal suntan, followed by their camels loaded with dates and bizarre objects. I had the impression that as they approached me they shed some of the warmth they had carried with them in the muddy folds of their burnousses. So one morning we set off, desperate, crossing, with more or less success, the flooding rivers, and heading straight for Biskra. Five days later, on February 28, I arrived at *El-Kantara*, on the edge of the Tell of Constantine, exhausted, frozen, drenched to the heart, but fully determined not to stop again until I saw the unmistakable sun of the south.

El-Kantara, the bridge, guards the defile and, so to speak, the sole gateway through which you can enter the Sahara from the Tell. This passage is a narrow rent that looks man made, in an enormous wall of rocks some three or four hundred feet high. The bridge, which was built by the Romans, crosses the cutting at an angle. Once you've crossed the bridge and have gone a hundred yards into the defile, you drop down along a steep slope to a charming village, watered by a deep watercourse and lost in a forest of twenty-five thousand palm trees. You are in the Sahara.

Beyond rises a double row of golden hills, the final upwellings of the ground, which, twelve leagues away, expire into the immense flat plain of the little desert of Angad, the first draft of the great desert.

Thanks to its special situation, El-Kantara, which is the first of the villages of the Sahara along this line, enjoys the rare privilege of being somewhat protected by its forest against the desert winds, and of being completely protected from the north wind by the high rampart of rocks it leans back against. As a result, the Arabs believe firmly that the mountain summit stops the winds from the Tell, that the rain comes to a stop there, and that winter does not venture beyond that wonderful bridge, which thus separates the seasons, winter from summer. Two countries, the Tell and the Sahara—and they offer by way of proof the fact that on one side the mountain is black and rain-colored, while on the other it is pink and the color of fine weather.

It was our last march but one, for the last march was to take us directly to Biskra. The morning had been icy cold; when we awoke, the thermometer under the cold tents of K'sour registered one degree above zero. I remember, although it happened five years ago, the tiniest details of that journey. It came close to becoming dreadful, for my friend A. S. almost cracked his skull when he handed me my rifle. I carried this fateful weapon across my shoulder and emptied it, having made a promise not to use it any more. There was certainly a little melancholy between us and, especially since the accident, we didn't speak. It was a gloomy place. We followed a rocky avenue, enclosed in two long walls of dark rocks, completely denuded of grass, barely lit by a sunless day. From time to time an eagle sitting on a ledge of the mountain would rise slowly at our approach and climb in a circular flight above our heads. The sky, covered in grey, took a rest from raining but the wind still came from the north. It threaded its way through the gorge and seemed intent on pursuing us. It was a little sharp breath, persistent, barely audible, and yet very uncomfortable. I remember it above all because of the strange noises it made in the empty barrels of my rifle. It sounded like the pealing of two bells ringing together in plaintive tones and not quite in unison. The sound was so slight that it seemed to come from far away and so strangely sad that for the rest of the day it disturbed me. It was only on the following day when I heard it again that I finally discovered what was causing it. At last we reached the defile; it was a few minutes short of six o'clock.

Doctor T. preceded us at a gallop on his limping horse, singing in languishing tones the pseudo-Arab song—in those days still new—of Khedoudja. He was the first to reach the bridge, took off his hat, and shouted to us, "Gentlemen, here we salute!"

Is it true that the first military column to cross that famous bridge in 1844 stopped in sudden admiration and that the bands burst into enthusiastic music? I know only what I've heard on that subject, but that evening the spectacle I beheld would have made me believe that the tale was true.

The palms, the first I had seen, the little golden village, huddled in the green foliage already heavy with the white flowers of spring, a young girl coming toward us, accompanied by an old man, in the splendid red costume and the rich necklaces of the desert, carrying a sandstone jug on her naked thigh; that first fair-skinned girl, tall and lovely, precociously combining childhood and womanhood; that old man, bent but not disfigured by a premature old age; the entire desert appearing to me thus in all its forms, in all its beauty, and in all its emblems was an amazing first sight. What was incomparable above all, was the sky; the sun was about to set, and it was turning gold and scarlet and covering with a fiery enamel a flock of little clouds which had broken free from the great black curtain stretched over our heads, clouds that were lined up like a fringe of foam on the edge of a stormy sea. Beyond the blue began, and then, to depths that had no limits, through unknown limpid space, you could see the celestial land of blue. Warm breezes wafted up to us with mingled, unknown odors, and mysterious airy music from the depths of that flowering village. The date palms, moving gently, swayed with golden rays in their fronds and under the peaceful forest you could hear the sounds of water mingled with the light rustling of the leaves, the songs of birds and the sounds of a flute. At the same time, an invisible muezzin began to chant the evening prayer, repeating it four times to the four points of the horizon, in passionate tones, with such accents that everything seemed to fall silent to hear him.

Banville

♦

Théodore de Banville (1823–1891), an effervescent and virtuoso poet whose witty verse enjoyed a considerable vogue during his lifetime, was also a prolific prose writer. Here he reveals his love of exuberant description in a prose that is limpid, supple, and witty.

TEXT USED: *Le Moniteur universel*, April 7, 1860.

PALM TREES
From La Mer de Nice (1860)

You go to Nice to see the olive trees, the rose bushes, and the golden oranges; to Monaco to see carob trees and euphorbia; to Menton for lemon trees that are loaded throughout the year with fruit and flowers. But, if you want to see palm trees that are really alive, you have to go all the way to Bordighera.

In 1584, the famous obelisk that stands in Rome on the Vatican square was still lying half-buried in the earth, next to the former sacristy of San Pietro. In less than a year, Sixtus the Fifth,[1] whose implacable will moved stones as it moved men, arranged for the immense monument to be dug up and moved to its ultimate destination, although hitherto its dimensions had discouraged the popes and their workmen. On the day on which Domenico Fontana[2] was to set the obelisk on its pedestal,

---

1. *Sixtus V:* Felice Peretti (1521–1590), pope from 1585 to 1590. A notable patron of the arts, he initiated the building of the Vatican Library.

2. Domenico Fontana (1543–1607), Italian architect and engineer. He designed the Sistine Library and helped complete the dome of Saint Peter's basilica, as well as re-erecting the obelisk in front of Saint Peter's, where it now stands.

an edict from the Holy Father announced that whosoever should make the slightest sound during the erection of the obelisk would be punished by death, for they must have feared that the murmuring of the crowd would disturb the workers, and prevent them from following the architect's instructions attentively. Thus, the gigantic work was accomplished before a silent crowd of statues and phantoms, dominated by the hard and thoughtful head of the apostolic Agamemnon, seated on a great crimson seat. But while the monolith was rising up at last, and the terrible silence was broken only by the whistling of the cables and pulleys, a sinister crack was suddenly heard. The obelisk remained motionless, then dropped a few inches; the ropes, loosened by the movement, no longer controlled the enormous mass. "Wet the ropes!" shouted a bold voice that set the blood rising in the pontiff's cheeks. Yet the advice was instantly acted on; the formidable column rose up, before a crowd trembling with admiration. But the Swiss Guards, obeying their orders, had already bought the guilty man before Sixtus the Fifth. He was the poor captain of a commercial vessel, a native of San Remo. This was the only occasion on which the redoubtable apostle drew back from committing a political error: despite the ferocious edict, the sailor Bresca was not executed, but received the title of captain of the papal army, with the right to fly the papal flag on his craft. Then, and this was even more valuable, Sixtus the Fifth granted him, for himself and his descendants, the exclusive right to supply the palms used in Rome during Holy Week. That is why Bordighera today is covered with palm trees cultivated by the Brescas, and that is why I set out for this fairy-tale village, too lovely for mortal eyes. I had read twenty times in all the available guide books the little story about the obelisk on Saint Peter's square, but I learned to love it only when I read it written in a rich and moving style in J. Ruffini's[3] novel *Doctor Antonio*. The eminent Italian publicist furnished Bordighera with a heroine, as idealized as the most exquisite maidens of Sir Walter Scott; and the memory of Lucy Davenne, the sweet friend of Speranza, is henceforth inseparable from the flower-strewn countrysides in which the poet exiled her one spring. I did not come across her white dress in the little tracks where the acanthus grows, but I saw the precious trees that gave Sir John Davenne the idea of including among his glass houses a palm house, and I do not believe that human eyes can be bewitched by enchantments more wonderful than that.

Your first impression is such a dazzle of living and succulent greenery that the amazed eye wanders as in one of those delirious symphonies in which the musician's fury imposes on all nature the color and accent

3. Giovanni Ruffini (1807–1881), best known as a librettist for Italian operas, especially for his connection with Donizetti.

of his dream. From the sea shore to the depths of the countryside, in gardens, nurseries, staged terraces, divided by small, green, murmuring streams, the palms launch up into the skies their immense straight fronds, bold, luxuriant, scarcely moved by the warm wind, as sublime as Glory, and, like Prayer itself, avid for ether and azure. "To the stars! To the stars!" so those noble fronds seem to cry, scorning the earth and sharing the human soul's hunger for azure and its thirst for the infinite. Among the gardens, some scarcely leave the ground; the trunkless palms seem mere sprays of greenery; in others, the trees, more than two or three centuries old, are giants with terrifying plumes; at your feet, you have new-born palms, already proud, for, no sooner are they born than this august foliage feels the pride of its imperishable destiny; above your head are the great palm trees, slender, bold, crowned with leaves like the massive columns of an imaginary temple. Some lean over the road like a Genie about to take flight. Others clamber up the masonry that hides their view of the sky; their feet scarcely touching a disintegrating wall, they leap into space, completely supported in the air, which seems to lend them wings. And all this is so cool, so rich, so green, that the mind is deceived into thinking these branches are oceans, streams, rivers, cascades of greenery. On other occasions, our imagination transforms them into saints, troops of warriors and angels equipped with all they need to conquer a heavenly Jerusalem. Nothing bears so intensely the stamp of eternity as these palm trees, which slowly, so slowly, but with an implacable and confident thrust, rise up toward the abyss that attracts them. Each year adds a few inches more to the trunk, formed merely by the base of each cut frond, and over our heads there waves an entire world of these trees, which are already as big as triumphal columns. Many are so old and have seen so many centuries come and go that their trunks, which were formerly rough and composed of layer on layer of scales, have become as smooth and as hard as a column made of marble. Certain palm trees, too, wearied no doubt by some remarkable effort, have lain right down, stretched on their stomachs on the ground, like a pilgrim wearied unto death; but even in these cases, the foliage still gazes at the vast plains of blue, as if expressing a longing for God, a longing that never sleeps in ardent souls, even when they are enveloped in the mourning cloaks of sleep.

Many a passer-by has spoken of Bordighera in terms of Africa. No comparison could be less accurate. Bordighera, rather, is cool and fresh, its greenery as shining and extravagant as that of an English forest in the month of June. Some have imagined they saw a miniature version of virgin forests in those agglomerations of leaves and limbs that fight for light; but on the contrary, it is in the nature of groups of palm trees to form architectural combinations which are as regular as if they had stepped from the mind of an inspired artist. These are living Alhambras,[4] mosques of greenery, palaces that grow by the hour, and these gardens whose vegetation overflows with life and richness, offer shapes as artful as those of the rigid Le Nôtre,[5] but intoxicated with enthusiasm, drowned in joy. The loveliest garden of Bordighera, mingling great palms with ancient olive trees, belongs to the French consul; he masterminds one of the largest olive oil–producing concerns in the region, installed in the very garden of the consulate, and lives like a king of Ithaca[6] in the days of the heroes. The French coat of arms, hanging on the façade of the house, is in no way demeaned by the oil presses that surround it, for these industries, which are exactly as they were in the days of the Bible or the Odyssey, have maintained the noble character of primitive times. Moreover, when you gaze at the immense palm trees, silhouetted against the sky, your mind cannot evoke anything vulgar or prosaic. You see again Rembrandt's angel launched into full light in its terrifying flight, and all those angels of Spanish painters who carry to dying martyrs the reward for their sublime virtues. Happy dwellers of Bordighera, beaten by the sounding billow! Happy, happy Bresca! While others sell ironmongery or baskets, the Brescas deal in something essentially heroic and ideal. As merchants, they supply paradise, the seven heavens illumined by a radiant love, the very sanctuary in which is placed the flaming Throne, and their clients are celestial archangels who sing of unending glory on harps that tremble with delight. A single one of these branches is the envy of ages and the admiration of the universe, and the Brescas possess thousands of them in their forests of sacred verdure, able to heal more bleeding wounds than the soldiers of truth and faith have received since the world began. I admired the beds of geraniums and violets, but how much more grandiose are those fields of emerald that supply the stores of heaven and the granaries of paradise!

---

4. *Alhambras:* The Alhambra, a castle on the hill above Granada, was the last stronghold of the Moorish kings in Spain. Famed for the beauty of its architecture and its gardens, it symbolized, for nineteenth-century French writers, an earthly paradise.

5. André Le Nôtre (1613–1700) was the French landscape gardener who perfected the French version of the formal garden. His most famous gardens are at Vaux-le-Vicomte and Versailles.

6. *Ithaca:* A Greek island in the Ionian sea; the home of Homer's Odysseus.

SHORT STORIES

Mérimée

Prosper Mérimée (1803–1870) was an archaeologist and writer whose story
Tamango *is often seen not merely as ushering in a new era in French short-
story writing, but providing a model for the genre, such as we conceive of it
today. His ability to convey both the exotic and the fantastic through the eyes
of an apparently down-to-earth narrator has earned him a particular place
in the history of the fantastic. His spare, unemotional prose frequently contains
puns and hidden personal jokes, inviting the reader to exercise considerable
caution in interpreting what is being told. Indeed, he began his writing career
with two hoaxes, one purporting to be a series of plays written by a Spanish
woman, Clara Gazul, the second claiming to be translations of Illyrian songs.
While his later short stories avoid such ludic traps for the unwary, they do
contain several playful allusions to Mérimée himself, depicted somewhat ironically as the scholar and intellectual whose knowledge is insufficient in the face
of the fantastic, the primeval, or even sexual passion.*

FURTHER READING: *Carmen and Other Stories*, tr. Nicholas Jotcham (Oxford: Ox-
ford University Press, 1989).
TEXT USED FOR "THE VENUS OF ILLE": *Colomba* (Paris: Charpentier, 1850).
TEXT USED FOR "LOKIS": *Dernières* Nouvelles (Paris: Calmann-Lévy, 1881).

THE VENUS OF ILLE (1837)

Ἰλεὼς ἦν δ' ἐγώ, ἔστω ὁ ἀνδριας
καὶ ἤπιος, ουτως ἀνδρεῖος ὤν.

ΛΟΥΚΙΑΝΟΥ ΦΙΛΟΨΕΥΔΗΣ[1]

---

1. This quotation is from Lucian, the Greek satirist and rhetorician of the second century AD.
These lines, from his work *The Lover of Lies*, mean: "And I said: 'Let the statue be gracious and
kindly, since it is so lifelike.' "

I was making way down the last slope of Mount Canigou and, although the sun had already set, I could make out on the plain the houses of the little town of Ille,[2] toward which I was headed.

"I'm sure," I said to the Catalan who had been my guide since the preceding day, "I'm sure you know where Monsieur de Peyrehorade lives?"

"Do I know it!" he cried out, "I'm as familiar with his house as I am with my own; and if it weren't so dark, I'd point it out to you. His is the finest house in all Ille. He has money and that's for sure, M. de Peyrehorade has; and he's marrying his son to someone who's even richer than he is."

"And is the wedding to take place soon?" I asked him.

"Soon! It could well be that the violins have already been ordered for the festivities. This evening, perhaps, tomorrow or the next day—how should I know! They're having it at Puygarrig since it's Mlle Puygarrig that the son is to wed. Oh yes, it's going to be splendid!"

It was my friend M. de P. who had recommended I visit M. de Peyrehorade. He spoke of him as a highly educated specialist in ancient sites, and someone whose helpfulness knew no bounds. He would be delighted to show me all the ruins within a radius of ten leagues. I had been counting on him to show me the area around Ille, which I knew to be rich in monuments dating from antiquity and from the middle ages. This was the first time anyone had mentioned the wedding to me, and it threw all my plans into disarray. I'm going to make a nuisance of myself, I thought to myself. But they were expecting me; I'd been announced by M. de P., and so it was imperative that I present myself.

"Shall we take a bet, sir," my guide said to me when we had reached the plain, "shall we bet a cigar that I can guess what you're going to do at M. de Peyrehorade's?"

"But," I answered, holding out a cigar to him, "it's not particularly hard to guess. At this time of night and when you've covered six leagues in the Canigou, the thing to do is have supper."

"Sure, but tomorrow? . . . Come on, I'm willing to bet you've come to Ille to see the idol. I guessed you were when I saw you making a portrait of the saints at Serrabona."

"The idol? What idol?" The word *idol* had aroused my curiosity.

"What? You mean to say they didn't tell you at Perpignan that M. de Peyrehorade has taken an idol from the earth?"

"You mean an earthen statue, a statue in terra cotta, in clay?"

"Not at all. This one is certainly copper, enough to make a pile of

---

2. *Ille:* This little town in southwestern France is west of Perpignan, in a region formerly known as Roussillon. Mount Canigou rises straight up from the plain to reach an altitude of over 9,100 feet.

coins. She weighs as much as a church bell. She was lying deep in the earth, at the foot of an olive tree, when we took her."

"You were there when they uncovered her?"

"Yes, sir, I was. Two weeks ago, M. de Peyrehorade told Jean Coll and me to uproot an old olive tree that had frozen last year, since it was a very hard winter, as you know. Well, Jean Coll was really going at it, hammer and tongs, when he brought down his mattock and I heard a 'bong' sound. It was as if he had struck a bell. 'What ever is that?' I said to myself. We went on digging and digging, and suddenly there appeared a black hand, which seemed to be a dead person's hand sticking out of the ground. Well as for me I was really scared. I took myself off to M. de Peyrehorade, and I said to him, 'Boss, there are dead people under the olive tree! We ought to call in the priest.' 'What dead people?' he asked. Along he comes and he'd no sooner set eyes on the hand than he cried out, 'An antique! an antique!' You'd have thought he'd found a treasure. And there he was with the mattock and his hands, hurling himself into the task and doing almost as much work as the two of us put together."

"And what did you find in the end?"

"A great black woman, more than half naked, if you'll excuse the expression, sir, all in bronze. M. de Peyrehorade told us it was an idol from pagan days, from the time of Charlemagne, would you believe it!"

"I see what it must be . . . Some Holy Mother of God covered in bronze from a monastery that was destroyed."

"A Holy Mother of God! Well I ask you! I'd have certainly recognized a Holy Mother of God. This one is an idol, I'm telling you. You can see it just by looking at her. It's as if she's staring at you. When you look at her, I can tell you, you lower your eyes."

"Are the eyes white? They're probably encrusted in the bronze. Perhaps it's a Roman statue."

"Roman! That's the word. M. de Peyrehorade says it's Roman. Ah, I can see you're as much of a scholar as he is."

"Is it complete and in a good state of preservation?"

"Oh! sir, there's nothing lacking at all. It's even finer and better finished than the bust of Louis-Philippe in painted plaster that we have in the town hall. But even so, this idol's face doesn't appeal to me. She looks evil, and she is, too."

"Evil? Whatever has she done to hurt you?"

"Well, she hasn't hurt me, precisely. But you'll see. There were four of us got together to stand her upright, and M. de Peyrehorade, who was also pulling on a rope, although he hasn't got much more strength than a pullet, the good man! We got her upright after a real struggle. I was just picking up a big tile to wedge under her, when caboom! she fell straight back all of a heap. I called out, 'Look out back there,' but not fast enough, as it happened. Jean Coll didn't have time to get his leg out of the way . . . "

"And he was wounded?"

"Snapped in two like a stick, his poor leg did. Damn it all, when I saw that I was absolutely furious. I wanted to pound the statue with my mattock, but M. de Peyrehorade held me back. He gave Jean Coll some money, but all the same he's still in bed since that happened two weeks ago, and the doctor says he'll never walk on that leg as he does on the other. It's a crying shame; he was our best sprinter, and after M. de Peyrehorade's son the sharpest player at tennis. You should have seen how sad M. Alphonse de Peyrehorade was, because Coll was the one who used to give him a game. It used to be wonderful to see them sending each other's ball back. Bang! Bang! They never touched the ground."

Chatting in this way we entered the town of Ille, and I was soon in the presence of M. de Peyrehorade. He was a little old man who was still full of life and energy. His wig was powdered and his nose was red, and he seemed a jovial and fun-loving sort. Before opening M. de P.'s letter, he installed me before a laden table and introduced me to his wife and son as a famous archeologist who was to save the Roussillon area from the oblivion in which it was sinking through the indifference of the learned.

While I ate with a hearty appetite, for nothing makes you so sharp-set as the keen mountain air, I examined my hosts. I have already said a word or two about M. de Peyrehorade, and I should add that he was the very soul of vivacity. He talked, ate, got up, ran to his library, brought me books, showed me engravings, filled my glass. He couldn't be still for two minutes at a stretch. His wife, who was a trifle on the plump side, as happens to the majority of Catalan women once they've turned forty, struck me as a dyed-in-the-wool provincial who cared for nothing but running her house. Although the supper would have been more than enough for at least six, she ran to the kitchen, had some pigeons killed, got the cook to fry some corn-meal cakes, opened heaven knows how many pots of jam. In an instant the table was loaded with dishes and bottles, and I would certainly be dead of indigestion if I had even so much as tasted all I was offered. But at every dish I refused, there were floods of apologies. They feared I must find myself very uncomfortable at Ille. The provinces have so few resources, and Parisians are so hard to please!

Amidst the comings and goings of his parents, M. Alphonse de Peyrehorade sat as still as a statue. He was a large young man of twenty-six, with handsome, regular features, but a face that lacked expression. His athletic waist and muscles fully justified his local reputation as an indefatigable hand-tennis player. That evening he was elegantly dressed, his clothes based exactly on the engraving in the latest number of the *Fashion Journal*. But he seemed to me to be uncomfortable in his clothes: he was as stiff as a post in his velvet collar and could only turn his whole body at once. His coarse, sunburned hands, his short nails, contrasted oddly with his outfit. They were workman's hands appearing out of a dandy's sleeves. Moreover, although he gazed at me from head to toe with intense curiosity, given that I was a Parisian, he addressed me only once in the whole evening, and that was to ask me where I had bought my watch chain.

"Well now, my dear guest," M. de Peyrehorade said to me as supper came to an end, "You belong to me now, you know, for you're in my home. I'm not going to let go of you until you've seen everything of interest in our mountains. You must get to know our Roussillon,[3] and then you'll pay it full justice. You've got no idea what I'm going to show you. Phoenician monuments, monuments from the time of the Celts, the Romans, the Arabs, monuments from the age of Byzantium, you'll see everything, from mountains to molehills. I'll take you everywhere, and I'm not going to let you off seeing a single brick."

An attack of coughing forced him to stop talking. I took advantage of this to tell him I'd be distressed to disturb him at a time of such importance for his family. If he were willing to give me his excellent advice on the excursions I should undertake, I could, without giving him the trouble of going with me . . .

"Oh, you're talking of the lad's wedding," he exclaimed, interrupting me. "Fiddlesticks! It'll take place the day after tomorrow. You'll celebrate with us, as part of the family, for his fiancée is in mourning for an aunt whose estate she's inherited. So there'll be no feast, no dancing . . . It's a shame . . . You could have seen our Catalan women dancing. . . . They're pretty girls and you might have felt the urge to imitate our Alphonse. People say one wedding brings others . . . By Saturday, the young people will be married and I'll be free, so we can set out on our wanderings. I'm sorry to have to inflict on you the boredom of a provincial wedding. For a Parisian whose appetite for feasts has been dulled . . . and what's worse, this is a wedding without dancing! But still, you'll see a bride . . . a bride. That'll be something to write home about . . . But you're a serious man and don't look at girls any more. But I've better things than that to show you. Have I got something to show you! . . . I'm keeping something really surprising to show you tomorrow."

"Well, you know," I said to him, "it's pretty hard to have a treasure in the house without the world at large getting to know about it. I think I can guess what surprise you have for me. But if it's your statue that

---

3. *Roussillon:* This area, which has now combined with the former Cerdagne to form the *département* known as the West Pyrenees, owed its unity as a historical entity to the Catalan language and culture. Its relatively gentle climate has made it renowned for its fruits and vegetables, as well as for its wines.

you're going to show me, the description my guide gave me of it only whetted my appetite and prepared me to admire it."

"Ah! He told you about my idol, for that's what they call my beautiful Venus Tur . . . But I'm not going to tell you another word about it. Tomorrow, when it's light, you'll see it and you'll tell me if I'm right to think it's a masterpiece. You really couldn't arrive at a better moment. It has inscriptions that I, ignoramus that I am, explain in my own way . . . but a Parisian expert! . . . You may well mock my interpretation . . . for I've written a piece about it . . . I have indeed . . . old provincial archeologist that I am, I've launched myself into it . . . I want to make the presses groan . . . If you were so kind as to read it for me and correct it, I might be able to hope . . . For instance, I'd really like to know how you'd translate this inscription on the base: *cave* . . . But I don't want to ask you anything yet! Let's leave it to tomorrow! Leave it to tomorrow! Not a word on Venus today."

"You're quite right to abandon your idol, Peyrehorade," his wife said. "You ought to see that you're stopping the gentleman from eating. Come on, the gentleman has seen much more beautiful statues than yours in Paris. In the Tuileries there are dozens of them, and they're in bronze."

"Well there you have the ignorance, the blessed ignorance, of the provinces!" M. de Peyrehorade broke in. "Imagine comparing an admirable statue from antiquity to Coustou's[4] dull pieces!

> *I count religion but a childish toy*
> *And hold there is no sin but ignorance.*[5]

"Would you believe that my wife wanted me to melt down my statue to make a bell for the church? That's because she'd have been its godmother. Melt down a masterpiece by Myron,[6] sir!"

"Masterpiece, masterpiece! A fine masterpiece she created! Breaking a man's leg!"

"My dear, you see this leg?" said M. de Peyrehorade in resolute tones, stretching out his leg in its silk sock. "Well, even if my Venus had broken this leg, I wouldn't regret it."

"Goodness gracious! Peyrehorade, how ever can you say such a thing? Fortunately the man's making progress . . . And yet I can't bring myself to look at a statue that causes such accidents! Poor old Jean Coll!"

---

4. *Coustou:* Two brothers of this name, Nicolas (1658–1733) and Guillaume (1677–1746), were highly regarded sculptors with statues held by the Louvre, Notre Dame, and the Tuileries gardens.

5. *I count . . . :* Mérimée parodies two lines from Molière's play *Amphytrion*, a parody replaced in this translation by lines from Marlowe's prologue to *The Jew of Malta*, which provide an appropriate parallel.

6. *Myron:* An Athenian sculptor of the 5th century B.C. His *Discus Thrower* and *Marsyas* are known through Roman copies.

"Wounded by Venus, sir," said Peyrehorade, with a guffaw. "He's been wounded by Venus, and the oaf complains about it! *Veneris nec praemia noris.*[7] Who has not been wounded by Venus?"

Monsieur Alphonse, who understood French better than Latin, gave a knowing wink and looked at me as if to ask: "Did you get the joke, Parisian?"

Supper had finished. I hadn't eaten anything for a whole hour. I was weary, and I couldn't hide my frequent yawns. Madame de Peyrehorade was the first to notice and announced that it was time for bed. That was the cue for countless apologies about the poor bed I was to have. It wouldn't be what I was used to in Paris. Things are so uncomfortable in the provinces! The Roussillonnais needed all the indulgence they could get. It was no good protesting that after a long walk in the mountains a bale of straw would be a delightful bed as far as I was concerned. They went on begging me to forgive poor country folk for not treating me as well as I could have desired. At last I went up to the room they had chosen for me, accompanied by M. de Peyrehorade. The stairway, whose upper steps were of wood, led to the middle of a corridor onto which opened several bedrooms.

"On the right," my host told me, "is the suite I've chosen for the future Madame Alphonse. Your room is at the end of the corridor on the other side. You'll appreciate," he added, with what he hoped passed for a knowing look, "you'll appreciate that a young couple needs some privacy. You're at one end of the house, and they're at the other."

We went into a well-furnished room, where the first object my eyes lit on was a bed seven feet long, six feet wide and so high that you needed a set of steps to reach it. When my host had shown me where the bell pull was and had assured himself that the sugar bowl was full, that phials of eau de cologne were in their place on the wash-stand, and had asked me several times if there was anything I needed, he wished me good night and left me alone.

The windows were closed. Before undressing, I opened one so that I could breathe in the fresh night air, which is so delicious after a long supper. Opposite me was the mountain of the Canigou, which is always spectacular but which seemed to me that evening to be the most beautiful mountain in the world, lit as it was by a brilliant moon. I spent a few moments gazing at its wonderful outline and was about to shut my window when, as I lowered my eyes, I caught sight of a statue on a pedestal twenty yards or so from the house. It had been placed at the corner of an evergreen hedge which separated a small garden from a vast and perfectly flat square, which I later learned was the town's tennis

---

7. *Veneris nec praemia noris:* This quotation is from Virgil's *Aeneid* (IV.33) and means: "And shall you not know the gifts of Venus?"

court. This land, which belonged to M. de Peyrehorade, had been given by him to the commune, at the urgent request of his son.

I was too far away to discern the statue's expression; I could merely judge its height, which seemed to me to be in the neighborhood of six feet. At that moment two town rascals were crossing the tennis court fairly close to the hedge and whistling the pretty Roussillon tune "*Mountain treats.*" They stopped to look at the statue; one of them even addressed it aloud. He spoke in Catalan, but I had been in the Roussillon long enough to be able to understand more or less what he was saying.

"So there you are, you minx!" (The Catalan term was more energetic than that.) "There you are!" he was saying. "So you're the one who broke Jean Coll's leg! If you were mine, I'd break your neck for you."

"Nonsense! What would you break it with?" said the other. "It's made of brass, and it's so hard that Etienne broke his file on it when he tried to mark it. It's brass from the time of the pagans; and it's harder than anything you like to think of."

"If I had my cold chisel (it seemed he was a locksmith's apprentice), I'd soon pop out her great white eyes, as I'd pop an almond out of its shell. There's more than a hundred sous worth of silver in there."

They walked a few paces away.

"I've got to bid the idol goodnight," said the larger of the apprentices, stopping abruptly.

He bent down, probably to pick up a stone. I saw him stretch out his arm and hurl something, and immediately a loud blow vibrated on the bronze. At the same instant the apprentice clapped his hand to his head, crying out in pain.

"She threw it back at me," he shouted.

My two rapscallions took to their heels at top speed. It was self-evident that the stone had ricocheted from the metal and had punished the rascal for his outrage on the goddess.

I shut the window, laughing with all my heart.

"Yet another Vandal punished by Venus! May all those who destroy our old monuments get their heads broken just like that!" And on that charitable request, I fell asleep.

It was broad day when I woke up. Standing by my bed stood, on one side, M. de Peyrehorade, in his dressing gown, and on the other a man-servant sent by Madame, holding a cup of hot chocolate.

"Come on, Parisian! Time to get up! That's your lazy folk who live in our nation's capital for you!" my host said, as I quickly dressed. "It's eight o'clock and he's still in bed. Now I've been up since six o'clock. This is the third time I've come upstairs, I crept to your door on tiptoes: no one, not a single sign of life. It would make you ill if you slept too long at your age. And there's my Venus that you still haven't clapped eyes on! Come on, drink this cup of Barcelona chocolate . . . That's real contraband, that is . . . The sort of chocolate you can't get in Paris. Get your strength up, because once I get you face to face with my Venus we won't be able to tear you away."

Five minutes later I was ready, by which I mean half shaved, poorly buttoned, and burned by the chocolate I had gulped down boiling hot. I went down to the garden and found myself standing in front of an admirable statue.

It really was a Venus, and a wonderfully beautiful one at that. The upper part of her body was bare, according to the general custom used in antiquity to represent the great gods and goddesses. Her right hand, raised to the level of her breast, was turned, palm inwards, the thumb and first two fingers stretched out, the other two fingers slightly bent. The other hand, held near her hip, lifted the drapery that covered the lower part of the body. The statue's attitude recalled that of the mora[8] player generally called, for reasons unknown to me, Germanicus. It may well have been the intention to represent the goddess playing at mora.

However that may be, you could not find a more perfect body than that of this Venus. Nothing could be smoother and more voluptuous than her contours, nothing more elegant and more noble than the drapery. I had been expecting something dating from the Roman decadence: what I saw was a masterpiece from the great age of sculpture. What struck me above all was the exquisite truth of shape, a truth so great that you might imagine them molded on a real woman, if nature ever produced such perfect models.

Her hair, raised above her brow, looked as if in the past it had been gilded. Her head, small as are those of almost all Greek statues, was slightly bent forward. As for the features, I could never find words to describe how strange they were, of a type recalling no ancient statue that I could remember. She did not possess that calm, severe beauty of Greek sculptors, who systematically impart a majestic immobility to all the features. Here, to the contrary, I observed to my surprise that it had been the artist's obvious intention to portray malice bordering on evil. All the features were slightly contracted, the eyes were somewhat oblique, the mouth raised at the corners, the nostrils slightly flared. Disdain, irony, cruelty could all be read on this face, which was nevertheless incredibly lovely. Truly, the more you looked at that admirable statue, the more you felt distressed that such marvelous beauty could be found together with a complete absence of sensitivity.

"If the model ever existed," I said to M. de Peyrehorade, "And I doubt that heaven ever produced such a woman, how I pity her lovers! She

---

8. *Mora:* In this game, the hand is briefly raised, with the opponent having to guess how many fingers were extended.

must have taken pleasure in making them die of despair. There's something ferocious in her expression, and yet I have never set eyes on anything so lovely."

"It is Venus in her might, attached to her prey!"[9] exclaimed M. de Peyrehorade, satisfied with my enthusiasm.

The hellish irony of her expression was, so it seemed, increased by the contrast of her eyes, encrusted with silver and gleaming brightly under the blackish-green patina that time had given to the entire statue. Those glittering eyes produced a certain illusion of reality, of life. I remembered what my guide had told me, that she made those who looked at her lower their eyes. That was almost literally true, and I couldn't contain a movement of rage against myself for feeling somewhat discomforted before that bronze figure.

"Now that you've admired everything in detail, my dear colleague in antiquology," said my host, "let's embark, if you agree, on a scientific talk. What's your opinion of that inscription that you may not yet have noticed?"

He showed me the statue's base, and there I read these words:
Cave amantem.

"Quid dicis, doctissime?"[10] he asked me, rubbing his hands in glee. "Let's see if we can reach agreement on the meaning of this *cave amantem.*"

"Well," I answered, "there are two meanings. You could translate, 'Be wary of him who loves you—mistrust lovers.' But I'm not certain whether *cave amantem* used in that way is really good Latin. Looking at the lady's diabolical expression, I'd be more tempted to believe that the artist wanted to warn the spectator against this terrible beauty. So I would translate, 'Take care if *she* should love you.'"

"Humph!" said M. de Peyrehorade. "Yes, that is an admirable meaning but, by your leave, I prefer the first translation, which I would however expand. You know who Venus's lover was?"

"There are several."

"Yes, but the principal one was Vulcan. Don't you think the intention was to say: 'Despite all your beauty, despite your haughty airs, you'll have a smithy, an ugly cripple for your lover.' That's a deep lesson, sir, to teach flirts!"

I couldn't help smiling, so far-fetched did this translation seem to me.

"Latin is a terrible language with its conciseness," I remarked, to avoid giving my archeologist a flat contradiction, and I stepped back several paces to get a better view of the statue.

---

9. *Venus:* This verse from *Phèdre* is probably Racine's most frequently quoted line.

10. *Quid dicis:* "What do you have to say, most learned one?" This quotation is from Molière's *Malade imaginaire.*

"Just a minute, colleague!" said M. de Peyrehorade, grasping my arm, "You haven't seen everything yet. There's another inscription. Climb on the base and look at the right arm." So saying, he helped me to mount.

I grasped the Venus's neck, rather unceremoniously, for I was beginning to grow familiar with her. For a moment I even stared her in the face and found that close up she was even more evil and even more lovely. Then I realized that there were engraved on the arm some letters in what seemed to me to be an ancient cursive script. By staring through my spectacles I spelled out what follows, and as I did so, M. de Peyrehorade repeated each word as I pronounced it, with gestures and inflections that were full of approval. This, then is what I read:

> Veneri tvrbvl. . . .
> evtychus Myron[11]
> imperio fecit

After the word Tvrbvl in the first line, it seemed to me that there were some letters that had been worn away; but Tvrbvl was perfectly legible.

"Which is to say. . . . ?" asked my beaming host with a malicious smile, for he really thought I wouldn't get out of that Tvrbvl so easily.

"There is one word I can't yet explain," I said. "All the rest is easy. Eutyches Myron made this offering to Venus at her command."

"Wonderful! But Tvrbvl, what do you make of that? What is Tvrbvl?"

"Tvrbvl is a real problem. I'm trying in vain to find some well-known epithet applied to Venus to help me out. Come, tell me what you think of Tvrbvlenta? Venus who disturbs and agitates . . . You can see I'm still preoccupied by her evil expression. Tvrbvlentam, that's not too bad an epithet for Venus," I added modestly, for I myself wasn't particularly satisfied with my explanation.

"Turbulent! Venus turbulent! Venus the noisy! Oh so you think my Venus is a dance-hall Venus? Not one bit. She's a high-society Venus. Listen and I'll explain this Tvrbvl. But promise me at least that you won't spread my discovery around too much before my monograph has been published. The thing is, I'm really proud of this little discovery . . . You really must leave us poor provincials a few stalks to glean. You're so rich, you scholars of Paris!"

From the top of the pedestal on which I was still perched, I gave him my solemn word that I would never be so unworthy as to divulge his discovery.

"Tvrbvl, sir," he said coming up close and lowering his voice lest anyone else hear him, "For Tvrbvl read Tvrbvlnerae."

"I'm none the wiser."

"Listen closely. One league from here, at the foot of the mountains,

---

11. *Eutychus Myron:* One of Mérimée's many in-jokes. Eutychus is the equivalent of Mérimée's own first name, Prosper.

there is a village called Boulternère. That's a corruption of the Latin word Tvrbvlnerae. There's nothing so common as inversions of that sort. Boulternère, sir, was a Roman town. I'd always suspected it but I'd never had proof. Now this is the proof. This Venus was the local divinity of the city of Boulternère and this word Boulternère, which I've just shown to be of ancient origin, proves something very curious, which is that Boulternère, before being a Roman city, was a Phoenician city!"

He paused for a moment to catch his breath and take pleasure in my surprise. I managed to control a powerful urge to laugh.

"Yes, indeed," he went on, "Tvrbvlnera is pure Phoenician, TVR you should pronounce TOUR . . . *Tour* is the same word as SOUR, wouldn't you agree? *Sour* is the Phoenician word for Tyr; I don't need to remind you what the word means. BVL is Baal; *Bâl, Bel, Bul* merely indicate slight differences in pronunciation. As for NERA, that does pose the odd problem. I'm tempted to believe, since I can't find a Phoenician word, that it comes from the Greek word *nhroz*, meaning damp, marshy. So it seems to be a hybrid word. To justify *nhroz*, I'll show you when we visit Boulternère how the mountain streams gather there and form foul marshes. On the other hand, the ending ERA could have been added much later in honor of Nera Pivesuvia, the wife of Tetricus, who could have been a benefactress of the city of Turbul. But, given the marshes, I prefer the etymology *nhroz*."

He took a pinch of tobacco with a satisfied air.

"But let's leave the Phoenicians and come back to the inscription. This is my translation: 'To the Boultenère Venus Myron dedicates at her orders this statue which he has made.' "

I refrained from criticizing his etymology, but I wanted to show that I too was capable of penetrating insights, and I said to him: "One moment, sir! Myron dedicated something, but I see no proof that it was this statue."

"What ever do you mean? Wasn't Myron a famous Greek sculptor? His talent would have been passed on through his family. It's one of his descendants who must have made this statue. There's no doubt about that."

"But," I answered, "I can see a little hole on the arm. I believe it was used to attach something, a bracelet for instance, that this Myron gave to Venus as an expiation. Myron was a star-crossed lover. Venus was angry with him; he appeased her by dedicating to her a gold bracelet. Note that *fecit* is very often used for *consecravit*. They're synonymous terms. I could show you several examples if I had Gruter or Orelli[12] with me. It's perfectly natural that a lover should see Venus in a dream

---

12. *Gruter or Orelli:* The first of these, Jan van Gruyere (1560–1627), was a Dutch humanist and archaeologist; the second, Johann Kaspar von Orelli (1787–1849), was a Swiss philologist. Both wrote important works on the deciphering of ancient inscriptions.

and imagine that she has ordered him to give her statue a gold bracelet. Myron dedicated a bracelet to her . . . Then the barbarians or perhaps some sacrilegious thief . . . "

"Ah! It's obvious you've written novels," exclaimed my host as he stretched out a hand to help me down. "No, sir, it's certainly a work of the school of Myron. Just look at the craftsmanship and you'll have to agree."

Just then he caught sight of a white mark a little above the Venus's breast. I saw a similar mark on the fingers of her right hand, which as I supposed then had been touched in the stone's trajectory, or perhaps a fragment had broken lose in the impact and ricocheted against the hand. I told my host the story of the insult I had witnessed, and the swift punishment that had ensued. He laughed loudly at that, and comparing the apprentice to Diomedes,[13] he expressed the wish that he, like the Greek hero, would see all his companions changed into white birds.

The dinner bell interrupted this classical discussion, and just as on the previous day I was obliged to eat enough for four. Then M. de Peyrehorade received some of his farmers, and while he was meeting them, his son took me to see a barouche that he had bought at Toulouse for his fiancée, and which I hardly need say I admired. Then I went with him to the stable, where he spent half an hour of my time praising his horses to me, telling me their genealogy and naming the prizes that they had won in local horse races. Only then did he begin to talk to me about his future wife, using as transition a gray mare he was planning to give her.

"We'll see her today," he told me. "I don't know if you'll think her pretty. You're fussy, you Parisians, but everyone here and in Perpignan considers her charming. The good thing about her is that she's well-to-do. Her aunt from Prades left her all her possessions. Oh! How happy I'm going to be."

I was deeply shocked to see a young man appear more moved by the dowry than the beauty of his future wife.

"You're an expert in jewelry," M. Alphonse went on. "What's your opinion of this? Here's the ring I'll be giving her tomorrow."

As he spoke, he drew from the first joint of his little finger a large ring embellished with diamonds and shaped like two joined hands, an allusion which struck me as infinitely poetic. The work was old but in my opinion the ring had been reworked to stud it with diamonds. On the inside curve could be read these words written in Gothic letters: *Sempr' ab ti*, meaning always with thee.

"It's a pretty ring," I said to him. "But the diamonds that have been added have taken something from its character."

---

13. *Diomedes:* A hero of the siege of Troy, where he wounded Venus. In revenge, she transformed his companions into white birds.

"Oh, but it's far prettier like that," he answered with a smile. "There's twelve hundred francs worth of diamonds there. My mother gave it to me. It's a ring that's been in the family and is very old . . . It dates from the days of chivalry. My grandmother used to wear it, and she got it from her grandmother. God knows when it was made."

"The custom in Paris," I told him, "is to give a very simple ring, generally consisting of two different metals, like gold and platinum. Look, this other ring, the one you're wearing on this finger, would be very suitable. This one, with its diamonds and its hands worked in bas-relief, is so heavy that you couldn't wear a glove over it."

"Oh! Madame Alphonse will work something out. But I still think she'll be pretty pleased to have it. Twelve hundred francs on your finger is pretty agreeable. This little ring," he added, looking with a satisfied air at the plain ring he wore on his hand, "this little ring was given me by a woman in Paris one Shrove Tuesday. Ah! How I threw myself into things when I was in Paris, two years ago! Now that's the place to have fun!" And he gave a sigh of regret.

We were to dine that day in Puygarrig, in the home of the future bride's parents. We boarded the barouche and set off for the castle, which was about a league and a half from Ille. I was introduced and welcomed as a family friend. I shan't speak of the dinner or the ensuing conversation, in which I took little part. M. Alphonse, sitting beside his future wife, spoke a word in her ear every quarter of an hour. As for her, she barely raised her eyes, and every time her fiancé spoke to her, she blushed modestly but answered him straightforwardly.

Mademoiselle de Puygarrig was eighteen years old. Her slender, supple figure formed a sharp contrast with the bony form of her robust fiancé. She was more than beautiful, she was seductive. I admired the perfectly natural way in which she spoke; and her kindly expression, which was not entirely free from a slight degree of malice, just like the Venus, reminded me willy-nilly of my host's statue. In making this mental comparison, I wondered if the fact that one would of course have to admit that the statue was superior in beauty did not stem from the tigerish expression she wore, for energy, even in evil passions, always arouses in us a sense of amazement and a kind of involuntary admiration.

"What a shame," I thought as we left Puygarrig, "That such a pleasant person should be rich and that her dowry should make her the object of the attentions of a man unworthy of her!"

On our way back to Ille I found myself unsure what to say to Mme Peyrehorade, but I felt I should every so often make some sort of conversation, so I remarked: "You're really tough-minded people in Roussillon! A wedding on a Friday! In Paris we'd be too superstitious; no one would dare take a wife on such a day."

"Don't talk about it!" she exclaimed. "If it had been up to me, we would of course have chosen a different day. But Peyrehorade wanted it to be a Friday, and we had to let him have his way. But it disturbs me all the same. What if something went wrong? There must be a reason for people being afraid of a Friday."

"Friday!" exclaimed her husband. "But that's Venus's day! An excellent day for a wedding. You can see, my dear colleague, that I think of nothing but my Venus. On my word of honor, it's for her sake that I chose a Friday. Tomorrow, if you like, on the day before the wedding, we'll make her a little sacrifice. We'll sacrifice two doves to her, and if I only knew where to find some incense . . . "

"For Heaven's sake!" his wife interrupted, deeply scandalized. "Incense for an idol! That would be an abomination! What would people say about us?"

"At least," said M. de Peyrehorade, "you'll allow me to place on her head a crown of roses and lilies: *Manibus date lilia plenis*.[14] You can see, dear sir, that the constitution carries no weight. We don't have freedom of worship."

It was decided that on the following day everyone was to be ready and fully dressed at ten o'clock. Once we had taken our chocolate, we would return to Puygarrig. The secular wedding was to take place at the town hall, the religious ceremony in the chapel at the chateau. After that came lunch, and then we would do whatever we pleased until seven o'clock. At seven, we'd return to Ille, to the Peyrehorades' house, where the two families were to share supper. The rest would follow its natural course. As dancing was impossible, they would eat as much as they could.

As early as eight o'clock I found myself sitting before the Venus, a pencil in my hand, making my twentieth attempt to draw the statue's head, and failing each time to capture her expression. M. de Peyrehorade bustled to and fro around me, giving me advice, repeating the Phoenician etymologies, then placing roses on the statue's pedestal. In tragi-comic tones, he expressed his hopes for the couple who were to live under his roof. Toward nine, he went back in to get ready for the wedding, and at that moment M. Alphonse appeared, tightly bound in a new suit, wearing white gloves, polished shoes, chiseled buttons, and a rose in his button hole.

"Will you do my wife's portrait?" he said as he bent over my drawing. "She's pretty, too."

At that moment a match began on the court I've already mentioned, and it immediately attracted M. Alphonse's attention. As for me, tired and losing all hope of conveying that diabolical expression, I soon left my drawing to watch the players. There were among them some Span-

---

14. *Manibus date lilia plenis:* "Give handfuls of lilies." The quotation is from Virgil's *Aeneid* (VI.883).

ish mule drivers who had arrived the day before. They were from Aragon and Navarre, and almost all were marvelously skillful. So the people of Ille, although they were encouraged by the presence and advice of M. Alphonse, were pretty swiftly beaten by these new champions. The French spectators were filled with consternation. M. Alphonse looked at his watch. It was only nine-thirty. His mother had not yet done her hair. He did not hesitate any longer. He took off his jacket, borrowed a waistcoat, and challenged the Spaniards. I watched him with a smile and some degree of surprise.

"It's a question of national honor!" he said.

It was then that I thought him really fine. He was impassioned. His clothes, which had taken all his attention just a few minutes ago, no longer mattered to him. A few minutes earlier he'd have been afraid to turn his head for fear of spoiling his cravat. Now he gave no thought to his curled hair and his finely tucked jabot. And his bride? . . . Well, I have to say that had it been necessary, he would probably have postponed the wedding. I saw him quickly pull on a pair of sandals, roll up his sleeves, and, with an assured air, put himself at the head of the defeated team, like Caesar rallying his troops at Dyrrachium.[15] I leapt over the hedge and settled myself comfortably in the shade of a great tree so that I could have a good view of both sides.

Contrary to all expectations, M. Alphonse missed the first ball. It is true that it came whizzing along the ground, hurled with surprising strength by an Aragonese who seemed to be the leader of the Spaniards.

He was a man of about forty, thin and wiry, six feet tall, and almost as dark in color as the bronze of the Venus.

M. Alphonse flung his racket to the ground in fury.

"It's this damned ring!" he exclaimed. "It's squeezing my finger and made me miss an easy ball."

With some difficulty, he removed his diamond ring; I went over to take it for him, but he was quicker than I, and ran to the Venus, slipped the ring on her ring finger and took up his place again at the head of the Illois.

He was pale, but calm and resolute. From that moment on he did not make a single error, and the Spaniards were roundly trounced. The spectators' enthusiasm was a fine thing to see. Some shouted joyously and threw their caps in the air; others shook his hands, calling him the honor of the country. Had he repelled an invasion, I doubt that he would have received livelier or more sincere congratulations. The disappointment of the defeated added even more to the intensity of his victory.

---

15. *Dyrrachium:* Pompey defeated Caesar here in 48 B.C. but was in turn defeated at the battle of Pharsalus later that year.

"We'll have other matches, old chap," he said to the Aragonese condescendingly. "But I'll give you a few points' lead."

I would have liked M. Alphonse to be a little more modest and was almost hurt by his rival's humiliation.

The giant Spaniard felt this insult deeply. I saw him blanch under his dusky skin. He gave his racket a glum look, while gritting his teeth, then in a muffled voice he murmured: "*Me lo pagarás.*"[16]

M. de Peyrehorade's voice interrupted his son's triumph. My host, greatly surprised not to find him supervising the preparation of the new carriage, was even more amazed to discover him covered with sweat and grasping a racquet in his hand. M. Alphonse ran to the house, washed his face and hands, donned his new coat once more, put on his polished shoes, and five minutes later we were trotting briskly on our way to Puygarrig. All the town's tennis players and a large number of onlookers followed us with shouts of joy. The strong horses that pulled us could only just keep ahead of these intrepid Catalans.

We were at Puygarrig and the procession was about to set off for the town hall when M. Alphonse, slapping his brow, whispered to me, "What a mess! I forgot the ring! It's still on the Venus's finger, devil take it. Just don't tell my mother. Perhaps she won't notice anything."

"You could send someone," I suggested.

"Not likely! My servant remained behind at Ille, and I don't trust that lot at all. Twelve hundred francs worth of diamonds might well tempt more than one of them. Besides, what would people think here if they knew I was so absent-minded? I'd be covered with scorn! They'd call me the Venus's husband. . . . Let's just hope no one steals it! Fortunately the idol scares those rascals. They don't dare come within arm's length of her. Ah well! I doesn't matter. I have another ring."

The two ceremonies, the civil and the religious, went off with all suitable pomp, and Mademoiselle de Puygarrig accepted the Parisian milliner's ring without realizing that her betrothed was sacrificing for her sake a pledge of love. Then we sat down to lunch and drank, ate, and even sang at great length. I felt for the bride when all this coarse joy burst out around her, but she put up with it better than I would have hoped, and her embarrassment showed neither naivety nor pretense.

Perhaps difficult circumstances stimulate courage in different people.

All in good time the lunch ended, around four o'clock. The men went walking in the park, which was magnificent, or watched the Puygarrig peasants dancing on the castle lawn, decked out in their Sunday best. This filled in a few hours. Meanwhile the women were very busy around the bride, who showed off her presents. Then she changed her outfit, and I noticed that she covered her beautiful hair with a bonnet

---

16. *Me lo pagarás:* "You'll pay me for that!"

and a plumed hat, for women are always eager to don those items of clothing that usage forbids them to wear when they are still unmarried.

It was almost eight o'clock when we got ready to return to Ille. But first we witnessed a heart-rending scene. Mademoiselle de Puygarrig's aunt, who had been a mother to her, an elderly and very devout woman, was not to travel to Ille with us. When we were ready to leave, she gave her niece a sermon about her duties as a wife, a sermon which resulted in floods of tears and endless embraces. M. de Peyrehorade compared this separation to the rape of the Sabine women. Eventually, however, we left, and on the way we all did our best to amuse the bride and make her laugh, but our efforts were in vain.

At Ille, supper awaited us. And what a supper! If this morning's coarse joy had offended me, I was far more offended by the dubious jokes and innuendoes made about the groom and above all the bride. The groom, who had disappeared for a moment before taking his place, was pale and icily serious. He drank copious amounts of vintage Collioure wine, which is almost as strong as brandy. I was sitting beside him and thought it my duty to warn him: "Be careful. It's said that wine . . . " And I added something stupid to put myself on a par with the other guests. He pushed my knee and said to me softly: "When we leave the table . . . I have a few words to say to you."

His solemn tone surprised me. I looked at him more attentively and noticed a strange alteration in his features.

"Do you feel ill?" I asked him.

"No."

Meanwhile, amidst shouts and applause, a child of about eleven, who had slipped under the table, showed the guests a pretty white and pink ribbon he had just taken from the bride's ankle. That's what they call a garter. It was immediately cut into pieces and distributed to the young men, who used them to adorn their buttonholes, following an old practice still maintained in certain patriarchal families. This made the bride blush to the whites of her eyes. But her embarrassment was brought to a pitch when M. de Peyrehorade, after calling for silence, sang to her a few lines of Catalan poetry, impromptu, according to him. This is their meaning, if I seized it correctly:

"What has happened, my friends? The wine I drank must have made me see double. There are two Venuses here . . . "

The groom abruptly turned his head with a look of terror that made everyone roar with laughter.

"Yes," went on M. de Peyrehorade. "There are two Venuses under one roof. One I found in the earth like a truffle; the other has come down from the skies to share her belt among us."

He meant her garter.

"My son, choose the Roman Venus or the Catalan Venus, whichever you prefer. The scoundrel takes the Catalan Venus, and he has the best share. The Roman Venus is black, the Catalan Venus is white. The Roman is cold, but the Catalan sets all who approach on fire."

This conclusion aroused such a cheer, such noisy applause, and so much laughter that I thought the ceiling would fall on our heads. Around the table there were only three serious faces, those of the bride and groom and my own. I had a pounding headache and, anyway, for some reason weddings always make me sad. Moreover, that particular wedding disgusted me somewhat.

M. Alphonse drew me into the window bay and said to me without looking at me: "You'll laugh at me . . . But I don't know what I've . . . I'm bewitched! Devil take me!"

The first thought to cross my mind was that he thought himself threatened by the misfortune that Montaigne and Madame de Sévigné discuss:[17] "The whole of love's realm is full of tragic stories etc." I said to myself, "And I thought that such accidents only befell the intelligent."

"You've drunk too much wine, my dear M. Alphonse," I said to him. "I warned you."

"Yes, that may be. But it's something much worse than that."

His voice was broken. I thought him completely drunk. "You know my ring?" he went on after a silence.

"Well, has it been taken?"

"No."

"So you've got it then."

"No. I can't get it off that devil of a Venus's finger."

"Well! You just didn't pull hard enough."

"Yes I did . . . but the Venus bent her finger."

He stared at me with a haggard expression, clinging to the window catch to avoid falling over.

"What a story! You must have pushed the ring on too hard. Tomorrow you can get it off using pincers. But be careful not to spoil the statue."

"No, I tell you. The Venus pulled her finger back, bent it over. She's closed her hand, do you see what I mean? She's my wife, it seems, because I gave her my ring . . . She doesn't want to give it back."

I was seized by a sudden shiver, and for a moment I was covered in goose bumps. Then as he sighed deeply I smelled the wine on his breath, and all my emotion subsided.

The wretch, I thought, he's dead drunk.

"You know about antiques, sir," the bridegroom went on in pitiful tones. "You know that sort of statue. There may be a spring, some trick, that I don't know. Would you go and see?"

---

17. *Montaigne and Mme de Sévigné:* Both writers discuss states of temporary sexual impotence in men.

"Of course. Come with me."

"No, I'd rather you went alone."

I left the room. The weather had changed during supper and the rain had begun to pour down. I was about to ask for an umbrella when a thought stopped me in my tracks. What an ass I would be, I said to myself, to go and verify what a drunk has told me! Perhaps, moreover, he just wanted to play some crude joke on me to make me a laughing stock for these provincials. The least that can happen to me is that I'll be drenched to the skin and catch a good cold.

From the door I glanced at the statue, which was streaming with water, and I went up to my room without returning to the parlor. I went to bed. But sleep was slow in coming. The day's events kept passing before my eyes. I thought of that young girl, who was so lovely and so pure, and who had been abandoned to a brutish drunkard. What a horrible thing these marriages of convenience are! A mayor puts on a tricolor scarf and a curé dons his stole, and that is how more than one honest lass is delivered to the Minotaur![18] What can two people who do not love each other find to say to each other at such a moment, a moment two lovers would buy at the cost of their lives? Can a woman ever love a man when she has seen him behave coarsely once? First impressions cannot be erased, and I am sure that this M. Alphonse really deserves to be hated . . .

During my monologue, of which I am giving a much shortened version, I had heard much coming and going in the house, doors opening and shutting, and vehicles leaving. Then I thought I heard the light steps of several women on the stairs leading to the end of the corridor opposite my room. This was probably the bride's escort taking her to bed. Then the steps went back down the stairs. Madame de Peyrehorade's door shut. How disturbed and uneasy that poor girl must be, I thought. I twisted and turned angrily in my bed. A bachelor plays an unenviable role in a house where there is a wedding.

Silence had reigned for some time before it was broken by heavy steps climbing the stairs. The wooden steps creaked noisily.

"What a brute!" I exclaimed. "I bet he falls down the stairs."

Everything became calm again. I took a book to set my thoughts on a different track. It contained the local statistics and was embellished by a study written by M. de Peyrehorade on the druidic monuments in the area around Prades. At the third page, I feel asleep over it.

I slept badly and woke several times. It must have been about five in the morning, and I had been awake about twenty minutes when the rooster crowed. Day was about to break. Then I distinctly heard the

---

18. *Minotaur:* This mythical monster, with the head of a bull and the body of a man was kept in the labyrinth in Crete, and fed on the flesh of seven youths and seven maidens sent every year by Athens as tribute. The Minotaur was killed by Theseus.

same heavy steps, the same creaking of the stair that I had heard before falling asleep. That struck me as odd. Yawning, I tried to guess why M. Alphonse was getting up so early. I could not think of any good reason. I was about to close my eyes again when my attention was again aroused by strange stamping noises and soon the ringing of bells and the noise of doors being flung open, and then I could make out confused shouts.

My drunkard must have set fire to something! I thought as I leapt from my bed.

I dressed quickly and went into the corridor. From the opposite end came cries and lamentations and a heart-rending voice rising above all the others said, "My son, my son!" It was obvious that an accident had befallen M. Alphonse. I ran to the bridal chamber. It was full of people. The first sight that struck my eyes was the young man, half-dressed, and lying across the bed, whose frame had been broken. He was completely white and motionless. His mother wept beside him. M. de Peyrehorade was bustling about, rubbing his temples with eau de cologne or putting salts to his nose. Alas! His son had died long since. On a sofa at the other end of the bedroom, was the bride, suffering from terrible convulsions. She was uttering inarticulate cries, and it was all that two strong servant girls could do to control her.

"My God!" I shouted, "what ever has happened?"

I went over to the bed and lifted the unfortunate young man's body. It was already stiff and cold. His teeth were clenched and his blackened face expressed the most terrible anguish. It was all too clear that his death had been violent and his suffering terrible. Yet there was no trace of blood on his clothes. I opened his shirt and saw on his chest a livid mark that continued around his ribs and across his back. It looked as if he had been embraced in a grip of iron. My foot landed on something hard under the rug; I bent over and saw the diamond ring.

I dragged M. and Mme de Peyrehorade into their room and then I had the bride carried there. "You still have a daughter," I told them. "It's your duty to care for her." Then I left them alone.

It seemed to me beyond doubt that M. Alphonse had been the victim of assassins who had found a way of entering the bride's room during the night. Those bruises on the chest and their circular pattern still worried me greatly, for a stick or an iron cudgel could not have produced them. Suddenly I remembered having heard that ruffians at Valence used long leather bags filled with fine sand to beat those they had been paid to murder. Immediately I remembered the mule driver and his threat. Yet I hardly dared think he would exact such terrible revenge for a light-hearted joke.

I wandered about the house, looking everywhere for traces of a forcible entry and not finding them anywhere. I went down to the garden to see if the assassins could have got in that way but could find no incontrovertible evidence. Yesterday evening's rain had, moreover, so soaked the soil that it couldn't have retained a clear print. Nevertheless I did catch sight of a few footprints deeply imprinted in the earth. They ran in two contradictory directions, but along the same line, setting out from the corner of the hedge next to the tennis court and reaching the house door. These could have been the prints left by M. Alphonse when he went to get his ring from the statue's finger. But it also has to be said that the hedge was less dense there than elsewhere, and it could have been at this point that the murderer had broken through it. Walking back and forth in front of the statue, I stopped for a moment to look at it. This time, I'll confess, I found it impossible to contemplate its expression of ironic wickedness without a feeling of terror; and, as my head was full of the horrible scenes I had just witnessed, I had the impression that I was looking at an evil goddess applauding the ill fortune that had befallen this house.

I returned to my room and stayed there until midday. Then I went out and asked after my hosts. They were a little calmer. Mademoiselle de Puygarrig, or I should say, M. Alphonse's widow, had regained consciousness. She had even spoken to the state prosecutor from Perpignan, who was currently on tour at Ille, and this magistrate had received her account of events. He asked me to give my own account. I told what I knew, and did not hide from him my suspicions against the Aragonais mule driver. He ordered him to be arrested immediately.

"Did you glean anything from Mme Alphonse?" I asked the prosecutor when my deposition had been written out and duly signed.

"That unfortunate young woman has been driven mad," he told me with a sad smile. "Mad! Completely mad! This is what she says happened: She had been in bed for several minutes and had pulled the bed curtains when the bedroom door opened and some one came in. At that time Mme Alphonse was at the far side of the bed, with her face turned to the wall. She didn't move, convinced that this must be her husband. After a moment, the bed groaned as if it had received an enormous weight. She was terrified but dared not turn her head. Five minutes, perhaps ten . . . she cannot be sure of the time, passed in this way. Then she made an involuntary movement, or else the person who was in the bed made one, and she felt the touch of something cold as ice, those are her words. She huddled on the far side of the bed, trembling all over. Shortly thereafter, the door opened for the second time, and someone came in, saying 'Good evening, little wife.' Soon afterwards someone opened the curtains. She heard a muffled cry. The person in bed beside her sat up and appeared to stretch her arms out. She turned her head . . . and saw, so she says, her husband kneeling by the bed, his head level with the pillow, between the arms of a kind of greenish giant who was hugging him with all her strength. She said, and she repeated this twenty times, the poor woman! she said that she recognized in this giant . . . can you guess? the bronze Venus, M. de Peyrehorade's statue . . . Since it's been in the region everyone has been dreaming about it. But let me go back to the story this poor madwoman told me. When she saw this, she fainted, and she had probably already lost her mind a few minutes before. She is quite incapable of saying how long she remained unconscious. When she returned to her senses, she saw the phantom again, or the statue, as she keeps saying, motionless, legs and lower body in the bed and between its arms her husband, motionless. A rooster crowed. Then the statue left the bed, dropped the corpse and went out. Madame Alphonse pulled on the bell, and you know what happened next."

The Spaniard was brought before us. He was calm and defended himself with a great deal of control and presence of mind. Moreover, he made no attempt to deny the comment I had overheard, but he explained it by saying that all he'd meant by that was that on the following day, once he had rested, he would win a tennis match against the man who had defeated him. I remember that he added: "An Aragonais, when he has been insulted, doesn't wait for the following day to exact revenge. If I had thought M. Alphonse intended to insult me, I would have plunged my dagger into his belly right away."

His shoes were compared with the prints found in the garden. His shoes were far too big.

Finally, the innkeeper at whose inn the man was lodging confirmed that he had spent the whole night rubbing down and giving medicine to one of his mules which had fallen ill.

Moreover, this Arogonais had a good reputation and was well known in the area, where he came every year to ply his trade. He was allowed to go free, therefore, and apologies were made to him.

I was forgetting the deposition of a servant who was the last to have seen M. Alphonse alive. That was at the point when he was about to go upstairs to his wife, and, calling the servant to him, had asked with a worried expression if he knew where I was. The servant replied that he had not seen me. Then M. Alphonse had sighed and stayed for a good minute without speaking, before saying: "Well, let's go! The devil has no doubt taken him, too!"

I asked this man whether M. Alphonse had been wearing his diamond ring when he spoke. The servant hesitated before replying and then said that he did not think so, but that he hadn't paid the matter any attention. "If he was wearing that ring on his finger," he added, reconsidering, "I would certainly have noticed it, for I thought that he had given it to Mme Alphonse."

As I questioned this man, I felt a little of the superstitious terror that Mme Alphonse's statement had spread throughout the household. The state attorney looked at me with a smile, and I was careful not to insist.

A few hours after the funeral of M. Alphonse, I prepared to leave Ille. M. de Peyrehorade's carriage was to take me to Perpignan. Although he was in a bad way, the poor old man wanted to accompany me to his garden gate. We passed through it in silence, he hardly capable of movement, leaning on my arm. When we were about to separate, I cast a final look at the Venus. I could see quite well that my host, although he did not share the terror and hatred it inspired in part of his family, would want to get rid of an object that would remind him constantly of a terrible misfortune. It was my intention to engage him to place it in a museum. I was hesitating over whether to raise the matter, when M. de Peyrehorade mechanically turned his head in the direction in which he could see me staring. He caught sight of the statue and burst into tears. I embraced him, and without daring to say a single word, I climbed into the carriage.

Since my departure I have not heard of any new information shedding light on this mysterious catastrophe.

M. de Peyrehorade died a few months after his son. In his will he bequeathed his manuscripts to me, and I may publish them one day. I did not find the monograph relating to the Venus' inscriptions.

P.S. My friend M. de P. has just written to me from Perpignan to tell me the statue no longer exists. After her husband's death, the first thing Mme de Peyrehorade did was to have it melted down to constitute a bell, and in that new form she serves at the Ille church. But, adds M. de P., it seems that bad luck pursues those who possess this bronze. Since the bell has been ringing at Ille, the vines have frozen twice.

LOKIS (1869)

I

"Théodore," said Professor Wittembach, "Would you be so kind as to hand me that notebook bound in parchment, on the second shelf above the desk. Not that one, the little octavo volume. That's where I've collected all the notes from my journal of 1866 or at least those that have to do with Count Szémioth."

The professor put on his glasses, and in the midst of the most profound silence, he read the following:

Lokis

with this Lithuanian proverb by way of epigraph:

> *Miszka su Lokiu*
> *Abu du tokiu.*

When the first translation of the Holy Scriptures into the Lithuanian language was brought out in London, I published, in the *Scientific and Literary Gazette* of Königsberg, an article in which, while according full justice to the efforts of the learned interpreter and the pious intentions of the Biblical Society, I believed it my duty to point out a few errors and draw attention to the fact that this version would be useful only to part of the Lithuanian people. Indeed, the dialect used there can be understood only with difficulty by the inhabitants of the districts in which Low Lithuanian, commonly called *Zmudz*, is spoken, and by that I mean in the palatinate of Samogitia, for there the language may well be even closer than High Lithuanian to Sanskrit.[19] This remark, despite the enraged attacks on me that it produced from a certain professor who is well known at the university of Dorpat, was an illumination for the honorable members of the administrative council of the Biblical Society, who had no hesitation in making me a flattering invitation to direct and oversee the translation into Samogitian of the Gospel according to Saint Matthew. At that stage I was too busy with my studies on the Transuralic languages to undertake a work which would have included all four gospels. So, postponing my marriage to Miss Gertrude Weber, I went to Kowno (*Kaunas*) with the intention of bringing together all the published or manuscript linguistic documents in the Zmudz language that I could lay hands on, not neglecting of course popular poetry, *daïnos*, and tales and legends, *pasakos*, which would provide me with the basis for a Zmudz vocabulary, a task which would, of necessity, have to precede that of translation.

I had been given a letter for the young Count Michel Szémioth, whose father, or so I was assured, had owned the famous *Catechismus Samogiticus* of Father Lawicki, a work so rare that its very existence has been questioned, notably by the Dorpat professor to whom I have already alluded. In his library could be found, according to information I had been given, an old collection of *daïnos*, as well as poems in the ancient Prussian tongue. Having written to Count Szémioth to explain why I was coming, I received the most kindly of invitations to come and stay in his castle at Médintiltas for as long as my research might take. He concluded his letter by saying in the most gracious manner that he took pride in speaking Zmudz almost as well as his peasants did and that he would be happy to work with me in an enterprise that he described as *great* and interesting. Like some of the richest landowners in Lithuania, he claimed to be a member of the Evangelical sect, of which I have the honor to be a minister. I had been informed that, while the count was not free from certain bizarre characteristics,

19. Lithuanian is one of the Baltic sub-family of the Indo-European group of languages. The Lithuanian dialects are said to resemble Sanskrit, although their grammar recalls more closely that of the Slavonic languages.

he was very hospitable, a friend of the sciences and the arts, and particularly well-disposed to those who cultivated them. I set off therefore for Médintiltas.

I was received at the steps of the castle by the count's majordomo, who immediately led me to the suite prepared to receive me. "The count," he told me, "regrets being unable to dine with his honored guest this evening. He is tormented by a migraine, a condition to which, unfortunately, he is somewhat subject. Unless the honored professor would prefer to be served in his bedroom, he will dine with Dr. Froeber, who is the countess's physician. Dinner will be served in an hour's time. Formal dress is not worn. If the honored professor has orders for me, here is the bell." And he departed, giving me a deep bow.

The suite of rooms was vast, well furnished, decorated with mirrors and gilding. On one side it looked out on the castle's garden, or rather its park, and on the other on the great court. Despite the announcement "Formal dress is not worn," I thought I had better take my black suit from my trunk. I was in shirt sleeves, engaged in unpacking my small amount of baggage, when the sound of a vehicle drew me to the window that overlooked the court. A fine carriage had just entered. It contained a lady in black, a gentleman, and a woman dressed in the fashion of the Lithuanian peasant women, but so tall and strong that at first I was tempted to take her for a man in disguise. She was the first to descend from the carriage; two other women, no less robust in appearance, were waiting on the steps. The gentleman leaned toward the lady in black, and to my great surprise unbuckled a large leather belt that attached her to her place in the carriage. I noticed that this lady's long white hair was in great disorder and that the lady's wide-open eyes seemed lifeless. She seemed a waxen figure. After unbuckling her, the lady's companion spoke to her, hat in hand, with much respect, but she seemed not to pay him the slightest attention. Then he turned toward the servants with a slight nod of the head. Immediately the three women seized the lady in black, and despite her attempts to cling to the carriage, they lifted her as if she were a feather, and carried her into the castle. The scene was witnessed by several of the castle's servants, who seemed to consider it perfectly normal. The man who had been in charge of the operation drew out his watch and asked if dinner would soon be served.

"In a quarter of an hour, doctor," he was told. I had no difficulty in guessing that this was Doctor Froeber, and that the lady in black was the countess. From her age I concluded that she was Count Szémioth's mother, and the precautions taken in looking after her indicated that her wits were gone.

A few instants later, the doctor himself came into my room. "Since the count is unwell," he said to me, "I'm obliged to introduce myself directly to our guest. Doctor Froeber, at your service. Delighted to meet a scholar whose worth is known to all those who read the *Scientific and Literary Gazette* of Königsberg. Would it suit you to take dinner now?"

I responded to his compliments as best I could and told him that if it was time to go to dinner I was ready to follow him.

As soon as we went into the dining room, a butler, in accordance with Northern customs, offered us a silver tray loaded with liqueurs and some savory, highly spiced foods calculated to whet our appetites.

"Allow me, Professor," the doctor said to me, "to recommend, in my role as doctor, a glass of this *starka*, a real Cognac brandy which has been in the oak for forty years. It's the mother of liqueurs. Take a Drontheim anchovy: there's nothing better for opening and preparing the digestive tubes, and they are among the most important of our organs . . . And now, let's eat. Why don't we speak German? You are from Königsberg, and I from Memel,[20] but I went to the university of Jena. That would put us both at our ease, and the servants, who speak only Polish and Russian, won't understand us."

At first we ate in silence, then, after taking a first glass of madeira, I asked the doctor if the count was frequently incommoded by the indisposition that had deprived us of his presence that day.

"Yes and no," said the doctor. "It all depends on where he's been."

"What do you mean by that?"

"When he takes the road to Rosienie, for instance, he returns with a migraine and a foul temper."

"I myself went to Rosienie without suffering such a misfortune."

"Well, professor," said the doctor with a laugh, "that's because you're not in love."

I sighed as I thought of Miss Gertrude Weber.

"So it's at Rosienie," I asked, "that the count's fiancée lives?"

"Yes, in that neighborhood. Fiancée? I know nothing of that! A real flirt! She'll make him lose his mind, just as his mother lost hers."

"I'd be right in thinking that Madame the Countess is . . . ill?"

"She's a lunatic, sir, a lunatic! And I must have been the greatest lunatic of all to come here."

"Let's hope your care will restore her to health."

The doctor shook his head as he examined attentively the color of a glass of Bordeaux that he held in his hand. "You see in me, professor, a man who was surgeon major to the Kalouga regiment. At Sebastopol[21] we worked from dawn to dusk amputating arms and legs; I won't mention the bombs that were falling as thick as flies settling on a flayed

---

20. *Memel:* The Lithuanian town of Klaipeda.
21. The major operation of the Crimean War took place at Sebastopol, the main base of the Russian Black Sea fleet, from October 1854 to September 1855.

horse; well! poorly housed and poorly fed as I was, I wasn't bored as I am here, where I eat and drink the best there is, where I'm housed like a prince, and paid like a court doctor . . . But freedom, my dear professor! Just imagine, with that she-devil I never have a minute to myself . . . "

"Has she been in your care for long?"

"Less than two years; but she has been mad for at least twenty-seven years, from before the time the count was born. You didn't hear the story at Rosienie or at Kowno? Well listen, for it's a case I want to write up one day as an article for the *Journal Médical de Saint-Pétersbourg*. She went mad from terror . . . "

"From terror? Is that possible?"

"From terror. She's one of the Keystut family . . . Oh! in that family there's no marrying below one's class. We're all descended from Gédymin.[22] So, Professor, three days . . . or maybe two days after her wedding, which took place in the very castle in which we are now dining (your health!), the count, the present count's father, was going hunting. Our Lithuanian ladies are true Amazons, as well you know. The countess went hunting, too . . . She either remained behind the hunters or got ahead of them, I don't know which, but suddenly the count saw the countess's little cossack, a child of twelve or fourteen, racing toward him at a full gallop. "Master," he said, "a bear is dragging the mistress away!" "Where?" asked the count. "Over there," said the little cossack. All the hunters rushed toward the place he indicated; no countess! Her strangled horse on one side, on the other her cloak torn to shreds. They search everywhere, beat the bushes hither and yon. At last a huntsman calls out, "There's the bear!" And indeed, there was the bear crossing a clearing, still dragging the countess, no doubt so that it could eat her at its leisure in a thicket, for those animals are fond of their food. Like monks, they like to eat in peace. Since he'd been married only two days, the count was very gallant and wanted to hurl himself at the bear, his hunting knife in his hand, but, dear sir, a Lithuanian bear can't just be stabbed like a stag. Fortunately, the count's blunderbuss bearer, a rather worthless lout, who was so drunk that day that he couldn't tell a hare from a hind, took aim with his rifle from more than a hundred paces without bothering to wonder whether the bullet would hit the animal or the woman . . . "

"And killed the bear?"

"Instantly. Only drunks can pull off such things. And, also, there are magic bullets. We have wizards here who sell them at a good price . . . The countess was badly scratched, unconscious I need hardly add, and

---

22. *Gédymin:* Considered the true founder of Lithuania. He reigned from 1316 to 1341, opening the country up to European influence and extending his domain into Byelorussia and the Ukraine. It was under him that Vilnius became the capital of Lithuania.

had a broken leg. She was carried away and regained consciousness, but her reason had left her. They took her to St. Petersburg. There was a great consultation, with four doctors bedizened with all the decorations you can imagine. According to them, the countess was pregnant, and it was likely that when she was delivered there would be a favorable crisis. She was to be kept in fresh air, in the country, given curds and whey, and codeine . . . A hundred rubles were given to each doctor. Nine months later, the countess gives birth to a perfectly formed boy; where's the favorable crisis? Ah well, yes indeed . . . She's twice as mad as before. The count shows her their son. That never fails to have an effect . . . at least in novels.

"It's an animal! Kill it, kill it!" she screamed out, and was on the point of wringing the boy's neck. Since then she has alternated between dazed madness and raging insanity. Strong tendency to suicide. We're forced to tie her in when we take her to get some fresh air. It takes three strong serving girls to hold her. Yet, Professor, pray note this fact: when I've used all my skills without making her obey me, I do have a means of calming her. I threaten to cut her hair . . . In the past, I believe, she had very lovely hair. Vanity! That's the last human sentiment to have remained with her. Isn't it strange? If I could treat her as I pleased, I might well heal her."

"How so?"

"By beating her soundly. I've used that method to heal a score of peasant girls in a village in which there was an outbreak of that weird Russian madness, a form of hysteria referred to as *howling*. A woman starts howling and her friend howls. After three days have gone by, the whole village is howling. By dint of beating them, I overcame it. Have some of the hazel hen, it's wonderfully tender. The count never wanted me to give it a try."

"What! You really wanted him to agree to so terrible a cure?"

"Oh! He hardly knew his mother, and, in any case, it's for her own good. But tell me, Professor, would you ever have believed that fear could drive a person out of their wits?"

"The countess's situation was hideous . . . Think of finding yourself in the claws of so ferocious an animal!"

"Well, her son's a different case altogether. Less than a year ago he found himself in exactly the same position and thanks to his self-control he escaped miraculously well."

"From a bear's claws?"

"From a she-bear's claws, the biggest she-bear we've seen in a long time. The count wanted to attack her with his hunting spear in hand. Boff! With a sweep of her paw she thrusts aside the hunting spear, seizes the count, and throws him to the ground as easily as I could throw down this bottle. He, cunning devil, feigns death . . . The she bear sniffed him, again and again, then instead of tearing him apart, licked him. He had the presence of mind not to move, and she went on her way."

"The bear must have thought he was dead. Indeed, I've heard that such animals don't eat carrion."[23]

"Well, that's a bit of lore you'd rather take on trust than put to the test; but, talking of fear, let me tell you an anecdote about Sebastopol. There were five or six of us around a jug of beer that someone had just brought us, behind the ambulance of the famous fifth bastion.[24] The sentinel shouted: 'A bomb!' We all flung ourselves flat on the ground, no, not all of us, a certain . . . but there's no point in telling you his name . . . a young officer who had just arrived among us stayed on his feet, raising his full glass just at the moment when the bomb exploded. It beheaded my poor comrade André Speranski, a fine lad, and smashed the jug. Fortunately, the jug was almost empty. When we stood up again after the explosion, we saw our friend in the midst of the smoke, draining the last mouthful of his beer, as if nothing had happened. We thought him a hero! The next day I met captain Ghédéonof on his way from the hospital. He said to me, 'I'm dining with you today, and to celebrate my return I'll pay for the champagne.' We sat down to eat. The young officer who'd drunk his beer was there. Someone opened a bottle near him. Bang! The cork hit him in the temple. He screamed aloud and passed out. You have to realize that our hero had been devilishly scared the first time, and that if he'd drunk his beer instead of taking cover, it's because he'd lost his head, and all he was capable of performing was that mechanical gesture, of which he was totally unaware. Indeed, Professor, the human machine . . . "

"Doctor," said a servant who entered the hall, "Jdanova says that my lady won't eat."

"Devil take her!" grumbled the doctor. "I'm coming. When I've got that she-devil to eat, Professor, we could, if you like, have a hand of 'preference' or 'dupe'."

I expressed my regrets at not knowing either game, and when he went off to see his patient, I returned to my room and wrote to Mlle Gertrude.

II

It was a warm night, and I'd opened the window that looked out over the park. Once I'd written my letter, I found I had no desire to sleep,

---

23. Both the idea that bears do not eat carrion and the belief that their cubs are born shapeless and have to be licked into shape by their mothers had been widely held convictions since the middle ages.

24. *Fifth Bastion:* This was the western fortification of the Sebastopol defenses.

so I began to revise the Lithuanian irregular verbs and to seek out the causes for those irregularities in Sanskrit. In the midst of this absorbing work, a tree fairly close to my window was violently shaken about. I heard dead branches cracking, and I had the impression that some heavy animal was trying to climb it. My mind full of the doctor's stories about bears, I got up, somewhat shaken, and a few feet from my window could make out in the foliage, a human head, fully lit by the light from my lamp. The apparition lasted a mere instant, but the extraordinary brightness of the eyes that met my gaze struck me more than I have words to tell. I made an involuntary leap backwards, then ran to the window and asked the intruder in stern tones what he wanted. He, however, climbed down in all haste and, seizing a large branch in his hands, swung from it and then dropped to the ground before immediately disappearing. I rang, and a servant came in. I told him what had just happened. "No doubt the honored professor was mistaken." "I'm certain of what I'm saying. I'm afraid there is a thief in the park." "That's impossible, sir." "So it must be someone belonging to the household?" The servant stared but made no answer. Then he asked if I had any orders for him. I told him to close the window, and I went to bed.

I slept very well and had no dreams of bears or thieves. The next morning, as I was just finishing my ablutions, someone knocked on the door. I opened it and found myself looking at a very tall and handsome young man wearing a Bukharian dressing gown and carrying a long Turkish pipe.

"I've come to offer my apologies, Professor, for having given so poor a welcome to so honored a guest. I am Count Szémioth."

I quickly replied that on the contrary it was my duty to thank him most humbly for his magnificent hospitality and asked him if he was cured of his migraine.

"More or less," he answered. "Until the next crisis," he added with a melancholy expression. "Are you tolerably comfortable here? You have to remember you are in the land of barbarians. One can't be fussy in Samogitia."

I assured him that I was wonderfully comfortable. As I spoke to him, I could not refrain from looking at him with a curiosity that I myself found impertinent. There was something strange in his gaze that reminded me, despite myself, of that of the man I had seen the previous evening climbing the tree . . . But what is the likelihood, I asked myself, that Count Szémioth would be climbing trees at night?

His brow was high and well developed, although a trifle narrow. His features were very regular, save that his eyes were too close together, and it seemed to me that between one tear duct and the other there was no room to fit an eye, in accordance with the canon of the Greek sculptors. His gaze was piercing. Our eyes met several times in spite of ourselves, and we looked away with a certain embarrassment. Suddenly the count burst out laughing and said, "You've recognized me!"

"Recognized you?"

"Yes. You caught me yesterday when I was behaving like an utter rascal."

"Oh! Count!"

"I'd been very ill all day, locked in my study. In the evening I felt better so I went for a walk in the garden. When I saw your light on, I yielded to a moment of curiosity . . . I ought to have introduced myself, but the situation was so ridiculous . . . I was ashamed and took to my heels . . . I do hope you forgive me for having disturbed you in the middle of your studies?"

All this was said in a tone that was meant to be light-hearted, but he blushed and was obviously ill at ease. I did all in my power to persuade him that I retained no unfortunate impression from that first glimpse and, to bring the subject to an end, I asked him if it was true that he owned the Samogitian catechism of Father Lawicki.

"It's possible, but to be honest I've only a vague knowledge of my father's library. He loved old and rare books. As for me, I hardly read anything but modern works. But we'll look for it, Professor. So you want us to read the Bible in Zmudz, do you?"

"Don't you think, count, that a translation of the scriptures into the language of the country would be desirable?"

"Of course, but if you'll permit me this little remark I'll tell you that among those who know no language other than Zmudz there is not a single person who can read."

"That may be, but with your excellency's permission I would like to say that the greatest difficulty in learning to read stems from the lack of books. When the Samogitian peasants have a printed text they'll want to read and they'll learn to do so. That's what happened to many a savage . . . not that I want to apply that epithet to those who live in this country . . . Moreover, isn't it deplorable that a language can disappear without leaving any trace? For the last thirty years, Prussian has been nothing more than a dead language. The last person who knew Cornish died the other day . . ."

"Sad," interrupted the count. "Alexander von Humboldt[25] used to tell my father that when he was in America he met a parrot that was the only creature to know a few words of the language of a tribe that today has been completely wiped out by smallpox. Would you allow me to call for our tea to be brought here?"

While we took our tea the conversation focused on the Zmudz lan-

25. Count Alexander von Humboldt (1769–1859) was one of the most influential scientific figures of the nineteenth century.

guage. The count criticized the way in which the Germans had printed Lithuanian texts, and he was perfectly justified in doing so. "Your alphabet," he said, "does not suit our language. You have neither our J nor our L nor our Y nor our E. I have a collection of *daïno*s that were published last year in Königsberg, and I have the greatest difficulty guessing what the words must be, because they're so strangely written."

"Your excellency is no doubt referring to the *daïno*s of Lessner?"

"Yes. It's pretty flat poetry, isn't it?"

"He could perhaps have found better examples. I agree that, as it stands, the collection's only interest is linguistic, but I think that if one searched hard one would succeed in gathering rather sweeter flowers among your popular poems."

"Alas! For all my patriotism I find that hard to believe."

"A few weeks ago, someone at Vilnius gave me a really fine ballad. Moreover, it's historical . . . It's remarkably poetic . . . Would you permit me to read it? I have it in my briefcase."

"Gladly."

He sank down in his armchair after having asked my permission to smoke. "I can't understand poetry unless I smoke," he said.

"This one is called *Boudrys's three sons*."

"Boudrys's three sons?" exclaimed the count with a movement of surprise.

"Yes. Boudrys, as your excellency knows better than I, is a historical figure."

The count stared at me with his curious gaze. Something beyond definition, at once timid and wild, which produced an almost painful effect, when you weren't used to it. I quickly began reading to escape that gaze.

Boudrys's three sons.

In the castle courtyard old Boudrys summoned his three sons, true Lithuanians as he himself was. He said to them: My sons, feed your war horses and prepare your saddles; sharpen your sabres and hone your javelins. It is said that at Vilnius war has been declared on the three corners of the world. Olgerd is to march against the Russians; Skirghello against our neighbors the Poles; Keystut will fall upon the Teutons.

You are young, you are strong, you are bold. Go and fight. May the gods of Lithuania protect you! This year I will not fight, but let me give you a piece of advice. There are three of you, and there are three ways that open before you.

Let one of you accompany Olgerd into Russia to the shores of Lake Ilmen under the walls of Novgorod. Ermine furs and brocaded materials are to be found in profusion there. In the merchants' shops you will find as many rubles as there are blocks of ice in the river.

Let the second of you follow Keystut in his ride. Let him tear to pieces the cross-bearing rabble! There, amber is as common as the sand in the sea. Their linen cannot be equaled for luster and color. There are rubies in the clothes of their priests.

Let the third cross the Niemen with Skirghello. On the far side, he will find crude agricultural tools. But on the other hand, he will be able to take his choice among fine lances and strong shields, and he will bring back a bride.

The girls of Poland, my sons, are the most beautiful of all captives. Playful as cats, and white as cream! Below their black brows their eyes gleam like two stars.

When I was young, half a century ago, I brought back from Poland a lovely slave who became my wife. Many years have passed since her death, but I cannot look at that side of the hearth without thinking of her.

He blessed the young men, who were already armed and mounted. They left. Autumn came, then winter, and they did not return . . . Already old Boudrys thought them dead.

Then there came a snowstorm, and a rider approached, covering some precious burden with his black cloak.—"It's a sack," said Boudrys. "Is it full of rubles from Novgorod?" "No father. I bring you a daughter-in-law from Poland."

In the middle of the snowstorm a rider approached, and his cloak swelled with some precious burden. "What is that my child? Is it yellow amber from Germany?" "No father. I bring you a daughter-in-law from Poland."

The snow flurries fell and a rider approached hiding in his cloak some precious burden . . . But before he had shown his booty, Boudrys invited his friends to a third wedding.

"Bravo, Professor!" the count exclaimed, "Your pronunciation of Zmudz is wonderful, but who gave you that charming *daïno?*"

"A young lady whose acquaintance I had the honor of making at Vilnius, at the house of Princess Katazyna Paç."

"Her name?"

"*Panna* Iwinska."

"Miss Ioulka!" the count exclaimed. "The little scamp! I should have guessed! Dear Professor, you know Zmudz and all manner of erudite languages, you've read all the old books, but you allowed the wool to be pulled over your eyes by a little girl who has read nothing but novels. She translated into more or less correct Zmudz for you one of Miçkiewicz's[26] prettiest ballads, which you haven't read because it's no older

---

26. Adam Miçkiewicz (1798–1855) was considered Poland's finest poet, and was the leader of the Polish Romantic movement. In exile he championed his country's nationalism and liberty, at a period when Poland no longer figured on the political map of Europe.

than I am. If you like, I'll show it to you in Polish, or if you prefer an excellent Russian translation, I'll give you Pushkin's."[27]

I admit I was stunned. What a delight for the professor from Dorpat, if I had published as an original the *daïno* about Boudrys's sons![28]

Instead of delighting in my discomfiture, the count, with exquisite politeness, rapidly changed the conversation.

"So you know Miss Ioulka, then?"

"I had the honor of being introduced to her."

"And what is your opinion of her?"

"A delightful young lady."

"You are kind enough to find her so."

"She is very pretty."

"What! Don't you think she has the loveliest eyes in the world?"

"Yes . . ."

"Her skin is extraordinarily white . . . I recall a Persian *ghazel*[29] in which a lover celebrates the fineness of his mistress's skin. 'When she drinks red wine,' he says, 'you can see it running down her throat.' *Panna* Iwinska reminds me of that Persian poem."

"Perhaps Miss Ioulka does present that characteristic, but I'm not so certain she has blood in her veins . . . She has no heart . . . She is as white as snow and as cold, too!"

He stood up and strode around the room for some time without speaking, and, so it seemed to me, struggling to hide his emotion. Then, abruptly stopping he said, "I'm sorry. We were talking, I think, about popular poetry."

"Yes, indeed, Count . . ."

"You must at least agree that she translated Mićkiewicz most attractively . . . 'Playful as a cat . . . white as cream . . . her eyes gleam like two stars . . .' It's a perfect description of the young lady. Don't you think so?"

"Entirely, Count."

"And as for that trick she played . . . inappropriate, no doubt, . . . the poor child is bored living with an old aunt . . . She's leading the life of a nun."

"At Vilnius she went into society. I saw her at a ball given by the officers of the regiment of . . ."

"Ah! yes, young officers, that's the society she needs . . . Laughing

---

27. Alexander Pushkin (1799–1837), the great Russian writer, was well known and highly respected in nineteenth-century France.

28. *an original daïno:* This is a typical in-joke, of the sort Mérimée enjoyed. As a young man he invented a series of thirty-two ballads, entitled *La Guzla,* which he published as the work of a Dalmatian poet. Some of these ballads were translated by Mićkiewicz and Pushkin, both of whom took them for authentic examples of Serbian folk poetry. Later, however, Mérimée himself translated and published a poem he believed to be an original work by Pushkin, but which was in fact the latter's translation of Mićkiewicz's ballad "The Three Boudrys."

29. *ghazel:* A short lyric poem; this form is widely used in Arabic, Persian, and Turkish poetry.

with one, gossiping with another, flirting with all of them . . . Would you like to see my father's library, Professor?"

I followed him to a large gallery housing many books which were well bound but rarely read, as one could tell from the dust that covered them. Consider my delight when one of the volumes I took out of a dresser turned out to be the *Catechismus Samogiticus*. I couldn't prevent myself from crying out in pleasure. A mysterious kind of attraction must be working on us, all unbeknownst to us. . . . The count took the book, and having leafed through it carelessly, he wrote on the front page: *To Professor Wittembach, a gift from Michel Szémioth*. Words fail me here to express the transports of gratitude I felt, and I made a mental promise that after my death this precious book would adorn the library of the university from which I graduated.

"Please consider the library your study," the count said to me. "No one will disturb you here."

III

The following day, after lunch, the count suggested we go on an outing. The goal was to visit a *kapas* (this is what the Lithuanians call the tumuli to which the Russians give the name *kurgan*) which was very well known in the area because in the past, the poets and wizards—one cannot distinguish between them—used to gather there on certain solemn occasions.

"I have a very gentle horse I can offer you," he told me. "I'm sorry I can't take you in the carriage; but to tell the truth the path we're to follow would be impracticable in a carriage."

I would have preferred to stay in the library and take notes, but I considered it would be wrong to express any desires contrary to those of my generous host, and I accepted. The horses were awaiting us at the bottom of the stairs, while in the courtyard a valet held a dog on a leash. The count stopped for a moment, and, turning toward me, said, "Professor, are you knowledgeable about dogs?"

"I know very little about them, your excellency."

"The mayor of Zorany, where I have some land, has sent me this spaniel, of whom he speaks very highly. Would you allow me to take a look at it?" He called the servant who brought the dog to him. It was a very handsome animal. Already familiar with the servant, the dog leaped about gaily and seemed full of fire; but when it came within a few paces of the count, it put its tail between its legs, leaped backwards, and seemed overwhelmed with sudden terror. The count patted it, which made it howl in the most heart-rending way, and, after considering it for some time with a knowing eye, he said, "I think he'll be fine. Take good care of him." Then he mounted his horse.

"Professor," said the count, as soon as we reached the avenue leading from the castle, "You've just witnessed that dog's fear of me. I wanted you to see it with your own eyes . . . Since you're a scholar, you ought to be able to work out the answer to riddles . . . Why are animals afraid of me?"

"Truly, count, you're paying me too much honor in taking me for an Œdipus. I'm merely a poor professor of comparative linguistics. It could be that . . . "

"You should know," he broke in, "that I never whip either my horses or my dogs. I'd feel ashamed to aim even a single blow at a poor animal that has done something silly without realizing what it had done. And yet you wouldn't believe the aversion horses and dogs have for me. To get them used to me, I have to put in twice as much work and twice as much time as any one else would. Take the horse you're riding now, it was ages before I tamed him, but now he's as gentle as a lamb."

"I believe, Count, that animals are physiognomists, and that they can tell right away if someone they see for the first time likes them or not. I suspect that you like animals only for the services they can perform for you, whereas some people have a natural love of certain animals, who realize that fact immediately. As for me, to give you an example, I have had a particular love of cats ever since I was a child. It's rare for a cat to run away from me when I go to pet one, and no cat has ever scratched me."

"That's quite possible," said the count. "Indeed, I don't have what people call the love of animals . . . They're hardly worth more than humans . . . I'm taking you, Professor, into a forest that's currently the flourishing empire of animals, the *matecznik*, the great womb, the great factory of creatures. Yes, according to our national traditions, no one has ever been able to plumb the depths or reach the heart of these woods and marshes, except, of course, poets and magicians, who can go everywhere. Here the animals live in a republic . . . or under a constitutional government, I couldn't tell you which of the two. Lions, bears, moose, *joubrs*, that's our word for aurochs, all live together in harmony. The mammoth still lives here and enjoys great prestige. He is, or so I believe, the speaker of their parliament. They have a very strict code of behavior, and when they find an animal who's vicious, they judge it and send it into exile. That animal then finds it's out of the frying pan and into the fire, for it has to venture into the land of men. Few survive."

"A most exceptional legend," I exclaimed, "but, Count, you were talking of aurochs. Caesar describes this noble animal in his *Commentaries*, and the Merovingian kings hunted it in the forest of Compiègne, but can it really be found in Lithuania, as I've heard tell?"

"Indubitably. My father himself killed a *joubr*, with a government permit, of course. You may have seen its head in the great hall. I myself have never seen one, and I believe they're very rare. On the other hand, we have hordes of wolves and bears here. It's in case of an encounter with one of those gentlemen that I brought this instrument (he showed me a Circassian *tchékhole* that he wore across his shoulders), and my groom carries across his saddle pommel a double-barreled carbine."

We were starting to go into the forest. Soon the very narrow path we'd been following disappeared. At every moment, we were forced to track around enormous trees whose low branches blocked our passage. Some of these, which had died of old age and fallen over, presented us with a kind of rampart crowned by a frieze of fronds which was impossible to climb over. Elsewhere we encountered deep ponds covered with water lilies and duckweed. Further on, we saw clearings in which the grass gleamed like emeralds; but woe betide anyone who might venture there, for that rich and deceptive vegetation normally hides abysses of mud into which horse and rider would disappear for ever . . . The difficulties of the route had interrupted our conversation. I gave all my attention to following the count, and admired the imperturbable skill with which he guided himself without a compass and always found the perfect direction for heading toward the *kapas*. It was obvious that he had spent many years hunting in these wild forests.

At last we caught sight of the tumulus in the center of a large clearing. It was very high, surrounded by a ditch which was still clearly recognizable despite all the scrub and the landslides. It looked as if a dig had already taken place there. On the top I noticed the remains of a stone construction, part of which had been burned. A noticeable quantity of ash mingled with coal, and here and there some shards of coarse pottery, showed that a fire had been maintained on the summit of the tumulus over a considerable period of time. If one accepts popular tradition, human sacrifices were celebrated on the *kapas* in the past; but there's hardly any dead religion to which people do not attribute those unspeakable rites, and I doubt that one could justify such a judgment with regard to the ancient Lithuanians if one used historical records.

The count and I were coming down from the tumulus on our way back to our horses, which we'd left on the other side of the ditch, when we saw an old woman coming toward us, leaning on a stick and carrying a basket in her hand.

"Good gentlemen," she said to us as she came up to us, "charity in the name of the Lord. Give me enough to buy a glass of brandy to warm my poor body."

The count threw her a silver coin and asked her what she was doing in the wood so far from any habitation. Her only response was to show him her basket which was full of mushrooms. Although my botanical knowledge is very limited, I had the impression that several of those mushrooms belonged to poisonous species. "My good woman!" I said to her. "I hope you're not planning to eat that?"

"My good lord," replied the old woman with a sad smile, "poor people eat anything the blessed Savior gives them."

"You don't know our Lithuanian stomachs," said the count. "They're plated with tin. Our peasants eat all the mushrooms they can find and are all the healthier for it."

"At least don't let her eat that *agaricus necator* I see in her basket," I exclaimed.

And I stretched out my hand to take one of the most poisonous of mushrooms, but the old woman swiftly pulled the basket out of my reach. "Take care!" she said, in a frightened tone. "They're guarded! . . . *Pirkuns! Pirkuns!*"

Pirkuns, I should say in passing, is the Samogitian nickname given to the divinity that the Russians call *Perun*, the Slavs' version of Jove the Thunderer. If I was amazed to hear the old woman invoke a pagan god, I was even more surprised to see the mushrooms heaving about. The black head of a snake came out and rose at least a foot above the basket. I leapt back, and the count spat on it over his shoulder in accordance with a superstition of the Slavs, who believe that this will avert bad luck, much in the manner of the Romans of antiquity. The old woman put the basket on the ground, crouched down beside it, then, with her hand stretched out to the snake, she pronounced a few words I couldn't understand and that appeared to be some sort of spell. For a moment the snake remained motionless then, twining itself around the old woman's haggard arm, it disappeared into the sleeve of her sheepskin cloak, which, with a tattered shirt, composed, I fully believe, the entire costume of this Lithuanian Circe. The old woman looked at us with a little laugh of triumph, like a conjurer who had just performed a difficult trick. There was in her face that mixture of sharpness and stupidity you find so often in self-styled wizards, most of whom are merely rascals and knaves.

"Here," the count said to me, "you have a sample of *local color*, a witch who charms a snake at the foot of a *kapas*, in the presence of an erudite professor and an ignorant Lithuanian aristocrat. It would make a fine subject for a genre painting by your compatriot Knauss . . . [30] Do you have a yen to have your fortune told? This would be a perfect opportunity for it."

I told him I had absolutely no intention of encouraging such practices. "I'd prefer," I added, "to ask her whether she knows anything about the curious tradition you mentioned to me. My good woman," I said to the old woman, "did you ever hear anything about a section of this forest in which the animals live in a community free from the control of man?"

The old woman nodded her head, and with a little laugh that seemed half-stupid, half-cunning, she announced, "That's where I've just been. The animals have lost their king. *Noble*, the lion, has died. They're going

---

30. Ludwig Knauss (1829–1910), a German genre painter, famed for his realism.

to elect someone to replace him. Go there, you could perhaps be their king."

"Whatever are you saying, old mother?" exclaimed the count, bursting into laughter. "Have you any idea whom you're talking to? Don't you know that this gentleman is (how the devil does one say professor in Zmudz?) this gentleman is a very learned man, a sage, a bard."

The old woman looked at him closely. "I was wrong," she said. "You're the one that ought to go there. You'll be their king and not him. You are big, you are strong, you have claws and teeth . . . "

"What do you say about these epigrams she's firing off at us?" the count asked me. "Do you know how to get there, my little mother?"

She waved toward a part of the forest.

"Oh yes?" returned the count. "And the marsh? How do you go about crossing it? I should tell you, Professor, that in that direction lies an uncrossable marsh, a lake of soft mud covered with green grass. Last year, a stag I'd wounded threw himself into that accursed marsh. I watched him sink in, slowly, ever so slowly . . . Two minutes later, I could see only his antlers; soon everything had disappeared, and two of my dogs together with him."

"But I don't weigh very much," said the old woman, with a snicker.

"I bet you cross the marsh without the slightest difficulty, on a broomstick."

A flash of rage glinted in the old woman's eyes. "My good lord," she said, adopting the drawling, nasal tone characteristic of beggars, "couldn't you give a pipe of tobacco to a poor old woman?—You'd do better," she added, dropping her voice, "seeking out the passage across the marsh than going to Dowghielly."

"Dowghielly!" exclaimed the count, blushing. "Whatever do you mean?"

I couldn't help noticing that this name produced an extraordinary effect on him. He was clearly embarrassed. He lowered his head, and, to hide his emotion, made a great fuss about opening his tobacco pouch, which hung from the handle of his hunting knife.

"No, don't go to Dowghielly," repeated the old woman. "The little white dove isn't what you need. Isn't that so, Pirkuns?" At that moment, the head of the snake appeared through the neck of the old cape and stretched itself up to his mistress's ear. The reptile, no doubt trained to perform this trick, moved its jaws as if it were talking. "He says I'm right," added the old woman.

The count put in her hand a fistful of tobacco. "Do you know who I am?" he asked her.

"No, my good lord."

"I am the owner of Médintiltas. Come and see me one of these days. I'll give you tobacco and brandy."

The old woman kissed his hand, and quickly strode away. In an instant she was lost from sight. The count remained thoughtful, knotting and untying the ribbon that bound his tobacco pouch, without really realizing what he was doing.

"Professor," he said to me after a fairly long silence, "you're going to find me ridiculous. That old jade knows me better than she claims to, and the path she's just shown me . . . After all, there's nothing especially surprising in all that. I'm really well known in this area. The old rascal must have seen me often on the way to the castle of Dowghielly . . . There's a young woman of marriageable age there, and so she's drawn the conclusion that I'm in love with the girl . . . Then some handsome lad must have bribed her to foretell a sinister fate for me . . . All of that is perfectly obvious, and yet, in spite of myself, her words have shaken me. I'm almost frightened by them . . . You're laughing. Quite right! The truth is that I'd planned to go and ask if we could dine at the Dowghielly castle, and now I'm hesitating about it . . . What an ass I am! Look, Professor, you be the one that decides. Shall we go or not?"

"I'm certainly going to be careful not to offer any opinion," I answered him with a laugh. "Where marriage is concerned, I never give advice."

We had returned to our horses. The count leaped athletically into his saddle and, dropping the reins, exclaimed, "We'll let the horse choose for us!" The horse showed not the slightest hesitation. It immediately set out along a little path that after a few twists and turns joined a paved road that led to Dowghielly. Half an hour later we had reached the castle stairway.

At the noise our horses made, a pretty blonde head appeared at a window between two curtains. I recognized the traitorous translator of Miçkiewicz. "Welcome!" she said. "You couldn't have come at a better time, Count Szémioth. A dress from Paris has just this minute arrived for me. You won't recognize me, I'll be so lovely."

The curtains closed. As we climbed the stairway, the count muttered between his teeth, "It's certainly not for my sake that she's débuting that dress!"

He introduced me to Mme Dowghiello, *Panna* Iwinska's aunt, who received me very warmly and talked to me about my most recent articles in the Königsberg *Literary and Scientific Gazette*.

"The professor," said the count, "has come to complain to you about Mlle Julienne, who played a very naughty trick on him."

"She's a child, Professor. You must forgive her. I'm frequently in despair over her foolishness. Now, when I was sixteen, I was better behaved than she is at twenty. But at heart she's a good girl, and she has all the qualities of a truly serious person. She's a very good musician, she paints flowers divinely, she has an equally good knowledge of French, German, and Italian . . . She embroiders . . . "

"And she writes poetry in Zmudz!" added the count with a laugh.

"She's quite incapable of such a thing!" exclaimed Mme Dowghiello, whom we were obliged to tell about her niece's prank.

Mme Dowghiello was educated and knew her country's ancient treasures. I found her conversation singularly delightful. She read many of our German reviews and had very sound notions of linguistics. I confess I didn't notice how long it took Mlle Iwinska to dress, but it seemed long to the count, who stood up, sat down again, stared out of the window, and drummed with his fingers on the glass like a man at the end of his patience.

Finally, after three quarters of an hour, there appeared, with a French governess in her wake, Mlle Julienne, wearing with grace and pride a dress whose description would demand much deeper knowledge than I possess.

"Aren't I beautiful?" she asked the count, turning round slowly so that he could see her from all sides. She looked neither at the count nor at me, but only at her dress.

"Ioulka!" exclaimed Mme Dowghiello, "you haven't said hello to the professor, who's just been complaining about you."

"Oh! Professor!" she exclaimed with a charming little pout. "Whatever have I done? Are you going to put me in the corner?"

"We'd be putting ourselves there," I replied, "were we to deprive ourselves of your presence. I'm far from complaining; on the contrary, I congratulate myself for having learned, thanks to you, that the Lithuanian muse has been reborn, more dazzling than ever."

She lowered her head, and putting her hands in front of her face, but taking care not to disorder her hair, she said, "Forgive me and I'll never do it again!" in the tone of a child who has just stolen jam.

"I won't forgive you, dear *Panni*," I told her, "until you've carried out a certain promise you kindly made me at Vilnius, at the house of Princess Katazyna Paç."

"What promise was that?" she said, lifting her face with a laugh.

"You haven't already forgotten it? You promised me that if we met in Samogitia, you would perform for me a certain local dance you praised highly."

"Oh! The russalka![31] I'm delicious in that, and here we have the very man I need for it!"

She ran to a table on which lay books of music, leafed through one of them rapidly, put it on the piano stand and turned to her governess. "Here, my love, *allegro presto*." And she herself, without bothering to sit down, played the ritornelle to give the tempo. "Come here, Count Michel, you're too much of a Lithuanian not to be able to dance the russalka well, but dance as if you were a peasant, you understand me?"

---

31. Russalka, a water nymph, according to Russian folklore.

Madame Dowghiello tried to remonstrate with her, but it was in vain. The count and I insisted. He had his reasons, for his role in this dance was a very pleasant one, as you will soon see. The governess, after a few attempts, said she thought she could play this kind of waltz, however bizarre it seemed to her, and Mlle Iwinska, having pushed aside a few chairs and a table that might have gotten in her way, seized her partner by the collar of his coat and led him to the middle of the room. "You should understand, Professor, that I am a russalka, at your service." She made a deep curtsey. "A russalka is a water nymph. There's one in all those ponds of black water that grace our forests. Don't go near them! The russalka comes out, and she's even prettier than I am, if that's possible. She carries you off to the bottom of the pond, and there, so it seems, she eats you up . . . "

"A real siren!" I exclaimed.

"He," Mlle Iwinska continued, pointing to Count Szémioth, "is a young fisherboy, a real simpleton, who offers himself to my claws while I, to make this delightful situation last a bit longer, dance around him, fascinating him . . . Oh, but to do it well I'd need a sarafan.[32] What a pity! . . . You'll have to forgive this dress, which has no character, no local color . . . Oh! And I'm wearing shoes, you can't dance the russalka in shoes! and with heels, what's more!"

She lifted her dress and gracefully shaking her pretty little foot, at the risk of showing a little of her leg, she sent her shoe flying to the end of the room. The second followed the first, and she stood on the parquet floor in her silk stockings. "All set!" she said to the governess and the dance began.

The russalka turns around and around her partner. He stretches out his arms to grasp her, she slips under them and eludes his grasp. It's all very graceful and the music has movement and originality. The dance ends when the partner attempts to seize her in order to kiss her, and she leaps forward, strikes him on the shoulder, and he falls as if dead at her feet . . . But the count improvised a variant, which consisted in seizing hold of the little tease in his arms and kissing her well and truly. Mlle Iwinska gave a little cry, blushed deeply, and collapsed on the sofa with a sulky expression, complaining that he had squeezed her like the bear he was. I could see that the comparison didn't please the count, for it reminded him of his family's misfortune. His brow darkened. As for me, I thanked Mlle Iwinska most warmly and praised her dance, which struck me as very ancient in character, recalling the sacred dances of the Greeks. I was interrupted by a servant announcing the General and Princess Veliaminof. Mlle Iwinska leapt from the sofa to her shoes, thrust her feet into them swiftly, and ran to meet the princess, to whom she made two deep curtseys, one after the other. I noticed that after

---

32. *sarafan:* A large scarf, often with colorful decoration.

each one she cleverly adjusted the back half of her shoe. The general brought two aides de camp and, like us, had come to request the pleasure of dining informally. In any other country, I believe that the mistress of a house would be somewhat embarrassed to find six unexpected guests, all of them hungry, but the abundance and hospitality that reigns in Lithuanian homes is such that I truly think dinner wasn't delayed by more than half an hour. The only problem was that there were too many hot and cold pastries.

IV

We had a very cheerful dinner. The general provided some particularly interesting details concerning the languages spoken in the Caucasus, some of which are Indo-European and others Uralic-Altaic, even though there exists a remarkable homogeneity of habits and customs among the different racial groups. I myself was forced to speak of my journeys because Count Szémioth congratulated me on my riding skills and said that he had never met a minister or a professor who could have carried out so easily the long ride we had just made, so I was obliged to inform him that when I'd been asked by the Bible Society to carry out a study of the language spoken by the Charrúas, I'd spent three and a half years in the republic of Uruguay, almost constantly on horseback and living on the pampas among the Indians. This was how it came about that I told the story of how, when I'd spent three days completely lost on those endless plains and had no food or water left, I was reduced to do what the gauchos who accompanied me did—to bleed my horse and drink its blood.

All the women screamed in horror. The general pointed out that the Kalmucks employed the same trick in similar circumstances. The count asked me what I had thought of that drink.

"In moral terms," I replied, "I found it deeply disgusting; but physically it did me a lot of good, and it's thanks to that drink that I have the honor of dining here today. Many Europeans, by which I mean whites, who have lived for a long time with the Indians, get quite used to it and even acquire a taste for it. My excellent friend Don Fructuoso Rivera,[33] who is president of the republic, rarely lets pass an opportunity to satisfy that taste. I remember that one day, when he was on his way to the parliament in full dress uniform, he passed in front of a ranch where a mare was being bled. He stopped, dismounted from his horse, and asked for a *chupón*, that is a mouthful, after which he gave one of his most eloquent speeches."

"Your president is a disgusting monster!" exclaimed Mlle Iwinska.

"Forgive me, dear lady," I told her, "but he's a very distinguished man,

---

33. Rivera (1778–1854), a president of Uruguay, had been assisted by French forces.

an outstanding intellect. He speaks several very difficult Indian languages extremely well, above all Charrúa, which is particularly hard because of the countless forms the verb takes, depending on whether it is transitive or intransitive, and even depending on the social relationships between the people speaking."

I was about to give a few rather curious details about the mechanism of Charrúan verbs, but the count interrupted me to ask where you had to bleed horses in order to drink their blood.

"For goodness sake, my dear professor," exclaimed Mlle Iwinska with an air of comic terror, "don't tell him. He's the sort that would kill his entire stable and then go on to eat us when no more horses remained."

On that sally, the ladies left the table, laughing, to go and prepare the tea and coffee, while we men smoked. After a quarter of an hour or so, the general was invited to go to the salon. We were all about to follow him, but we were told that the ladies wanted only one of us at a time. Soon we heard great bursts of laughter and applause coming from the salon. "Mlle Ioulka is up to her old tricks," said the count. Then he was sent for; fresh laughter, fresh applause. After him it was my turn. When I went into the salon all present had assumed an expression of seriousness which didn't bode at all well. I expected some trick to be played.

"Professor," the general asked me with his most official air, "these ladies claim that we gave their champagne too warm a welcome and are willing to admit us among them only after making us pass a test. You must allow us to blindfold you, and then you are to touch that wall with your finger. Are you in a condition to follow a straight line?"

"I think so, General."

Mlle Iwinska immediately put a blindfold over my eyes and held it tightly behind. "You're in the middle of the salon," she said, "stretch out your hand . . . Good! I bet you can't touch the wall."

"Forward march!" said the general.

It was a distance of only five or six paces. I went forward very slowly, convinced I would bump into a rope or a stool, treacherously placed in my path to make me trip. I could hear stifled laughter which added to my embarrassment. At last I thought I must be very close to the wall, but at that moment my finger, which I had held out in front of me, suddenly plunged into something cold and sticky. I grimaced and leapt backwards, making all those present burst out laughing. I tore off my blindfold, and saw beside me Mlle Iwinska holding a pot of honey, into which I had put my finger in the belief that I was about to touch the wall. My consolation lay in seeing the two aides de camp go through the same test and perform no better than I had.

During the remainder of the evening, Mlle Iwinska constantly gave vent to her wild mood. Unceasingly mocking, always mischievous, she would take now one of us, now someone else for the butt of her jokes.

Yet I noticed that she most frequently addressed the count who, it must be said, never got nettled, and even seemed to take pleasure in her teasing. On the contrary, when she turned her humor against one of the aides de camp he frowned, and I could see his eye glint with that dark fire that had a hint of something truly terrifying in it. "Mad as a cat and white as cream." It struck me that in writing that line Miçkiewicz had sought to paint a portrait of *Panna* Iwinska.

V

We went to bed fairly late. In many large Lithuanian houses, you can see splendid silverware, fine furniture, precious Persian rugs, and yet there isn't, as in our dear Germany, a good featherbed to offer a weary guest. Rich or poor, gentleman or peasant, a Slav is perfectly capable of sleeping on a plank. The castle of Dowghielly was no exception to this rule of thumb. In the room to which the count and I had been taken, there were only two sofas covered with leather. That didn't worry me at all, for in my travels I had often slept on the bare earth, and I rather scorned my host's exclamations concerning his compatriots' lack of civilization. A servant came to pull off our boots and gave us dressing gowns and slippers. The count, having removed his coat, strode about for a little in silence, then standing next to the sofa on which I was already lying, he asked me, "What do you think of Ioulka?"

"I think she's charming!"

"Yes, but such a flirt! . . . Do you think she's really attracted to that little blond captain?"

"The aide de camp? . . . How on earth would I know?"

"He's an ass . . . and therefore women like him."

"That's a conclusion I'd deny, count. Do you want me to tell you the truth? Mlle Iwinska is much more concerned to please Count Szémioth than all the aides de camp in the entire army."

He blushed without replying, but it seemed to me that my words had given him real pleasure. He strode up and down a little while longer in silence then, after looking at his watch, he said, "Goodness me, we really ought to go to sleep; it's late."

He took his rifle and his hunting knife, which had been placed in our room and placed them in a cupboard from which he removed the key. "Would you mind keeping this?" he asked me, handing me the key, much to my surprise. "I could easily forget it. You've certainly got a better memory than I have."

"The best way of not forgetting your weapons," I said, "would be to place them on that table by your sofa."

"No . . . Look, I'll be open about this. I don't like having arms near me when I'm sleeping . . . I'll explain. Once when I was in the hussars at Grodno, I was sleeping in a room with a comrade. I'd put my pistols on a chair beside me. That night, I was awakened by the sound of a shot. I had the pistol in my hand. I had fired, and the bullet had gone a mere two inches from my comrade's head . . . I don't remember what I was dreaming about."

That story disturbed me somewhat. I was fairly certain I wouldn't get a bullet in the head, but when I considered how tall my companion was and how Herculean his build, and when I thought of his sinewy arms with their black hair, I couldn't help recognizing that he was quite capable of strangling me with his bare hands if he happened to have a nightmare. Nevertheless, I was careful not to reveal any disquiet, although I placed a light on a chair near my sofa and began to read Lawicki's *Catechism*, which I had brought with me. The count wished me good night, stretched out on the sofa, turned over five or six times, and then seemed to fall asleep, although he was curled up like the lover Horace talks of who, enclosed in a trunk, knocks his head against his bent knees:

> *. . . Turpi clausus in arca,*
> *Contractum genibus tangas caput.*[34]

From time to time he sighed deeply, or produced a kind of nervous rattle that I attributed to the strange position he had adopted for sleeping. An hour or so went by in this way. I myself was falling asleep. I had closed my book and was stretching out as best I could on my sofa, when a strange sneering laugh from my neighbor made me shudder. I looked at the count. His eyes were closed, but his body trembled, and his half open lips let fall a few barely articulated words: "Very fresh! . . . Very white! . . . The professor doesn't know what he's saying. . . . Horses aren't worth anything . . . What a delicious morsel! . . . " Then he began to bite ferociously at the cushion under his head, at the same time roaring so loudly he woke up.

As for me, I remained motionless on my sofa and pretended to sleep. Yet I watched him. He sat up, rubbed his eyes, sighed sadly and remained for an hour without changing his position, apparently absorbed in his reflections. Nevertheless I was very uncomfortable, and I made a mental promise never again to sleep in the same room as the count. Finally, however, weariness gained the upper hand over my disquiet, and when the servants came into our room the next morning we were both soundly asleep.

VI

After lunch we returned to Médintiltas. There, having found Dr. Froeber alone, I told him that I believed the count was ill, that he suf-

---

34. *Turpi . . . :* this is from Horace's *Satires* (II.7.ll.60–62): "Or will you rather crouch with your head between your knees, locked ignobly in some chest where a maidservant, party to her mistress's wrongdoing, hid you?"

fered from dreadful dreams, that he might indeed be a sleepwalker, and that he could well be very dangerous in such a state.

"I've been aware of all that," the doctor told me. "Although he has the build of an athlete, he has the nerves of a pretty woman. Perhaps he takes after his mother in that regard. She was the devil of a handful this morning . . . I don't set much store by those stories of the fears and desires experienced by pregnant women, but one thing is certain: that the countess is a maniac, and that mania can be passed on from parent to child . . . "

"But," I went on, "the count is perfectly rational. He's fair-minded, he's cultivated, far more than I would have believed, I admit; he loves reading . . . "

"Agreed, agreed, my dear sir, but he is often strange. Sometimes he locks himself away for days at a stretch, sometimes he prowls about at night; he reads incredible books . . . on German metaphysics, physiology, goodness knows what else. Just yesterday a whole package of them arrived for him from Leipzig. Should I tell you what I really think? Every Hercules needs a Hebe.[35] There are some very pretty peasant girls around here . . . On Saturday evening, after their bath, you'd take them for princesses. Every single one of them would be proud to distract the count. At his age, devil take it, I myself . . . No, he hasn't got a mistress, he isn't married, and that's a mistake. He needs an outlet."

The doctor's gross materialism shocked me profoundly, and I brought an abrupt stop to the conversation by saying that I profoundly hoped the count would find a wife worthy of him. I admit that it was not without a feeling of surprise that I had learned from the doctor that the count had such a taste for philosophical studies. That officer of the hussars, that passionate hunter, reading German metaphysics and worrying his head over physiology, now that really set my thoughts topsyturvy. But the doctor had indeed told the truth, as I was to discover that very day.

"How do you explain, Professor," he said to me abruptly toward the end of dinner, "how do you explain the *duality* or the *duplicity* in our natures? . . . "

And as he saw that I didn't fully understand him, he went on, "Haven't you ever found yourself at the top of a tower, or else beside a precipice, and experienced the simultaneous and contradictory urge to hurl yourself into the void, and the feeling of absolute terror?"

"Well, that can be explained by purely physical causes," said the doctor. "First, the weariness you feel after an upward climb provokes a rush of blood to the brain which . . . "

"Let's have no more talk of blood, doctor!" exclaimed the count im-

---

35. Hebe was the goddess of youth. When Hercules became a god, he was granted Hebe as his bride.

patiently. "Let's take a different example. You're holding a loaded fire-arm. Your best friend is there. You suddenly imagine putting a bullet in his head. You're filled with the greatest horror at the idea of a mur-der, and yet the idea came to you. I believe, gentlemen, that if all the thoughts that occurred to us in the space of an hour . . . I believe that if all *your* thoughts, Professor, for I consider you a scholar, were written down, they might well fill an in-folio volume, on the basis of which there would not be a single lawyer who could not successfully demand that you be expelled from the country, not a single judge who wouldn't put you either in prison or in a madhouse."

"That judge, Count, would surely condemn me for having spent more than an hour this morning looking for the mysterious law according to which Slavic verbs take a future sense when they are used with a preposition, but if by chance I had had a different thought, what proof would it furnish against me? I am no more master of my thoughts than I am master of the external accidents that suggest those thoughts to me. The fact that a thought leaps into my mind does not allow one to conclude that I contemplated putting that thought into action, far less that I resolved to do so. I have never considered killing someone, but if the thought of a murder did cross my mind, isn't my reason there to banish it?"

"It's all very well for you to talk of reason, but is it always there—as you say—to guide us? If reason is to speak and be obeyed, there must be reflection, that is, time and composure. Does one always have both at one's disposal? In a battle, I see a ricocheting bullet coming toward me, I swing round and leave room for the bullet to reach my friend, for whom I would have given my life if I had had the time to reflect . . . "

I tried to talk to him about his duty as a man and as a Christian, of the necessity for us to imitate the warrior of the Scriptures, who is al-ways ready for combat; finally I pointed out to him that in constantly struggling against our passions we acquire new strength to diminish and dominate them. I fear I succeeded only in reducing him to silence, and he didn't appear convinced.

I spent a further two weeks at the castle. I made a second visit to Dowghielly, but we didn't spend the night there. As on the first occa-sion, Mlle Iwinska behaved like a mischievous and spoiled child. She exerted over the count a kind of fascination, and I had no doubt he was in love with her. Nevertheless, he knew her faults well, and he had no illusions about her. He knew her to be flirtatious, frivolous, indifferent to anything that didn't amuse her. Often I perceived that he was suf-fering inwardly at the realization that she was so irrational, but as soon as she treated him with the slightest affection he forgot everything, his face lit up, he beamed with joy. He wanted to take me on a final visit to Dowghielly on the eve of my departure, perhaps because I could then stay and talk to the aunt while he strolled in the park with the niece, but I had a lot of work to do and had to excuse myself, however hard he tried to persuade me. He returned for dinner, although he had told us not to wait for him. He sat down but could not eat. Throughout the meal he was gloomy and in a bad mood. From time to time, his eyebrows drew together and his eyes assumed a sinister expression. When the doctor left to go to the countess, the count followed me to my room and told me what was on his mind.

"I truly repent," he exclaimed, "having left you so that I could go and see that madcap who merely mocks me and who likes only such faces as are new. But fortunately it's all over between us, I'm completely fed up with her, and I'll never see her again . . . " He strode up and down for a while, as he was wont to do, then went on: "Perhaps you thought I was in love with her? That's what that fool of a doctor thinks. No, I've never loved her. Her laughing face amused me. Her white skin was a pleasure to look at . . . Those are the only good points she has . . . especially her skin . . . No brains at all. I've never seen in her anything but a pretty doll, something that's good to look at when you're bored and you don't have a new book . . . Doubtless you could call her a beauty . . . Her skin is wonderful! . . . Professor, the blood under that skin must be better than a horse's, don't you think?"

And he burst out laughing, but it was a laugh that was painful to listen to.

The next day I took my leave of him and continued my exploration in the north of the Palatinate.

VII

Those explorations took about two months, and I can say that there is hardly a town in Samogitia in which I did not stop and where I did not collect some documents. Allow me to seize this opportunity to thank the inhabitants of that province, especially the gentlemen of the church, for the truly eager assistance they granted my research, and the excellent contributions with which they enriched my dictionary.

After spending a week at Szawlé, my plan was to embark at the port of Klaypeda (which we call Memel) in order to go back home, when I received from Count Szémioth the following letter, which one of his messengers brought me:

Professor,
Allow me to write to you in German. I would probably commit even more solecisms if I were to write to you in Zmudz, and you would lose any esteem you had for me. I do not know if you have much esteem for me anyway, and the news I have to tell you may well not increase it. Without any more beating around the bush, let me say I'm getting married, and you can guess whom I'm marrying. Jove laughs at lovers' vows. *So does Pirkuns, our Samogitian*

Jove. So it's Mlle Julienne Iwinska that I shall wed on the eighth of next month. You would be the kindest of men if you were to come to the wedding. All the peasants from Médintiltas and the environs will come to my home to eat a few oxen and countless pigs, and when they're drunk they'll dance in the meadow, you know, the one on the right of the avenue. You'll be able to see costumes, and they'll be costumes worthy of your attention. You would give me the greatest pleasure if you would come, and Julienne would be delighted, too. I will add that your refusal would throw us into the worst of predicaments. You know I belong to the Evangelical church, as does my fiancée. Well, our minister, who lives thirty leagues away, is stricken with gout, and I very much hope you will be willing to preside in his place. I am, Professor, your most devoted,
    Michel Szémioth.

At the bottom of the letter, as a postscript, a rather attractive feminine hand had added in Zmudz: "I, the muse of Lithuania, write in Zmudz. Michel is quite impertinent to cast doubts on whether or not you will approve. Truly I'm the only girl mad enough to want a lad like him. You'll see, Professor, on the eighth of next month, a rather *chic* bride. That's not Zmudz, that's French. Now just don't go daydreaming during the ceremony!"

Neither the letter nor the postscript pleased me. I felt the engaged couple showed an unpardonable frivolity for so solemn an occasion. But how could I have refused? I will also admit that the spectacle the count had announced was very tempting for me. It seemed quite likely that among the large number of gentry who would gather at the castle of Médintiltas, I could not fail to meet educated people who would provide me with useful information. My Zmudz glossary was very rich, but the meaning of a certain number of words I'd learned from the mouths of coarse peasants remained wrapped in relative obscurity for me. All those considerations combined to provide a powerful reason for me to agree to the count's request, and I told him that on the morning of the eighth I would be at Médintiltas. How deeply I was to regret that decision!

VIII

As I entered the avenue leading to the castle, I saw a large number of ladies and gentlemen in morning dress, gathered on the stairway or wandering in the paths that led through the park. The courtyard was full of peasants in their Sunday best. The castle was festively adorned; everywhere there were flowers, garlands, flags, and festoons. The majordomo led me to the room that had been prepared for me on the ground floor, begging my pardon for not being able to offer me a finer one, but there were so many people at the castle that it would have been impossible for me to keep the suite I had occupied during my first visit, and which had been reserved for the wife of a noble marshal. Moreover my new room was very acceptable, overlooking the park and situated immediately below the count's suite. I quickly dressed for the ceremony and donned my robe, but neither the count nor his fiancée appeared. The count had gone to collect her from Dowghielly. They should have been back long before, but a bride's preparations are no small matter, and the doctor informed those present that, since dinner would take place only after the religious ceremony, those whose appetites were too ferocious would be well advised to take all necessary precautions by taking advantage of a certain buffet heaped with cakes and all kinds of liqueurs. I noticed on that occasion how much a little delay can set malicious tongues wagging; the mothers of two pretty maids who had been invited to the wedding were unstinting in their snide attacks on the bride.

It was after midday when a salvo of mortars and firearms signaled her arrival, and soon thereafter a gala coach turned into the avenue, drawn by four magnificent horses. From the foam that covered their chests, it was easy to see that the delay was no fault of theirs. The coach contained only the bride, Mme Dowghiello, and the count. He stepped out and gave Mme Dowghiello his hand. Mlle Iwinska, with a most graceful movement that revealed all her childish coquetry, pretended that she wanted to hide under her shawl to escape the curious glances that surrounded her on all sides. All the same, she stood up in the coach and was about to take the count's hand, when the lead horses, frightened perhaps by the rain of flowers the peasants threw at the bride, but perhaps also feeling that strange terror that Count Szémioth inspired in animals, reared and plunged. One wheel struck the stone at the foot of the stairway, and for a moment it seemed there would be an accident. Mlle Iwinska gave a little cry. But we were soon reassured. The count, seizing her in his arms, carried her to the top of the steps as easily as if he had been holding in his arms a mere dove. We all applauded his skill and his chivalrous gallantry. The peasants shouted out formidable "Hoorays," the bride blushed deeply, and laughed and trembled simultaneously. The count, in no hurry to free himself of his charming burden, seemed to triumph in showing her to the surrounding crowd . . .

Suddenly, a tall woman, pale and thin, with her clothes all awry, her hair disordered and her every feature distorted with terror, appeared at the top of the stairs, without anyone knowing where she had come from.

"The bear!" she screamed in a high voice, "get the bear! Where are your guns! He's making off with a woman! Kill him! Fire! Fire!"

It was the countess. The bride's arrival had attracted everyone to the stairs, to the courtyard, or to the castle windows. Even the women watching the poor madwoman had forgotten their orders. She had escaped and, unobserved by anyone, had made her way to the midst of the crowd. It was a most painful scene. She had to be carried away despite her loud protestations and all her resistance. Many of the guests were unaware of her illness. Explanations had to be given. For a long time their was much quiet whispering. All the faces looked sad. It was a sign of bad luck! That was the decision of those who were superstitious, and there are a great many of them in Lithuania.

Nevertheless, Mlle Iwinska requested five minutes to prepare herself and don her bridal veil, an operation that took a good hour. That was more than enough to allow those who had been ignorant of the countess's illness to learn the cause and all the details.

At last the bride reappeared, magnificently adorned and covered with diamonds. Her aunt presented her to all the guests, and when the time had come to move to the chapel, to my great surprise, Mme Dowghiello, in the presence of the entire company, slapped her niece's cheek, hard enough to make those who might have been looking elsewhere swing around. This blow was received with the most complete resignation, and no one seemed surprised by it, but a man in black wrote something on a piece of paper he had brought, and several of those present appended their signatures with the most indifferent expressions. It was only at the end of the ceremony that I learned the key to this riddle. Had I guessed it, I would not have failed to oppose this hateful practice with all the strength of my sacred ministry, for its purpose is to lay the grounds for a divorce case by suggesting that the marriage took place only as a result of material violence carried out against one of the signatories to the contract.

After the religious service, I believed it was my duty to address a few words to the young couple, attempting to place before their eyes the gravity and the sanctity of the engagement that had just united them, and as I still had weighing on my heart the ill-worded postscript written by Mlle Iwinska, I reminded her that she was entering a new life—one no longer accompanied by youthful joys and pleasures, but full of serious duties and grave trials. It seemed to me that this part of my speech produced a profound effect on the bride, as on all those present who knew German.

Salvoes of firearms and shouts of joy greeted the wedding procession as we left the chapel, and then we went into the dining room. The meal was splendid, appetites were sharp, and at first all that could be heard was the sound of knives and forks, but soon, with the help of champagne and of Hungarian wines, people began to chat, to laugh, and even to shout. The bride was toasted with much enthusiasm. Scarcely had we sat down again than an old gentleman with white mustaches stood up and said with a tremendous voice, "It is a great sorrow to me to see that our old customs are disappearing. Never would our fathers have drunk that toast in crystal glasses. We used to drink it in the bride's shoe and even in her boot, for in my days brides wore boots of red leather. Let us show, friends, that we are still true Lithuanians. And you, my lady, be so kind as to give me your shoe."

The bride replied with a blush and a stifled little laugh, "Come and get it, sir . . . but I won't reciprocate with your boot."

The old gentleman didn't have to be asked twice, but knelt down gallantly and removed a little shoe of white satin with a red heel, which he filled with champagne and drank so quickly and skillfully that no more than half of it ran over his clothes. The shoe went from hand to hand, and all the men drank from it, but not without difficulty. The old gentleman demanded the shoe back as if it were a precious relic, and Mme Dowghiello ordered a chamber maid to come and repair the disorder in her niece's outfit.

This toast was followed by many others, and soon the guests became so noisy that it no longer struck me as suitable to remain with them. I slipped away from the table without anyone paying me any attention, and I went to breathe in the fresh air outside the castle. But even there I came across a sight which could hardly be called edifying. Most of the servants and peasants, who had been given all the beer and brandy they wanted, were already drunk. There had been fights and broken heads. Wallowing here and there on the meadow were drunkards deprived of all feeling, and the general aspect of the festivities was that of a battlefield. I would have been curious to see the peasant dances from closer up, but most of them were performed by brazen gypsies, and I didn't think it suitable to venture into that hurly-burly. So I went off to my room, read for a bit, then undressed and soon fell asleep.

When I awoke, the castle clock was striking three. The night was clear, although the moon was somewhat veiled by a light mist. I tried to go back to sleep, but to no avail. As is my custom in such a situation, I decided to take up my book and study, but I couldn't find my matches within reach. I got up and was feeling my way around my room, when an opaque and very large body fell in front of my window and landed with a muffled thud in the garden. My first thought was that it was a man, and I assumed that one of those drunkards must have fallen from the window. I opened my own window and looked out. I could see nothing. At last I lit a candle and, having gone back to bed, revised my glossary until a servant brought me some tea.

Toward eleven I went to the salon, where I found many weary eyes and faded complexions. I learned that people had indeed left the table very late. Neither the count nor the young countess had yet appeared. At half past eleven, after many nasty jokes, people began to murmur, softly at first but soon fairly loud. Doctor Froeber took it upon himself to send the count's valet to knock at his master's door. After a quarter of an hour the man came back down and, somewhat shaken, reported to the doctor that he had knocked more than a dozen times without obtaining any reply. Mme Dowghiello, the doctor, and I discussed what we should do. The valet's nervousness had disturbed me. The three of us went upstairs with him. In front of the door we found the young countess's chamber maid in a most agitated state and certain that an accident had happened, for my lady's window had been found wide open. I remembered with a shock of fear the heavy body that had fallen in front of my window. We knocked loudly. No reply. At last the valet brought an iron bar, and we broke down the door . . . No! I do not have the heart to describe the scene that met our gaze. The young countess lay dead on the bed, her face terribly lacerated, her chest torn open, drenched in blood. The count had disappeared, and no one since has heard anything of him.

The doctor examined the young woman's dreadful wound. "No steel blade," he said "made this wound. . . . It's a bite . . . "

The professor closed his book and gazed thoughtfully at the fire.

"And that's the end of the story?" asked Adelaide.

"The end!" said the professor in mournful tones.

"But," she went on, "why did you call it *Lokis*? Not a single one of the characters has that name."

"It's not a man's name," said the professor . . . "Come, Théodore, do you understand the meaning of Lokis?"

"I haven't a clue."

"If you had steeped yourself in the laws concerning the transformation of Sanskrit into Lithuanian, you would have recognized in Lokis the Sanskrit *arkcha* or *rikscha*. In Lithuanian the name Lokis is given to the animal the Greeks call *arktos*, the Romans *ursus*, and the Germans *Bär*.

Now you can understand my epigraph:

Miszka su Lokiu
Abu du tokiu.

You know that in the tale of Reynard the Fox the bear is called *damp Brun*. Among the Slavs, he is called Michael, Miszka in Lithuanian, and this nickname almost always replaces the generic name, Lokis. It's in the same way that the French have forgotten their neolatin word "goupil" or "gorpil" and have replaced it with that of "renard." I could quote you many more examples . . . "

But Adelaide pointed out that it was late, and the party broke up.

Balzac

◆

Honoré de Balzac (1799–1850) was a prolific, ebullient, and extraordinarily energetic writer whose novels played a uniquely important role in determining our contemporary image of the genre. Although he began by writing historical chronicles in the style of Walter Scott, who enjoyed enormous popularity in France in the first decades of the nineteenth century, he soon switched to recording his own times. Convinced that the objects we use, the clothes we wear, and the houses we inhabit reveal much about our personalities, he filled his novels and short stories with detailed descriptions that reveal a love both of the material world and of the language that can be used to represent it. Studded with neologisms and nonce-words, richly evocative and often highly comic, his writing aims to convey all the complexities of the society in which he lived. Early in the 1840s he began developing a complex and highly ambitious plan to interconnect his series of loosely connected novels and tales. This would allow him to cover the experiences and morals of French people throughout the kingdom, old and young, men and women, from peasants to the aristocracy. His Human Comedy *moreover is marked by its recurring characters, figures whose familiarity to the reader of other Balzac novels increases that sense of the real which he so frequently and so ambitiously strove to convey. Fascinated by the power of evil, he created an array of manipulative men and women whose vision of society is notoriously cynical. Accused of preferring evil to good, Balzac responded somewhat unconvincingly that his series, if read in its entirety, would be found to contain as many good as evil characters, but, like Milton, he could not help rendering the devil in more charismatic terms than his angelic heroes and heroines. While his plots are often sprawling, Balzac's evocation of character and his eye for idiosyncrasies make his writing compulsive reading.*

FURTHER READING: There are countless translations of Balzac's novels. A representative sampling might include *Old Goriot, Cousin Bette, Lost Illusions,* and *The Lily of the Valley.*

BIOGRAPHY: Graham Robb, *Balzac: A Life* (New York: Norton, 1994); André Maurois, *Prometheus: The Life of Balzac* (New York: Carroll and Graf, 1983). TEXT USED: *Histoire des Treize* (Paris: Calmann-Lévy, 1887).

THE GIRL WITH THE GOLDEN EYES (1834–1835)

[. . .] On one of those lovely spring mornings when the leaves are not yet green but when they have begun to unfold, when the sun begins to make the roofs blaze and the sky is blue, when the population of Paris comes out of its honeycombs to hum along the boulevards, or flows like a thousand-hued serpent down the Rue de la Paix toward the Tuileries, greeting the festivities that nature begins all over again, on one of those happy days then, a young man, as lovely as the day on that particular day, dressed tastefully, of easy manners, (let's tell his secret) a love child, the natural son of Lord Dudley and the renowned Marquise de Vordac, strolled along the great avenue of the Tuileries. This Adonis, whose name was Henri de Marsay, was born in France, where Lord Dudley had come to marry off the young woman, who was already carrying Henri, to an old gentleman called Monsieur de Marsay. This faded butterfly, who had already almost withered right away, recognized Henri as his own son in exchange for the usufruct of shares worth 100,000 francs, which were established in the name of his putative offspring; this was a folly that did not cost Lord Dudley dear, for at that time the French shares cost him 17 francs and 50 centimes a year. The old gentleman died without having known his wife. Madame de Marsay then married the Marquis de Vordac, but before she became a marquise she worried her head very little about her child and Lord Dudley. First, the war that had been declared between France and England had separated the two lovers, and fidelity *in the face of all odds* was not and never will be in vogue in Paris. Then, the success she won as an elegant, pretty woman who was universally adored stifled in the heart of the Parisian the sentiments of the mother. Lord Dudley took no more care of his progeny than the mother did. The swift infidelity of a young girl who had been ardently loved may well have inspired in him a kind of aversion for everything associated with her. Moreover, it may also be that fathers love only those children whom they have had ample time to get to know. This is a social belief of the greatest importance for the peace of mind of families and that all bachelors must support, for it proves that paternity is a feeling the wife raises in a hothouse through her behavior and her laws.

Of the two men, poor Henri de Marsay found a father only in the man who was not obliged to be a father at all. Monsieur de Marsay's paternity was quite naturally very incomplete. In the natural order of things, children have a father only during a very few minutes; and the gentleman imitated nature. The good man would not have sold his name had he not possessed certain vices. So he devoured, in gambling dens, and drank elsewhere, without a shred of remorse, the few semesters the National Treasury paid to shareholders. Then he handed the child over to an old sister of his, a Mademoiselle de Marsay, who looked after him very carefully, and, on the meager pension her brother allotted her, gave him a tutor, an abbot without a penny to bless himself with, who assessed the young man's future and resolved to pay himself back, from the 100,000 francs worth of shares, for the care he would give his charge, toward whom he grew to feel real affection. By chance this tutor was a true priest, one of those men of the cloth cut out to become cardinals in France or Borgias under the tiara. He taught the child in three years what he himself had learned in ten at his college. Then this great man, Abbot de Maronis, completed his pupil's education by making him learn about civilization under all its guises: he nourished him on his own experience, rarely took him to churches, which at that time were closed, escorted him sometimes to the theater, more often to brothels. He took human emotions apart for him, piece by piece, taught him about politics in the heart of the very salons where in those days it was being cooked up, enumerated government strategies for him, and tried, out of friendship for a fine but abandoned nature, a nature that had ample prospects, to offer a virile replacement for his mother. Is the Church not the mother of orphans? The pupil responded to all this care. This worthy man died a bishop in 1812 with the satisfaction of having left under heaven a child whose heart and mind were so well fashioned at the age of sixteen that he could twist a man of forty around his finger. Who could have expected to meet a heart of bronze and a brain steeped in alcohol under a more seductive exterior than the old painters—those naive artists—gave the serpent in the earthly paradise? And I have told you nothing yet. For the good scarlet devil had acquainted his favorite pupil with certain people in Parisian high society who were worth as much in the young man's hands as a further 100,000 shares. And finally, this priest, corrupt but diplomatic, an unbeliever but a scholar, perfidious but amiable, apparently weak but as vigorous intellectually as he was physically, was so truly useful to his pupil, turned such a blind eye on his vices, was so good a calculator of all kinds of strength, so deep when it was necessary to make some human deduction, so youthful at table, at Frascati,[1] at . . . goodness knows where else, that the grateful Henri de Marsay hardly ever felt the slightest tenderness by 1814 except when he saw the portrait of his dear bishop, the only bit of portable property the prelate had been able to leave him. This priest was an admirable example of those men of genius

---

1. *Frascati:* This famous restaurant and gambling house attained mythical status, symbolizing riches and fame.

who will save the Catholic, apostolic, and Roman church, compromised at this point in time through the weakness of its recruits, and through the old age of its pontiffs—but so the Church wills it. The European war prevented the young de Marsay from becoming acquainted with his true father, whose name it is doubtful he knew. As a child who had been abandoned, he did not know Mme de Marsay any better. Naturally he felt little grief over the death of his putative father. As for Mademoiselle de Marsay, his sole mother, he erected for her on her death a very pretty little tomb in Père Lachaise cemetery. Monsignor de Maronis had guaranteed this old beribboned bonnet one of the best places in heaven, so that, when he saw she was glad to die, Henri shed some selfish tears, mourning her for his own sake. Seeing this grief, the abbot dried his pupil's tears by pointing out to him that the good old spinster had taken her snuff in a disgusting manner and had become so ugly, so deaf, and so dull that he owed death a debt of gratitude. The bishop had his pupil declared to have come of age in 1811. Then, when de Marsay's mother remarried, the priest chose through a family counsel, one of those honest, brainless idiots he had encountered through the confessional, and he charged him with administering the boy's fortune, whose revenues he applied to help the community in its need, but whose capital he wanted to preserve.

Toward the end of 1814, Henri de Marsay therefore owed no one on earth any obligation, and was as free as a bird without a mate. Although he had turned twenty-two, he scarcely seemed seventeen. Generally speaking, the least generous of his rivals considered him the most attractive boy in Paris. From his father, Lord Dudley, he had taken the most amorously deceptive pair of blue eyes; from his mother, the most abundant head of black hair; from both of them, pure blood, the complexion of a young maiden, a gentle and modest air, a slender and aristocratic figure, and very fine hands. For a woman, just to see him was to be mad about him; you know what I mean? It was to be smitten with one of those desires that eat into the heart but that you forget because of the impossibility of satisfying it, since in Paris the common run of women lack tenacity. Few of them repeat to themselves as men do the motto—I SHALL PERSEVERE—of the house of Orange. Under this freshness of life, and despite the limpid clarity of his eyes, Henri had the courage of a lion and the dexterity of a monkey. At ten paces he could send a bullet through a knife blade; he rode on horseback in a way that brought to life the fable of the centaur; he could drive a four-in-hand gracefully; he was as supple as Cherubino[2] and as calm as a sheep, but he knew how to defeat a man from the suburbs at the terrible games of French boxing or quarterstaff. And then, he played the piano

---

2. *Cherubino:* The character in Beaumarchais's play and Mozart's opera *The Marriage of Figaro,* who represents the adolescent in love with love.

well enough to become a performer if he ever fell on hard times, and owned a voice which would have earned him 50,000 francs a season from Barbaja. Alas, all these wonderful gifts and these attractive failings were tarnished by a horrible vice: he believed neither in men nor in women, neither in God nor in the Devil. Capricious Nature had begun endowing him with gifts; the task had been successfully completed by a priest.

In order to make this adventure comprehensible, I have to add at this point that Lord Dudley naturally found many women willing to make copies of his delicious portrait. His second masterpiece of this type was a young girl called Euphemia, the daughter of a Spanish lady, raised in Havana, brought back to Madrid with a young Creole woman from the West Indies, with all the ruinous tastes one acquires in the colonies. Fortunately she was married to an old and powerful and rich Spanish lord, Don Hijos, the Marquis of San-Réal, who, since the French troops had occupied Spain, had come to live in Paris on the Rue Saint Lazare. As much through thoughtlessness as out of respect for the innocence of youth, Lord Dudley did not inform his children of the relationships he had created for them hither and yon. This is a slight inconvenience of civilization, but since it has so many advantages we should take the rough with the smooth. Lord Dudley, let me add, to save me from returning to this subject, took refuge in Paris in 1816 in order to avoid the pursuit of British justice, which, where the Orient is concerned, protects only the merchandise. The wandering lord caught sight of Henri and asked who he was. Then, when he heard his name, he said, "Oh! He's my son! What a pity!"

That's the tale of the young man who toward the middle of April in 1815 was nonchalantly strolling along the great avenue of the Tuileries like all those animals who, knowing their strength, walk in peace and majesty. Middle-class women swung round quite naively to see him again, ladies did not turn around but simply waited for him to come back again, and etched in their memories, to remember, when it was needed, that suave figure which would not have been unworthy of the most beautiful among them.

"Now, what are you doing here on a Sunday?" the Marquis de Ronquerolles asked Henri as he went past.

"There's a fish on the line," the young man answered.

This exchange of thoughts took place by means of two meaningful glances and without either Ronquerolles or de Marsay giving any indication that they knew each other. The young man examined the strollers with that swift glance and rapid ear characteristic of a Parisian who at first glance seems to see and hear nothing. At that moment, a young man came to him, seized him familiarly by the arm and said to him: "How are things with you, my good de Marsay?"

"Excellent," de Marsay replied with that air that seems affectionate, but that between young Parisians proves nothing as regards either the present or the future.

Indeed, the youth of Paris are unlike those of any other town. You can divide them into two classes: the young man who has something, and the young man who has nothing; or the young man who ponders, and the young man who squanders. But let's be clear on this, we're talking only of those native-born Parisians who lead the delightful life of elegance. There are indeed a few other young men, but these are children who conceive of Parisian life only at a late stage and who remain its dupes. They do not speculate, they study, they grind away, according to the others. Finally you can also find certain young men, rich or poor, who embrace careers and pursue them undeviatingly. These are rather like Rousseau's Emile,[3] citizen fodder, and never appear in society. Diplomats impolitely call them fools. Fools or no, they increase the number of those mediocre people under whose weight France is currently collapsing. They are always there, always ready to spoil public and private affairs with the flat trowel of mediocrity, while they plume themselves on their powerlessness, which they call morals and probity. These kinds of winners of social Prizes for Excellence infest the administration, the army, the bench, the chambers, the court. They diminish and flatten the country, and constitute what could be seen as the lymph in the political body, weighing it down and making it flabby. These honest men call men of talent immoral rogues. If those rogues charge for their services, at least they serve; while the others cause harm and are respected by the mob, but, fortunately for France, the gilded youth stigmatizes them constantly by calling them blockheads.

So, at first sight, it is natural to consider as quite distinct these two species of young men who lead the elegant life, an amiable company to which Henri de Marsay belonged. But those observers who are not satisfied to remain on the surface of things will be quickly convinced that the differences are purely moral, and that there is nothing so misleading as that pretty shell. Nevertheless, all of them take precedence over everyone else, speak (without rhyme or reason) of things, men, literature, and the fine arts, have constantly on their lips the year's quislings, interrupt a conversation to slip in a pun, pour scorn on knowledge and the scholar, despise all those whom they do not know or all those whom they fear, and set themselves above everything, constituting themselves as the supreme judges over everything. All of them would pull the wool over their father's eyes and would be ready to pour crocodile tears on their mother's breast, but in general they believe in nothing, speak ill of women, or put on a show of modesty, while in reality they are carrying out the orders of some foul courtesan or haggard

---

3. The French philosopher Jean-Jacques Rousseau (1712–1778) wrote a pedagogical treatise named for its central character, Emile.

crone. All of them are decayed to the bone through calculations, deprivations, and a brutal desire to succeed, and if they were suspected of suffering from kidney stones, an examination would find that all of them have such stones, but in their hearts. In their normal state they have the most attractive exteriors, bring friendship into play under any excuse, and are all equally inspiriting. The same ill-natured banter dominates their changing jargon, they aim at bizarreness in their outfits, they glory in repeating the stupidities of this or that fashionable actor, and begin with scorn and impertinence, whomever they may be conversing with, in order to win as it were the first round in that game; but woe betide anyone who isn't able to let them tear out one of his eyes so that he can tear out both of theirs. They seem equally untouched by the country's fortunes and by its plagues. In a word, they are all like that pretty white foam that crowns the flood of tempests. They dress, they dine, they dance, they amuse themselves on the day of the battle of Waterloo, during the cholera, or while a revolution rages. Finally, they certainly all spend the same amount, but this is where the contrast begins. Of this floating fortune they spend so pleasantly, some have the capital and others expect it; they have the same tailors, but the bills of the latter group await payment. Then if one group, like so many sieves, receive countless ideas without retaining any, the other group compare those ideas and assimilate all that are sound. If one group think they know everything, yet know nothing and understand everything, lend everything to those who need nothing and offer nothing to those who need something, the other group study in secret the thoughts of others and put their money, like their madness, where they will earn high interest. One group no longer have any faithful impressions, because their souls, like a mirror grown tarnished with use, no longer reflect any image; the others are economical with their senses and their life, although they appear to throw them out the window as liberally as the others. The first group, trusting in a hope, devote themselves without conviction to a system blown by the wind and moving against the current, but they leap onto another political boat when the first begins to lose headway; the second group measure the future, examine it, and see in political fidelity what the English see in commercial probity, an element of success. But where the young man who owns something makes a pun or a fine phrase when a throne is overturned, the one who has nothing makes a calculation in public, or performs a base act in private, and succeeds while continuing to shake his friends' hands. One group never believe in the abilities of others, consider all their own ideas brand new, as if the world had been made the day before, they have boundless self-confidence, and have no more ferocious enemy than themselves. But the others are armed with a constant distrust of those men whose value they correctly gauge, and are deep enough to have one thought more than the friends they exploit. Then, each night, when their heads lie on the pillow, they weigh men as a miser weighs gold. One group grow angry at an unimportant piece of impertinence, but let themselves be teased by diplomats who make them pose before them while they pull these puppets' main strings, their self-pride; while the second group force others to respect them, and choose their own victims as they choose their own protectors. Then, one fine day, those who had nothing, have something; and those who had something, have nothing. The former consider their friends who have achieved a position in life to be sly and heartless but also as men to be reckoned with. He is someone to be reckoned with! is the vast praise handed out to those who succeed, however they do so, in politics, in love, or in money. Among them can be found certain young men who play this role starting from a position of being in debt; naturally they are more dangerous than those who play it without having a penny.

The young man who called himself Henri de Marsay's friend was a madcap fresh from the provinces. He was learning from other young men who were then in fashion how to make a hole in his inheritance. He did, however, have one last cake to eat in the provinces, an ironclad establishment. He was quite simply an heir who had moved directly from his slender hundred francs a month to his father's entire fortune, and who, while he didn't have wit enough to see he was the object of mockery, was good enough a mathematician to stop when he'd spent two thirds of his capital. In Paris, he had come to discover, for the price of a few notes of a thousand francs each, the art of not overly respecting one's gloves, of listening to wise meditations on the wages to pay servants, and seeking out what was the best contract to conclude with them. He was eager to be able to talk about his horses and his Pyrenean dog in the correct terms, and to learn how to recognize according to her dress, her walk, or her slipper, to what species a woman belonged, to study écarté,[4] brush up on a few fashionable words, and conquer through his stay in the Parisian world the authority he would need later on to import to his province the taste for tea and for silver in the English patterns, and to give himself the right to despise everything around him for the rest of his life. De Marsay had shown a liking for him in order to use him in society, as a bold speculator makes use of an agent whom he trusts. True or false, de Marsay's friendship provided Paul de Manerville with a position in society while he for his part thought himself very cunning in exploiting his intimate friend in his own way. He lived in his friend's reflected glory, walked constantly under Henri's umbrella, wore his boots, and gilded himself with Henri's glory. When he stood beside Henri or even walked with him he seemed to be saying to himself, "Don't insult us, we're real tigers!" He often allowed himself to say complacently, "If I asked for such and such from

---

4. *écarté:* A popular card game.

Henri he's good enough a friend to do it . . . " But he was careful never actually to ask him for anything. He feared him, and his fear, although imperceptible, worked on others and served de Marsay's ends. "De Marsay's really great," Paul used to say. "Ha, ha, you'll see, he'll become whatever he takes it into his head to become. I wouldn't be surprised to find that one day he'd become minister for foreign affairs. Nothing can stop him." Then he would make of de Marsay what corporal Trim[5] used to make of his bonnet, a perpetual gambling stake. "Ask de Marsay, you'll see!"

Or else: "The other day, we were hunting, de Marsay and I. He didn't want to believe I could, but I leaped over a bush without moving from the saddle!"

Or else: "De Marsay and I were with some women the other day and, on my word of honor . . . etc."

So Paul de Manerville could be classed only in the great, famous, and powerful family of fools on their road to success. One day he would be a politician, but for the moment he wasn't even a young man. His friend de Marsay defined him in the following way: "You want to know what Paul is? Well, Paul . . . is Paul de Manerville."

"I'm surprised to find you here," he said to de Marsay, "on a Sunday."

"I was about to make the same remark to you."

"Something's afoot?"

"Could be . . . "

"Hmmm . . . "

"I can certainly tell you without compromising my passion. And too, a woman who comes to the Tuileries on a Sunday has no real value, aristocratically speaking."

"Ha! Ha!"

"Hush, or I won't say another word. You laugh too loud, people will think we've dined too well. Last Thursday, here, on the terrace that goes past the Feuillants convent, I was strolling along without thinking of anything. But when I reached the gate to Rue Castiglione, by which I was planning to leave, I found myself face to face with a woman or rather a young person who, if she didn't exactly fling her arms around my neck, refrained from doing so less out of common decency than through one of those feelings of astonishment that cut off your arms and legs, run down your spinal cord and stop in the soles of your feet, riveting you to the ground. I've often produced such effects, it's a kind of hypnotism that becomes very powerful when there's a complete case of elective affinities. But it wasn't a case of stupefaction, and she wasn't just a common girl. Morally speaking her expression seemed to say: 'What! You here, my ideal man, the idol of my thoughts, the cynosure of my dreams at night and in the morning? How do you come to be

---

5. *Trim:* Character in Lawrence Stern's *Tristram Shandy.*

here? Why this morning? Why not yesterday? Take me, I'm yours, and so forth!' Well, I said to myself, here's another! So I looked at her closely. Ah! Paul, physically speaking that stranger is the most adorably feminine woman I have ever met. She belongs to the type of woman the Romans called *fulva* or *flava*, the woman of fire. What struck me most of all at the outset and what still sets me on fire are two yellow eyes like those of tigers: a yellow the color of gleaming gold, living gold, thinking gold, gold that loves and is absolutely determined to slip into your wallet!"

"No one's talking about anything else!" exclaimed Paul. "She sometimes comes here, she's *the girl with the golden eyes*. That's the nickname we've given her. She's about twenty-two years old, and I used to see her here when the Bourbons[6] were here, but with a woman who's worth a hundred thousand times more than she is."

"Hold your tongue, Paul! It's impossible for any woman, whoever she might be, to outdo that girl, who's like a cat that wants to come and rub against your legs, a pale girl with ash-colored hair, delicate in appearance but who must have downy threads on the third phalanx of her fingers; and along her cheeks there's a pale down whose line, which glows with light on a fine day, begins at the ears and finishes on her collar."

"Oh! But the other one, de Marsay! She has dark eyes that have never shed a tear, but that burn; black brows that meet and give her an expression of hardness belied by the network of lines on her lips, on which a kiss would not settle, lips that are passionate and cool; a Moorish complexion that warms a man as if he were standing in full sunlight: but, word of honor, she's just like you!"

"You're flattering her!"

"An upright figure, the soaring figure of a corvette built for racing, and that bounds up to a merchant steamer with an entirely French impetuosity, bites it, and sinks it in less time than you can bat an eye."

"Well, after all, what do I care about the one I didn't see?" went on de Marsay. "Since the time I started studying women, my unknown is the first whose virgin breast, and whose ardent and voluptuous forms have embodied for me the one woman of my dreams! She is the original of the wild painting called *Woman Caressing Her Chimera*, the hottest and most infernal inspiration ever produced by the genius of antiquity: a holy poem prostituted by those who have copied it for frescos and mosaics for a mass of middle-class men who see in this cameo a mere trinket, something to hang on their watch chains, whereas she is woman in her entirety, an abyss of pleasures into which one falls without ever reaching the end, an ideal woman who can sometimes be seen in Spain or Italy but almost never in France. Well, I saw that girl with the golden

---

6. *Bourbons:* Branch of the French royal family that came to power in 1814.

eyes, that woman caressing her chimera a second time, I saw her here on Friday. I guessed that she would come back the following day at the same time. I was not mistaken. I took it into my head to follow her without letting her see me, to study the indolent walk of the woman of leisure, in whose movements can be detected a dormant eroticism. Well, she turned round and saw me, adored me afresh, trembled again, shivered. But then I noticed the real Spanish duenna who guards her, a hyena whom some jealous man has clothed in a dress, some she-devil amply paid to guard that soft creature . . . Oh then the duenna aroused in me more than mere love, she aroused my curiosity. On Saturday no one came. Here I am today waiting for this girl whose chimera I am, and asking for nothing better than to pose as the monster in the fresco."

"Here she is," said Paul, "everyone is turning round to look at her . . . "

The stranger blushed and her eyes glittered when she caught sight of Henri, she closed them and went past.

"You're trying to tell me she notices you?" exclaimed Paul de Manerville jokingly.

The duenna stared closely at the two young men. When the stranger and Henri met for the second time, the young woman brushed past him and her hand squeezed the young man's hand. Then she turned round and smiled passionately at him. But the duenna pulled her away very quickly, toward the gate to Rue Castiglione. The two friends followed the young girl, admiring the magnificent curve of her neck, to which the head was joined by a combination of vigorous lines, and from which sprang back a few spirals of short, curly hair. The girl with the golden eyes had that slender, curved, nicely articulated foot that offers so many attractions to hungry imaginations. As a result she was elegantly shod and wore a short dress. During this part of the journey, she turned round every few seconds to see Henri again and appeared to follow only regretfully the old woman to whom she seemed simultaneously a mistress and a slave: she could beat her black and blue, but she couldn't dismiss her. All that was perfectly obvious. The two friends reached the gate. Two liveried valets unfolded the steps of a tasteful coupé, covered with coats of arms. The girl with the golden eyes boarded first, took the side from which she would be seen when the carriage turned around, put her hand on the door, and waved her handkerchief, unbeknownst to the duenna, and without a care for the scandalized responses of curious bystanders said publicly to Henri through waves of her handkerchief, "Follow me . . . "

"Have you ever seen anyone drop a handkerchief better?" Henri said to Paul de Manerville.

Then, catching sight of a cab about to depart after having brought people to the gardens, he signaled to the driver to wait.

"Follow that carriage, see what street and what house it goes into, and I'll pay you ten francs. Farewell, Paul."

The cab followed the coupé. The coupé went to Rue Saint-Lazare and drove into one of the loveliest private houses in the area.

De Marsay was no scatterbrain. Any other young man would have obeyed the whim to find out a few things about a girl who so perfectly embodied the most luminous ideas oriental poetry has expressed about women. But, too cunning to compromise away the future of this promising affair by doing any such thing, he told his cab to continue down Rue Saint-Lazare, and bring him back to his hotel. On the following day, his chief valet, Laurent, a lad as crafty as a Figaro[7] of old-fashioned comedy, waited in the vicinity of the stranger's hotel for the letters to be delivered. In order to spy out the land more comfortably and prowl around the house, he had taken a leaf out of the book of those policemen who want to disguise themselves well; having once brought back a man's outfit from a visit to the Auvergne,[8] he attempted to adopt the appearance of an Auvergnat. When the mailman who was doing the Rue Saint-Lazare delivery that morning happened to pass by, Laurent pretended to be a messenger attempting to remember the name of someone to whom he was meant to deliver a package, and consulted the mailman. At first deceived by appearances, this highly picturesque person who crops up in the midst of Parisian civilization informed him that the hotel in which the girl with the golden eyes was living belonged to Don Hijos, the Marquis de San Réal, a member of the Spanish nobility. Naturally the man from the Auvergne had no business to carry out with the marquis.

"My package," he said, "is for the marquise."

"She's out of town," said the mail man. "Her letters are being redirected to London."

"So the marquise isn't a young girl who . . . "

"Ah!" said the mailman, interrupting the servant and looking at him attentively, "if you're a messenger, I'm a dancer."

Laurent showed a few gold coins to the whistle-carrying mailman who began to grin. "Look, here's the name of your quarry," he said, taking from his leather bag a letter bearing a London stamp and on which the following address—Miss Paquita Valdès, rue Saint Lazare, Hotel Saint Réal, Paris—was written in a thin scrawl that betrayed a woman's handwriting.

"Would you be willing to contemplate a bottle of chablis, together with a filet sautéed with mushrooms and preceded by a few dozen oysters?" asked Laurent, who wanted to win over the mailman's valuable friendship.

---

7. *Figaro:* Character who typifies cunning dexterity and the ability of the servant classes to outwit their upperclass masters. He appears in the *Barber of Seville* and in *The Marriage of Figaro.*

8. *Auvergne:* A predominantly agricultural region in southwestern France. The inhabitants of this area, the *Auvergnats,* were known for their accent and their rustic nature.

"At nine-thirty, when I've finished my rounds. Where?"

"At the corner of Chaussée-D'Antin and Neuve-des-Maturins, at the inn called the Forty-fived Wine," said Laurent.

"Listen, friend," said the mailman when he met up with Laurent again, one hour after this meeting, "if your boss is in love with this girl, he's going to give himself an awful lot of work. I doubt you'll succeed in seeing her. I've been a mailman in Paris for twenty years now, and I've had the opportunity to see a lot of entry systems! But I can tell you, without fear of contradiction from my fellow workers, that there's no entry more mysterious than the Marquis de San Réal's. No one can get into that hotel without some password, and you can see the house was chosen deliberately for the way it's set between courtyard and garden so as to avoid sharing a wall with any other house. The doorman is an old Spaniard who never utters a word of French but really stares at people, just as intensely as Vidocq[9] would, to see if they are thieves or not. If this first doorman could be deceived by a lover, by a thief, or by you, without wishing to suggest any odious comparisons, well, when you came to the first room, which is closed by a glass door, you'd still meet a majordomo surrounded by lackeys, an old joker who's even wilder and more curmudgeonly than the doorman. If someone goes through the main entrance, my majordomo comes out, waits for him on the peristyle, and puts him through an interrogation as if he were a criminal. It happened to me, and I'm only a mailman. He took me for someone from the demitasse in disguise," he added, laughing at his malapropism. "As for the servants, don't hold out any hope of getting much from them: I think they're dumb, no one in the district has caught wind of their words. I don't know what wages they pay them to keep them from talking or drinking, the fact of the matter is they're unapproachable, either because they're afraid of being shot down, or because they have an enormous sum to lose if they're indiscreet. Even if your master is sufficiently in love with Miss Paquita Valdès to overcome all those obstacles, he certainly won't outwit Dona Concha Marialva, the duenna who accompanies her and who would put her under her skirts rather than leave her. Those two women give all the appearance of being sewn together."

"Well, worthy mailman," said Laurent, after having drunk some wine, "what you tell me there confirms what I've just learned. On my faith as an honest man, I thought people were joking. The fruit-seller across the street told me that during the night dogs were set loose in the gardens and their food hung from stakes, too high for them to reach. The result is, those damned animals think anyone who might go in is planning on eating it, and they'd tear them into shreds. You'll tell me it

---

9. *Vidocq:* Balzac based his character Vautrin on this complex criminal.

would be possible to throw them rissoles but they've been trained, so it seems, to eat nothing from anyone but the caretaker."

"Baron Nucingen's porter, whose garden borders that of the marquis, told me that was the case," said the mailman.

"Good, my master knows him," Laurent said to himself. "Do you know," he went on, eyeing the mailman, "that I belong to a master who's pretty special and if he got it into his head to kiss the soles of an empress, she'd just have to knuckle down and let him have his way? If he were to need you, as I hope he does, since he's a generous man, could we count on you?"

"You certainly can, M. Laurent, my name is Sparro. You spell it just like the bird—S-P-A-R-R-O, ro, Sparro."

"I see," said Laurent.

"I live at number 11, Rue Trois Frères, on the fifth floor," went on Sparro. "I have a wife and four kids. If what you need from me doesn't infringe on my conscience and my administrative duties—you know what I mean!—then I'm all yours."

"You're a good man," Laurent told him, shaking his hand.

"Paquita Valdès must be the mistress of the Marquis de San Réal, King Ferdinand's friend. He's an old Spanish corpse, eighty years old, and he's the only one capable of taking such precautions," said Henri when his valet told him the outcome of his research.

"Sir," said Laurent, "unless you go in by balloon, no one can get into that hotel."

"What a fop you are! Do I need to get into the hotel to have Paquita, given that Paquita wants to get out?"

"But, sir, you're forgetting the duenna."

"We'll lock her up for a few hours, that's what we'll do with your duenna."

"Well then, we'll have Paquita!" said Laurent, rubbing his hands together.

"Listen you scoundrel! I'll condemn you to entertaining Concha if you push your insolence so far as to talk like that about a woman before I've had her. Concentrate on dressing me, I'm going to go out."

For a moment Henri remained deep in joyful thought. It should be said in praise of women that he obtained all those whom he deigned desire. And what opinion could we have of a woman without a lover who could resist a young man armed with beauty, which is the body's soul, armed too with both moral strength and monetary fortune, the two things that alone have real power? But because he had triumphed so easily, de Marsay could not fail to grow bored with triumph, and as a result he'd been rather bored these past two years or so. When he dived into the depths of pleasure, he brought back more sand than pearls. So he'd reached the stage, as monarchs do, of begging fate to give him some difficulty to overcome, some undertaking that would make him exploit his inactive mental and physical powers. Although Paquita Valdès offered him the wonderful combination of perfections that hitherto he had enjoyed only separately, the attraction of passion was almost nonexistent in him. A constant satiety had weakened his heart's power to love. Like old men or those grown indifferent, he no longer felt any whims except those that were bizarre, no tastes except those that were destructive, no fantasies but those that, once satisfied, left no good memory in his heart. Where young men are concerned, love is the most beautiful of sentiments; it makes life blossom in the soul; through its sun-like power it ripens the loveliest inspirations and the greatest thoughts. In all matters, it is the first fruit that has the most delicious taste. Where mature men are concerned, love becomes a passion: strength leads to abuse. Where old men are concerned, love becomes vice: impotence leads to extremes. Henri was simultaneously old, mature, and young. To give him back the emotions of true love he, like Lovelace, needed a Clarissa Harlowe.[10] Without the magical reflection of this undiscoverable pearl, he could experience only passions sharpened by some Parisian vanity, bets taken with himself to lead a particular woman to a particular depth of corruption, or adventures that stimulated his curiosity. Laurent's information had just set an enormous price on the girl with the golden eyes. It would be a question of waging war on a secret enemy, one who seemed as dangerous as he was skillful, and to carry off the victory Henri would need all the powers he had at his disposal. He was going to play out that old comedy that will always be new, in which the main characters are an old man, a young girl, and a lover: Don Hijos, Paquita, Marsay. If Laurent was every bit as good as Figaro, the duenna still seemed beyond corruption. Thus, the play in life was more tightly constructed by chance than it had ever been by any playwright! But then, isn't chance a great genius anyway?

"We're going to have to play our cards just right," Henri said to himself.

"Well," Paul de Manerville said to him as he came in, "what's the score? I'm going to have lunch with you."

"Very well," said Henri, "it won't shock you if I get dressed in front of you?"

"You're joking!"

"We're taking such an English view of things these days that we could well end up as hypocritical and prudish as they are," Henri replied.

Laurent had placed so many utensils in front of his master, so many

---

10. Lovelace is the principal male character in Richardson's novel *Clarissa Harlowe* (1748). He is presented as the archetypal libertine, while Clarissa herself is the archetype of feminine purity.

different items of furniture, so many pretty things, that Paul could not refrain from saying, "But, this'll keep you occupied for two hours!"

"No!" replied Henri, "two and a half."

"Well, since there's just the two of us and we can tell each other everything, just explain to me why a man as superior as you are, for you are superior, should want to blow out of all proportion a self-importance that can't be at all natural. Why spend two and a half hours grooming yourself when all you have to do is spend fifteen minutes in a bath, run a comb through your hair, and get dressed? Come on, tell me what it's all about."

"I must be really fond of you, you great fat-head, to confide such high ideas in you," said the young man, whose feet at that moment were being brushed with a soft brush covered in English soap.

"But I've sworn the most sincere attachment to you," answered Paul de Manerville, "and I especially like you when I see how much more superior to me you are . . . "

"You must have noticed this, that is, if you are able to observe any moral fact," went on de Marsay without giving any other reply than a glance to Paul's declaration. "Do you know why women like conceited fops? You see, it's because conceited fops are the only men who take care of themselves. Well, if you take too much care of yourself, isn't that a sign that what you're caring for in yourself is someone else's property? The man who doesn't belong to himself is the very man that women long to have. Love is in essence a thief. I'm not talking about that excessive cleanliness that drives them wild. Have you ever found one who's conceived a passion for a man who doesn't care for his body, even if he's a remarkable man? If such a thing happens, we have to attribute it to the fantasies of a pregnant woman or those mad ideas that pop into everyone's head from time to time. On the other hand I've seen very remarkable men cut dead because they didn't take any care of themselves. A conceited fop who busies himself over his own body is preoccupied by stupid and small things. And what is a woman? A small thing, a conglomeration of stupidities. Isn't it true that you say two words at random and set her thinking for four hours? She's certain the fop will become preoccupied with her, because he's not occupied with great things. She'll never be neglected for glory, ambition, politics, art, those great whores who are a woman's rivals. What's more, fops have the courage to cover themselves in ridicule to please a woman. Of course her heart is full of rewards for a man made ridiculous out of love. Finally, a fop can be a fop only if he has some reason for being so. It's women who promote us to that rank. The fop is the colonel of love, he has lucky encounters, he has a regiment of women under his command. My dear, in Paris, everyone knows everything and a man can't be a fop for nothing. You who have only one woman and who are perhaps right to have only one, could you be a fop? You wouldn't even make yourself ridiculous, it would kill you. You'd become a walking prejudice, one of those men inescapably condemned to do one thing and one thing only. You would symbolize stupidity as M. de Lafayette[11] symbolizes America, M. de Talleyrand,[12] diplomacy, Désaugiers,[13] songs, M. de Ségur,[14] romances. If they move outside their genre no one believes in the value of what they're doing. That's what we're like in France! Always completely unjust. M. de Talleyrand may well be a great financier, M. de Lafayette may well be a tyrant, Désaugiers may be a good administrator. You could have forty women next year, and in public no one would believe that you'd had even a single one. That's how it comes about that foppery, my friend, is the sign of an indisputable dominance over the female of the species. A man who is loved by several women is regarded as having superior qualities. And then it's a question of who'll get him, the poor thing! But do you think it's nothing to have the right to arrive in a salon, to look at all those present from the top of one's cravat or through one's lorgnon, and to be allowed to despise the most superior of men if he's wearing a waistcoat that's behind the times? Laurent, you're hurting me! After dinner, Paul, we'll go to the Tuileries to see the adorable girl with the golden eyes."

When, having enjoyed an excellent meal, the two young men strode up and down the terrace of the Feuillantines and the grand Avenue of the Tuileries, they could find no trace of the sublime Paquita Valdès on whose behalf fifty of the most elegant young men in Paris, drenched in perfume, cravatted to the ears, wearing boots and spurs, were walking back and forth, flicking their whips, talking, laughing, and kicking up the devil of a din.

"No bite," said Henri, "but I've just had the most excellent idea in the world. That girl gets letters from London, we must bribe the mailman or get him drunk, open a letter, read it, naturally, slip in a little love note and seal it again. The old tyrant, the *crudel tiranno* no doubt knows the person who writes the letters that come from London and doesn't worry about them any more."

The following day, de Marsay came again to stroll in the sunlight on the terrace of the Feuillantines and saw Paquita Valdès there. Passion had already made her appear more lovely in his eyes. He fell madly in love with those eyes whose rays seemed just like those emitted by the sun and whose ardor perfectly encapsulated that perfect body in which everything was designed for pleasure. De Marsay burned to brush close

---

11. Marie Joseph Lafayette (1757–1834), general and politician who took part in the American War of Independence.

12. *Talleyrand:* Charles Maurice de Talleyrand-Périgord (1754–1838), brilliant and wily French politician and diplomat.

13. Antoine Désaugiers (1772–1827), French song writer and vaudeville performer.

14. *Ségur:* Possibly Philippe Paul Ségur (1780–1873), historian.

by the dress of that seductive girl when they met in their walks, but his attempts were always frustrated. At one point when he had gone past the duenna and Paquita in order to be on the right side of the girl with the golden eyes when he turned round again, Paquita, no less impatient, stepped forward quickly, and de Marsay felt her press his hand both so swiftly and so meaningfully, that he thought he had received an electric shock. In a second all the emotions of his youth welled up in his heart. When the two lovers looked at each other Paquita appeared ashamed, she dropped her eyes so as not to see Henri's eyes, but her glance slipped under her lids to look at the feet and shape of the one whom women before the Revolution used to call their conqueror.

"I'll definitely have that girl as my mistress," Henri said to himself.

Following her to the end of the terrace, in the direction of Place Louis XV, he caught sight of the old Marquis de San Réal, who was strolling along, propped up by his servant, walking with all the precaution of a bad-tempered old gout sufferer. Doña Concha, suspicious of Henri, made Paquita go between herself and the old man.

"Oh, you," Marsay muttered to himself as he sent a glance of scorn to the duenna, "if we can't get you to give in, will put you to sleep with a bit of opium. We know our mythology, and we know the fable about Argus."[15]

Before getting into her carriage, the girl with the golden eyes exchanged with her lover a few glances which left Henri in no doubts and a state of rapture. But the duenna caught sight of one of those glances and said a few sharp words to Paquita, who threw herself into the carriage with an expression of despair. For several days Paquita paid no more visits to the Tuileries. Laurent, who, on his master's orders, kept watch around the hotel, learned through the neighbors that neither the two women nor the old man had gone out since the day when the duenna had surprised a glance between Henri and the girl placed under her care. The very weak link that had existed between the two lovers was therefore already broken.

A few days later, without anyone knowing how he'd done it, de Marsay attained his ends. He'd acquired a seal and some wax exactly like the seal and the wax on the letters sent from London to Miss Valdès, he had paper identical with the paper her correspondent used, and all the tools and irons needed to stamp on them the official stamps of the French and English mail services.

"Dear Paquita, I won't attempt to paint for you in words the passion you have inspired in my heart. If I am happy enough to have you share it, let me tell you that I have found way of corresponding with you. My

---

15. According to Greek legend, the fabulous creature Argus had 100 eyes. Hera set him to watch over Io, of whom she was jealous. Hermes managed to charm him to sleep and slayed him. Hera then placed his eyes in the peacock's tail.

name is Adolphe de Gouges, and I live on Rue de l'Université, at number 54. If you are too closely watched to write to me, if you have neither paper nor pen, I will know by your silence that this is the case. So if tomorrow between eight in the morning and ten in the evening you have not thrown a letter over your garden wall into the garden of the Baron de Nucingen,[16] where someone will wait for it throughout the day, at ten in the morning on the following day a man who is entirely devoted to me will slip two vials over the wall for you from the end of a rope. Make sure you are walking by there at that time. One of the two vials will contain opium to put your Argus to sleep. You need only give her six drops of it. The other will contain ink. The ink vial is of cut glass, whereas the other is smooth. Both are flat enough for you to hide them in your corset. Everything I have done already to succeed in corresponding with you must tell you how much I love you. If you were to doubt that, I swear to you that to obtain a meeting of one hour with you I would give my entire life."

"And they believe such words, those poor creatures!" de Marsay said to himself, "but they're right to do so. What would we think of a woman who would not be seduced by a love letter accompanied by such well-laid plans?"

This letter was delivered by Monsieur Sparro, the mailman, on the following day, toward eight in the morning, and handed it to the doorman of San Réal's hotel.

To get closer to the field of battle, de Marsay had come to dine with Paul, who lived on Rue de la Pépinière. At two o'clock, at the moment when the two friends were laughingly telling each other about the discomfiture of a young man who had wanted to lead an elegant life without an established fortune, and while they wondered how it would all end, Henri's coachman came in search of his master at Paul's place and introduced to him a mysterious person who was insisting on talking to him. This person was a mulatto from whom Talma[17] could certainly have drawn inspiration for the role of Othello, had he ever met him. Never had an African face better expressed the grandeur in revenge, the swiftness of suspicion, the promptness in carrying out a thought, the strength of the Moor and his childlike failure to reflect. His dark eyes had the fixity of a raptor's eyes, and they were set, like those of a vulture, in a bluish membrane devoid of lashes. His brow, low and small, had a menacing air. Obviously, this man was under the yoke of a single, dominant thought. His sinewy arm did not belong to him. He was followed by a man whom all imaginations, from those that shiver in

---

16. The Baron de Nucingen is the great banker in Balzac's *Comédie humaine*.

17. François-Joseph Talma (1763–1826), a famous French tragic actor, did much to restore realism to the French stage after the excesses of tragedy in the late eighteenth century.

Greenland to those who sweat in New England, will paint according to this description: "He was an unhappy man." This expression will allow everyone to guess what he was like and to imagine him according to the individual ideas of each country. But who will imagine his white lined face, burned red at the extremities, and his long beard? Who will see his yellowy, string-like cravat, his gray shirt collar, his thoroughly worn hat, his greenish coat, his pitiable trousers, his wrinkled waistcoat, his false gold pin, his muddy boots, whose laces had trailed in the mud? Who will understand him in all the immensity of his present and past suffering? Who? Only the Parisian. A man who is wretched in Paris is an utterly wretched man, for he still feels some joy in discovering how completely wretched he is. The mulatto seemed to be one of Louis XI's executioners leading a man out to be hanged.

"Whoever fished those two knaves up for us?" asked Henri.

"Heavens above!" said Paul, "one of them sends shivers down my spine."

"Who are you, you there, the one that looks the most civilized of the two of you?" said Henri, looking at the unhappy man.

The mulatto kept his eyes fixed on the two young men, with the air of someone who understood nothing but who nevertheless attempted to guess something from the gestures and the movements of the lips.

"I'm a public scribe and an interpreter. I live at the Law Courts and my name is Poincet."

"Very well. What about him?" said Henri pointing to the mulatto.

"I do not know. He speaks only a kind of Spanish patois, and he's brought me here to try to reach an agreement with you."

The mulatto drew from his pocket the letter written by Henri to Paquita and gave it back to him, at which Henri threw it into the fire.

"Well, the plot begins to thicken," Henri said to himself. "Paul, leave us alone for a moment."

"I interpreted that letter for him," said Poincet as soon as they were alone. "When I'd done that, he went off somewhere or other. Then he came back to find me in order to bring me here. He's promised me two louis."

"What do you have to say to me, Chinaman?" asked Henri.

"I didn't put in the Chinaman," said the interpreter as he awaited the reply from the mulatto.

"He says," the interpreter went on after listening to the unknown man, "that tomorrow evening you must be on the Boulevard Montmartre, near the café. You'll see a carriage, in which you will mount saying to the man who opens the door for you the word *cortejo*, a Spanish word meaning lover," added Poincet as he sent a glance of congratulations to Henri.

"Very well!"

The mulatto was about to pay two louis, but de Marsay would not allow it and paid the interpreter himself. While he paid him, the mulatto added a few words.

"What does he say?"

"He's warning me that if I commit a single indiscreet act, he will strangle me. He's nice, but he really looks as if he could do it."

"I'm sure he can," replied Henri. "He would do it as easily as he says it."

"He adds that the person who sent him begs you, for your sake and for hers, to act with the greatest prudence, because if any daggers are raised at your heads they will plunge into your hearts and no human power will be able to protect you."

"He said that! All the better, it will make it more fun.—You can come in, Paul!" he shouted to his friend.

The mulatto who had not stopped watching Paquita Valdès's lover with magnetic attention, went away, followed by the interpreter.

"At last, a truly romantic adventure," Henri said to himself when Paul came back. "By taking part in a few, I've at last met in Paris an intrigue accompanied by serious circumstances and major dangers. Devil take it! How danger makes women bold! Hamstring a woman, attempt to go against her wishes, all you do is give her the right and the courage to overcome in a moment all the barriers that otherwise she would take years to leap! Sweet creature, let's see you leap. Die? Poor lass! Daggers? A woman's imagination! They all feel the need to make their little joke seem all the better. Moreover we'll give it some thought, Paquita! We'll give it some thought, dear child! Devil take me, but now I know that lovely girl, that masterpiece of nature is mine, the adventure has lost some of its savor."

Despite his flippant words, the young man had reappeared in Henri de Marsay. So as not to suffer too much in waiting for the following day, he had recourse to exorbitant pleasures: he gambled, dined, supped with friends; he drank like a fish, ate like a glutton, and won some ten or twelve thousand francs. He left the Rocher de Cancale at two in the morning, slept like a baby, woke up the next morning fresh and pink, and dressed to go to the Tuileries with the plan of riding on horseback after seeing Paquita in order to work up a good appetite for dinner, so that he could make the hours pass more quickly.

At the appointed hour, Henri was on the boulevard, saw the vehicle, and gave the password to a man who seemed to him to be the mulatto. When he heard the word, the man opened the door and quickly unfolded the steps. Henri was carried so swiftly through Paris, and his thoughts left him so little ability to pay attention to the streets through which he passed, that he did not know where the carriage stopped. The mulatto led him into a house in which the stairway was next to the coach door. The stairway was dark as was the landing on which Henri was obliged to wait for a while, during the time it took the mulatto to open the door of a damp, stinking, lightless apartment, whose rooms, barely lit by the candle his guide found in the antechamber, seemed to him empty and poorly furnished, like those of a house whose owners are traveling. He recognized the sensation he always felt when reading the novels of Ann Radcliffe,[18] in which the hero walks through cold rooms, rooms that are dark, uninhabited and in some gloomy and deserted spot. At last the mulatto opened a door. The state of the old furniture and the faded drapes with which this room was adorned made it appear like the salon of a brothel. There was the same pretention to elegance and the same conglomeration of things in poor taste, the same dust and dirt. On a couch covered in red Utrecht velvet, beside a smoking chimney, in which the fire had been buried under ashes, sat an old woman. She was fairly badly dressed, and wore on her head one of those turbans that English women invent when they reach a certain age and that would have enormous success in China, where the artist's highest ideal is monstrosity. This salon, the old woman, the cold hearth, everything would have frozen love, had Paquita not been there on a love seat. She was wearing a voluptuous peignoir, free to send wherever she wished the glance of her golden flame-like eyes, free to show her arched foot, free in all her luminous movements. This first meeting was what all first meetings are when they take place between passionate people who have swiftly leaped over the distances between them, and who desire each other ardently without, for all that, knowing each other. It's impossible to avoid a few harsh notes at first in such a situation, which is embarrassing up to the moment when the two souls reach the same pitch. If desire gives boldness to the man and predisposes him to let nothing deter him, on pain of being effeminate, the mistress, however violent her love may be, is frightened to find herself so swiftly at her goal and faced with the necessity of giving herself, something which for many women is like a fall into an abyss at the bottom of which they do not know what they may find. The woman's involuntary coldness contrasts with her admitted passion and of necessity reacts on the most amorous lover. These ideas which often float like vapors around the two souls create therefore a kind of fleeting illness. In the sweet journey that two beings undertake through the fine countries of love, this moment is like a heath that must be crossed, a heath without heather, alternatively hot and humid, full of burning sand, broken up by marshlands, a heath that leads to agreeable copses covered with roses, where love and its train of pleasures unfolds on carpets of fine greenery. Often the witty man finds himself inflicted with a stupid laugh as his sole reply to everything; his wit is, so to speak, frozen under the icy compression of

---

18. Ann Radcliffe (1764–1823), British novelist famous for her gothic novels, particularly *The Mysteries of Udolfo* and *The Italian*.

his desires. It would not be beyond the bounds of possibility for two creatures, each equally beautiful, witty and passionate, to begin by exchanging the most stupid of clichés until chance, a word, the trembling of a certain glance, the sharing of a spark, made them recognize the happy transition that would lead them into the flower-strewn pathway along which you don't walk but roll, and yet you manage not to fall. This state of mind is always in direct proportion to the violence of the feelings. Two creatures who love each other weakly will experience nothing like this. The effect of this crisis could also be compared to that produced by the ardor of a clear sky. At first glance, nature seems covered with a gauze veil, the azure sky seems black, the most intense light seems like darkness. In Henri, as in the Spanish girl, there was an equal violence, and that law of statistics, according to which two identical forces cancel each other out when they meet might also be true in the moral domain. And, too, the embarrassment of the moment was greatly increased by the presence of the old mummy. Love takes fright or delight in everything, for love everything has a meaning, everything predicts either happiness or gloom. This decrepit old woman was there, as if to offer a possible outcome, symbolizing the horrible fish tail with which the symbolic geniuses of Greece completed the bodies of the Chimaeras and Sirens, whose upper body is so seductive and so deceptive, as are all passions in their early moments. Although Henri was, while not a strong intellect, since such a description is always made ironically, nevertheless a man of extraordinary powers, a man as great as any man can be when he lacks faith, all these circumstances taken together affected him. Moreover the strongest men are naturally the most easily impressed and as a result the most superstitious, if, that is, you can give the name of superstition to the reaction of the initial moment, which doubtless offers a foretaste of the final outcome, which the individual perceives in causes that remain hidden to other eyes.

The Spanish girl took advantage of this moment of stupor to indulge herself in the ecstasy of that endless adoration that seizes a woman's heart when she truly loves and finds herself in the presence of an idol she has fruitlessly longed for. Her eyes were full of joy and happiness. Sparks leaped from them. She was under his charm and felt no fear in drinking in a happiness she had long dreamed of. She seemed to Henri at that moment so wonderfully lovely that all that phantasmagoria of rags, old age, worn red drapes, green mats lying before the arm chairs, the badly polished red tiles, and all that unhealthy, ailing luxury immediately disappeared. The salon was filled with light, and it was only through a cloud that he now saw the terrible harpy, immobile and silent on her red sofa, her yellow eyes betraying the servile sentiments that misfortune inspires or that vice engenders when you've fallen under its thrall, and it deadens you as it despotically spurs you on. Her eyes had the cold gleam of those of a caged tiger that knows itself to be powerless and is obliged to suppress its longing to destroy.

"Who is that woman?" Henri asked Paquita.

Paquita made no reply. She indicated that she knew no French and asked Henri if he spoke English. De Marsay repeated his question in English.

"She's the only woman I can trust, although she's sold me once already," Paquita said calmly. "My dear Adolphe, she's my mother, a slave bought in Georgia for her rare beauty, although little of that now remains. She speaks only her mother tongue."

The woman's attitude and her desire to guess, from her daughter's gestures and those of Henri, what was happening between them, suddenly became clear to the young man, put at ease by this explanation.

"Paquita," he said, "will we then never be free?"

"Never," she answered sadly. "What's more, we have very few days left for each other."

She lowered her eyes, looked at her hand, and counted with her right hand on the fingers of her left hand, thus showing Henri one of the finest pairs of hands he had ever seen.

"One, two, three . . . "

She counted up to twelve. "Yes, we have twelve days."

"And then?"

"Then," she said, lost in thought, like a weak woman faced with the executioner's ax and killed in advance by a fear that strips her of that splendid energy that nature seemed to have given her with the sole aim of increasing her pleasures and converting the most vulgar delights into endless poetry.

"Then," she repeated. Her eyes remained fixed on what seemed to be a far-away object, full of danger. "I don't know," she said.

This girl is mad, Henri said to himself, and he too fell into strange musing.

Paquita seemed engrossed in something other than him, like a woman torn equally between remorse and passion. Perhaps she held in her heart another love that she alternately forgot and remembered. In an instant, Henri was assailed by a thousand contradictory thoughts. For him, this girl had become a mystery. But when he contemplated her with the knowing attention of the man who has grown sated with pleasure, and hungers for new pleasures, like that Oriental king who demanded that a new pleasure be created for him, a horrible thirst that seizes hold of great souls, Henri recognized in Paquita the richest organization that Nature had delighted in creating for the purpose of love. Leaving aside the soul, what he imagined to be the workings of that machine would have terrified anyone but de Marsay; but he was fascinated by that rich harvest of promised pleasures, by that constant variety in happiness, that all men dream of finding and that every loving woman aims for, too. He was maddened by the thought that infinity could be rendered palpable and transported into the most excessive pleasures of a human being. He saw all this in Paquita more clearly than he had ever seen it, for she revealed herself to him quite contentedly, happy to be admired. De Marsay's admiration became a secret rage, and he revealed it completely by darting at her a glance that the Spanish girl understood, as if she were quite used to receiving such glances.

"If you were not to be mine alone, I would kill you!" he exclaimed.

When she heard this, Paquita covered her face with her hands and cried out naively, "Holy Mother of God, what have I got myself into?"

She stood up, flung herself on the red sofa, buried her head in the rags covering her mother's breast, and wept there. The old woman received her daughter without changing her immobility, without showing her any emotion. The mother possessed in the highest degree that gravity of wild tribes, that statuesque impassibility over which observation is powerless. Did she love her daughter, or did she not? No answer. Under that mask smoldered all human feelings, good and bad, and with such a creature anything might happen. Her glance moved slowly from her daughter's fine hair, which covered her like a mantilla, to Henri's face, watching it with a kind of inexpressible curiosity. She seemed to be wondering what magic charm had brought him there, what caprice of nature had created so seductive a man.

"These women are toying with me!" Henri said to himself.

At that instant, Paquita lifted her head, and sent him one of those glances that go straight to the soul and burn it. She seemed to him so lovely, that he swore that he would possess this treasure trove of beauty.

"Paquita, be mine!"

"Do you want to kill me?" she said fearfully, palpitating, disturbed, but brought back to him by some inexplicable force.

"Would I kill you!" he said with a smile.

Paquita cried out in terror, said a word to the old woman, who seized Henri's hand with an air of authority, then took her daughter's, looked at them for a long time, and gave them back with a horribly meaningful nod of the head.

"Be mine this evening, this instant, follow me, don't leave me, I want it, Paquita! Do you love me? Then come!"

At that moment he said to her a thousand meaningless words with the speed of a torrent leaping between rocks and repeated the same sound under a thousand different forms.

"It's the same voice!" said Paquita in melancholy tones, too softly for Henri to hear, "and . . . the same ardor," she added.

"Yes, yes," she said, abandoning herself to passion with an intensity nothing could express. "Yes, but not this evening. This evening,

Adolphe, I gave too little opium to Concha; she could wake up, and then I'd be lost. At this moment, the entire household thinks I'm asleep in my bedroom. Two days from now, be at the same spot, give the same password to the same man. He's my adopted father. Christemio adores me and would die for me in agonies without his torturers tearing from him a single word against me. Farewell," she said, seizing Henri around the waist and twining herself around him like a snake.

She thrust her body against his, brought his head to hers, offered him her lips, and took a kiss that made them both so giddy that de Marsay believed the earth was opening at his feet. Paquita cried out, "Go now!" in a voice that revealed all too clearly how little she was in control of herself. But she kept him, while she went on crying out to him, "Go now!" and led him slowly to the stairs.

There the mulatto, his white eyes flaming at the sight of Paquita, took the torch from his idol's hands, and led Henri to the street. He left the flame under the vault, opened the gate, put Henri back in the carriage, and set him down on the Boulevard des Italiens, all with a wonderful rapidity. The horses seemed to have hell itself in their bellies.

This scene was like a dream for de Marsay, but one of those dreams that, as they fade, leave in the soul a feeling of supernatural pleasure, a pleasure a man pursues for the rest of his life. A single kiss had been enough. No rendez-vous has taken place in a more decent way, none has been more chaste, even cold, none in a place the details of which were more horrible, before a more hideous goddess; for that mother had remained in Henri's imagination as something infernal, crouching, cadaverous, vicious, wildly ferocious, something the fancy of poets and painters had not yet divined. Indeed, never has a rendez-vous irritated the senses more, none has ever revealed bolder pleasures, none has been better able to make love leap from its center to spread like an aura around a man. It was dark, mysterious, gentle, tender, at once constricting and expansive, a coupling of the horrible and the celestial, of paradise and hell, and it went to de Marsay's head like wine. He was no longer himself, yet he was still great enough to be able to resist the intoxicating effects of pleasure.

In order for you to reach a full understanding of his behavior at the end of this story, it is essential that I explain how his soul had been enlarged at the age when young men ordinarily grow smaller, mingling with women or being too preoccupied by them. His soul had grown through a combination of secret circumstances that invested him with an immense unknown power. This young man held in his hand a scepter more powerful than that of modern kings, all of whom are held in check by laws when they attempt to carry out their slightest will. De Marsay exercised the autocratic power of the oriental despot. But this power, so stupidly employed in Asia by men little better than beasts, was multiplied tenfold by European intelligence and French wit, which is the sharpest of all intellectual instruments. Henri could do whatever he wanted in the interests of his pleasures and his vanities. This invisible action on the social world had clad him in a real but secret majesty, free of pomposity and tightly furled. He judged himself, not as Louis XIV might have judged himself, but as the proudest of the caliphs, the pharaohs, the most arrogant Xerxes[19] who believed himself of divine race, judged themselves when they were imitating God by veiling themselves from their subjects' sight, under the pretext that to look at them would lead to death. Thus, without the slightest remorse for the fact that he was both judge and interested party, de Marsay coldly condemned to death the man or woman who had seriously offended him. Although it was often pronounced almost lightheartedly, the decision was irrevocable. An error was a misfortune similar to that caused by lightning when it falls on a happy Parisian woman in her coach, instead of crushing the old coach driver who is taking her to her rendez-vous. Thus the deep, bitter joking that distinguished the conversation of this young man generally caused sufficient terror; no one felt any desire to push him. Women fall profoundly in love with those men who describe themselves as pashas and who seem to be accompanied by lions, or those who proclaim themselves torturers, and walk about surrounded by the machinery of terror. This gives these men a particular certainty in all their actions, a certainty of power, a pride in their gaze, a leonine consciousness that for women embodies the type of strength they all dream about. This was what de Marsay was like.

Happy now about his future, he became once again young and supple, and when he went to bed he had thoughts only of love. He dreamed of the girl with the golden eyes as passionate young people are wont to dream. There were monstrous images, weird, impalpable things full of light, images revealing invisible worlds. But they never fully revealed those worlds, for a veil came between them and the viewer, and changed the optical conditions. The following day and the day after, he disappeared without anyone finding any trace of him. His power was his own only under certain conditions, and so it came to pass that during those two days he was a simple soldier in the service of the devil to whom he owed his talismanic existence.[20] But at the stated hour in the evening, on the boulevard, he waited for the carriage, which was not late in coming. The mulatto went up to Henri to say to him, in French, a sentence he seemed to have learned by heart: " 'If you want to come,' she told me, 'you must agree to let me cover your eyes.' "

And Christemio showed him a white silk scarf.

"No!" said Henri, whose omnipotence suddenly rebelled.

---

19. *Xerxes:* King of Persia from 486 to 465 B.C. A tyrannical ruler and compulsive builder.
20. *the devil:* This person is Ferragus, the leader of the criminal gang to which Henri belongs.

And he moved as if to climb into the carriage. At a gesture of the mulatto, the carriage departed.

"Yes!" shouted de Marsay, enraged at the thought of losing the happiness he had promised himself. Moreover, he saw how impossible it was to effect a compromise with a slave whose obedience was as absolute as that of an executioner. Then, too, what was the point of venting his rage on this passive instrument?

The mulatto whistled, the carriage returned. Henri leaped swiftly aboard. Already a few rubberneckers were clustering stupidly on the boulevard. Henri was strong and wanted to play a trick on the mulatto. When the carriage set off at a fast trot, he seized the mulatto's hands in order to overpower him and retain the exercise of his faculties, so that he could find out where they were going. The attempt was in vain. The mulatto's eyes sparked in the gloom. The man howled with fury, broke free, and flung de Marsay back with an iron fist, nailing him, so to speak, to the back of the carriage. Then with his free hand he pulled out a triangular dagger, and let out a piercing whistle. The coach driver heard the whistle and stopped. Henri was unarmed and was forced to submit. He stretched his head toward the scarf. This submissive gesture calmed Christemio, who bound his eyes with a respect and care that revealed a kind of veneration for the man loved by his own idol. But, before taking this precaution, he defiantly returned his dagger to a side pocket and buttoned his jacket up to the chin.

"This Chinaman would've killed me!" de Marsay said to himself.

The carriage was again moving rapidly forward. There remained only one resource for a young man who knew Paris as well as Henri did. To discover where he was going, all he had to do was concentrate and count, by the number of gutters they crossed, the streets they passed as they went along the boulevards, so long as the carriage continued to move straight ahead. He could thus recognize the side street down which the carriage headed on its way either to the Seine or to the heights of Montmartre and guess the name or position of the street where his guide stopped. But the violent emotion caused by his struggle, the fury engendered by his compromised dignity, the thoughts of revenge in which he indulged, the suppositions that came into his mind as a result of the careful attention this mysterious girl had taken in bringing him to her, all this prevented him having the kind of attention—common among blind men—he would have needed to concentrate his intelligence, and all this likewise destroyed the perfect insight of memory. The journey lasted half an hour. When the carriage came to a halt, it was no longer on a street. The mulatto and the coach driver seized Henri bodily, lifted him, put him in a kind of litter, and carried him across a garden in which he smelled flowers and the special odor of trees and vegetation. The silence that reigned there was so deep that he could distinguish the noise made by a few drops of water as they fell from the wet leaves. The two men carried him into a stairway, made him get up, and, guiding him with their hands, led him through several rooms. Then they left him in a room whose atmosphere was heavy with perfume and where he felt a thick carpet under his feet. A woman's hand pushed him onto the divan and undid the blindfold. Henri saw Paquita before him, but Paquita in all the glory of her voluptuous womanhood.

The half of the bedroom in which Henri found himself described a circular line, soft and gracious and in stark contrast to the other half, which was perfectly square. In the middle of the square section gleamed a chimneypiece in white and gold marble. He had come in by a side door hidden behind a rich tapestry and opposite a window. The semicircle was adorned with a real Turkish divan, that is to say, a mattress placed on the floor, but a mattress as big as a bed, a divan some fifty feet around, in white cashmere, adorned with black and flaming red silk pompons in a diamond pattern. The headboard of this immense bed rose several inches above the numerous cushions that enriched it yet further with their tasteful ornamentations. The bedroom was hung in red fabric, on which was placed an Indian muslin, fluted like a Corinthian column, with folds that were alternately convex and concave, and bound at the top and bottom by a band of red fabric with black arabesques. Under the muslin, the red turned to pink, the color of love, which was repeated in the window curtains. These were in Indian muslin, lined with pink taffeta and adorned with red fringes mingled with black. Six vermillion brackets, each of which supported two candles, were attached to the wall and placed at equal distances to illuminate the divan. The ceiling, in the middle of which hung a chandelier in dull silver, gleamed white, and the cornice was gilded. The carpet resembled an Eastern shawl with oriental designs evocative of Persian poetry, on which slave hands must have worked. The furniture was covered in white cashmere, adorned by black and red designs. The clock, the candelabras, everything was in white and gold marble. The only table there had a cashmere tablecloth. Elegant flower pots contained roses of all the different varieties, with flowers that were either white or red. In a word, the slightest detail seemed to have been the object of loving care. Never had riches so coquettishly hidden themselves away to become elegance, to express grace, to inspire pleasure. Everything there would have warmed the coldest individual. The glimmering light from the hangings, whose color changed according to the direction of your gaze, becoming either completely white or utterly pink, harmonized with the effect of light diffused by the diaphanous folds of the muslin, producing a cloudy appearance. Our souls feel some strange attachment for white, love delights in red, and gold flatters the passions, having the power to make all our fancies come true. Thus everything vague and mysterious in man himself, all the unexplained affinities were caressed in their involuntary sympathies. There was in this perfect harmony a concert of colors to which the soul replied with sensual, indeterminate, floating ideas.

Surrounded by a vaporous atmosphere, heavy with exquisite perfumes, Paquita, wearing a white peignoir, with her feet bare, and with orange blossoms in her black hair, appeared kneeling before Henri, adoring him as if he were the god of this temple to which he had deigned to come. Although de Marsay was used to seeing all the refinement of Parisian luxury, he was surprised at the sight of this shell, which resembled the conch shell in which Venus was born. Either through the contrast between the shadows from which he had come and the light that now bathed his soul, or through a rapidly performed comparison between this scene and that of the first meeting, he experienced one of those delicate sensations that true poetry provides. When he saw in her bower this girl who had been brought into being by a fairy's wand, this girl with her warm-colored complexion, her soft skin which was turned a light gold by the reflections from the red colors and by the effusion of some vapor of love which made it gleam as if she had received the rays of lights and colors, his rage, his desires for revenge, his wounded vanity, all disappeared. Like an eagle swooping on its prey, he seized her round the waist, sat her on his lap and felt with an unspeakable intoxication the pleasurable pressure of her plumply developed beauty sweetly enveloping him.

"Come, Paquita!" he whispered.

"Speak up! You can speak without fear," she said to him. "This retreat has been built for the purposes of love. No sound escapes from it, because its ambitious architecture has been planned to retain the accents and music of the beloved voice. However loud the cries, they cannot be heard outside these walls. Someone could be killed in here, and their pleas would be just as much in vain as if they had been made in the middle of the great desert."

"But who ever is it who has understood jealousy and its needs so well?"

"Never ask me about that," she answered, as she undid the young man's cravat, with an incredibly gentle gesture, no doubt so that she could look at his throat.

"Yes, there's the throat I love so much!" she said. "Do you want to give me pleasure?"

This question, rendered almost lascivious by its intonation, drew de Marsay from the reverie into which he had been plunged by Paquita's despotic reply, forbidding him to make any attempt to discover the unknown being who floated over them like a shadow.

"And if I insist on knowing who reigns here?"

Paquita looked at him, trembling.

"So it isn't me," he said standing up and flinging the girl aside, so that she fell back on her head. "I want to be the only one, wherever I am."

"The resemblance is striking, it's striking," said the poor slave, terrorized.

"Who do you take me for then? Will you answer?"

Paquita stood up gently, her eyes swimming with tears, and went in search of a dagger which she took from one of the two ebony chests and offered to Henri with a submissive gesture that would have melted a tiger's heart.

"Give me a feast of the sort men give when they love," she said, "and while I sleep, kill me, for I cannot answer you. Listen: I'm like a poor animal attached to a stake; I'm amazed that I've been able to throw a bridge over the abyss that separates us. Fill me with joy and then kill me. Oh, no, no," she said, joining her hands together, "don't kill me! I love life! Life is so beautiful for me! If I'm a slave, I'm also a queen. I could deceive you with words, tell you I love no one but you, prove it to you, take advantage of my temporary power to tell you: 'Take me as one enjoys the scent of a garden one walks past in the palace of a king.' Then, having displayed a woman's cunning eloquence and lifted you on the wings of pleasure, after having satisfied my thirst, I could have you thrown into a well where no one would find you. It's a well that was constructed in order to satisfy the needs of revenge without having to fear the revenge of the law, a well full of lime which would burst into fire to consume you without a single scrap of you remaining to be found. You'd remain in my heart, mine for ever."

Henri looked at the girl without trembling, and this fearless gaze filled her with joy.

"No, I won't do it! You haven't fallen into a trap but into the heart of a woman who loves you, and it is I who will be thrown into the well."

"All this seems extremely strange to me," de Marsay told her as he looked at her. "But you strike me as a good young woman, with a weird nature. You are, on my faith as an honest man, a living riddle that seems very hard to guess."

Paquita understood not a word the young man was saying; she looked at him sweetly, opening eyes that could never be stupid since they contained so much pleasure.

"Listen, my darling," she said, returning to her first thought, "do you want to give me pleasure?"

"I'll do everything you want me to, and even things you don't want me to do," answered de Marsay with a laugh as he rediscovered his foppish ease, resolving to let himself drift with his good luck without looking either behind or ahead. And it may also be that he counted on his power and his ability as a man used to good fortune in love to be able to dominate this girl a few hours later and extract all her secrets from her.

"Well then," she said to him, "let me dress you to my liking."

"Go ahead," said Henri.

Paquita joyously went and took from one of the two chests a dress of red velvet in which she clothed de Marsay, then she put on his head a woman's bonnet and wrapped a shawl around him. In abandoning herself to these follies, performed with a childlike innocence, she laughed a convulsive laugh, and looked like a bird beating its wings; but she said nothing more than that.

If it's impossible to paint the indescribable delights of these two lovely creatures that the heavens had made on a day of joy, it is perhaps necessary to find a metaphysical translation for the extraordinary and almost fantastic impressions experienced by the young man. What men who find themselves in de Marsay's social position, and who live as he lived, can best recognize is a girl's innocence. But, and this is strange, if the girl with the golden eyes was a virgin, she was certainly not innocent. This very bizarre union of the mysterious and the real, of shadow and light, of the horrible and the beautiful, of pleasure and danger, of paradise and hell—which we have already encountered in this adventure—continued in all aspects of the capricious and sublime creature de Marsay enjoyed. All the most knowledgeable aspects of the most refined pleasure, all that Henri had ever learned about that poetry of the senses called love, was exceeded by the treasures unfolded by this girl, whose gleaming eyes contained not the slightest lie in connection with all the promises they made. She was an oriental poem, in which gleamed the sun that Saadi[21] and Hafiz[22] placed in their capering verses. Yet neither the rhythm of Saadi nor that of Pindar[23] could have expressed the ecstasy and the confusion which seized this delicious girl when Henri brought an end to the error in which a hand of iron had forced her to live.

"I'm dead!" she said, "I'm dead! Adolphe, take me to the ends of the earth, to an island where no one will find us. Make sure our flight leaves not the slightest trace! We would be followed into hell itself. God! It's daybreak. You must escape! Will I ever see you again? Yes, tomorrow, I want to see you again tomorrow, even if obtaining that happiness meant assassinating all my servants. We'll meet again tomorrow."

She seized him in her arms with an embrace that contained a mortal terror. Then she pushed a button which appeared to be connected to a bell and begged de Marsay to allow himself to be blindfolded.

"And if I refused, or if I wanted to stay here?"

"You'd be causing my death all the more swiftly," she said, "since now it's certain I'll die for you."

---

21. *Saadi:* Sa'di of Shirâz (c.1215–1292?), Persian poet and popular moralist.

22. *Hafiz:* Hâfiz (1326?–1390), the greatest lyric poet of Persia.

23. Pindar (518–438 B.C.) was a Greek choral lyric poet famed for his depiction of races and athletic games.

Henri allowed himself to be led away. There is, in the man who has just been filled with pleasure, a slide into forgetfulness, a certain ingratitude, a longing for freedom, a fancy to go and take a walk, an element of scorn and perhaps even disgust for his idol—in a word, inexplicable feelings that make him treacherous and ignoble. It was no doubt the sure knowledge of that affection which is vague but really exists in souls that are neither illuminated by celestial light nor scented with holy balm, that brings us that pertinacity of feelings that dictated to Rousseau the adventures of Lord Edward and that bring the letters in *La Nouvelle Héloïse* to an end.[24] If Rousseau obviously drew inspiration from Richardson's works, he moved away from them in countless details that make his magnificent monument original. He recommended it to posterity through great ideas which are difficult to extract through analysis when, in your youth, you read this book with the aim of discovering in it the warm portrayal of the most physical of our feelings, whereas serious writers, philosophical writers use images only when they result from or are demanded by a great thought. And the adventures of Lord Edward constitute one of the most Europeanly delicate ideas in the whole work.

Henri, then, found himself under the sway of that vague sentiment that true love never feels. He needed, so to speak, the persuasive decree of comparisons and the irresistible attraction of memories to bring him back to a woman. True love reigns above all in the memory. Can a woman who has failed to engrave her memory in a man's soul, either by abundant pleasure or by strength of sentiment, ever be loved? Unbeknownst to Henri, Paquita had established herself in his memory by both means. But at that moment, abandoning himself entirely to the weariness of joy, that delicious melancholy of the body, he could scarcely analyze his own heart by seizing again on his lips the taste of the most intense pleasures that had yet taken root there. He found himself on the boulevard Montmartre at daybreak, glanced stupidly at the horses as they galloped off, drew two cigars from his pocket, lit one from the lantern of a woman selling brandy and coffee to the workers, street children, and market gardeners, indeed all that Parisian population whose life begins before daybreak. Then he strolled off, smoking his cigar, his hands in his trouser pockets, revealing a truly dishonorable carelessness.

"What an excellent thing a cigar is! Now there's something a man will never grow tired of!"

At that moment, the girl with the golden eyes, on whom all the elegant youth of Paris doted, scarcely commanded a second thought from him. The idea of death, that the lovely creature who recalled the houris[25] of Asia through her mother, Europe through her education, and the

---

24. *La Nouvelle Héloïse*: Jean-Jacques Rousseau's famous epistolary novel of love and duty.
25. *Houris:* The black-eyed damsels of the Islamic paradise.

tropics through her birth, had expressed amid all the pleasures she was experiencing, and the fear which had several times darkened her brow seemed to him to be one of those deceptions through which all women attempt to make themselves interesting.

She is from Havana, the most Spanish country in the entire New World; she preferred, therefore, to play at being terrified rather than complaining to me about her sufferings, her difficulties, her duties, or flirting with me, as Parisian women do. I swear on her golden eyes that I really feel I need a sleep.

He saw a cab for hire, standing beside Frascati and waiting for any gamblers that might come out. He roused himself, took the cab home, went to bed, and fell asleep with the sleep of the unjust, a sleep which, through a bizarre twist of fate that no songwriter has yet exploited, is just as deep as the sleep of the innocent. Perhaps this is the result of that proverbial axiom: if you go too far East you end up in the West.

Toward midday, de Marsay stretched his arms as he woke up, and felt himself attacked by one of those canine hungers that all old soldiers can remember experiencing the day after a victory. So he was pleased to see Paul de Manerville standing before him, for nothing is more agreeable under such circumstances than eating with friends.

"Well," his friend said to him, "we all thought you must have been locked away for the past ten days with the girl with the golden eyes."

"The girl with the golden eyes! But I no longer give her the slightest thought. On my word, I've got other cats to skin."

"Ah! You're being discreet."

"Why not?" laughed de Marsay. "My friend, discretion is the cleverest of all calculations. Listen . . . But no, I'm not going to tell you anything. You never tell me anything, and I'm not willing simply to give away the treasures of my diplomacy at a complete loss. Life is a river that allows one to carry out a trade. By all that is most sacred on earth, by cigars, I am no professor of social economics brought down to the level of fools. Let's have lunch. It's less expensive to buy you a tuna omelette than to waste my gray matter on you."

"You're counting the pennies where your friends are concerned?"

"My friend," said Henri, who could rarely refrain from ironic comments, "as you may, just like anyone else, need discretion at some stage or other, and as I'm very fond of you . . . Yes, indeed I am! On my word of honor, if all you needed was a thousand franc note to keep you from blowing your brains out, you'd find it here, for we haven't yet mortgaged anything on that, have we Paul? If you were to duel tomorrow, I'd measure out the distances and load the pistols, just to be sure you'd be killed according to the rules. And lastly, if anyone other than me should take it into their head to speak ill of you behind your back, they'd have to deal with a pretty rough gentleman who happens to live in my skin. That's what I call a friendship that stands up to all tests. Well, when you need discretion, my boy, you should know there are two kinds of discretion: active and negative. Negative discretion is the kind chosen by fools, who use silence, negation, a withdrawn air, the discretion of closed doors, a real powerlessness! Active discretion works by affirmation. If, this evening, at the Circle, I were to say: 'On a gentleman's honor, the girl with the golden eyes isn't worth what she costs me,' everyone would exclaim as soon as I left: 'Did you hear that ass try to make us believe he'd already had the girl with the golden eyes? That's how he wants to get rid of his rivals. Not exactly a clumsy device.' But it's a dangerous and vulgar ruse. However enormous the stupidity that we let slip, there are always dunces who can believe in it. The best of discretions is the one that clever women use when they want to pull the wool over their husbands' eyes. It consists in compromising a woman we don't care about, or whom we don't love, or don't possess, in order to preserve the honor of the woman we love enough to respect. This is what I call the screen woman.—Ah, here's Laurent. What have you got for us?"

"Oysters from Ostend, my Lord . . . "

"One day, Paul, you'll know how amusing it is to deceive the world by hiding the secret of your affections from it. I get an immense kick out of escaping from the stupid jurisdiction of the masses, who never know either what they want or what others are making them want, who take the means for the result, who in turn love and condemn, construct and demolish! What a joy it is to impose emotions on the masses and have nothing imposed on oneself, to dominate them and never obey them! If anything can make you proud, isn't it the power you've acquired by yourself, a power of which you are the cause, the effect, the principal, and the result! Well, no one knows whom I love, or what I want. It may be known whom I have loved and what I would have wanted, as one knows the plots of plays that have run their course. But letting someone see what cards I'm holding at present. . . . That would be weakness and dupery. I know nothing more despicable than strength deceived by skill. I'm initiating myself with a laugh into the task of an ambassador, that is, if diplomacy is as hard as life is! I doubt that it is. Are you ambitious? Do you want to make something of yourself?"

"Oh, Henri, you're mocking me. As if I weren't mediocre enough to succeed in everything."

"Good, Paul. If you go on mocking yourself, you'll soon be able to mock everyone else."

After they had lunched, while they were smoking de Marsay's cigars, he began to see the events of the night in a strange light. As with many great minds, his perspicacity wasn't spontaneous, and he didn't see the depths of things immediately. As in all natures endowed with the faculty of living intensely in the present, of squeezing the juice from it and devouring it, his second judgement needed a sort of sleep in order to identify itself with the causes. Cardinal Richelieu[26] was just like that, which does not mean that he lacked the gift of foresight needed to conceive great things. De Marsay found himself in exactly that situation, but at first he used his powers only to further his leisure, and became one of the deepest of our current politicians only when he had steeped himself in the pleasures all young men think of first when they have money and power. A man is toughened in such a school; he uses a woman up so that she may not use him up. So at that moment, de Marsay realized he had been the plaything of the girl with the golden eyes, once he saw that night in its entirety, a night whose pleasures had begun as a trickle and ended by pouring out in torrents. Only then was he able to read that page whose effects had been so glittering, only then could he guess the hidden meanings. The purely physical innocence of Paquita, the astonishment of her joy, a few initially obscure words that were now clear, words that had burst from her in the midst of her pleasure, everything revealed to him that he had posed for another person. As social corruption was unknown to him, and as he professed a complete indifference toward all caprices and believed them justified by the very fact that they were capable of achieving satisfaction, he was not horrified by vice; he knew it as one knows a friend, but he was hurt to find he had been vice's fodder. If his presumptions were correct, he had been outraged in the very depths of his being. The mere suspicion of this threw him into a fury, he gave the roar of a tiger mocked by a gazelle, the cry of a tiger combining with the strength of the animal the intelligence of a demon.

"Whatever's the matter?" asked Paul.

"Nothing's the matter!"

"If you had something against me, I wouldn't want you to answer with such an expression, or we'd certainly have to fight the next morning."

"I no longer fight duels," said de Marsay.

"That seems to me even more tragic. So you're assassinating people instead?"

"That's a travesty of words. I execute."

"My dear friend," said Paul, "your jokes are very black this morning."

"What can you expect? Pleasure leads to ferocity. Why? I don't know, and I'm not curious enough to want to seek out the cause.— These cigars are excellent. Give your friend a little tea.—You know, Paul, the life I lead is the life of a beast. Soon I really must choose some sort of future for myself, use my strength for something that's worth living for. Life is a strange comedy. I'm frightened by the inconsequence of our social order, and I laugh at it. The government cuts off the head of

---

26. *Richelieu:* Armand Jean du Plessis, cardinal de Richelieu (1585–1642), powerful politician during the reign of Louis XIII.

a poor devil who's killed a man and licenses creatures who dispatch, medically speaking, a dozen young men each winter. Morality has no power against a dozen vices that destroy society and that nothing can punish. Another cup? On my honor, man is a clown dancing on a precipice. They talk to us about the immorality of *Dangerous Liaisons*[27] and of some other book that has the name of a chamber maid, but there's a horrible, filthy, terrifying, corrupting book that's always open, that will never be closed, the great book of the world, and that's leaving aside another book a thousand times more dangerous, which consists of everything that men whisper in each other's ears, or women discuss behind their fans, each evening, during the ball."

"Henri, something really extraordinary is going on in your mind, that's for sure, and it's perfectly obvious despite your active discretion."

"Yes! Look, I've got to get through the time between now and evening. Let's go to the gambling parlors. Perhaps I'll be lucky enough to lose."

De Marsay got up, took a handful of bank notes, rolled them into his cigar box, dressed, and took advantage of Paul's carriage to go to the Foreigners' Club, where he spent the time until dinner in those alternating bursts of losing and winning that are the last resource of strong constitutions, when they have to exercise that strength in the void. That evening he went to the boulevard as arranged and complacently allowed his eyes to be covered with the blindfold. Then with that powerful willpower that only truly strong men have the ability to summon, he brought all his attention to bear on guessing what streets the carriage was following. He was more or less certain of being carried to Rue Saint Lazare, and of coming to a stop at the little garden gate of the San Réal hotel. When he went through that gate, as had happened the first time, and was placed again on the stretcher no doubt carried by the mulatto and the coach-driver, he understood from the crunch of sand under their feet, why such minute precautions were taken. Had he been free, or had he walked, he could have plucked a branch from a shrub, or have examined the kind of sand that would have clung to his boots, whereas, transported so to say aerially into an inaccessible hotel, his piece of good luck would once again be what it had been before, a dream. But it is man's misfortune that he can do only that which is imperfect, either for good or for evil. All his intellectual and physical productions are stamped with the mark of destruction. It had rained lightly, and the ground was damp. During the night, certain odors of plants are much stronger than during the day, and Henri could thus smell the perfume of mignonette along the path down which he was being carried. That clue ought to shed light in the inquiries he

---

27. *Dangerous Liaisons*: Choderlos de Laclos's powerful study of sexual power-play had been published in 1782.

promised himself he would make in order to recognize the hotel in which Paquita's bedroom was situated. He also studied the detours his bearers took inside the house and believed he could remember them. As on the previous evening, he found himself on the ottoman, before Paquita, who undid his blindfold. But he saw her pale and changed. She had wept. Kneeling like an angel in prayer, but like a sad and deeply melancholy angel, the poor girl no longer resembled the curious, impatient, bounding creature who had taken de Marsay on her wings to carry him to the seventh heaven of love. There was something so true in this despair veiled in pleasure that the terrible de Marsay felt within himself a sense of admiration for this new masterpiece of nature, and briefly forgot the main interest of this meeting.

"But what's the matter, my Paquita?"

"My dear," she said, "take me away, this very night, can you? Hurl me to some point where no one can say on seeing me, 'That's Paquita,' where no one answers, 'There's a girl here with a golden gaze and long hair.' There I'll give you the kind of pleasures you want to receive from me. Then, when you no longer love me, you can leave me, I won't complain, I won't say anything. Leaving me shouldn't cause you any remorse, for one day spent with you, a single day during which I'll have looked at you, will have been worth an entire lifetime for me. But if I stay here, I'm lost."

"I can't leave Paris, my sweet," Henri replied. "I don't belong to myself, but am bound by oath to the fate of several people who are as devoted to me, as I to them.[28] But I can create for you in Paris a safe place that no man's power can reach."

"No," she said, "you're forgetting the power of a woman."

Never had a sentence pronounced by a human voice expressed a more complete terror.

"Who could ever reach you if I stood between you and the world?"

"Poison!" she answered. "Already Doña Concha is suspicious of you. And," she went on, with tears gleaming down her cheeks, "it's perfectly easy to see I'm no longer the girl I used to be. Well, if you abandon me to the fury of a monster that will devour me, let your holy will be done! But come, give me all life's pleasures in our love. Moreover, I'll beg, I'll weep, I'll scream, I'll defend myself, and perhaps I may even escape."

"But who is it that you'll implore?"

"Hush!" Paquita answered. "If I'm pardoned it may well be as a result of my discretion."

"Give me my dress," Henri pleaded, insidiously.

"No, no," she replied violently, "stay what you are, one of those angels I was taught to hate, and in whom I saw only monsters, whereas you

---

28. *several people as devoted to me as I to them:* This is the gang of thirteen that plays an important role in Balzac's series of novels.

are the most beautiful thing under the sky," she added, caressing Henri's hair. "You don't know how stupid I am? I have learned nothing. From the age of twelve I've been shut away without seeing anyone. I don't know how to read or write. I speak only English and Spanish."

"How is it that you receive letters from London?"

"My letters! Look, here they are!" she said, taking a few pieces of paper from a long Japanese vase.

She handed de Marsay letters in which the young man saw to his surprise strange figures that resembled those of a puzzle, drawn in blood, expressing sentences full of passion.

"But," he exclaimed, as he admired these hieroglyphs created by a skillful jealousy, "are you under the power of a genie from hell, then?"

"From hell," she repeated.

"But how then were you able to go out . . . "

"Ha!" she answered, "that's what led to my downfall. I put Doña Concha in the position of having to decide between the fear of immediate death and future anger. I was devilishly curious, I wanted to break the bronze circle that had been drawn between me and the rest of creation. I wanted to see what young men were like, for the only men I know are Christemio and the marquis. Our coach driver and the valet that accompanies us are old men . . . "

"But you haven't always been locked away? For your health's sake you must have . . . "

"Oh!" she went on, "we used to go for walks, but that was at night and in the country, beside the Seine far from other people."

"Aren't you proud of being loved like that?"

"Not any more," she answered. "Although it's a very full life, a life spent hiding is merely a life of shadows in comparison with the light."

"What do you call light?"

"You, my lovely Adolphe! You, for whom I would give my life. All the passionate words spoken to me and inspired by me, I feel them all for you! At certain moments I understood nothing of existence, but now I know how much we love each other, and up to now I was loved, but I did not love. I'll leave everything for your sake, take me away. If you want, take me as one takes a toy, but let me stay with you until you break me."

"You won't have any regrets?"

"Not a single one!" she said, letting him read her eyes, whose golden color stayed pure and clear.

"Am I the one she loves best?" Henri said to himself, for if he could glimpse the truth of all this, he found himself disposed to forgive the offense in favor of so naive a love. "I'll find out," he said to himself.

If Paquita owed him no account of the past, the slightest memory was nevertheless a crime in his eyes. He therefore had the grim strength to keep his thoughts to himself, to judge his mistress, to study her while he abandoned himself to the most overwhelming pleasures that a Peri[29] descended from the skies had ever found for her beloved. Paquita seemed to have been created for love. Nature seemed to have taken special care in forming her. From one night to the next, her woman's genius had made the most rapid progress. Whatever the young man's power, however careless he might have been where pleasure was concerned, and despite being fully satisfied the night before, he found in the girl with the golden eyes that seraglio that the loving woman is able to create and that a man never renounces. Paquita responded to that passion for the infinite that all men feel if they are truly great, a mysterious passion so dramatically expressed in Faust and so poetically translated in Manfred,[30] and that drove Don Juan to rummage in women's hearts in the hope of finding there that boundless thought which so many specter hunters seek, that intellectuals think they perceive in knowledge and that the mystics find in God alone. The hope of finally having the ideal being with whom one could constantly struggle while never growing weary delighted de Marsay, who for the first time in a long while opened his heart. His nerves relaxed, his coldness melted in the atmosphere of this burning soul, his trenchant doctrines faded away, and happiness colored his existence as this bedroom was colored in white and pink. When he felt the spur of a higher pleasure, he was drawn beyond the limits in which he had hitherto always contained his passions. He did not want to be outstripped by this girl, who had been formed in advance for the needs of the soul by a love which, to some extent, was artificial. In that vanity that urges a man to remain the victor in all matters, he found the strength he needed to dominate the girl. But thrown beyond the line where the soul remains her own mistress, he lost himself in that delicious limbo that the vulgar so stupidly call the space of the imagination. He was tender, gentle, and communicative. He drove Paquita all but mad.

"Why don't we go to Sorrento, to Nice, to Chiavari, and spend all our lives like this? Would you like that?" he said to Paquita in a penetrating voice.

"Do I really ever need to say to me 'Would you like that?' " she exclaimed. "Do I have a will? If I have an existence outside you it is only in order to give you pleasure. If you want to choose a hiding place that is worthy of us, Asia is the only country where love can spread its wings . . ."

"You're right," went on Henri. "Let's go to India, where it is always spring, where the earth bears only flowers, where anyone can employ

---

29. *peri:* Originally a beautiful but malevolent sprite of Persian myth, but the word has come to be used of any lovely young woman.

30. *Manfred:* Central character of Byron's dramatic poem of this name (1817), archetype of the doomed, arrogant Romantic hero.

all the pomp and circumstance of sovereigns, without people criticizing, as happens in those stupid countries where the main goal is to achieve the dull dream of equality. Let's go to the country where you live among crowds of slaves, where the sun always shines on a place that stays white, where perfumes are scattered through the air, where the birds sing of love, and where those who can no longer love, die."

"And where lovers die together!" said Paquita. "But let's not wait until tomorrow to go: let's leave now, this instant; let's take Christemio with us."

"Indeed, pleasure is life's finest end. Let's go to Asia, but in order to leave, child, we need money, lots of money, and to get money one has to put one's affairs in order."

She understood nothing of that.

"Money? But we've piles this high of it here," she said, holding her hand up.

"That money isn't mine."

"So what?" she answered. "If we need it, let's take it."

"It doesn't belong to you."

"Belong!" she repeated. "But didn't you take me? When we've taken it, it will belong to us."

He burst into laughter. "What a poor little innocent you are! You know nothing of the world."

"No, but I do know this," she exclaimed, pulling Henri to her.

At the very moment when de Marsay was about to forget everything, and was conceiving the desire to commandeer this creature forever, he received in the midst of his joy a dagger blow that for the first time went right through his mortified heart. Paquita who had raised him vigorously in the air as if to gaze on him, had cried out, "Oh! Mariquita!"

"Mariquita!" exclaimed the young man with a roar. "Now I know everything that until this moment I didn't want to believe."

He leapt toward the chest that contained the long dagger. Fortunately for her and for him it was locked. His rage redoubled as a result of this obstacle, but he recovered his calm, went to get his cravat and walked up to her with so ferociously meaningful an air that, without knowing the crime she had committed, Paquita nevertheless understood that she was threatened with death. At that she flung herself in a single leap to the far end of the room to avoid the fatal noose that de Marsay wanted to put round her neck. A struggle ensued. The antagonists were equally supple, agile, vigorous. To end the struggle, Paquita threw a cushion at her lover's legs, making him fall over, and profited from the respite this advantage gave her to push the button of the bell cord. The mulatto arrived immediately. In the wink of an eye Christemio leapt on de Marsay, flung him to the ground, put his foot on Henri's chest with his heel pointing at his throat. De Marsay understood that if he struggled he would be crushed immediately at the slightest signal Paquita gave.

"Why did you want to kill me, my love?" she asked him.

De Marsay did not answer.

"What have I done to displease you?" she said to him. "Speak. Let's work it out."

Henri maintained the phlegmatic attitude of the man who feels himself defeated; his face revealed the cold, silent, completely English expression that reveals a man fully conscious of his dignity even in a moment of resignation. Moreover he had already thought, despite his outburst of rage, that it was not very prudent to get involved with the law by killing this girl spontaneously, and without having prepared the murder in a way that would ensure that he could do it with impunity.

"My love," said Paquita, "speak to me; don't leave me without a loving farewell! I don't want to go on feeling in my heart the terror you've just placed there. Will you speak?" she asked, stamping in anger.

The only response she got from de Marsay was a glance that said so clearly "You'll die!" that Paquita hurled herself at him.

"What! You want to kill me? If my death can give you any pleasure, kill me then!"

She gestured to Christemio, who lifted his foot from the young man, and he went away without revealing any expression that might suggest whether he thought well or ill of Paquita.

"There's a man for you!" said de Marsay, pointing to the mulatto with a somber gesture. "There is no devotion except for the devotion that obeys a friend without judging that friend. In that man you have a real friend."

"I'll give him to you if you want," she replied. "He'll serve you with the same devotion that he feels for me, if I order him to do so."

She waited for him to reply, then went on with a voice full of tenderness, "Adolphe, say one kind word to me. Dawn has almost broken."

Henri did not reply. This young man had a certain grimness about him, for everything that resembles strength is valued highly, and often men regard extravagance as divine. Henri was incapable of forgiving. The ability to fall in love all over again, which is certainly one of the soul's graces, was for him a nonsense. The ferocity of Northern men, when their English blood is dyed deeply enough, had been transmitted to him by his father. He was as unshakable in his good as in his bad feelings. Paquita's exclamation was all the more horrible for him in that he had been dethroned from the sweetest triumph that had ever swollen his masculine vanity. Hope, love, and all such emotions had been whipped up within him, and had burst into flame in his heart and mind; then these torches, which had been lit to illuminate his life, had been blown out by a cold wind. Paquita, stupefied, was so grief stricken that she had only the strength to give the signal that he should leave.

"This isn't necessary," she said, removing the blindfold. "If he doesn't love me any more, if he hates me, everything is over."

She waited for a glance, failed to obtain it, and fell down half-dead. The mulatto threw Henri a glance so horrifyingly meaningful that it sent a tremor, for the first time in his life, through this young man, who, as everyone acknowledged, was uncommonly bold. "If you don't love her deeply, if you cause her the slightest unhappiness, I'll kill you." That was the meaning of this rapid glance. De Marsay was led with almost servile care along a corridor lit by casement windows and at the end of which they went out by a secret door into a hidden stairwell that led to the garden of San Réal's house. The mulatto made him walk cautiously along an avenue of lindens that culminated in a little gate leading into a street, which at that hour was deserted. De Marsay took careful note of everything, the coach awaited him, and this time the mulatto did not accompany him. At the moment when Henri thrust his head out of the coach window to see the gardens and the hotel once more, he met Christemio's white eyes and exchanged a glance with him. On both sides this glance was a provocation, a challenge, the announcement of a war between savages, of a duel that took no note of the ordinary laws, in which treachery and perfidy were acceptable means. Christemio knew Henri had sworn to kill Paquita, and Henri knew that Christemio wanted to kill him before he could kill her. Both understood the other wonderfully well.

"The plot's thickening in an interesting way," Henri said to himself.

"Where are you going, sir?" the driver asked him.

De Marsay ordered the driver to take him to Paul de Manerville's.

For over a week Henri was absent from home, and no one was able to discover either what he did during this time or where he stayed. This retreat saved him from the mulatto's wrath and brought about the loss of the poor creature who had placed all her hopes in the man she loved as no creature on this earth has ever loved. On the last day of that week, toward eleven in the evening, Henri came in a carriage to the little gate of the garden belonging to the San Réal hotel. Three men accompanied him. The driver was obviously one of his friends, for he sat on his seat in the posture of a man who, like an attentive sentinel, wanted to catch the slightest sound. One of the other three stood outside the door in the street; the second remained standing in the garden, leaning against a wall; the last, who held a bunch of keys in his hand, went with de Marsay.

"Henri," his companion remarked to him, "we've been betrayed."

"By whom, my good Ferragus?"

"Not everyone is asleep," replied the Devourers' boss, "someone in the house must have neither drunk anything nor eaten anything. Look at that light."

"We have the plan of the house. Where is it coming from?"

"I don't need the plan to tell you that," said Ferragus. "It's coming from the marquise's bedroom."

"Ah!" exclaimed de Marsay. "She must have arrived from London today. That woman will have stripped me of everything, even my revenge! But if she's got in before us, my dear Gratien, we'll hand her over to the police."

"Just listen! It's all over with!" Ferragus remarked to Henri.

The friends listened and could hear weak cries that would have softened the breasts of tigers.

"Your marquise didn't realize that sounds would come out through the chimney," said the Devourers' boss, with the laugh of a critic enchanted to discover a fault in a work of great beauty.

"We alone can foresee all contingencies," said Henri. "Wait for me, I want to see how things are proceeding up there, so that I can discover how they go about their domestic quarrels. In God's name, it sounds as if she's got her on a slow fire."

De Marsay leaped lightly up the stairs that he knew so well and recognized the bedroom door. When he opened the door, he had that involuntary shudder that the most determined man experiences at the sight of shed blood. The spectacle that greeted his eyes had moreover more than one reason to astonish him. The marquise had calculated her revenge with that perfidious perfection that distinguishes the weaker animals. She had hidden her rage in order to be certain the crime had been committed before she punished it.

"Too late, my love!" said the dying Paquita, whose pale eyes turned toward de Marsay.

The girl with the golden eyes was dying drowned in blood. The flaming torches, a delicate perfume that could just be detected, a certain disorder in which a man used to love affairs could not fail to recognize the kinds of follies committed in all passions, revealed that the marquise had questioned the guilty party most cunningly. This white apartment, which set off the blood to such advantage, betrayed a lengthy struggle. Paquita's hands had left their imprint on the cushions. Everywhere she had clung to life, everywhere she had defended herself, and everywhere she had been struck. Entire shreds of the wall hangings had been ripped off by bloodstained hands, hands that doubtless had struggled at length. Paquita must have tried to climb onto the ceiling. Her naked feet had left their tracks along the back of the divan on which she had apparently run. Her body, which her torturer had filled with dagger holes, spoke of the determination with which she had clung to a life Henri had made dear to her. She was lying on the ground, and as she died had bitten the muscles in the arch of Madame de San Réal's foot as the latter clung to her bloodstained dagger. The marquise had had strands of hair torn out, she was covered with bites, several of which were bleeding, and her torn dress revealed her half-naked, her breasts scratched. She was sublime in such disarray. Her avid and furious face breathed in the odor of blood. Her gasping mouth was half-open and her nostrils were not wide enough for all the air she wanted to draw in. Certain animals when driven to fury leap on their enemy and kill it, then, tranquil in victory, seem to forget it. Others prowl around their victim, keep it, in fear that it may be taken from them, and, like Homer's Achilles, go nine times around Troy, dragging their enemy by the feet. This was what the marquise was like. She did not see Henri. For one thing, she knew so well that she was alone that she had no fear of witnesses. Moreover, she was too intoxicated with the warm blood, too animated by the struggle, too exalted to have seen the whole of Paris if Paris had formed a circle around her. She would not have felt a lightning bolt. She had not even heard Paquita's last sigh and thought the dead girl could still hear her.

"Die unabsolved!" she was saying to her. "Go to Hell, you monster of ingratitude. Belong to no one henceforth but the Devil. For the blood you gave him, you owe me all of yours! Die, die, suffer a thousand deaths. I have been too kind: I took only a moment to kill you, I would have liked to make you feel all the pain you leave with me. I shall live! I shall live unhappy, reduced to loving no one but God!" She looked at her. "She's dead!" she remarked after a pause and swung around violently. "She's dead! I'll die of grief!"

The marquise went to throw herself on the divan, overwhelmed with a despair that robbed her of speech, and this movement allowed her to see Henri de Marsay.

"Who are you?" she asked, running at him with her dagger held high.

Henri seized her arm, and thus they were able to gaze into each other's face. A horrible surprise sent a frozen chill through their blood, and they trembled like terrified horses. Indeed, two Menechmians[31] would not have appeared more alike. Both asked at the same time, "Lord Dudley must be your father?" Each nodded in agreement.

"She was faithful to the blood," said Henri, pointing to Paquita.

"Her guilt is as slight as it could possibly be," answered Margarita-Euphémia Porrabéril, who threw herself on Paquita's body with a cry of despair. "Poor girl! Oh! I wish I could bring you back to life. I was wrong, forgive me, Paquita! You're dead and I'm alive! I'm the unhappier of the two of us!"

At that moment the horrible face of Paquita's mother appeared.

"You're going to tell me you didn't sell her to me so that I could kill

---

31. *Menechmians:* Two people who are exactly like each other. The allusion is to Plautus' *Menechmi.*

her," shouted the marquise. "I know why you've come out of your den. I'll pay you double for her. Be quiet."

She took a bag of gold from the ebony chest and threw it disdainfully at the feet of that old woman. The sound of money had the power to sketch a smile on the motionless visage of the woman from Georgia.

"I've come just in time for you, my sister," said Henri. "The police will have questions for you . . . "

"They won't ask me any questions," answered the marquise. "There's only one person who could demand that I account for the girl. Christemio is dead."

"And the mother," said Henri, pointing to the old woman, "won't she go on blackmailing you?"

"She comes from a country where women are not human beings but things that one treats as one likes, one can sell them or buy them or kill them, in a word, one uses them for one's whims, as you make use of a chest of drawers here. Moreover, she has a passion that makes all her other passions its servants, a passion that would have stifled her maternal feelings if she had ever loved her daughter, a passion . . . "

"Which passion?" said Henri sharply, interrupting his sister.

"Gambling! God keep you from it!" the marquise replied.

"But who will help you," asked Henri, pointing to the girl with the golden eyes, "to get rid of the traces of that whim of yours, for which the law would not forgive you?"

"I have her mother," answered the marquise, pointing to the old Georgian woman whom she ordered with a gesture to remain.

"We'll meet again," said Henri, who thought of his friends' concern and felt he must leave.

"No, brother," she said, "we'll never meet again. I'm going back to Spain to put myself in the Convent of Those Who Grieve."

"You're still too lovely and too young," said Henri, taking her in his arms and kissing her.

"Farewell," she said. "Nothing consoles us for the loss of what seemed to us to be the infinite."

A week later, Paul de Manerville met de Marsay in the Tuileries on the Feuillantines terrace.

"Well, what's become of our lovely girl with the golden eyes, you great rascal?"

"She's dead."

"What killed her?"

"Her chest."

Paris, March 1834–April 1835

Gautier

◆

Théophile Gautier (1811–1872), the poet to whom Baudelaire dedicated The
Flowers of Evil, *set out to become a painter, but was prevented from following that career by poor eyesight. His poetry and his prose writing, especially
his criticism, reflect his early love of color and shape, and although he later
settled into a kind of poetry in which form is of paramount importance, his
early enthusiasm for Romanticism can still be detected in his short stories and
in his novels* Mademoiselle de Maupin *and* Le Capitaine Fracasse. *An
ebullient character, his works reflect an enthusiasm for the exotic, for the un-
explainable, and for erotic love. In later life, he was influential mainly as a
critic of literature and art, and he played an important role in establishing the
careers of several younger writers. His short stories contain some of his finest
prose—supple, dynamic, and strikingly visual. His exploitation of the fantastic in such tales enabled him to explore the labyrinthine workings of the mind
and to illuminate much of the darker side of Romantic sexuality.*

FURTHER READING: *Mademoiselle de Maupin* (New York: Pyramid, 1955).
BIOGRAPHY: Joanna Richardson, *Théophile Gautier, His Life and Times* (London:
M. Rheinhardt, 1958).
TEXT USED: *Nouvelles* (Paris: Charpentier, 1845).

THE LOVE OF A DEAD WOMAN (1845)

You ask me, brother, whether I have ever loved. I have. It's a strange
and terrible tale, and although I am now sixty-six, I hardly dare stir up
the embers of that memory. I have no wish to refuse anything you ask
of me, but I would not relate such a story to anyone less tried and true
than you are. What happened was so odd that I find it impossible to
believe that it happened to me. For more than three years I was the
plaything of a strange and diabolical illusion. I, a poor country priest,
dreamed every night (pray God it was a dream) that I led the life of

a damned soul, the life of a man of the world, of a Sardanapalus.[1] A single over-kindly glance almost destroyed my soul; but at last, with the help of God and my guardian angel, I succeeded in driving out the evil spirit that had taken control of my being. My daytime existence had been complicated by a nocturnal existence of an entirely different nature. By day, I was a priest working for the Lord. I was chaste, concerned with prayers and with holy matters. At night, as soon as I had closed my eyes, I became a young nobleman, a fine connoisseur of women, dogs, and horses; proficient at gambling, drinking, and blaspheming. And when I would awaken at dawn, it seemed to me, on the contrary, that I was falling asleep and merely dreaming I was a priest. That somnambulist's life has left me with memories of objects and words against which I am defenseless, and although I have never left the walls of my parsonage, people listening to me would be more likely to consider me a man who had tried everything and had retreated from the world to the church, a man who had turned to religion in the hope of ending in the bosom of the Lord a life which had been too agitated rather than a humble seminary student grown old in a parish the world has passed by, deep in the woods, and having no links with worldly matters.

Yes, I have loved, as no one in the world has loved, with a wild and furious love, so violent that it astonishes me that my heart did not burst asunder. Oh, those nights! those nights!

From my earliest childhood, I felt a vocation for the priesthood. As a result, all my studies had that goal in mind, and my entire life, up to the time I turned twenty-four, was nothing but a long novitiate. Once my theological studies had been completed, I passed through all the lower orders one by one, and my superiors judged me worthy, despite my great youth, to take the final and formidable step. The day for my ordination was set for the week of Easter.

I had never gone out into the world. For me, the world consisted of the domain of the college and the seminary. I was vaguely aware of the existence of something called woman, but I did not expend any thought on it. My innocence was complete. I saw my elderly and invalid mother only twice a year. That was the entire extent of my relations with the world outside.

I had no regrets, I felt not the slightest hesitation about this irrevocable engagement. I was full of joy and impatience. Never has a young fiancé counted the hours with a more feverish impatience: I could not sleep for longing, and would dream that I was conducting mass. In my eyes, the world had no beauty greater than being a priest. I would have

---

1. *Sardanapalus:* Fictional Assyrian king, used as the epitome of debauchery. With the enemy at his gates, he is supposed to have ordered the destruction of his horses and women slaves, and to have set fire to himself. Delacroix painted this scene in *The Death of Sardanapalus.*

refused to be a king or a poet. My ambition could conceive of nothing higher.

I'm telling you this to show you the extent to which what happened to me ought not to have happened to me, and to show you that the fascination to which I fell victim was quite inexplicable.

When the great day came, I walked to the church with a step so light that I felt I walked on air or that there were wings on my shoulders. I considered myself an angel, and was astonished at the somber and preoccupied faces of my companions, for several of us were taking our vows.

I had spent the night in prayer, and was in a state bordering on ecstasy. The bishop, a venerable old man, seemed to me to be God the Father brooding on his eternity, and through the vaults of the church I could see heaven.

You are familiar with the details of the ceremony: the blessing, the communion in its two forms, the placing of the oil on the aspirant's palms, and finally the holy sacrifice offered up together with the bishop. I will not dwell on that. Oh how right Job is, and how imprudent are they who do not seal a pact with their eyes! As chance would have it, I raised my head, which until that moment I had kept bowed, and before me I saw, so close that I could have touched her, although in reality she was a fair way off and on the far side of the altar rail, a young woman of exceptional beauty, dressed in clothes of regal magnificence. It was as if scales had fallen from my eyes. I felt like a blind man who had suddenly recovered his sight. The bishop, who a moment before had been so radiant in my eyes, suddenly faded, the candles grew dim on their golden chandeliers as stars do in the light of dawn, and the entire church was overwhelmed in darkness. The charming creature stood out against that background of darkness like an angelic revelation. She seemed illuminated with a light all her own. She seemed to shed light rather than just receive it.

I lowered my eyelids, determined not to raise them any more. I wanted to escape from the influence of outside objects, for it was increasingly difficult to concentrate, and I barely knew what I was doing.

A moment later I opened my eyes again, for through my lashes I could see her glimmering in all the colors of the rainbow, in that purplish penumbra you see if you look at the sun.

Oh! She was so lovely! When the greatest painters pursue ideal beauty in heaven, they bring back to earth the holy portrait of the Madonna, but they do not even come close to depicting the fabulous reality I perceived. Neither the poet's verses nor the painter's palette could give the slightest idea of it. She was fairly tall, with the figure and bearing of a goddess. Her hair was of a soft blond, spreading over her head and cascading down her temples like two rivers of gold. She seemed a queen in a crown. Her brow, transparent and so white it seemed blue, spread out broad and serene above the arcs of her eyebrows, which were almost brown, a rarity which added even more to the effect of her sea green eyes, which possessed a gleam and vivacity that were almost unbearable. What eyes! A lightning bolt from them would determine a man's destiny; they had a vitality, a limpidity, an ardor, a shining moistness about them that I have never seen in any human eye; rays like arrows burst from them, and I distinctly saw those arrows plunge into my heart. I do not know whether the flame that lit them came from heaven or hell, but surely it came from one or the other. That woman was an angel or a demon, and perhaps both at the same time. She certainly did not issue from Eve, the universal mother. Teeth of the most beautiful orient glittered in her red smile, and at every inflection of her mouth little dimples appeared in the pink satin of her adorable cheeks. As for her nose, it was utterly regal in its finesse, and its arrogance revealed she was of the noblest birth. An agate gloss played on the smooth, lustrous skin of her half-covered shoulders, and strings of large blond pearls, almost identical in shade to that of her neck, fell on her breast. From time to time she would raise her head with the undulating movement of a snake or a strutting peacock, lending a slight shiver to the high embroidered ruff that enveloped it like a silver trellis.

She wore a dress of orange-red velvet, and from her wide sleeves with their ermine lining issued patrician hands of infinite delicacy, with long, plump fingers so perfectly transparent that light came through them as it does through the fingers of Dawn.

All these details are still as present in my mind as if they dated from yesterday, and although I was deeply disturbed, nothing escaped my attention. The slightest nuance, the little black dot at the corner of her chin, the almost invisible down on the corner of her lips, the velvet softness of her brow, the trembling shadow of her lashes on her cheeks, all this I seized with astonishing lucidity.

As I watched, I felt doors opening within me that had until that moment been closed. Blocked vents burst out in all directions and allowed glimpses of unknown horizons. Life appeared to me in an entirely different light. I had just been born into an entirely different way of thinking. A terrifying anguish clawed at my heart. Every minute that passed seemed to me a single second and an entire century. Yet the ceremony went on, and I was carried far, far away from the world whose entrance my nascent desires were furiously besieging. Yet I said yes when I longed to say no, when everything within me revolted and protested against the violence my tongue was inflicting on my soul. An occult power tore the words from my throat in spite of me. This may perhaps be why so many girls walk to the altar with the firm intention of scandalously refusing the husband imposed on them, and not a single one puts her plan into action. This no doubt is why so many poor novices take the veil although they had been determined to tear it into pieces when the moment came to take their vows. You dare not cause a scandal in front of everyone, you dare not disappoint the hopes of so many people. All those firm wills, all those searching glances, seem to weigh down on you like a leaden cope. And then, measures have been taken, everything has been so well decided in advance, it's all so irrevocable already that your thoughts yield under the weight and collapse completely.

The lovely stranger's expression changed as the ceremony progressed. At first tender and caressing, it gradually assumed an air of scorn and unhappiness, as if she were grieved to find she had not been understood.

I made an effort that would have been enough to tear a mountain from its roots, trying to scream that I had no wish to be a priest; but it was in vain, my tongue remained glued to my mouth and it was impossible for me to express my will through even the slightest of negative movements. I was wide awake, in a state resembling that of nightmares, where you long to cry out a word on which your entire life depends, but all in vain.

She seemed aware of the martyrdom I was going through, and as if to encourage me she sent me a glance rich in superb promises. Her eyes were a poem in which every glance formed a song. She was saying to me, "If you are willing to be mine, I will make you happier than God himself in his heaven; the angels will envy you. Tear asunder that shroud in which you are about to bury yourself away; I am beauty, I am youth, I am life. Come to me and together we will be love. What could Jehovah offer in recompense? Our life will flow past like a dream and will consist of eternal kisses. Throw the wine from that chalice, and you will be free. I shall take you to unknown islands. You will fall asleep on my breast, in a bed of solid gold and under a silver tent; for I love you and I want to take you from your God, before Whom so many noble hearts pour forth floods of love which never reach Him."

It seemed that these words were carried to me on a rhythm of endless sweetness, for her eyes seemed to have a sound of their own, and the sentences they conveyed to me echoed in the depths of my heart as if an invisible mouth had whispered them to my soul.

I felt ready to renounce God, and yet my heart mechanically performed the actions demanded by the ceremony. The beautiful woman sent me a second glance so full of supplication and desperation that keen-edged blades pierced my heart, and I felt I had more daggers in my breast than did our lady of sorrows.

It was over and done. I was a priest.

Never has a human face painted a more poignant anguish; the young girl who sees her fiancé die suddenly at her side, the mother standing by the cradle that no longer carries her child, Eve sitting on the threshold of the door to paradise, the miser who finds a stone where his treasure used to be, the poet who mistakenly drops into the fire the only manuscript of his finest work, do not look more distressed or more inconsolable. All the blood drained away from her face, turning it as white as marble; her lovely arms dropped down by her body as if the muscles had lost all their force, and she leaned against a pillar, for her legs buckled and slid from under her. As for me, deathly pale, my brow drenched with a sweat more bloody than that of Calvary, I staggered out through the church door; I was choking; the vaults were collapsing on my shoulders, and it felt as if my head were supporting all on its own the entire weight of the cupola.

As I was about to cross the threshold, a hand suddenly caught hold of mine, a woman's hand! I had never touched one. It was as cold as a snake's skin, and the imprint burned my hand like the mark of a red-hot iron. It was she. "You wretch! You wretch! What have you done?" she whispered to me and then she disappeared into the crowd.

The old bishop went past. He sent me a severe glance. I had the strangest expression you could possibly imagine. I grew pale, I blushed, my eyes were dazzled. One of my friends took pity on me, seized my elbow, and led me away. I would have been incapable of finding the way to the seminary on my own. In the bend of a road, while the young priest was looking the other way, a Negro page, strangely clad, came up to me and, without stopping, handed me a little wallet with decorated gold edges, signaling to me that I should keep it hidden. I slipped it into my sleeve and held it there until I was alone in my cell. I sprang open the lock. It contained only two sheets of paper, with these words: "Clarimonde, at the Concini Palace." At that stage I knew so little of worldly matters, that, despite her fame, I did not know Clarimonde's name, and I had not the slightest idea of where the Concini palace was. I made a thousand guesses, each more extravagant than the last, but to tell the truth, provided I could see her again, I was not at all worried about what she might be and whether she was a great lady or a courtesan.

The love that had been born so recently had taken root indestructibly in me. I did not even consider trying to tear it from my soul, so impossible did I feel such a task to be. The woman had completely taken control of me. A single glance from her eyes had been enough to change me. She had let me know what she wanted of me, and I no longer existed in myself but in and through her. I committed a thousand extravagant acts. I kissed the place on my hand where she had touched it, and I repeated her name for hours on end. I had only to close my eyes to see her as distinctly as if she had been really present, and I said to myself the words she had spoken in the church doorway: "You wretch! You wretch! What have you done?" I understood the full horror of my position, and the dismal, terrible aspects of the state I had just embraced were all too clear to me. To be a priest! To be chaste, not to love, to distinguish neither sex nor age, to turn away from all beauty, to tear out your own eyes, to crawl under the glacial shadow of cloister or church, to see only the dying, to watch over unknown corpses, and to wear your own mourning in the form of the cassock, so that your clothes provide the material for your coffin!

And I felt life rising within me like an underground lake that swells and overflows; my blood beat strongly in my veins, my youth which had been oppressed for so long suddenly burst out like the aloe that takes a hundred years to flower and opens with a clap of thunder.

How could I manage to see Clarimonde again? I had no excuse to leave the seminary, for I knew no one in the town. I was not even to remain there, and I was waiting only to be told what parish would become mine. I tried to break through the bars on the window, but it was terrifyingly high, and since I had no ladder it was not to be thought of. Moreover, I could leave only at night, and even so how ever would I guide myself through the inextricable labyrinth of streets? All those difficulties, which others would have made nothing of, were immense for me, a poor seminary boy, who had only just fallen in love, who had no experience, no money, and no clothes.

Oh, if only I were not a priest, I could have seen her every day. I would have been her lover, her husband, I repeated to myself in my blindness. Instead of being wrapped in a mournful shroud, I would have clothes of silk and velvet, golden chains, a sword and plumes as handsome young knights did. My hair, instead of being dishonored by a generous tonsure, would play around my neck in wavy curls. I would have a fine waxed mustache; I would be a gallant. But one hour spent before the altar, a few words barely uttered, had cut me off forever from the world of the living, and I myself had sealed the stone on my tomb, my own hand had pushed home the bolt on my prison!

I went to stand by the window. The sky was admirably blue, the trees had donned their springtime garb; nature was on parade with an ironic joy. The square was full of people, coming and going, young dandies and youthful beauties, couple by couple, strolled in the direction of the park and the bowers. Journeymen went by singing drinking songs. All was movement, life, energy, and a gaiety that made my own mourning and solitude stand out all the more starkly. A young mother on a doorstep played with her child. She kissed its little pink mouth which still bore the pearls of milk drops, and teasingly treated it to a thousand of those divine childish tricks that mothers alone can find. The father who stood some distance away, smiled gently at this charming group, his arms crossed to press his joy to his heart. I could not bear to watch this spectacle. I closed the window and threw myself on my bed with dreadful hatred and jealousy in my heart, biting my fingers and my blanket as if I were a tiger that had been fasting these three days.

I do not know how long I stayed like that, but as I spun round in a furious spasm, I caught sight of Abbot Serapion[2] standing in the middle of my room and looking at me with close attention. I was ashamed of myself, and dropping my head on my breast, I hid my eyes behind my hands.

"Romuald, my dear friend, there's something very strange in the way you're behaving," he said after a few minutes of silence. "Your behavior really defies explanation! You, so pious, so calm, so gentle, you're flinging yourself about your room like a wild beast. Be careful, brother. Do not listen to the devil's suggestions. The evil spirit, enraged that you have always devoted yourself to the Lord, prowls round you like a starving wolf and is making one last attempt to draw you to him. Instead of allowing yourself to be struck down, my dear Romuald, make yourself an armor of prayers, a shield of mortifications, and struggle valiantly against our enemy. You will defeat him. Virtue needs to be tested, and gold that has passed through the crucible is all the purer for it. You should be neither afraid nor discouraged. Those souls that are most surely guarded and strengthened have all passed through such moments. Pray, fast, meditate, and the evil one will withdraw."

Abbot Serapion's words restored me to my senses, and I became somewhat calmer. "I have come to tell you that you've been appointed to the parish of C***. The priest who used to hold it has just died, and his worship the bishop has charged me with installing you there; be ready to leave tomorrow." I replied with a nod that I would be ready, and the abbot withdrew. I opened my missal and began to read the prayers. But the lines soon blurred under my eyes, the thread of my thoughts grew tangled in my mind, and the book slipped from my hands without my noticing it.

Leave tomorrow without having seen her again! Add yet another impossibility to all those that had already come between us! Lose for all eternity the hope of finding her again, except by a miracle! Write to her? Who would take my letter to her? Given my damned role as a priest, to whom could I open my heart, whom could I trust? I felt a dreadful anxiety. Then, what Abbot Serapion had told me about the devil's tricks came back to my mind: the strangeness of the adventure, the beauty of her eyes, the burning touch of her hand, the way the sight of her had disturbed me, the sudden change that had taken place within me, the way my piety had instantly faded, all that was clear proof of the devil's presence, and that satin-soft hand may well have been only the glove with which he covers his claws. These ideas threw me into a great terror. I picked up the missal which had dropped from my lap to the ground, and I began to pray again.

---

2. *Serapion:* The choice of this name is a tribute to the German Romantic writer E. T. A. Hoffmann, whose tales of the fantastic were very popular in France at this time, and who called one of his collections of short stories *The Serapion Brothers.*

The following day, Serapion came to collect me. Two mules were waiting at the door, loaded with our few possessions. He mounted one and I the other, somewhat inexpertly. As we traveled through the streets of the town, I looked at all the windows and balconies in the hopes of seeing Clarimonde, but it was still too early and the town had not yet opened its eyes. My glance tried to plunge behind the blinds and through the windows of every palace we went past. Serapion probably attributed this curiosity to the admiration aroused in me for the architecture, for he slowed his mount's pace to give me time to look. At last we reached the town gate and began to climb the hill. When we had reached the summit I turned around to cast one final look at the place where Clarimonde lived. The shadow of a cloud covered the whole town; its blue and red roofs blended in to a general half-tint from which arose, here and there, what seemed to be white balls of foam, the smoke of early morning. Through a curious optical effect, a single ray of light picked out a golden blond building rising above the neighboring constructions, which were completely drowned in the mist. Although it was more than a league away it seemed right next to us. You could make out the slightest detail, the turrets, the platforms, the casement windows, and even the wind vanes with their dove tail shapes.

"What is that palace I see down there, caught in a beam of sunlight?" I asked Serapion.

He put his hand above his eyes and looked, then said, "It's the former palace of Prince Concini, who gave it to the courtesan Clarimonde. Horrible things happen there."

At that instant I thought I saw, I don't know whether in truth or through an illusion, a slender, white form gliding along the terrace and glinting for an instant before fading from view. It was Clarimonde!

Oh! Did she know that at that very moment, from the top of the rough road which took me far from her, and along which I could never return, I brooded ardently and anxiously over the palace in which she lived, the palace that a mocking play of light seemed to bring closer to me as if to invite me to enter it as its master? No doubt, she knew, for her soul was too closely harmonized with mine not to feel the slightest commotions I experienced. It was surely that feeling that had driven her, wrapped in the thin veils she wore at night, to show herself at the top of the terrace in the icy dew of morning.

The shadow engulfed the palace, and all I could see now was a motionless ocean of roofs in which nothing could be distinguished but an undulation of hills and valleys. Serapion touched his mule, and mine instantly fell into step with it. A turn in the path hid from me forever the town of S . . . , for I was never to return to it. After three days of travel through gloomy countryside, we saw through the trees the steeple cock of the church I was to serve. After following several tortuous streets lined with thatched cottages and gardens, we arrived in front of the facade, which could hardly be described as magnificent. A porch adorned with a few ornamental ribs and two or three coarsely hewn sandstone pillars, a tiled roof, and some buttresses of the same sandstone, and that was all. To the left was a cemetery full of tall grass with a large iron cross in the middle; on the right, in the shadow cast by the church, the parsonage. This was a house of extreme simplicity and arid cleanliness. We went in. A handful of hens were pecking at a few grains of oats scattered on the floor. Obviously used to the black robes worn by men of the church, they were not alarmed at our presence and scarcely moved aside to let us pass. A hoarse, rough barking could be heard, and we saw an old dog bound toward us.

This was my predecessor's dog. His eye was dull, his coat was gray, and he had all the symptoms of the greatest age a dog can reach. I patted him gently with my hand, and immediately he began to walk beside me with an undescribable air of satisfaction. An elderly woman who had been the former curé's housekeeper came to meet us straightaway and, having led me into a low room, she asked me if I intended to keep her. I replied that I would keep not only her but also the dog, the hens, and all the furniture her master had left her after his death, which filled her with transports of delight, for the abbot immediately gave her the price she wanted for them.

Once I was installed, Abbot Serapion returned to the seminary. So I remained alone and with no support except for myself. The thought of Clarimonde began to obsess me again, and however hard I tried to drive it away, I was unsuccessful. One evening, as I strolled along the box-lined paths of my little garden, I thought I saw through the hedgerow the shape of a woman who was watching my every movement. Through the leaves there seemed to glint two sea green eyes. But it was merely an illusion, and when I crossed over to the other side of the path, I found nothing but a footprint in the sand, a print so small you would have thought it left by a child. The garden was surrounded by very high walls. I explored all its corners and found no one. I have never been able to explain this circumstance which was, moreover, a mere bagatelle in comparison with the strange events that were about to befall me. Thus I lived for a year, meticulously fulfilling all the duties of my position, praying, fasting, exhorting, and caring for the ill, giving alms to the point where I reduced myself to the most indispensable necessities. But I felt deep within myself an extreme aridity. The fountain of grace was sealed up against me. I experienced none of the happiness that the accomplishment of a holy mission brings with it. My mind was elsewhere, and Clarimonde's words often came to my lips like a kind of involuntary refrain. O brother, meditate deeply on this! Because I had once raised my eyes to look at a woman, because of a fault that seems so minor, I experienced for several years the most unhappy agitation. My life was thrown into constant disarray.

I won't burden you any longer with those inner defeats and those victories which were always followed by yet deeper relapses. Let me pass straight on to a circumstance that proved decisive. One night someone rang violently at my door. The old housekeeper went to open it, and a man the color of copper, richly clad but in a fashion foreign to us and carrying a long dagger, appeared in the light of Barbara's lamp. Her first movement was one of fear, but the man reassured her and told her he needed me immediately for a matter concerning my ministry. Barbara led him in. I was about to go to bed. The man told me his mistress, a very great lady, was on the point of death and wanted a priest. I answered that I was ready to follow him. I took with me all I needed for extreme unction and went out in great haste. At the door I found two horses as black as night itself, cavorting impatiently and blowing onto their breast bands long floods of smoke. He held my stirrup for me and helped me to mount, then he leapt onto the other horse by merely placing one hand on the saddle bow. He clenched his knees and loosened his horse's reins, and it set off like an arrow. He was holding my horse by the reins, so it too set off at a gallop, and both horses kept perfectly in step with each other. We devoured the ground; the earth rushed beneath us, gray and striped, while the black silhouettes of trees fled like a routed army. We crossed a forest so opaque and glacial in its darkness that I felt a shiver of superstitious terror run over my skin. The plumes of sparks our horses' shoes struck from the stones as we passed left a blaze of fire, and if anyone had seen us so late at night they would have taken my guide and me for two ghosts riding a nightmare. From time to time two will-o'-the-wisps crossed our path and the jackdaws whimpered piteously in the depths of the woods, in which could be seen glinting here and there the phosphorescent eyes of wild cats. The horse's manes flew out more and more wildly, the sweat dripped from their flanks, and the breath burst noisily and urgently from their nostrils. But when he realized they were faltering, the rider would revive them by making a guttural cry that was utterly inhuman, and the wild race would begin again. At last the whirlwind stopped. A black mass, starred with several gleaming points of light, suddenly arose before us. Our horses' hooves rang out more noisily on an iron pathway, and we came in under a dark vault which yawned between two enormous towers. There was great movement in the castle. Servants with flares in their hands crossed the courtyard in all directions, and lights went up and down the stair wells. I glimpsed a confused mass of immense architectural shapes, columns, arcades, stairs, and ramps, a construction whose luxurious nature was both regal and fairy-like. A Negro page, the very one who had given me Clarimonde's wallet, and whom I instantly recognized, helped me dismount, and a majordomo clad in black velvet and with a golden chain around his neck and an ivory walking stick in his hand, came to meet me. Large tears trickled from his eyes and poured down his cheeks over his white beard. "Too late!" he said with a shake of his head. "Too late, revered father! But if you've been unable to save her soul, at least come and watch over the body." He took me by the arm and led me to the dead woman's room. I wept as bitterly as he did, for I had realized that the dead woman was none other than that Clarimonde I had so deeply and so madly loved. A kneeling stool was set by the bed, a bluish flame trembling from a bronze hook shed through the room a weak and doubtful light. Here and there the light set some sharp corner of a piece of furniture or a cornice glimmering mothlike in the dark. On the table, in a chiseled urn, there was a faded white rose whose petals, save one that still clung on, had fallen to the foot of the vase like perfumed tears. A broken black mask, a fan, all manner of disguises, were draped over arm chairs and revealed that the dead woman had arrived in this place unexpectedly and without announcing her arrival. I knelt without daring to glance at the bed, and set about reciting the psalms with great fervor, thanking God that He had set a tomb between the idea of this woman and myself, so that I could add her name to my prayers, a name henceforth sanctified by death. But little by little that impetus slowed down, and I fell into reverie. This room had nothing about it that suggested a death chamber. Instead of the fetid and corpse-like air I was accustomed to breathing when I watched over the dead, languorous fumes of Eastern essences, a trace of the perfume of love and woman, swam softly in the warm air. That pale light seemed more like a carefully maintained half-light produced for sexual pleasure than the yellow reflections of the lamps which usually tremble beside the bodies of the departed. I thought of the extraordinary coincidence that had allowed me to rediscover Clarimonde at the moment when I was to lose her forever, and a sigh of regret escaped my breast. I had the impression that someone behind me had sighed, too, and I swung round involuntarily. It was an echo. In that movement, my eyes fell on the bed, which until then they had avoided. The red damask curtains with their large flowers, held up by gold tassels, revealed the dead woman lying full length with her hands joined on her breast. She was covered with a blindingly white linen veil that the dark crimson of the curtains set off all the more intensely, and its exceptional fineness hid nothing of the charming form of her body, allowing the eyes to follow the lovely undulating lines, recalling those of a swan, lines death itself had been unable to stiffen. She looked like an alabaster statue that a skillful sculptor had created to place on a queen's tomb, or perhaps a maiden who had fallen asleep and on whom the snow had fallen.

I could bear it no longer. This bedroom air intoxicated me, that feverish scent of half-faded rose went to my head, and I strode around the room, stopping each time I came before the bedstead to gaze at the graceful dead woman under her transparent shroud. Strange thoughts rushed through my mind. I imagined she was not truly dead, and that this was merely a pretense she had employed to attract me to her castle and to tell me of her love. At one point I even thought I saw her foot move under the whiteness of the veils and disturb the straight lines of her shroud.

And then I said to myself, "Is it really Clarimonde? What proof have I? Could the black page not have moved to the service of another woman? I'm truly mad to be so distraught and so agitated." But the beating of my heart replied, "It is indeed her, it is indeed her." I went up to the bed and looked with redoubled attention at the object causing me such uncertainty. Dare I confess? The perfection of her shape, purified and sanctified though it was by the shadow of death, aroused me sexually more than I should have allowed, and her repose seemed so like sleep that anyone could have been misled. I forgot that I had come there to perform a funereal task, and I imagined that I was a young husband entering his bride's room, while she hides her face in modesty and is unwilling to let herself be looked at. Crushed with grief, wild with joy, trembling with fear and pleasure, I leaned toward her and took the corner of the sheet; I lifted it slowly, holding my breath for fear of arousing her. My veins beat with such strength that I could hear them whistling in my temples, and my brow dripped with as much perspiration as if I had been lifting a marble tombstone. It was indeed Clarimonde, as I had seen her at the church at the time of my ordination. She was just as charming, and death in her case seemed merely an additional seduction. The pallor of her cheeks, the loss of pinkness in her lips, her long lashes which were lowered and whose brown fringe was etched against that whiteness, all gave her an expression of melancholy, chastity, and thoughtful suffering that was unspeakably seductive. Her long, unbound hair in which a few little blue flowers were still mingled, made a pillow for her head, and their curls protected the nakedness of her shoulders. Her lovely hands, purer and more transparent than the Eucharist, were folded in an attitude of pious repose and silent prayer, which corrected whatever might have been too seductive, even in death, about the exquisite roundness of her naked arms, whose pearl bracelets had not been removed. For a long time I remained absorbed in silent contemplation, and the more I looked at her the less I could believe that life had abandoned that lovely body forever. I do not know whether it was an illusion or the reflection of the lamp, but it seemed that the blood began to flow again under the dull pallor, and yet she continued to lie perfectly still. I touched her arm gently; it was cold, and yet no colder than her hand on the day when she had brushed mine under the church portico. I resumed my position, with my face bent over hers as I dropped on her cheeks the warm dew of my tears. Oh! How bitterly I felt my despair and my powerlessness! What suffering there was in watching over that corpse! I would have liked to be able to gather my life into a parcel to give to her. I longed to blow over her frozen remains the flame that devoured me. The night was passing, and as I felt we were nearing the moment of eternal separation, I could not refrain from giving myself that sad and final sweetness of pressing a kiss on the dead lips of the woman who had had all my love. O miracle! A light breath mingled with my breath, and Clarimonde's mouth replied to the pressure of mine. Her eyes opened and regained some of their sparkle, she sighed, and unfolding her arms she flung them around my neck with an expression of inexpressible delight. "Oh, it's you, Romuald," she said in a voice as sweet and as full of languor as the last vibrations of a harp. What ever are you doing? I have waited for you so long that I have died. But now we are betrothed I'll be able to see you and visit you. Farewell, Romuald, farewell! I love you, that's all I wanted to tell you, and I return to you the life that you gave me for a minute with your kiss. May we meet again soon."

Her head fell back but she still circled me with her arms as if to hold me. A furious whirlwind broke through the window and swirled into the room; the last petal of the white rose trembled for a little like a wing at the end of its stalk, then dropped and flew out through the opening window, carrying with it Clarimonde's soul. The lamp went out, and I fell in a faint on the breast of the beautiful dead woman.

When I regained consciousness I was lying in my bed in my little bedroom in the parsonage, and the former curé's old dog was licking my hand as it lay outside the blanket. Barbara was fussing around the room with a senile trembling, opening and shutting drawers, or shaking powders into glasses. When she saw me open my eyes, the old woman gave a cry of joy, the dog barked and waved his tail, but I was so weak that I could not say a single word or make the slightest movement. I have since discovered that I remained like that for three days, giving no sign of life other than an almost imperceptible respiration. Those three days have no place in my life. I do not know where my spirit went during that time. I have retained no memory of it. Barbara told me that the same man with the copper complexion who had come to seek me out during the night had brought me back in the morning in a closed litter and had returned immediately. As soon as I could summon my thoughts, I went over in my mind the circumstances of that fatal night. At first I thought I had been the victim of a magic trick. But real and palpable circumstances soon destroyed any such supposition. I could not believe it was all a dream, since Barbara had seen as I had the man with the two black horses, and she described his appearance and dress exactly. Nevertheless, no one knew a castle in the neighborhood that corresponded to the description of the castle where I had rediscovered Clarimonde.

One morning I saw Abbot Serapion come in. Barbara had informed him that I was ill, and he had come in all haste. Although this speed revealed his affection for me and his interest in me, his visit did not bring me the pleasure it should have. The abbot's eyes had a penetration and an inquisitorial air that embarrassed me. I felt disturbed and guilty in his presence. He had been the first to discover my spiritual distress, and I resented his clearsightedness.

While he asked me, with honey-sweet hypocrisy, how I was feeling, he fixed on me two eyes as yellow as a lion's and plunged his gaze into my heart as if measuring it. Then he asked me several questions about how I was running my parish, whether I was happy there, how I spent my time when my duties left me free, if I had made any acquaintances among the local inhabitants, what my favorite books were, and a thousand other such details. I answered all that as briefly as I could, and without waiting for me to finish he himself moved on to other topics. This conversation obviously had no connection with what he really wanted to say. Then, without any preparation, and as though it were an item of news he had just remembered at that instant and was afraid he might forget later, he said in a clear and vibrant voice that resounded in my ear like the trumpets of the Day of Judgement: "The great courtesan Clarimonde died recently, as the result of an orgy that lasted eight days and eight nights. It was infernally splendid. They renewed the abominations practiced in the feasts of Balthazar[3] and Cleopatra. What an age we live in, good God! The guests were served by dark-skinned slaves speaking an unknown language. They strike me as being real demons; the livery worn by the lowliest of them would have provided an emperor with clothes he could wear at a gala. There have always been the strangest tales about that Clarimonde, and all her lovers have come to a miserable and violent death. People have said she is a ghoul, a female vampire; but it's my belief she was Beelzebub in person."

He fell silent and looked at me more attentively than ever, to see the working of his words on me. I had been unable to withhold a movement when I heard him pronounce Clarimonde's name, and the news of her death—along with the grief that it caused me through its strange coincidence with the nocturnal scene I had witnessed—troubled and frightened me in ways that were reflected in my face, despite all my efforts at control. Serapion threw me an anxious and severe glance, then said to me, "My son, I must warn you that you have one foot over an abyss. Take care not to fall into it. Satan has long claws, and tombs are not always faithful. Clarimonde's burial stone should be sealed with a triple seal, for it is said that this is not the first time she's died. May the Lord watch over you, Romuald!"

---

3. *Balthazar* (Belshazzar): Babylonian king who saw the words "Mene, tekel, peres" appear on the wall, written by a disembodied hand, as he was indulging himself in his final orgy. It was at that moment that his enemy entered Babylon (Daniel 5).

With these words, Serapion walked slowly to the door, and I did not see him again, for he left for S*** almost immediately afterwards.

I recovered completely and assumed my usual tasks once more. The memory of Clarimonde and the old abbot's words were constantly in my mind, but no bizarre event occurred to confirm Serapion's gloomy predictions, and I began to believe that his fears and my terror had both been exaggerations. But one night I had a dream. Scarcely had I drunk the first few gulps of sleep when I heard the curtains of my bed slide open while the curtain rings resounded loudly against the railing. I sat up abruptly on my elbow and saw the shadow of a woman standing before me. I recognized Clarimonde immediately. She carried in her hand a little lamp in the form of those that are placed on tombs, and its light gave to her slender fingers a pink transparency that continued while fading imperceptibly into the milky opaque whiteness of her bare arm. All she wore was the linen shroud which had covered her death bed, and she crushed the folds to her breast as if embarrassed to be wearing so little, but her small hand was not equal to the task. She was so white that the color of her shroud blended with that of her flesh under the pale rays of the lamp. Enveloped in this fine material, which betrayed all the contours of her body, she looked more like an antique marble statue of a bather than a living woman.

Dead or alive, statue or woman, shadow or substance, her beauty remained the same. Only the green glimmer of her eyes was somewhat dulled and her mouth which had been so red, was now merely a pale and delicate pink, almost the color of her cheeks. The little blue flowers I had noted in her hair had withered and lost almost all their petals, but that took nothing from her charm, a charm so great that despite the strangeness of what was happening and the inexplicable way in which she had come into my room, I did not feel a moment's terror.

She set the lamp on the table and sat on the foot of my bed, then leaned over me, saying in that voice that was simultaneously silvery and velvety and that she alone possessed, "I have kept you waiting a long time, my dear Romuald, and you must have thought I had forgotten you. But I have come from far away and from a place from which no one has hitherto returned. The country I come from has neither moon nor sun. It's only the distance of a shadow, but there's no path and no road, no earth for feet, no air for wings, and yet I am here for love is stronger than death and will finally vanquish it. Oh what grim faces and terrible things I saw on my journey! How hard it was for my soul, forced back into this world by the power of my will, to find its body again and reinstall itself. What efforts it took for me to raise the tombstone that had been placed over me! Look! The palms of my poor hands are still quite bruised from their struggles! Kiss them and make them better, my love!" She placed both of her cold palms, one after the other, on my mouth; and indeed I kissed them several times, and she watched me do so with a smile of indescribable pleasure.

I confess to my shame that I had completely forgotten the advice of Abbot Serapion and what behooved a man of my condition. I had fallen without any resistance and at the first attack. I had not even attempted to repulse the tempter. The coolness of Clarimonde's skin penetrated my own, and I felt shivers of sensual pleasure running over my entire body. Poor girl! Despite all I had seen I still found it hard to believe she was a devil. At least she didn't look like one, and never has Satan kept his claws and his horns better hidden. She had folded her heels beneath her and crouched down at the side of my bed in a position full of carefree coquetry. From time to time she ran her little hand through my hair and rolled it into curls as if she were seeing what I would look like with a different hair style. I allowed her to do so with the most culpable complacence, and she accompanied all of this with the most charming chatter. Remarkably, I felt no astonishment at such an extraordinary adventure, and with the facility one possesses in visions to admit as quite simple, events which are really very odd, I saw nothing in it that wasn't completely natural.

"I loved you long before I saw you, my dear Romuald, and I sought you out everywhere. You were my dream, and I caught sight of you in the church at the fatal moment. I immediately said to myself, 'It's him!' I sent you a glance into which I'd put all the love I'd felt in the past, that I felt at that moment, and that I was still to feel for you. It was a glance that would have damned a cardinal, that would have made a king kneel at my feet in front of his entire court. You remained unmoved and preferred your God to me. Oh! How jealous I am of God, for you loved Him, and you still love Him more than you love me! Oh, what an unhappy wretch I am! I shall never have your heart for myself alone, I whom you brought back to life with a kiss, Clarimonde the dead, who for your sake has forced open the doors of the tomb and who has come to devote to you a life she began again in order to make you happy!"

All these words were interrupted by wild caresses that so dazed my senses and my reason that I was not afraid to console her by expressing the most dreadful blasphemy, and telling her that I loved her as much as I loved God Himself.

Her eyes came back to life and shone like chrysoprases. "Truly? Really and truly? As much as God!" she said, enfolding me in her lovely arms. "If that is so, come with me, follow me where I lead you. You'll leave behind those horrible black clothes. You'll be the proudest and most envied of knights, and you will be my lover. To be the avowed lover of Clarimonde, she who has refused a pope, that's really fine! Oh, how good and happy our life will be, the golden life we're going to lead! When will we leave, my lord?"

"Tomorrow! Tomorrow!" I cried deliriously.

"Tomorrow it'll be then!" she replied. "I'll have time to change my clothes, for this outfit is somewhat succinct and would be of no value on a voyage. I'll also need to go and warn my servants, who think I'm truly dead and who are as grief-stricken as they can be. Money, clothes, carriages, everything will be ready. I'll come for you at the same time as tonight. Farewell, dear heart." And she touched my brow with her lips. The lamp went out, the bed curtains closed again, and I no longer saw anything. A leaden dreamless sleep fell upon me and kept me motionless until the following morning. I awoke later than usual, and the memory of that extraordinary vision disturbed me all day long. I finally convinced myself that it was nothing but vapors created by my overheated brain. Yet the sensations had been so intense that it was hard to believe they hadn't been real, and it was not without some apprehension about what would happen that I went to bed, having prayed to God to send all evil thoughts far away from me and to protect the chastity of my sleep.

I soon fell deeply asleep and my dream continued. The curtains parted, and I saw Clarimonde not as she had been the last time, pale in her pale shroud and with death's violets on her cheeks, but gay, lively, and elegant, in a superb traveling outfit in green velvet adorned with gold frogs and lifted up on one side to reveal a satin skirt. Her fair hair escaped in large curls from under a broad hat of black felt decked with white feathers whimsically curved. In her hand she held a little whip that ended in a golden whistle. She touched me lightly with it and said, "Well then, my fine sleeper, is this how you get ready? I expected to see you out of bed. Get up quickly, we have no time to lose." I leaped down from the bed.

"Come, get dressed, and let's go," she said, pointing out to me a little packet she had brought with her. "The horses are growing bored and are champing at the bit. We ought to be ten leagues away by now!"

I dressed quickly, and she herself handed me the items of clothing, laughing uproariously at my clumsiness, and showing me what they were used for whenever I made a mistake. She brushed my hair, and when all was ready she handed me a little Venetian crystal pocket mirror with a silver filigree border and said to me, "What do you think of yourself? Do you want to take me into your service as your personal valet?"

I was no longer the same man, and I didn't recognize myself. I was no more like myself than a completed statue is like a stone block. My former face seemed only to be a coarse first draft of the one the mirror reflected. I was handsome, and my vanity was discernibly flattered by that metamorphosis. Those elegant clothes, that rich embroidered waistcoat, made me into an entirely different person, and I admired the power of a few yards of material tailored in a certain way. The spirit of my suit penetrated my own, and within ten minutes I had become fairly conceited.

I strode around my room several times, to get used to my new clothes. Clarimonde gazed at me with an air of maternal pride and seemed very satisfied with her handiwork. "That's enough play for the moment! Let's go, Romuald! We've a long distance to travel, and we'll take forever to get there." She seized my hand and dragged me off. All the doors opened before her the instant she touched them, and we passed by the dog without waking it.

At the door we found Margheritone. This was the groom who had already guided me. He held the bridles of three horses, all of them black as the first two had been, one for me, one for himself, and one for Clarimonde. Those horses must have been Spanish arabs, born from mares serviced by the zephyr breeze, for they moved as swiftly as the wind. The moon, which had risen at our departure in order to light our way, rolled in the heavens like a wheel that had broken free from its chariot. We saw it on our right leaping from tree to tree and panting from having run after us. We soon reached a plain where a vehicle harnessed to four vigorous animals awaited us near a thicket of trees. We got in and the postilions made them set off at a wild gallop. I put one arm around Clarimonde's waist, and one of her hands was enfolded in mine. She leaned her head on my shoulder, and I felt her half-naked breast touch my arm. Never had I felt such intense happiness. I had forgotten everything at that moment, and the memories of my time as a priest had grown as vague as the memories of my time in my mother's womb, so great was the fascination the evil spirit exerted over me.

From that night on, my nature split in two, so to speak, and there were two men within me, neither of whom knew the other. Sometimes I believed I was a priest who dreamed every night that he was a lord, and sometimes a lord who dreamed he was a priest. I could no longer distinguish the world of dreams from the waking world, and I didn't know where reality ended and illusion began. The pretentious and libertine young lord mocked the priest, while the priest detested the young lord's dissolute life. The image of two spirals wound within each other and intermingling without ever touching offers a very good illustration of that twin-headed life I led. Despite the strangeness of my situation, I do not believe that I stepped into madness for a single moment. I have always preserved very clear perceptions of my two existences. Only there was an absurd fact I could never explain; that is, that the sense of the same identity should exist in two men who were so different. This was an anomaly I did not realize, either because I believed I was the priest of the small village of ***, or because I thought I was Lord Romualdo, the acknowledged lover of Clarimonde.

Whatever the case may be, I was, or at least I believed myself to be, in Venice. I have not yet been able to unravel what was illusion and what was reality in that bizarre adventure. We were living in a great marble palace on the Canaleio, full of frescoes and statues, with two Titians from his best period in Clarimonde's bedroom, a palace worthy of a king. Each of us had a gondola and a gondolier in our own livery, we had a music room and a poet. Clarimonde had a sumptuous view of life, and there was in her nature something reminiscent of Cleopatra. As for me, I was living the life of a prince and kicking up as much dust as if I'd been a family member of one of the twelve apostles or the four evangelists of the most serene republic. I would not have stepped aside to let the doge pass by, and I don't believe that anyone, since the days when Satan fell from heaven, has been more arrogant or insolent than I. I would go to the ridotto, and would bet hellishly. I used to see the finest society in the world, ruined sons, women of the stage, crooks, parasites, braggadocios. But despite the extreme dissipation of the life I was leading, I remained true to Clarimonde. I loved her wildly. She would have aroused satiety itself, and made inconstancy constant. To have Clarimonde was to have twenty mistresses, so mobile was she, so changeable, so unlike herself—a real chameleon! She would make you commit with her the infidelity you might otherwise have carried out with others, because she could adopt the entire character, the movements, the type of beauty of the woman who seemed to please you at a particular moment. She repaid my life a hundredfold, and it was in vain that young noblemen and even old men of the council of ten made her magnificent propositions. One of the Foscari even went so far as to propose marriage; she refused everything. She had had her fill of money. All she wanted was love, a young, pure love that she had awakened, a love that was to be first love and last love. I would have been perfectly happy had an accursed nightmare not returned every night, a nightmare in which I believed myself to be a village priest mortifying his flesh and punishing himself for the excesses I had committed during the day. Reassured by the habit of being with her, I no longer gave much thought to the strange way in which I'd met Clarimonde. Yet, what the Abbot Serapion had said about her sometimes came back to me and unfailingly caused me some disquiet.

For some time Clarimonde's health had not been as good; she grew daily paler. The doctors who were summoned understood nothing about her malady and had no idea what to do. They prescribed a few pointless remedies, and did not return. Nevertheless, she grew visibly paler, and became colder and colder. She was almost as white and almost as dead as on that famous night in the unknown castle. I was in despair at seeing her slowly fade away like this. She, touched by my sorrow, would smile at me softly and sadly with that fatalistic smile of those who know they are going to die.

One morning I was sitting beside her bed and breaking my fast at a small table in order not to leave her for a single minute. As I cut into a piece of fruit, I accidentally cut my finger fairly deeply. The blood immediately burst out in crimson streams, and a few drops fell on Clarimonde. Her eyes lit up, her face assumed an expression of wild, savage joy that I had never seen in her. She leaped from the bed with animal agility, the litheness of a cat or a monkey, and flung herself on my wound, which she began to suck with an expression of unspeakable pleasure. She swallowed the blood in little mouthfuls, slowly and preciously as a gourmet savors a Sherry or a Syracuse wine. She half-closed her eyes, and the pupil of those green eyes became oblong instead of round. From time to time she stopped to kiss my hand, then she began again to press her lips to the lips of my wound to extract yet more red drops. When she saw that no more blood flowed from it, she got up, her eyes moist and shining, her skin pinker than a May dawn, her face full, her hand warm and moist, in a word more lovely than ever and in a state of perfect health.

"I'm not going to die! I'm not going to die!" she said, half mad with joy as she clung around my neck. "I'll be able to love you for a long time still. My life is in your life, and all that is mine comes from you. A few drops of your rich and noble blood, more precious and more efficacious than all the elixirs in the world, have given me back my life."

This scene long preoccupied me and inspired in me strange doubts about Clarimonde, and that very evening, when sleep had returned me to the parsonage, I saw Abbot Serapion, looking graver and more worried than ever. He looked at me attentively and said, "You're not content to lose your soul! You're trying to destroy your body as well! Unfortunate young man, what a trap you've fallen into!"

The tone in which he said those few words struck me profoundly. But, despite its keenness, this impression was soon diminished, and a thousand other cares erased it from my mind. Yet one evening I saw in my mirror, on whose treacherous position she had not calculated, that Clarimonde was tipping a powder into the glass of spiced wine she usually prepared me after our meal. I took the glass and pretended to drink it, then placed it on the sideboard as if to finish it at my leisure later. Taking advantage of a moment when my beauty had her back turned, I threw the contents under the table. After that, I retired to my room and went to bed, fully determined not to sleep, but to watch everything that transpired. I didn't have long to wait; Clarimonde came in her night dress, and, having removed her veils, lay down in the bed beside me. When she was sure I was sleeping, she bared my arm and drew a gold pin from her hair. Then she began to murmur softly, "A drop, just a little red drop, a bit of red at the tip of my needle! . . . Since you still love me, I must not die . . . Oh! my poor love, I'm going to drink your lovely crimson blood. Sleep, my only beloved, sleep my god, my child. I won't hurt you, I'll only take from your life what I need in order for my own not to fade away. If I didn't love you so much, I could find the resolve to take other loves, whose veins I'd drain, but since I've known you, everyone else repels me . . . Oh! what a lovely arm! how round it is! How white! I'll never dare prick that pretty blue vein." As she said this she sobbed, and I felt her tears rain down on my arm as she held it in her hands. At last she made up her mind, and gave me a little prick with her needle. She began to suck the blood that flowed from it. Although she had scarcely drunk a few drops, she was seized by the fear of exhausting me, and she carefully wrapped a little bandage around my arm, after rubbing the wound with an ointment that closed it immediately.

I could no longer entertain the slightest doubt. Abbot Serapion was right. Yet despite that certainty, I could not help loving Clarimonde. I would willingly have given her all the blood she needed in order to support her fallacious existence. Moreover, I wasn't very frightened. The woman in her protected me from the vampire, and what I had heard and seen reassured me completely. At that time my veins were so plump that they weren't likely to be rapidly drained, and I wasn't one to sell my life drop by drop. I would have opened my arm myself and said to her, "Drink! Let my love infiltrate its way into your body with my blood." I avoided making the slightest allusion to the narcotic she had given me or to the needle scene, and we continued to live in the most perfect harmony. Nevertheless, my priestly scruples tormented me more than ever, and I sought in vain for further kinds of punishment to overcome and mortify my flesh. Although all these visions came independently of my will, and although I took no part in them, I did not dare touch the body of Christ with hands so impure and a spirit defiled by such debauchery, whether real or dreamed. To avoid falling into those exhausting hallucinations, I tried to prevent myself from sleeping. I held my lids open with my hands and stood against walls, struggling with all my strength against sleep, but the sand of slumber soon rolled into my eyes and, seeing that the whole struggle was pointless, I let my arms fall in discouragement and lassitude while the current sucked me back into those treacherous dreams. Serapion exhorted me most vehemently, and harshly reproached me for my weakness and my lack of fervor. One day when I was more agitated than usual, he said to me, "There is only one way to free you of this obsession, and although it is extreme it must be taken. Great evils require great remedies. I know where Clarimonde was buried. We must dig up her body so that you can see in what a piteous state the object of your love is. You will no longer be tempted to lose your soul for a disgusting corpse devoured by worms and on the point of disintegrating into dust. Surely that will bring you back to your senses." As for me, I was so weary of this double life that I accepted. I wanted to know once and for all who was the dupe of an illusion, the priest or the lord, and so, to benefit one or the other, I was determined to kill one of the two men within me, or to kill both of them together, for such a life could not continue.

Abbot Serapion armed himself with a stake, a lever and a lantern and at midnight we set off for the cemetery of ***, whose placement and position he knew perfectly. Having held the light of the dark lantern over the inscriptions on several tombs, we at last reached a stone half-hidden under tall grass and devoured by moss and parasitical grasses, on which we could make out the opening words of this inscription: "Here lies Clarimonde, who during her life was the most beautiful woman in the world. . . . " "It's here," said Serapion, and, putting his lantern on the ground, he slipped the lever into the gap in the stone and began to lift it. The stone yielded, and he set to work with the stake. I watched him, blacker and more silent than night itself. He himself, bent over his ghastly work, streamed with sweat, gasped and breathed so rapidly that it seemed the death rattle of a dying man. It was a strange sight, and anyone who had seen us would have taken us for profane grave robbers rather than priests of the Lord. Serapion's zeal had in it something hard and wild that made him resemble a demon rather than an apostle or an angel, and his face with its large, austere features, deeply etched by the reflection of the lantern, was far from reassuring. I felt a freezing sweat form on my limbs, and my hair stood up painfully on my head. In the depths of my being I considered the severe Serapion's actions an abominable sacrilege, and I would have liked the flanks of the dark clouds that rolled ponderously above us to let fall a triangle of fire that would reduce him to a powder. The owls that had perched on the cypresses, alarmed by the light of the lantern, came and beat heavily against the pane with their dusty wings, making plaintive moans; foxes barked in the distance, and a thousand sinister noises broke from the silence. At last Serapion's shovel struck the coffin, whose planks reechoed with a dull and sonorous sound, the dreadful sound the void makes when you touch it. He flung open the lid, and I saw Clarimonde as pale as a marble statue, her hands joined. Her white shroud fell straight down from her head to her feet. A little red drop glistened at the corner of her pallid mouth. Catching sight of this Serapion flew into a fury: "Ah! There you are, you devil, you shameless courtesan, you drinker of blood and gold!" and he scattered holy water on the body and the coffin, on which he drew the form of a cross with his aspergillum. Poor Clarimonde had no sooner been touched by the holy water than her lovely body disintegrated into dust. She was no longer anything but a horribly shapeless mixture of ashes and half-burned bones. "There is your mistress, Lord Romuald," said the inexorable priest, as he showed me these grim remains. "Are you still tempted to promenade on the Lido or at Fusine with your fair one?" I lowered my head. My life had just collapsed in ruins. I returned to my parsonage, and Lord Romuald, the lover of Clarimonde, parted from the poor priest with whom he had so long kept such strange company. Only the next night I saw Clarimonde. She said to me, as she had the first time under the portico of the church: "Wretch! Wretch! What have you done? Why did you listen to that imbecile priest? Weren't you happy? And what had I done to you for you to violate my poor tomb and lay bare the misery of my emptiness? All communication between our souls and our bodies is henceforth broken forever. Farewell. You will miss me." She evaporated into the air like smoke, and I never saw her again.

Alas! She told the truth. I have missed her more than once, and I still miss her. My peace of soul was bought for a very high price. The love of God was only just enough to replace her. There, brother, you have the story of my youth. Never look at a woman, and walk with your eyes always riveted to the ground, for however chaste and calm you may be, it takes only a moment to make you lose all eternity.

Nerval

◆

Gérard de Nerval is the pseudonym of Gérard Labrunie (1808–1855), a French poet and prose writer who published a remarkable translation of Goethe's Faust *when he was twenty, traveled widely in Germany, Italy, and the Near East, but suffered a series of mental breakdowns between 1841 and his suicide in 1855. His collection of sonnets,* Les Chimères, *reveals a mind of exceptional complexity, a fascination with a syncretic view of history and myth, and a sensitivity to the suggestion of rhyme and image that make him one of the greatest poets of the century.* Aurélia, *his exploration in prose of the visions and dreams that led to his mental breakdown, is a work of powerful psychological insight, all the more poignant for its touches of humor and its rejection of any suggestion of self-pity. The extraordinary lucidity and poetic beauty of* Sylvie *render it a superb representation of the workings of memory, the multiple layers of the subconscious, and the revelatory qualities of dream.*

FURTHER READING: *Journey to the Orient*, tr. Norman Glass (New York: New York University Press, 1972)
TEXT USED: *Sylvie* (Paris: Giraud, 1854)

SYLVIE: MEMORIES OF THE VALOIS[1] (1854)

I. LOST NIGHT

I was leaving a theater where, every evening, I appeared in the wings in the full regalia of a suitor. Sometimes the house was full, sometimes it was empty. It mattered little to me whether I could feast my eyes on

---

1. *Valois:* This region to the north of Paris is named for the royal dynasty of France who reigned from 1328 to 1589.

orchestra stalls inhabited by a mere thirty or so loyal theater buffs, or on boxes decked with bonnets and outdated dresses, or whether I was part of an animated, trembling throng crowned at every level with flower-adorned outfits, sparkling jewels, and radiant faces. Indifferent to what was taking place in the house, my attention was scarcely captured by what took place on the stage either—except at the moment when, in the first or second act of one of that period's dull masterpieces, a well-known apparition illuminated the empty space, giving life with a breath and a word to those empty figures that surrounded me.

I felt I lived in her and that she lived for me alone. Her smile filled me with infinite bliss; the vibration of her voice, so soft and yet strongly inflected, made me tremble with joy and love. For me she possessed all the perfections, she was the answer to all my enthusiasms, all my caprices—as lovely as the day in the stage lights that lit her from below, pale as night when the lowered ramp left her lit from above by the rays from the chandelier and revealed her as more natural, shining in the shadows with the light of her beauty alone, like the holy hours that rise up each with a star on her brow, from the brown background of the frescoes at Herculaneum![2]

A whole year had gone by and still it had not even crossed my mind to inquire about what she might be outside the theater; I was afraid to disturb the magic mirror that transmitted her image to me, and the most I had done was to lend an ear to a few statements concerning, not the actress, but the woman. I took as little trouble to find out about these rumors as I would have about gossip that might have centered on the Princess of Eldium or the Queen of Trebizond, since one of my uncles, who had lived in the very last years of the eighteenth century and had led the kind of life one had to lead to know the century well, had warned me from an early stage that actresses were not women and that nature had omitted to give them a heart. No doubt he was speaking of those of his own time, but he had told me so many tales of his illusions and his disappointments and shown me so many portraits on ivory, so many charming medallions that he now used to adorn tobacco cases, so many yellowing letters and wilted favors that I had grown accustomed to thinking ill of all of them without keeping in mind the passing of time.

Those were strange times we were living in, like those that normally follow revolutions or accompany the decay of mighty reigns. It was no longer a time of heroic gallantry, of the kind seen during the Fronde;[3]

---

2. *Herculaneum:* One of the ancient towns on the Bay of Naples, destroyed in the eruption of Vesuvius in A.D. 79.

3. *The Fronde:* An uprising (1648–1653) during the ministry of cardinal Mazarin, during the minority of Louis XIV.

ours was not the elegant, ornamental vice that thrived under the Regency,[4] or the skepticism and wild orgies of the Directory;[5] this was an age marked by a mixture of activity, hesitation and laziness, of glittering utopias, philosophical or religious aspirations, vague enthusiasms, mingled with certain intimations of a renaissance; a time when we were bored with past discord and uncertain hopes—something like the times of Peregrinus[6] or Apuleius.[7] Material man longed for the bouquet of roses that was to regenerate him through the hands of lovely Isis;[8] the eternally young and pure goddess appeared to us in our dreams and made us ashamed of our wasted days. Yet we were not of the age to have ambitions, and the greedy carving up of positions and honors that was taking place at that time drove us away from possible spheres of activity. The only asylum that remained open to us was that ivory tower of the poets, up which we constantly climbed higher and higher to isolate ourselves from the throng. On those high peaks to which our masters led us, we at last breathed in the pure air of empty spaces, we drank oblivion from the golden chalice of legends, and found intoxication in poetry and love. A love, alas!, of vague shapes, of pink and blue shades, of metaphysical phantoms! Seen from close up, flesh-and-blood woman repelled our innocence; it was essential that she appear as a queen or goddess, and above all she must never come near us.

Nevertheless a few of us had little time for such platonic paradoxes, and through our dreams of a rejuvenated Alexandria they sometimes waved the torch of subterranean gods, lighting the darkness for an instant with their wake of sparks. This was why, when I left the theater with that bitter sorrow we experience on awakening from a dream, I liked to join a large group that took supper together, where all melancholy yielded before the unquenchable verve of a few striking minds, minds that were lively, tempestuous, and sometimes sublime—the sort of mind that has always been present in times of renovation and decadence, and whose conversations reached such a pitch that the more timid among us sometimes went to the windows to see whether the Huns, the Turks, or the Cossacks were at last arriving to bring the arguments of these rhetoricians and sophists to an abrupt end.

"Wisdom lies in wining and wenching!" That was the only opinion these young men held. One of them said to me, "I've been meeting you

---

4. *Regency:* Period of 1715 to 1723, when Philippe, duke of Orléans, set aside the will of Louis XIV to govern France during the minority of Louis XV.

5. *The Directory:* The constitution of 1795 invested executive power in five "Directors," one of whom retired every year. It survived a mere four years, coming to an end with Bonaparte's *coup d'état* in 1799.

6. Peregrinus, a writer who died around A.D. 167, was considered a charlatan.

7. *Apuleius:* Latin writer of the second century, author of *The Golden Ass.*

8. *Isis:* A principal goddess of ancient Egypt.

at the same theater for ages, now. Every time I go there, you're there. Which one do you go for?" Which one? To me it did not seem possible that one might go there for any but her. Nevertheless, I conceded a name. "Well!" said my friend indulgently, "over there is the happy man who has just accompanied her home, and who, faithful to the laws of our circle, may very well not go back to her until the night is over."

Without much emotion I turned my eyes toward the person he indicated. He was a young man, correctly dressed, with a pale and nervous face, passable manners and eyes imbued with melancholy and gentleness. He threw money onto a whist table and lost it with indifference. "What does it matter to me," I said, "whether it's him or anyone else? There had to be someone, and he strikes me as worthy of having been chosen." "And you?" "Me? I'm pursuing an image, nothing more."

On my way out, I went through the reading room, and mechanically looked at a newspaper. I think I wanted to see the figures for the stock exchange. In the ruins of my opulence there was a fairly high sum in the form of foreign stocks. The rumor had been abroad that these stocks, long neglected, were going to be honored. This had just taken place as the result of a change of ministry. The stocks were already valued very highly; I found myself rich again.

A single thought was inspired by this change in my fortunes: the woman I had so long loved could be mine if I wished. I could reach out and touch my ideal. Was it perhaps another illusion, an ironic printing error? But other papers gave the same news. The sum I had gained rose up before me like the gold statue of Moloch. "What would the young man I saw a moment ago have to say now," I thought, "if I were to take his place beside the woman he has left alone?" I trembled at this thought, and my pride rose up in rebellion.

No! Not in such a way and not at my age was love to be killed by money. I would not be a corrupter. Moreover, that was the thinking of another age. And who says that the woman was willing to be bought? My eyes wandered vaguely down the paper that I still held in my hand, and I read these two lines: "The Festival of the Bouquet in the Provinces.—Tomorrow, the archers of Senlis are to restore the bouquet to those of Loisy." These words, for all their simplicity, aroused in me a whole new series of impressions: it was a memory of a province long-forgotten, a far-off echo of the innocent festivals of youth. The horn and the drum resounded far off in hamlets and woods; young girls braided garlands and matched bouquets with colored ribbons, singing as they worked. A heavy cart, drawn by oxen, received gifts as it passed, and we, the children of the district, formed a procession with our bows and arrows, adorning ourselves with the title of knights—not knowing then that we were merely repeating down the centuries a druidic festival that had survived new monarchies and new religions.

II. ADRIENNE

I went back home to bed and could find no rest there. As I lay there, plunged in a half-sleep, all my youth went past me in the form of memories. This state, in which the mind still resists the bizarre combinations created by dreams, often allows you to see rushing by in a few minutes the most striking tableaux from a long span of years.

I conjured up before my eyes a chateau from the days of Henri IV,[9] with its pointed roofs covered with tiles and its reddish face with the corners embellished with yellowing stones, a large green square framed with elms and lindens whose foliage was shot through with the flaming rays of the setting sun. Girls danced in a circle on the lawn, singing old songs that had been handed down to them by their mothers, and in a French so naturally pure that one really felt one was living in that old country of the Valois kings, in which the heart of France had beaten for over a thousand years.

I was the sole boy in that circle, to which I had brought my companion, Sylvie, who was still very young, a little girl from the neighboring hamlet, so lively and so fresh, with her black eyes, her regular profile and her lightly tanned skin! I loved none but her, I saw none but her . . . at least until then! I had scarcely noticed in the circle in which we were dancing a tall, lovely blond girl, who was called Adrienne. Suddenly, in accordance with the rules of the dance, Adrienne stood alone in front of me in the middle of the circle. We were of the same height. We were told to kiss each other, and the dance and the chorus spun even more quickly than before. As I gave her that kiss, I could not refrain from pressing her hand. The long, curling rings of her golden hair touched my cheeks. From that moment I was seized with an unknown sense of unease.—The lovely girl had to sing in order to gain the right to re-enter the dance. Everyone sat down around her, and immediately, in a fresh, penetrating voice, a voice that was lightly veiled like the voice of girls from a foggy country, she sang one of those old romances full of melancholy and love, that always tell the misfortunes of a princess locked away in her tower through her father's decree as a punishment for having loved. The melody stopped at the end of each stanza with those trembling trills that bring out the best in young voices when they imitate, through a modulated shiver, the trembling voices of grandmothers.

As she sang, the shadows descended over the tall trees, and the growing moonlight fell on her alone, standing isolated within our rapt circle.—She fell silent, and no one dared break the silence. The lawn was covered with delicate, condensed vapors that draped their white flakes along the tips of the grasses. We thought we were in paradise.—At last

---

9. Henri IV (1553–1610), king of France from 1589 to 1610.

I stood up, ran to the chateau flower garden, where the laurel trees grew in great pottery vases on which cameos were painted. I brought back two branches, which we then braided into a crown and bound with a ribbon. I put this ornament on Adrienne's head, and the shining leaves gleamed on her blond hair in the pale beams of the moon. She recalled Dante's Beatrice smiling at the poet as he wandered on the threshold of paradise.

Adrienne stood up. Straightening her tall back, she bowed to us graciously, and ran back into the chateau.—We were told she was the granddaughter of one of the descendants of a family that had been allied with the former kings of France; the blood of the Valois ran in her veins. For this festal day she had been permitted to mingle with our games; we were never to see her again, for the following day she departed again for the convent at which she was a boarder.

When I came back to Sylvie, I realized she was crying. The crown I had given the lovely singer with my own hands was the cause of her tears. I offered to go and pick another one, but she said that she didn't want one, since she didn't deserve it. In vain I tried to defend myself. She did not say another word to me during the time it took me to take her back to her family.

I myself was summoned back to Paris to take up my studies once more, and I carried with me that double image of a tender friendship sadly interrupted, and of an impossible and vague love, a source of painful thoughts that the philosophy I learned at college was powerless to calm.

Adrienne's face alone remained triumphant—a mirage of glory and beauty, softening or sharing the hours of stern study. In the holidays of the following year, I learned that that lovely girl whom I had barely seen was destined by her family to lead the life of a nun.

III. RESOLUTION

That half-dreamed memory explained everything. My vague and hopeless love, conceived for a woman of the theater, a love that seized me every evening at the hour of the performance, and left me only when the time came for sleep, had its origins in the memory of Adrienne, that flower of the night which had opened in the pale light of the moon, a pink and golden phantom sliding over the green grass half-bathed in white vapors. The resemblance to a face that had been forgotten for years henceforth delineated itself with exceptional clarity. It was a pencil drawing faded by the passing years that suddenly became a painting, like those old sketches by great masters that you admire in a museum and for which you suddenly find elsewhere the glittering original.

To love a nun in the form of an actress!! . . . and if it was the same woman! It was enough to drive you mad. It's the kind of fatal attraction in which the unknown draws you to it like a will-o'-the-wisp flying over the reeds in stagnant waters . . . Let's find our footing again in reality.

And Sylvie, whom I loved so well, why have I forgotten her for these past three years? She was truly a pretty girl, the loveliest in all Loisy!

She exists, she is doubtless good and pure at heart. I can see once more her window where the vine twines around a rosebush, with the cage of warblers hanging on the left; I can hear the sound of her sonorous spindles and her favorite song:

The lovely girl was sitting
Beside the flowing stream . . .

She's still waiting for me . . . Who would have married her? She is so poor.

In her village and in those that surround it, there are good peasants in their smocks, with their rough hands and their thin faces, and their tanned skin! She loved me alone, the little Parisian that I then was, when I went to visit my poor uncle near Loisy, my uncle who is now dead. For the last three years I'd been frittering away in lordly fashion the modest sum he left me, a sum that should have lasted me an entire lifetime. With Sylvie I would have preserved it. Chance has given part of it back to me. There is still time.

What is she doing at this time of night? She's asleep . . . No, she's not asleep, for today it's the feast of the bow, the only night of the year in which you dance all night long. She is at the feast.

What's the time?

I had no watch.

In the midst of all the splendid pieces of bric-a-brac that in those days it was customary to group together to restore an apartment from the past to all its local color, there gleamed with a rejuvenated glow one of those shell clocks that date from the Renaissance, with its gilded dome surmounted by the figure of Time and supported by caryatids in the Medici style, which in their turn rest on horses that are half-rearing. The historical Diana, leaning on a stag, is in bas-relief under the clock face, on which the enameled figures indicating the hours are marked against inlaid enamel work. The mechanism, which was no doubt excellent, had not been wound for two centuries. When I bought this clock in Touraine, it was not in order to tell the time of day.

I went down to the caretaker's apartment. His cuckoo clock showed that it was one in the morning. In four hours, I said to myself, I can be at the Loisy ball. On the square in front of Palais-Royal there were still five or six cabs waiting for those who frequented the clubs and gaming houses. "To Loisy!" I said to the most obvious of these.

"Where's that?" "Near Senlis, eight leagues away." "I'll take you to the mail station," said the coach driver, who was less preoccupied than I was.

What a gloomy route that Flanders road is, a road that becomes beautiful only when it reaches the forest region. Two lines of monotonous trees go endlessly by, grimacing with their vague shapes; beyond are squares of green and plowed land, bordered on the left by the bluish hills of Montmorency, Écouen, Luzarches. Here is Gonesse, a vulgar town full of memories of the League[10] and the Fronde . . .

Beyond Louvres is a path bordered by apple trees whose flowers I have often seen gleaming in the night like stars on earth; this was the quickest route to the hamlets.–While the carriage climbs the hills, let's put some order into the memories of those days when I went there so often.

IV. A JOURNEY TO CYTHERA

A few years had passed. By now, the time when I had met Adrienne at the chateau was already nothing more than a childhood memory. I was back again at Loisy at the time of the patron saint's festival. Once again I joined the knights of the bow, taking my place in the company in which I had already participated. Young men belonging to the old families who, in that area, still own chateaux lost in the forests, and that have suffered more from time than revolutions, had arranged the festival. From Chantilly, Compiègne, and Senlis, joyful cavalcades came flocking, taking their place in the rustic procession of the companies of the bow. After the long procession through the villages and towns, after mass in the church, after competitions of skill and the distribution of the prizes, the victors had been invited to a meal held on an island shaded by poplars and linden trees in the middle of one of the ponds fed by the Nonette and the Thève. Flag-bedecked barks took us to the island, the choice of which had been determined by the existence of an oval temple with columns that was to serve as a dining hall for the feast. There, as at Ermenonville,[11] the country is scattered with these delicate edifices from the end of the eighteenth century where millionaire philosophers drew inspiration for their plans from the dominant taste of the day. I fully believe this temple had initially been dedicated to Urania.[12] Three columns had collapsed, carrying in their fall a part of the architrave; but the interior of the room had been cleared of rubble,

---

10. *The League:* This group was founded in 1576 to maintain the Catholic faith in France. It was organized by the Guise family, to keep the Protestant Henri IV from the throne.

11. *Ermenonville:* This village is closely associated with the philosopher Jean-Jacques Rousseau, who died there.

12. *Urania:* Muse of astronomy in Greek mythology.

garlands hung between the columns, and thus this modern ruin had been rejuvenated—a ruin that belonged to the paganism of Boufflers[13] or Chaulieu[14] more than to that of Horace.

The voyage across the lake had been designed as a reminiscence of Watteau's[15] *Voyage to Cythera*. Probably our modern costumes were the only thing that clashed with the illusion. The immense bouquet of the festival had been removed from the cart that carried it and placed on a great bark. The procession of girls clad in white that accompanied it according to custom had taken their places on the benches. That gracious *theorem*, which recalled the days of antiquity, was reflected in the calm waters of the pond that separated it from the bank of the island which glowed so pink in the evening light with its hedgerows of hawthorn, its colonnade, and its light foliage. All the barks landed at the same time. The basket which had been conveyed so ceremoniously was placed in the center of the table, and everyone took a seat, the most favored boys sitting next to girls: all that was needed was for the boy to know the girl's parents. That was why I found myself once more beside Sylvie. Her brother had already joined me again in the festivities and criticized me for not having visited the family for such a long time. I excused myself on the grounds of my studies, which kept me in Paris, and assured him I had come with the intention of visiting them. "No, it's me he's forgotten," said Sylvie. "We're village folk, and Paris is so far above us!" I wanted to kiss her to close her mouth, but she still bore me a grudge, and her brother had to intervene to make her offer me her cheek with an air of indifference. This kiss gave me no joy for it was one that many others had been favored with, since in this patriarchal country where everyone who passes is greeted, a kiss is nothing but an act of politeness between well-brought-up people.

The organizers of the festival had arranged a surprise. At the end of the meal, a wild swan flew away from the depths of the giant basket, having been held captive until that moment under the flowers which now its strong wings, breaking through the network of garlands and crowns, finally scattered in all directions. I had the good fortune to catch one of the finest of them, and Sylvie, wreathed in smiles, this time allowed herself to be kissed more tenderly than before. I understood that with this gesture I had removed the memory of another time. This time she had no need to share my admiration with anyone else, she had become so lovely! She was no longer the little village girl whom I'd passed over for someone who was older and more ready for the world's graces. Everything about her had improved. The charm of her

---

13. *Boufflers:* Stanislas Jean, chevalier de Boufflers (1738–1815), author of light poetry and short stories.

14. *Chaulieu:* Guillaume Amfrye, abbot of Chaulieu (1639–1720), poet.

15. Antoine Watteau (1684–1721), French painter particularly known for his scenes of lovers disporting themselves in rural landscapes.

dark eyes, which from childhood had been so seductive, had become irresistible. Under the arched curve of her brows, her smile, which suddenly lit up features that were regular and placid, had about it something of the Athenian. I admired those features, which bore comparison with the art of antiquity, in the midst of the rumpled faces of her companions. Her long, delicate hands, her arms that had grown whiter as they had grown rounder, her supple form, made her quite different from the girl I had known. I could not prevent myself from saying how much she'd changed, hoping that this would cover up my old and brief infidelity.

Everything smiled on me, moreover: her brother's friendship, the charming impression created by the feast, the evening hour, and the place itself—in which, through a highly tasteful whim, someone had reproduced a picture of the gallant traditions of days gone by. As long as we could, we escaped from the dance to chat about our childhood memories and to admire, as we dreamed together, the reflections of the sky in the shadows and on the water. Sylvie's brother had to tear us from this contemplation by saying that it was time to return to their village, which was some distance away.

V. THE VILLAGE

It was at Loisy, in the former guard's house. I accompanied them there and then returned to Montagny, where I was staying with my uncle. When I left the path to cross a little wood that separates Loisy from Saint-S . . . I soon entered a deep track that runs alongside the forest of Ermenonville; I then expected to meet some convent walls that one followed for a quarter of a league. From time to time the moon disappeared behind clouds, barely lighting the dark sandstone rocks and the heather that grew thick beneath my feet. To right and left were forest borders with no marked roads, and always in front of me those druidic rocks of the region that retain the memory of Herminius' sons, exterminated by the Romans! From the top of these sublime piles, I could see the far-off ponds standing out like mirrors on the misty plain, although I could not distinguish the lake where the feast had taken place.

The air was warm and full of scents; I resolved to go no farther but to await morning, lying down on clumps of heather.—When I woke up, I gradually recognized the features that lay near the place where I had wandered astray that night. On my left I could see the outline of the long line of the walls of the convent of Saint-S..., then on the other side of the cliff of the Gendarmes, with the breached ruins of the former Carolingian residence. Nearby, above the clusters of trees, the high ruins of the abbey of Thiers stood out against the horizon, with sections of wall pierced into clover-leaves and ogives. Beyond, the Gothic manor

of Pontarmé, surrounded by water as it had been in the past, soon reflected the first fires of day, while arising in the south could be seen the
high keep of La Tournelle and the four towers of Bertrand-Fosse on
the first hill of Montméliant.

The night had been sweet for me, and my mind dwelt only on Sylvie;
nevertheless the sight of the convent raised in me the passing notion
that it was perhaps the one where Adrienne lived. The ringing of the
morning bell still echoed in my ears and had no doubt awakened me.
For an instant I thought of glancing over the walls by climbing to the
highest point of the rocks. But on reflection, I abstained as if from some
profanation. As daylight increased, this empty memory was driven from
my mind, leaving only the rosy features of Sylvie. "Let's go and wake
her up," I said to myself, and I set off again on the path to Loisy.

Here's the village at the end of the track that follows the forest;
twenty thatched cottages with vines and climbing roses clinging along
the walls. Early-rising spinners, heads bound in red kerchiefs, work together in front of a farm. Sylvie is not among them. She is almost a
lady, now that she creates fine lace, whereas her parents have remained
good village folk. I went up to her bedroom without surprising anyone; she had already been awake for a long time and was moving the
spindles of her lace machine, which clicked gently on the green square
supported on her knees. "There you are, lazybones!" she said with her
marvelous smile, "I'm sure you've only just got out of bed!" I told her
of the sleepless night I had spent, of my vague wanderings through the
woods and rocks. She was kind enough to pity me for an instant. "If
you're not tired," she said, "I'll give you some more exercise. Let's go
and see my great aunt at Othys." Scarcely had I replied than she leaped
up joyously, arranged her hair in the mirror, and put on a hat of rustic
straw. Innocence and joy beamed from her eyes. We set out, following the banks of the Thève, through meadows dotted with daisies and
bachelor's buttons, then down beside the woods of Saint Lawrence,
sometimes crossing streams and hedgerows to shorten the journey. The
blackbirds were singing in the trees, and the titmice burst joyfully from
bushes we touched as we walked by.

Sometimes we would find beneath our steps the periwinkles Rousseau had so loved, opening their blue corollas amidst the long strands
of paired leaves, modest lianas that stopped my companion's quiet feet.
Indifferent to the memories of the Genevan philosopher, she searched
for richly flavored strawberries, while I told her of La Nouvelle Héloïse,[16]
several passages of which I recited by heart. "Is it pretty?" she asked.
"It's sublime." "Better than Auguste Lafontaine?" "More tender." "Oh!
Very well," she said, "I must read it. I'll tell my brother to bring it to

---

16. La Nouvelle Héloïse: Rousseau's famous novel of love and self-denial.

me the first time he goes to Senlis." And I went on reciting fragments of *La Nouvelle Héloïse* while Sylvie picked strawberries.

VI. OTHYS

As we left the wood, we came across great clumps of crimson fox-gloves; she made an enormous bouquet of them, saying to me, "They're for my aunt. She'll be so pleased to have these lovely flowers in her room." We only had a section of the plain to cross to reach Othys. The village steeple rose up against the bluish hills that go from Montméliant to Dammartin. The Thève once again murmured over the sandstone and pebbles, growing smaller as we came nearer its source, where it rests in the meadows, forming a little lake surrounded by flags and iris. We soon reached the first houses. Sylvie's aunt lived in a little thatched cottage built in rough sandstone rocks that were covered with trellises of hops and ivy. She lived alone on a few squares of land that the village folk had cultivated for her since the death of her husband. The arrival of her niece was a real cause for joy. "Hello, aunt! Your children are here!" said Sylvie. "And we're starving!" She kissed her tenderly, put the flowers in her arms and at last got around to introducing me by saying, "This is my beau!"

I kissed the aunt in my turn, and she said, "How sweet he is . . . So he's blond! . . . " "He has nice, fine hair," said Sylvie. "That won't last," said the aunt, "but you've got time on your side, and as you're dark, you make a good couple." "We've got to give him something to eat, Aunt," said Sylvie. And she rummaged through the cupboards and the hutch finding milk, black bread, and sugar, spreading out on the table without too much care the crockery plates and bowls embellished with large flowers and roosters with bright feathers. A Creil porcelain jug, full of milk in which strawberries were floating, became the centerpiece, and after she'd stripped the garden of a few handfuls of cherries and goose-berries, she placed two vases of flowers at each end of the tablecloth. But the aunt pronounced these fine words, "All that's just dessert. Now you must leave the rest to me." She took down the frying pan and threw a log into the high chimney. "I don't want you getting your hands in this!" she said to Sylvie, who wanted to help her. "I'm not having you spoil those pretty fingers that make lace that's lovelier than anything you'll find at Chantilly. You've given me some, and I know what I'm talking about." "Oh, yes, Aunt! Listen, if you've got some bits of old lace, they would provide me with models." "Well, go and look upstairs. There may be some in the chest of drawers." "Give me the keys," said Sylvie. "Bless you!" her aunt replied, "the drawers aren't locked." "That's not true. There's one that's always shut." And while the good woman cleaned the pan after putting it in the fire, Sylvie untied from her belt a little key of worked steel, which she showed me with an air of triumph.

I followed her, climbing quickly up the wooden stairway that led to the bedroom. O holy youth and holy old age! Who then would have thought to tarnish the purity of a first love in this sanctuary of faithful memories? The portrait of a young man of the good old days smiled with his dark eyes and his red lips in an oval portrait with a gilded frame, hanging at the head of the rustic bed. He wore the uniform worn by gamekeepers of the house of Condé; his half-military attitude, his pink, benevolent face, his pure brow under his powdered hair, imbued what might otherwise have been a mediocre portrait with the grace of youth and simplicity. Some modest artist invited to the princely hunting domains had applied himself to portraying him as best he could, as well as his young wife, who could be seen in another medallion, attractive, canny, upright in her open blouse with its braided ribbons, teasing a bird that sits on the tip of her finger. Nevertheless it was the same good old woman who at that very moment was doing the cooking, bent over the hearth fire. That made me think of the circus fairies who hide, under their wrinkled mask, an attractive face, which they reveal right at the end when the temple of love appears with its turning sun radiating with magic fire. "O you good aunt!" I exclaimed, "how pretty you were." "And what about me?" said Sylvie who had succeeded in opening the aforementioned drawer. In it she'd found a long taffeta dress which crackled as she unfolded it. "I'm going to see if it will fit me," she said. "Oh, it'll make me look like an old fairy!"

"The fairy of legends who never grows old! . . . " I said to myself. Already Sylvie had undone her calico dress and let it fall to her feet. The old aunt's thick dress was a perfect fit for Sylvie's slim figure. She asked me to button it for her. "Oh, look at these flat sleeves, aren't they ridiculous?" she said. And yet the lace-bedecked sleeves set off admirably her bare arms, and her breasts fitted perfectly in the pure lines of the corsage with its yellowing tulle and its old-fashioned ribbons, which had, all too briefly, enfolded the aunt's lost charms. "Hurry up! Don't you know how to button a dress, then?" Sylvie said to me. She looked just like the village bride in the painting by Greuze.[17] "You need some powder," I said. "We'll go and find some." Once again she ferreted around in the drawers. Oh, what riches! How good it all smelled, how it gleamed in bright colors and modest adornments! Two fans in mother-of-pearl, slightly broken, some papier mâché boxes adorned with Chinese motifs, an amber necklace, and hundreds of frills and furbelows, including a gleaming pair of little shoes in white drugget with buckles encrusted with Irish diamonds! "Oh! I want to put them on," said Sylvie, "if only I can find the embroidered stockings!"

---

17. Jean-Baptiste Greuze (1725–1805), French painter known for paintings that convey a moral.

A second later, we unfolded a pair of stockings in soft pink silk with green medallions; but the aunt's voice, accompanied by the singing of the pan, suddenly recalled us to reality. "Go down quickly!" said Sylvie, and despite my protests, she would not let me help her put her shoes on. Meanwhile the aunt had begun to pour into a plate the contents of the pan, a piece of fried bacon with eggs. Sylvie's voice soon summoned me back. "Get dressed quickly!" she said, and, completely dressed herself, she showed me the wedding clothes of the gamekeeper placed together on the chest of drawers. In a second I transformed myself into a bridegroom of the previous century. Sylvie was waiting for me on the stairs and we both went down holding hands. The aunt exclaimed as she spun around, "Oh my dear children!" and she began to cry, then smiled through her tears.—We were the very picture of her youth, a cruel and charming apparition. We sat down beside her, moved and almost serious, but we soon recovered our gaiety, for once the first moment had passed, the good old woman thought of nothing else but remembering the splendid ceremonies of her wedding. She even discovered in her memory the alternating songs that used to be sung in those days, and that were exchanged between one end of the wedding table and the other, as well as the naive wedding song that accompanied the married couple on their way home after the dance. We repeated those stanzas with their simple rhythms, with their hiatuses and the assonances common in those days; songs as loving and florid as the canticle of Ecclesiastes—we were the bride and groom for one fine summer morning.

VII. CHÂALIS

It's four in the morning. The road plunges down a fold in the hills and then rises up again. The carriage will pass through Orry, then La Chapelle. On the left, there's a road that runs past the Hallate woods. It's along that road that Sylvie's brother took me one evening in his cart to a local ceremony. I believe it was the evening of Saint Bartholomew's day.[18] Through the woods, along little-frequented roads, his little horse flew as if on its way to a witches' sabbath. We returned to the paved road at Mont-l'Evêque, and a few minutes later we stopped at the guard house at the former abbey of Châalis. Châalis! Yet another memory.

This old retreat of emperors now offers for our admiration nothing more than the ruins of its cloister with their Byzantine arcading, the last row of which still stands out against the ponds—the forgotten remains of pious foundations which were once part of those domains formerly called Charlemagne's farmlets. Religion in this region far from

---

18. *Saint Bartholomew's day:* The date of the massacre of Protestants executed under the orders of Charles IX on the night of August 23, 1572.

roads and towns has preserved special traces of the long period in which the cardinals of the house of Este stayed there in the days of the Medicis: its attributes and customs still have a trace of the gallant and the poetic, and you can breathe in an essence of the Renaissance under the chapel's arches with their fine ribs decorated by Italian artists. Figures of saints and angels stand out in pink on the vaults painted in soft blue, with an air of pagan allegory that makes one think of Petrarchan sentimentality and the fabulous mysticism of Francesco Colonna.

We were intruders, Sylvie's brother and I, in the special festivity taking place on that particular night. A person of very high birth owned the domain in those days, and had had the idea of inviting several local families to a kind of allegorical performance, in which some of the boarders in the nearby convent were to appear. This was not a reminiscence of the tragedies of Saint-Cyr, but went back to the first experiments in lyricism brought into France in the days of the Valois. What I saw performed was like a mystery play from the days of antiquity. The costumes, consisting of long dresses, were differentiated only by the colors of the azure sky, of the hyacinth, and of the dawn. The scene was the dwelling of angels on the ruins of a world that had been destroyed. Each voice celebrated one of the splendors of this extinguished globe, and the angel of death defined the causes of its destruction. A spirit came up from the depths, holding in its hand a flaming sword and summoning the others to come and admire the glory of Christ, victor of Hell. This spirit was Adrienne, transfigured by her costume as she was already transformed by her vocation. The halo of gilded cardboard that circled her angelic head seemed to us quite naturally a circle of light; her voice had gained in strength and range, and the endless grace notes of the Italian song embroidered the singing of birds on the severe phrases of a sumptuous recitative.

As I go over these details in my mind, I now wonder if they are real or if indeed I dreamed them. Sylvie's brother was a little tipsy that day. We had stopped for a few moments in the guard house, where—and this really struck me—a swan was spread-eagled on the door while inside were tall closets in sculpted walnut, a great clock inside its case, and award trophies of bows and arrows above a red and green paper target. A strange dwarf, wearing a Chinese bonnet, held in one hand a bottle and in the other a ring, and seemed to invite the archers to aim true. This dwarf, I fully believe, was cut out of sheet metal. But was the appearance of Adrienne as true as these details and the unquestionable existence of the abbey at Châalis? In any case, it really was the guard's son who took us into the room where the play was taking place; we were near the door, behind a large seated company that was gravely affected. It was the feast of Saint Bartholomew—strangely linked to the memory of the Medicis, whose arms, linked with those of the house of Este decorated these old walls. Perhaps this memory is an obsession! Fortunately the carriage has stopped on the road to Plessis; I escape from the world of revery and have only fifteen minute's walk to reach Loisy along roads that are little frequented.

VIII. THE LOISY BALL

I arrived at the Loisy ball at that melancholy yet still sweet hour when the lights grow dim and flicker at the approach of day. The lower trunks of the lindens were in darkness, but their tops were gradually turning a bluish shade. The shepherd's flute no longer had to struggle so strongly with the trills of the nightingale. Everyone was pale and in the thinning groups I had difficulty meeting faces I knew. At last I caught sight of Tall Lisa, a friend of Sylvie. She kissed me. "Haven't seen you for a long time, Parisian!" "Yes, it's been a long time." "And you chose such a time to arrive?" "I've come on the mailcoach." "You didn't hurry!" "I wanted to see Sylvie. Is she at the ball?" "She never leaves before dawn; she just loves dancing."

In a second, I was beside her. Her face looked tired, but her dark eyes still gleamed in the Athenian smile of days gone by. A young man stood close by her. She indicated to him that she'd sit out the next contredance. He withdrew with a bow.

Day was beginning to break. We left the ball, hand in hand. The flowers in Sylvie's hair drooped in her free-flowing locks. The bouquet in her corsage was also losing its petals in the crushed lace, which she herself had cunningly wrought. I offered to accompany her home. It was fully daylight, but the weather was gloomy. The river Thève murmured on our left, leaving in its bends eddies of stagnant water, in which blossomed yellow and white water lilies, and where there gleamed like daisies the delicate embroidery of the water stars. The plains were covered with sheaves and haystacks, whose perfume went to my head without intoxicating me, just as the cool scent of woods and hedgerows of flowering thorn had done in the past.

It did not occur to us to cross those woods again. "Sylvie," I said to her, "you don't love me any more!" She sighed. "My dear," she said, "you have to accept the inevitable. Things don't happen in life as we wish they would. In the past you talked to me of *La Nouvelle Héloïse*. I read it, and I trembled when the first thing I came across was this sentence: 'Every young girl who reads this novel will be lost.' But I read on, trusting to my good sense. You remember the day when we put on the old wedding clothes that belonged to my aunt? The engravings in the book also depicted the lovers in old costumes from the past, so that for me you were Saint Preux, and I saw myself in Julie. Oh! Why didn't you come back then? But I was told you were in Italy. You must have seen much prettier girls than me over there!" "Not a single one, Sylvie, who had your expression and the pure lines of your face. Though you don't know it, you're a nymph of antiquity. What's more, the woods of this region are just as lovely as those of the Roman countryside. Just over there you can find piles of granite that are no less sublime, and a waterfall that plunges from the top of the cliffs like that at Terni. I saw nothing there whose absence I could regret here." "And in Paris?" she asked. "In Paris . . . " I shook my head and didn't answer. Suddenly I thought of the empty image that had so long led me astray.

"Sylvie," I said, "let's stop here, do you mind?"

I threw myself at her feet; I confessed, weeping copiously, how irresolute and capricious I'd been; I mentioned the fatal specter that was passing through my life.

"Save me!" I added, "I've returned to you forever."

She turned toward me with tender eyes.

At that moment, our discussion was interrupted by a violent outburst of laughter. It was Sylvie's brother, who had caught up with us, with that good rustic gaiety which is an inevitable result of a night of festivities and had been developed beyond measure by numerous refreshments. He summoned the gallant I had seen at the ball, who was lost far away in thorn bushes and who soon caught up with us. This boy was hardly any more sure on his feet than his companion, and seemed even more embarrassed by the presence of a Parisian than by that of Sylvie. His open face, his deference, with its mixture of embarrassment, prevented me from bearing him a grudge for having been the dancer for whom Sylvie had lingered so late at the dance. I considered he didn't pose much of a danger.

"We must go home," Sylvie said to her brother. "Until this afternoon!" she said to me, giving me her cheek.

The gallant took no offense at that.

IX. ERMENONVILLE

I didn't have the slightest desire to sleep. I went to Montagny to see my uncle's house once more. A great sense of sorrow seized me as soon as I caught sight of the yellow facade and the green shutters. Everything seemed in the same state as it had in the past. The only difference was that I had to go to the farmer to get the door key. Once the shutters had been opened, I felt a sense of tenderness on seeing again the old furniture, preserved in the same state and occasionally polished, the tall walnut wardrobe, two Flemish paintings that were said to be the work of an old artist who was our ancestor; large prints after Boucher[19] and a whole series of framed illustrations to *Emile*[20] and *La Nouvelle Héloïse*, by Moreau;[21] on the table, a stuffed dog I had known when it was alive,

---

19. François Boucher (1703–1770), French painter who painted pastoral scenes.

20. *Emile* is Rousseau's evocation of an ideal education.

21. *Moreau:* Jean-Michel Moreau the Younger (1741–1814), French engraver who illustrated the works of Molière, Rousseau, and Voltaire.

a former companion of my rambles in the woods, perhaps the last carlin, for it belonged to that lost race.

"As for the parrot," the farmer told me, "he's still alive; I brought him back to my place."

The garden presented a magnificent sight of wild vegetation. There I recognized in a corner a child's garden I had traced out in days gone by. I went, trembling, into the study, where you could still see the little library full of selected books, old friends of the man who no longer lived, and on the desk, a few ancient remains that had been found in the garden, vases, Roman medallions, a local collection that had made him happy.

"Let's go and see the parrot," I said to the farmer. The parrot asked for his dinner as he had in his heyday, and looked at me with that round eye, bordered with a heavily wrinkled skin, that makes you think of the experienced gaze of the old.

Full of the sad thoughts inspired by this belated return to places I had loved so much, I felt the need to see Sylvie again, for she was the sole living and still young face that tied me to this region. I took the track to Loisy once more. It was midday; everyone was asleep, weary after the festivities. It suddenly occurred to me to divert myself with a stroll to Ermenonville, which was a league away along a forest path. It was a fine summer day. I took pleasure at first in the coolness of this track, reminiscent of the kind of avenue found in parks. The uniformity of the great, green oaks was broken only by the white trunks of birches with their rustling leaves. The birds were silent, and all I heard was the sound made by the woodpecker hammering the trees to make itself a nest. At one point, I risked going astray, for the posts whose fingers announce the different routes now only offer the occasional letter, and even those are almost worn away. Finally, leaving the *Desert* on my left, I reached the dance circle, where you can still see the old folks' seat. All the memories of the philosophy of antiquity, brought back to life by the former owner of the domain, came crowding back to me before that picturesque representation of *Anarcharsis* or *Emile*.

When I saw the water of the lake gleaming through the branches of willows and hazel trees, I recognized perfectly a place where my uncle, in his walks, had often led me; it's the *Temple of philosophy* that its founder did not have the joy of completing. It has the form of the temple of the Tiburtian sibyl, and, still standing, under the shelter of a group of pine trees, it reveals all those great names in the history of thought, beginning with Montaigne and Descartes, and stopping at Rousseau. This unfinished edifice is now a mere ruin, ivy curls gracefully around it, and thistles have invaded the buckled steps. There, when still a child, I saw festivals in which young girls, clad in white, came to receive their prizes for study and good behavior. Where are the rose bushes that used to circle the hill? The briars and the raspberry brambles hide the last plants as they return to their wild state. As for the laurels, have they been cut, as the young girls say in their song, when they no longer wish to go to the woods?[22] No, those bushes from mild Italy have perished under our foggy skies. Happily Virgil's privets still flower as if to support the master's words, inscribed above the door: *Rerum cognoscere causas!*[23]—Yes, this temple is falling down, as are so many others. People, in their forgetfulness or weariness, will no longer come to this place, and indifferent nature will take back the terrain that art claimed from it; but the thirst for knowledge will remain forever, the driving force behind all strength and all activity!

Here are the poplars of the island, and here is Rousseau's tomb, empty of its ashes.[24] O sage! You gave us the milk of the strong, and we were too weak for it to benefit us. We have forgotten your lessons, lessons our fathers knew, and we have lost the meaning of your words, the last echo of ancient wisdom. And yet, let's not lose heart, but let's turn our eyes, as you did in your final moment, toward the sun!

I saw the chateau once again, the peaceful water that bordered it, the waterfall that moaned in the rocks, and that roadway that linked the two parts of the village, with its corners marked by four dovecotes, its lawn spreading out like a savannah, dominated by shady slopes. Gabrielle's[25] tower is reflected from afar in the waters of an artificial lake starred with short-lived flowers. The foam boils and the insects strum. . . . I must escape from the perfidious air that arises from the powdery sandstone of the desert and the heaths where pink heather intensifies the green of the bracken. How lonely and melancholy it is! Sylvie's enchanted gaze, the wild races she ran, her joyful cries, gave so much charm in days gone by to the places I have just visited! In those days she was still a wild child, her feet were bare, her skin was tanned, in spite of her straw hat, whose broad ribbon floated at random with her locks of black hair. We used to go and drink milk at the dairy, and they would say to me, "What a pretty sweetheart you have, little Parisian!" Oh, in those days no peasant would have danced with her! She danced only with me, once a year, at the feast of the bow.

X. BIG CURLY

I set off again on the path to Loisy. Everyone had awakened. Sylvie was wearing the sort of clothes a young lady might wear, almost in the taste of the city. She led me up to her room with all the open inno-

---

22. *The laurels:* A reference to the folk song that begins: "We will go no more to the woods, the laurels have been cut."

23. *Rerum cognoscere causas:* The quotation is from Virgil's *Georgics* (II.490). The full line runs: "Happy are they who are able to discover the causes of things."

24. Rousseau's body, contrary to his wishes, lies not at Ermenonville, but in the Panthéon in Paris.

25. Gabrielle (1571–1599) was the daughter of Antoine d'Estrées. In 1590, Henri IV happened to spend a night at the Château de Cœuvres and fell in love with her.

cence of the past. Her eyes still sparkled in a smile full of charm, but the strongly marked curve of her brows occasionally gave her a serious look. The room was decorated with simplicity, but the furniture was modern. A mirror with a gilded border had replaced the ancient pier-glass in which could be seen a shepherd boy of the sort found in idylls, offering a bird's nest to a shepherd girl in blue and pink. The columned bed chastely covered with old striped chintz had been replaced by a bunk in walnut and decorated with an arrow-patterned curtain. In the window, in the cage where formerly there had been warblers, there were now canaries. I was eager to leave this room, in which I found no trace of the past. "You're not working on your lace-making today?" I asked Sylvie. "Oh, I don't make lace any more: there's no demand for it in the region. Even at Chantilly, the factory has closed." "So what do you do?" She went to a corner of her room and took out an iron instrument that resembled a long pair of pincers. "Whatever is that?" "That's what's called the machine. It holds the glove leather so you can sew it." "Ah! So you're a glove maker, are you, Sylvie?" "Yes, we work here for Dammartin. There's a lot of call for gloves at the moment; but I'm not going to do anything today. We can go wherever you choose." I turned my eyes in the direction of Othys. She shook her head, and I realized that the old aunt was no longer in the land of the living. Sylvie summoned a little boy and got him to saddle the donkey. "I'm still tired from yesterday," she said, "but an outing will do me good. Let's go to Châalis." So there we were, crossing the forest, followed by the little boy carrying a branch. Soon Sylvie wanted to stop, and I kissed her, urging her to sit down. Conversation between the two of us could no longer be very intimate. I had to tell her of my life in Paris, my travels . . . "How can one go so far?" she asked. "It's a question I ask myself when I see you again." "Oh, you just say that!" "Well, you must agree you weren't as pretty in those days as you are now." "I don't know about that." "Do you remember the time when we were children and you were the taller?" "And you were the better behaved?" "Oh! Sylvie!" "They put us on the donkey, one in each pannier." "And in those days we didn't say the formal *vous* to each other . . . Do you remember how you taught me to fish for crayfish under the bridges of the Thève and the Nonette?" "And do you remember your foster-brother, who one day had to drag you out of the *waaater?*" "Big Curly! He was the one who said you could walk across it, that *waaater!*"

I was eager to change the subject. This memory had suddenly brought back to my mind the time when I used to visit the region, clad in a little English suit that made the peasants laugh. Only Sylvie thought I was well dressed. But I didn't dare remind her of an opinion held so long ago. I don't know why my thoughts turned back to the wedding clothes we'd put on at the old aunt's house at Othys. I asked what had become of them. "Oh, my good old aunt!" said Sylvie. "She lent me her dress to go and dance at the Dammartin carnival, two years ago. The following year she was dead, the poor love!"

She sighed and wept, so I couldn't ask her about the circumstances that had led to her going to a masked ball, but I understood clearly enough that, thanks to her skills as a worker, Sylvie was no longer a peasant. Only her family had remained in that class, and she lived among them like a hardworking fairy, spreading prosperity around her.

XI. THE RETURN

The vista opened out when we left the wood. We had reached the edge of the ponds at Châalis. The cloister galleries, the chapel with its high ogival vaulting, the feudal tower, and the little castle that sheltered the love affair of Henri IV and Gabrielle were tinged in the red of the setting sun against the dark green of the forest. "It's a landscape worthy of Walter Scott,[26] isn't it?" said Sylvie. "And who's talked to you about Walter Scott?" I asked her. "What a lot you've read in these last three years! . . . As for me, I'm trying to forget books. What I find charming is seeing this old abbey again with you, where, when we were very small, we used to hide in the ruins. Do you remember, Sylvie, how frightened you were when the guardian told us the tale of the red monks?" "Oh, don't talk of it!" "Well, then, sing me the song of the beautiful girl stolen from her father's garden, under the white rose bush." "No one sings that any more." "Have you become a musician, then?" "A bit." "Sylvie, Sylvie, I'm sure you sing opera arias!" "Why should that worry you?" "Because I loved the old tunes, and you won't know how to sing them any more."

Sylvie modulated a few bars of an aria from a great modern opera . . . She was *phrasing*!

We had turned toward the nearby ponds. Here was the green lawn, surrounded by lindens and elm trees, on which we had so often danced! I was conceited enough to define the old Carolingian walls and deci- pher the coats of arms of the house of Este. "What about you, then! You've read a lot more than I have!" said Sylvie. "So you're a scholar, now, are you?"

I was stung by her reproachful tone. Until that moment I'd been looking for a good moment to renew the morning's moment of spon- taneity, but what could I say to her in the company of a donkey and a very alert small boy, who took delight in coming closer and closer to listen to a Parisian speak? Then I had the misfortune to tell her of the phantom I'd seen at Châalis and that had lingered in my memory. I took Sylvie to the very room in the castle where I had heard Adrienne sing. "Oh! Let me hear you!" I said to her, "Let your dear voice resound

---

26. Walter Scott (1771–1832), the Scottish writer, was immensely popular in France at this time.

under these vaults and drive away the spirit that torments me, whether that spirit is divine or truly fatal!" She repeated the words and the song after me:

Angels, come swiftly down
To the depths of purgatory. . . .

"It's awfully sad!" she said to me.

"It's sublime . . . I think it's by Porpora,[27] with words translated in the sixteenth century."

"I don't know," said Sylvie.

We came back along the valley, following the Charlepont path, which the peasants, who by nature aren't good etymologists, obstinately go on calling Châllepont. Sylvie, tired of the donkey, leaned on my arm. The road was deserted. I tried to talk of the things I had in my heart, but, I don't know why, I could find only commonplace expressions or, from time to time, some high-flown sentence from a novel—which Sylvie might well have read. So I stopped in utterly classic fashion, and she occasionally expressed surprise at these broken effusions. When we reached the walls of Saint-S . . . we had to watch our steps. You cross damp meadows through which ripple little streams. "What became of the nun?" I asked suddenly.

"Oh you're dreadful with your nun! Well . . . well . . . it all turned out badly."

Sylvie wouldn't tell me another thing about it.

Do women truly feel that certain words leave the lips without emanating from the heart? You wouldn't believe it, to see how easily they can be misled, when you think of the choices they most often make. There are men who can play the comedy of love so well! I could never do it well, although I know that certain women allow themselves to be deceived, knowing full well what is happening. Moreover, a love that goes back to childhood has something sacred about it. . . . Sylvie, whom I had seen grow up, was like a sister for me. I couldn't attempt to seduce her . . . An entirely different idea crossed my mind. At this moment, I said to myself, I would normally be at the theater . . . What would Aurélie (that was the actress's name) be performing in tonight? She must be playing the role of the princess in the new play. Oh! The third act, she's really moving in that! . . . And in the love scene in the second act! With the wrinkled young lead . . .

"A penny for your thoughts!" said Sylvie and she began to sing:

At Dammartin there were three young girls:
One of them is lovelier than the day . . .

---

27. Nicola Antonio Porpora (1686–1768), Italian composer and singing teacher whose compositions show off the voice of virtuoso singers.

"Oh! You wretch!" I exclaimed, "You see, you do still know the old songs."

"If you came here more often, I'd remember more of them," she said, "but one has to think of practical matters. You have your concerns in Paris, and I have my work. Let's not get home too late. Tomorrow I have to be up with the sun."

XII. OLD DODU

I was about to reply, I was on the point of throwing myself at her feet, I almost offered her my uncle's house, which I could have bought back, for he had had several heirs and that little property had not been divided up, but at that moment we reached Loisy. We were expected for supper. The onion soup radiated from afar its patriarchal odor. Some neighbors had been invited on this day after the feast. I immediately recognized the old woodcutter, old Dodu, who in evenings long gone had told tales that were either very funny or very frightening. By turns shepherd, messenger, game keeper, fisherman, even poacher, old Dodu in his spare time made cuckoo clocks and roasting spits. For a long period he had devoted himself to guiding English visitors to Ermenonville, leading them to the spots where Rousseau had meditated and telling them about his final moments. He had been the little boy the philosopher had employed to classify his herbs and whom he ordered to pick the hemlocks from which he extracted the sap and put it in his cup of milky coffee. The innkeeper of the Golden Cross was skeptical about this point, and that had given rise to long-lasting enmity. Old Dodu had long been accused of possessing a few very innocent secrets, such as being able to cure cows with a verse said backwards and a sign of the cross drawn on the left foot, but he had quickly renounced such superstitions—thanks to the memory, so he used to say, of Jean-Jacques's conversations.

"There you are, little Parisian!" old Dodu said to me. "Have you come to seduce our girls?" "Me, old Dodu?" "Do you take them to the woods while the wolf's away?" "Old Dodu, you're the one who's the wolf." "I was a wolf as long as I could find lambs, but now I meet only goats, and they certainly know how to protect themselves! But you Parisians, you know a thing or two! Jean-Jacques was quite right when he used to say, 'Man is corrupted in the poisonous air of the city.'" "Old Dodu, you know quite well that man can be corrupted anywhere."

Old Dodu began to hum a drinking tune. People tried in vain to make him stop before a certain ribald couplet that everyone knew by heart. Sylvie wouldn't sing for us, despite our pleas, saying that it was no longer done to sing at table. I had already noticed that last night's gallant was sitting on her left. There was something in his round face, his tousled hair, that was not altogether unfamiliar to me. He stood up and came to stand behind my chair, saying, "Don't you recognize me then, Parisian?" A kind woman, who had just come back for dessert after having served us, whispered in my ear, "Don't you recognize your foster brother?" Without this hint, I would have made a fool of myself. "Oh! It's you, *Big Curly*!" I said. "You're the one who pulled me out of the waaater!" Sylvie burst out laughing at this memory. "You're forgetting," the lad said as he gave me a hug, "that you were wearing a fine silver watch and when you came back you were much more worried about the watch than about yourself, because it wasn't working anymore. You said, 'The creature is drownded: it doesn't go tick-tock any more. What will my uncle say . . . ?' "

"A creature in a watch!" said old Dodu. "That's what they make children believe in Paris!"

Sylvie was sleepy, and I felt I had lost her. She went back up to her room and while I embraced her, she said, "Until tomorrow! Come and see us!"

Old Dodu had stayed at the table with Sylvain and my foster brother. We talked for a long time around a flask of ratafia from Louvres. "All men are equal," old Dodu said between two couplets, "I drink with a pastry cook as I would with a prince." "Where's the pastry cook?" I said. "Look beside you! A young man who is ambitious to establish himself."

My foster brother seemed embarrassed. I understood everything.—It was a stroke of bad luck for me to have a foster brother in a region made famous by Rousseau,[28] who wanted to get rid of wet-nurses!— Old Dodu told me that there was much talk of a marriage between Sylvie and *Big Curly*, who wanted to set up a pastry shop at Dammartin. I didn't ask any more questions. The coach from Nanteuil-le-Haudoin took me back to Paris the following day.

XIII. AURÉLIE

To Paris! The coach takes five hours to get there. I was in no rush, provided I could be there before evening. Around eight I was in my usual place. Aurélie radiated her inspiration and charm over lines which drew feeble inspiration from Schiller and were written by a current talent. In the garden scene, she became sublime. During the fourth act, in which she did not appear, I went to buy a bouquet at Mme Prévost's. I slipped into it a most tender letter signed "An unknown admirer." I said to myself, "Now that's something settled for the future," and the next day I was on the road for Germany.

What was I going to do there? I wanted to put my feelings back in

---

28. Rousseau was a passionate proponent of women breast-feeding their own babies, at a time when the middle classes and the aristocracy generally sent their infants out to be suckled by professional wet nurses. Despite Rousseau's eloquence, the practice continued through the nineteenth century.

order. If I were writing a novel, I would never be able to make my reader accept the story of a heart smitten with two simultaneous loves. It was my own fault that Sylvie was slipping through my fingers, but seeing her again for just one day was enough to elevate my soul again. Henceforth I would place her in the temple of wisdom like a smiling statue. Her gaze had stopped me on the edge of the abyss. I rejected even more forcefully the thought of presenting myself to Aurélie and struggling briefly with so many commonplace lovers who shone briefly beside her and then fell down again, broken. One day we'll see, I thought to myself, whether that woman has a heart.

One morning, I read in a newspaper that Aurélie was ill. I wrote to her from the Salzburg mountains. The letter was so steeped in German mysticism that I couldn't expect much success from it, and I didn't even ask for a reply. I did count a little on luck and on—*an unknown admirer.*

Months went by. In between my errands and my leisure I had undertaken to fix in poetic form the love of the painter Colonna for the lovely Laura, whose parents forced her to take the veil, and whom he loved until his death. Something in the subject was linked to my constant preoccupations. When I had written the last line of the play, my thoughts dwelt only on returning to France.

What can I say now that will not be the story of so many other people? I went through all the circles of those testing grounds known as theaters. "I have eaten the drums and cymbals" to quote the apparently meaningless sentence of Eleusis's initiates. No doubt it means that, when necessary, one must go beyond the limits of nonsense and absurdity. For me, the rational thing would be to conquer and fix my ideal.

Aurélie had accepted the leading role in the play I'd brought back from Germany. I shall never forget the day when she allowed me to read my play to her. The love scenes had been written with her in mind. I truly believe that I said them with all my soul, but above all with enthusiasm. In the conversation that took place after the reading, I revealed that I was the unknown admirer of the two letters. She said to me, "You're utterly mad. But come back and see me again . . . I have never succeeded in finding someone who knew how to love me."

O woman! You are in search of love! And I, what about me?

The following days, I wrote the tenderest letters, no doubt the most beautiful that she had ever received. I received from her letters that were full of reason. At one point she was touched, summoned me to her side, and admitted to me that it was hard for her to break a former attachment.

"If you truly love me for myself," she said, "you will understand that I can belong to one man alone."

Two months later, I received from her a letter that was most effusive.

I rushed to be with her.—In the intervening time someone had given me a precious piece of information. The handsome young man I had met one night at our circle had just joined the Algerian troops.

The following summer, there was a horse race at Chantilly. The theater troop in which Aurélie was acting was putting on a performance there. Once in the region, the company was under the stage manager's orders for three days. I'd won the friendship of this good man, a former Dorante of Marivaux's[29] comedies, and long the leading man in dramatic performances, whose last success had been the role of lover in the play imitated from Schiller, in which my opera glasses had revealed him to be so wrinkled. From close up, he seemed younger, and as he had remained slender, he still produced an effect in the provinces. He was full of energy. I accompanied the troupe in the role of dramaturge; I persuaded the theater manager to go and put on performances at Senlis and Dammartin. At first he was drawn to Compiègne, but Aurélie was of the same opinion as I was. The next day, while he was dealing with the owners of theaters and with the authorities, I hired some horses, and we took the pond road to Commelle in order to have lunch at the chateau of Queen Blanche. Aurélie, in a riding habit, and with her blond hair flying free, rode through the forest like a queen from bygone days, and the peasants stared in amazement. Madame de F . . . was the only woman they had seen who waved to them so imposingly and graciously. After lunch, we went down to villages recalling those of Switzerland, where the waters of the Nonette turn sawmills. Such sights, which were dear memories to me, interested her without holding her attention. My plan was to lead Aurélie to the chateau, near Orry, on that same green square where I had first seen Adrienne. She showed not the slightest emotion. Then I told her everything; I told her of the source of that love I had glimpsed at night and dreamed of later and now had found embodied in her. She listened to me seriously and then said, "You don't love me! You expect me to say, 'The actress is the same woman as the nun'; you're looking for drama, that's all, and the ending remains hidden from you. Come now! I won't believe another word you tell me!"

That comment was like a flash of lightning. Those strange enthusiasms I had so long felt, those dreams and tears, that despair and tenderness . . . was that not love after all? But then, what is love?

Aurélie performed that night at Senlis. I thought I detected in her an attachment for the stage manager, the wrinkled young leading man. He had an excellent nature and had rendered her various services.

Aurélie told me one day, "If you want to know whom I love, it's him!"

---

29. *Marivaux:* Pierre Carlet de Chamblain de Marivaux (1688–1763), French comic playwright, famed for renewing comedy by basing his plays on stories of budding love affairs.

XIV. FINAL PAGE

Such are the fantasies that charm us and lead us astray in the morning of our lives. I have tried to fix them without too much order, but many hearts will understand me. Illusions fall one after the other, like the peel of a piece of fruit, and that fruit is experience. Its taste is bitter, but it has something tart about it that strengthens us, if you'll forgive my old-fashioned way of putting it. Rousseau says that the sight of nature consoles one for everything. Sometimes I try to rediscover my groves of Clarens lost in the north of Paris, in the mists. All of that has changed so much!

Ermenonville! Land where the ancient idyll still flourished, an idyll translated for a second time in the fashion of Gessner![30] You have lost your only star, which gleamed for a while with a double beam. Alternatively blue and pink like the deceptive star Aldebaran, it was Adrienne or Sylvie, the two halves of a single love. One was the sublime ideal, the other sweet reality. What do your shadows and your lakes mean to me now, and even your desert? Othys, Montagny, Loisy, poor neighboring hamlets, Châalis (which is being restored)—you have kept nothing of the past! Sometimes I need to see those places of solitude and reverie once more. Once there, I sadly rediscover again within myself the fleeting traces of a time when what was natural was affected. Sometimes I smile, when I read on the flank of granite rocks certain lines of Roucher, which seemed sublime to me—or maxims demanding benevolence above a spring or a grotto consecrated to Pan. The ponds, dug at such cost, vainly offer their stagnant waters that the swan scorns. They are gone, the days when the Condé hunts went by with their proud amazons, when the horns answered each other from afar, multiplied by the echoes! . . . To reach Ermenonville today, you can no longer find a direct route. Sometimes I go there by way of Creil and Senlis, and sometimes through Dammartin.

Nowadays you can only reach Dammartin at evening. Then I go and sleep at "The Image of Saint John." Usually they give me a fairly clean room, hung in old tapestry and with a pier-glass above the mirror. This room is the last return to bric-a-brac, which I long ago renounced. You sleep warmly there under the eiderdown that's customary in the region. In the morning, when I open the window, framed in ivy and roses, I find to my delight a green horizon spreading for ten leagues, with the poplars lined up like armies. Here and there a handful of villages take shelter under the steep belfries, which are built, as the local saying has it, with bone pointing. First of all one can make out Othys, then Eve, then Ver; you could make out Ermenonville through the woods if it

---

30. Salomon Gessner (1730–1788), Swiss poet whose evocation of natural beauty paved the way for Romanticism.

had a belfry—but in this philosophical spot the church was of course neglected. Having filled my lungs with the pure air breathed on those plateaux, I go downstairs gaily, and pay a visit to the pastry cook. "There you are, Big Curly!"

"There you are, little Parisian!" We shake hands with the friendly exuberance of childhood, then I climb up a certain stairway where the joyful cries of two children greet my arrival. Sylvie's Athenian smile lights up her charmed features. I say to myself, "That may have been where happiness was to be found, and yet . . . "

Sometimes I call her Lolotte[31] and she finds in me some resemblance to Werther, apart from the pistols which are no longer in fashion. While Big Curly gets dinner ready, we take the children for a walk in the linden avenues that border the ruins of the chateau's old brick towers. In the playing fields of the companions of the bow, the little ones practice making their father's arrows plunge into the straw, while we read a few poems or a few pages of those very short books people no longer publish.

I almost forgot to say that on the day when the company Aurélie belonged to gave a performance at Dammartin, I took Sylvie to the show, and asked her if she didn't think the actress looked like someone she already knew. "Whom do you mean?" "Do you remember Adrienne?"

She burst into loud laughter and said, "What an idea!" Then, as if she reproached herself, she sighed and said, "Poor Adrienne! She died at the convent of Saint S . . . around 1832."

---

31. *Lolotte:* The reference is to the woman in Goethe's short novel *The Sufferings of Young Werther.* Werther loves Lolotte, who is already promised to another. While Werther shoots himself to death, Nerval's hero prefers a more placid outcome.

Maupassant

◆

Guy de Maupassant (1850–1893) is one of the finest and most prolific of French story writers. In the course of some eleven years of active writing he produced over six hundred short stories and six novels, before succumbing to psychological disorders, apparently the result of syphilis. Novels such as Pierre et Jean *and* Bel-Ami *have a surface appearance of realism, with a complex underlying network of metaphors and images that speak of the disintegration and insincerity of professed bourgeois values, and the impossibility of the ideal in human relationships. His tales are highly varied, ranging from stories about peasant life, studies of war-torn France, evocations of society's outlaws and misfits, sketches of the humdrum existence of minor civil servants, to ghost stories and reminiscences of sexual encounters.* Ball of Lard, *Maupassant's first published story, is typical in the careful realism of its descriptions, the unemotional sympathy it reveals for those who live on the edge of society, its contempt for hypocrisy, and its invitation to read on symbolic levels. As a psychological study of egotism and the ease with which people can convince themselves of the morality of actions they know to be merely expedient, it has rarely been matched.*

FURTHER READING: *The Diary of a Madman*, tr. Arnold Kellett (London: Pan, 1976).
TEXT USED FOR "BALL OF LARD": *Soirées de Médan* (Paris: Charpentier, 1880).
TEXT USED FOR "APPARITION": *Clair de lune* (Paris: Olendorff, 1891).
TEXT USED FOR "PAUL'S GIRL": *La Maison Tellier* (Paris: Victor-Havard, 1882).

BALL OF LARD (1880)

For several days now little pockets of the retreating army had passed through the town.[1] It wasn't a troop, just undisciplined hordes. The men's beards were long and dirty, their uniforms in tatters, and they

---

1. As a result of the French defeat in the 1870 war against the Prussians.

moved forward sloppily, stripped of their flags, lost from their regiments. All seemed overwhelmed, exhausted, incapable of forming a thought or making a decision, walking merely out of habit and collapsing with weariness as soon as they stopped. What you saw most of was the conscripts, peaceful folk, calm people of independent means, bent double under the weight of their rifles; small, alert members of the National Guard, easily terrified and readily moved to enthusiasm, as ready to attack as to flee; then, in the midst of these others, a few red-trousers, the remnant of a division reduced to exhaustion in a great battle; somber artillery men lined up with this rag-bag of foot-soldiers; and sometimes the gleaming helmet of a dragoon with leaden feet, struggling to keep up with the lighter step of the men of the line.

Legions of partisans, with heroic titles such as "Avengers of the Defeat," "Citizens of the Tomb," "Sharers of Death" went by in their turn, looking like bandits.

Their leaders, former cloth or grain dealers, erstwhile merchants of tallow or soap, turned soldiers by a whim of fate, appointed officers because their pockets were deep or their mustaches were long. Covered with weapons, with flannel, and with gold braid, they spoke in blaring voices, discussed plans of campaign, and claimed to be supporting single-handedly their dying country as it lay on their swaggering backs. But sometimes they feared their own soldiers, men used to dealing with burlap and rope, often excessively brave, debauched looters.

The Prussians were going to enter Rouen, so the rumor went. The National Guard, which had been doing some highly circumspect reconnoitering in the neighboring woods, sometimes gunning down its own sentinels and preparing for mortal combat when a little rabbit moved in the undergrowth, had gone home. Their weapons, their uniforms, all their murderous accoutrements, which in days gone by had aroused terror along the national highways for a radius of three leagues, had suddenly vanished.

The last French soldiers had indeed just crossed the Seine to reach Pont-Audemer via Saint-Sever and Bourg-Achard; and marching behind all the rest, the general, in despair, unable to attempt anything with these disparate rags and tatters, and in terror himself in this great defeat of a people used to conquering and disastrously beaten despite its legendary courage, went away on foot flanked by two aides-de-camp.

Then a deep calm, a terrified and silent expectancy hovered over the city. Many fat-bellied citizens, whose virility had been sapped by commerce, anxiously awaited the victors, trembling in fear that the enemy might consider using their cooking spits and the big kitchen knives as weapons.

Life seemed to have stopped. The shops were shut, the streets silent. Sometimes one of the citizens, intimidated by the silence, slipped rapidly past, hugging the walls.

The anguish of waiting made people long for the arrival of the enemy.

In the afternoon that followed the departure of the French troops, a few Uhlans,[2] who had come from goodness knows where, crossed the town at great speed. Then, a little later, a black mass of people came down Saint Catherine's hill, while two other invading floods appeared along the roads from Darnetal and Boisguillaume. The forerunners of each troop met up exactly at the same moment on the square in front of the Town Hall, and through all the adjoining streets the German army came, unfurling its battalions and making the streets resound with their harsh rhythmic step.

Orders shouted in an unknown guttural tongue rose up past houses that seemed dead and deserted, while behind the closed shutters eyes watched these victorious men who, through the "right of war," held in their hands the city, its fortunes, and their lives. In their darkened rooms, the inhabitants suffered that wild fear that is triggered by cataclysms, great deadly overturnings of the earth against which all wisdom and all strength are useless. For the same sensation recurs each time the established order of things is overturned, when people are no longer secure, when everything that was protected by the laws of men and nature is at the mercy of a ferocious brutality that has no conscience. The earthquake that crushes an entire nation under collapsing houses, the river that breaks its banks and rolls drowned peasants with the corpses of cattle and beams torn from roofs, or the glorious army massacring those who defend themselves and taking the rest prisoner, pillaging in the name of the sabre and thanking some god to the noise of cannon, are all terrifying plagues that overturn all belief in eternal justice, all the faith we've been taught to have in heavenly protection and human reason.

But at each door, small detachments were knocking, then disappearing into the houses. This was the occupation after the invasion. It was now the victors' duty to appear gracious in their behavior toward the vanquished.

After a while, once the first terror had faded, a new calm took hold. In many cases, the Prussian officer dined with the family. Sometimes he was well brought up and through politeness expressed pity for France, speaking of the repugnance with which he had taken part in this war. This sentiment earned him a degree of gratitude, but one day or another it might be necessary to rely on his protection. By treating him well, the family might perhaps get slightly fewer men to feed. And why should you offend a person on whom you are totally dependent? Such behavior would be less bravado than rashness. —And rashness is no longer one of the weak points of the middle classes of Rouen, as it was in the days of the heroic defenses for which the city is renowned. Indeed, people said, this being the final reason French urbanity could pro-

2. *Uhlans:* Prussian troops.

duce, that it was certainly permitted to be polite in one's own home provided that, in public, one didn't treat a foreign soldier with any familiarity. Outside the house, foreigner and host no longer recognized each other, but inside the house they enjoyed chatting, and the German would stay a bit longer each evening, warming himself at the communal hearth.

The town itself gradually resumed its usual appearance. The French still went out rarely, but the streets were swarming with Prussian soldiers. Moreover, the officers of the Blue Hussars, who arrogantly pulled their great instruments of war along the pavements, didn't seem to despise the simple citizens enormously more than the officers of the light infantry had when, the year before, they'd been drinking in those selfsame cafés.

And yet there was something in the air, something subtle and intangible, a strange intolerable atmosphere like a ubiquitous odor, the odor of invasion. It filled the houses and the public squares, it changed the taste of food, it made you feel you were traveling far from home among dangerous and barbarian tribes.

The victors demanded money, a lot of money. The inhabitants always paid up; anyway, they were rich. But the wealthier a Normandy shopkeeper grows, the more painful each sacrifice is, and the more he suffers at the sight of each part of his fortune passing into the hands of another.

Meanwhile, two or three leagues below the town, as you follow the river toward Croisset, Dieppedalle, or Biessart, sailors and fishermen often plucked from the river bed a bloated German corpse in its uniform, dead of a knife wound or a blow from a clog, his head bashed in by a stone or thrown into the water from the top of a bridge. The river mud buried these savage, legitimate, and unidentifiable acts of vengeance, these unrecognized feats of heroism, these silent attacks, more dangerous than the great public battles, and carrying no fame or glory.

Hatred of the Foreigner always provides arms for a few Intrepid souls who are ready to die for a Belief.

Finally, because the invaders, although they held the town in sway to their inflexible discipline, had not perpetrated any of the horrors that their reputation attributed to them along the length and breadth of their triumphant march, people grew bolder, and the demands of trade once again obsessed the hearts of local businessmen. Some of them had large interests tied up at Le Havre, which was occupied by the French army, and they wanted to try to reach the port by traveling overland to Dieppe and taking the boat from there.

They used the influence of those German officers whose acquaintance they had made, and they received authorization to leave from the commander-in-chief.

So, when a four-horse stage coach had been booked for the journey and ten people had signed on with the driver, it was decided to set out on a Tuesday morning before daybreak, to avoid any crowds.

For some time already the frost had been hardening the earth, and on the Monday, around three o'clock, heavy black clouds coming from the North brought snow, which fell constantly all that evening and throughout the night.

At half past four the next morning, the travelers assembled in the courtyard of the Hôtel de Normandie, where they were to embark on the coach.

They were still heavy with sleep and shivered with cold under their wraps. It was hard to see in the darkness, and the heavy winter clothing heaped on them made all these bodies look like obese curés wearing long cassocks. But two men recognized each other, a third came up to them, and they began chatting: "I'm bringing my wife," said the first. "I'm doing the same." "Me too." The first added, "We won't return to Rouen, and if the Prussians come close to Le Havre, we'll go to England." All had the same plans, being of like mind.

And still no one was preparing the coach for departure. A small lantern carried by a stable boy occasionally issued from one dark door to disappear immediately into another. The horses' hooves pawed the ground, muffled by their bedding straw, and a man's voice speaking to the animals and cursing could be heard in the depths of the building. A low ringing of bells indicated that the harness was being moved about; soon this murmur became a clear and continuous ringing, whose rhythm corresponded to that of the animal, sometimes stopping then beginning again with an abrupt shock accompanied by the dull thud of an iron-shod hoof striking the ground.

Suddenly the door closed. All noise stopped. The frozen passengers fell silent; they remained motionless and stiff.

A curtain of white flakes, falling continuously, glimmered as they fell to earth, obliterating shapes, powdering objects with a frozen lather; and now, in the great silence of the calm town as it lay buried under winter, nothing more could be heard than this vague, indescribable and floating rustle of falling snow, more a sensation than a sound, a mingling of light atoms that seemed to fill space and cover the world.

The man reappeared with his lantern, pulling at the end of a rope a sad horse that came reluctantly. He placed it beside the shaft, attached the harness, moved around it slowly to make sure all was tight, for he could use only one hand, since he was carrying his light in the other. As he went in search of the second animal, he noticed all these motionless passengers, already white with snow, and said to them, "Why don't you climb in? You'd at least be sheltered there."

It probably hadn't occurred to them, and they rushed to get in the coach. The three men installed their wives at the back before seating themselves, then the other vague and veiled shapes took the last places in their turn without exchanging a word.

The floor was covered with straw so deep that their feet sank into it. The women in the back, having brought little copper heaters with chemical coal, lit these machines and for a short while softly enumerated their advantages, repeating to each other things with which they had long been familiar.

At last, the coach was harnessed up, with six horses instead of four because pulling it would be more difficult, and a voice outside asked, "Everyone aboard?" A voice from within answered, "Yes." They set out.

The coach moved forward slowly, very slowly, the horses taking small steps. The wheels sank into the snow; the whole body of the coach groaned with soft cracking sounds; the animals slid, puffed, and steamed. The coach driver's gigantic whip cracked constantly, flying in all directions, knotting and unfolding like some slim snake, and suddenly lashing a bulging rump that immediately tightened under a more violent effort.

But it was growing imperceptibly lighter. Those soft flakes—which one of the passengers, a Rouen man to the core, had compared to a rain of cotton—no longer fell. A dirty light filtered through the dark and heavy-laden clouds that made the whiteness of the countryside all the more startling. You could see now a line of tall trees covered with hoar frost, now a thatched cottage with a hood of snow.

In the coach, the passengers looked at each other curiously in the grim light of that dawn.

Right at the back, in the best seats, slumbered on opposite sides, M. and Mme Loiseau, wholesale wine merchants from la Rue du Grand-Pont. The former salesman of a boss who'd been ruined in business, Loiseau had bought up the business and made his fortune. He sold very bad wine to small country stores for a very low price and was considered by his acquaintances and friends as a crafty rascal, a true son of Normandy, full of tricks and good cheer.

His reputation as a crook was so well established that when, one evening at the prefecture, M. Tournel, an author of fables and songs, a biting and clever mind, and a local star, suggested to some ladies who seemed to him to be dozing that they should all play a round of *Loiseau vole*,[3] the expression itself took flight through all the prefect's ballrooms, then, reaching those of the town, set all those provincial jaws to laughing for a whole month.

In addition, Loiseau was famous for his great array of practical jokes, the good or bad tricks he played; and no one could mention him without immediately adding "He's priceless, that Loiseau."

---

3. This means both "the bird flies" and "Loiseau steals." *Pigeon vole* is a children's game somewhat similar to "Mother may I?"

Small in stature, he presented a ballooning belly topped off by a red face between two greying mutton chops.

His wife was tall, stout, and obstinate, with a loud voice and a mind rapidly made up. She was the force of order and arithmetic in the business, which he animated with his joyous activity.

Beside them was seated the more worthy M. Carré-Lamadon, who belonged to a higher caste. He was a well-to-do man who had made his money in cotton, owned three cotton mills, was an officer of the Legion of Honor and a member of the General Council. Throughout the Empire he had led a benevolent opposition, merely in order to exact a higher price for rallying to the cause that he combatted with the weapons of politeness, as he himself called them. Mme Carré-Lamadon, who was much younger than her husband, was the consolation of officers from good families who were sent to the Rouen garrison.

She sat opposite her spouse, very small and sweet, extremely pretty, wrapped up in her furs and staring with distraught eyes at the coach's deplorable interior.

Her neighbors, the Count and Countess Hubert de Bréville, bore one of the most ancient and noble names in Normandy. The Count, an old gentleman of prepossessing appearance, attempted through various tricks of dress, to intensify his natural resemblance to King Henry IV,[4] who, according to a legend that brought the family glory, had got with child a lady de Bréville, whose husband, as a result, had been made a count and a provincial governor.

A colleague of M. Carré-Lamadon on the General Council, Count Hubert represented the Orleanist[5] party in the department. The story of his marriage to the daughter of a small-arms dealer in Nantes had remained a mystery. But as the countess was very impressive, made an impeccable hostess, and was even believed to have been loved by one of Louis-Philippe's sons, the entire nobility courted her, and her salon remained the most prestigious in the region, the only one to retain the old forms of gallantry, and to which it was difficult to obtain an entry.

The fortune of the Brévilles, which was entirely in real estate, was reputed to earn them some five hundred thousand pounds a year. These six people occupied the back of the coach, the domain of those members of society whose income was assured, who were calm and strong, worthy people, whose authority is beyond dispute and who have Religion and Principles.

Through a strange whim of fate all the women were on the same bench, and the countess had for two further neighbors a couple of nuns who were counting their long rosaries as they muttered Paters and Aves.

---

4. *Henri IV:* King of France from 1589 to 1610.

5. *Orleanist:* The younger branch of the Bourbon line, the Orleanists had ruled France through Louis-Philippe from 1830 to 1848.

One was an old woman with a face disfigured by smallpox, as if she had received at point-blank range a blast of shotgun fire full in the face. The other, who looked very sickly, had a pretty, invalid's face above a tubercular chest eaten away by that devouring faith that creates martyrs and visionaries.

Opposite these two nuns, a man and a woman drew the glances of everyone in the coach.

The man was well known. He was Cornudet the Red, the terror of respectable people. For twenty years he had been dipping his great red beard into the beer mugs of all the left-wing cafés. With his friends and comrades he had gone through a pretty good fortune he'd inherited from his father, a former confectioner, and he impatiently awaited the coming of the Republic to obtain at last the position he had earned through so many revolutionary drinks. On the fourth of September,[6] perhaps as the result of a joke, he believed he had been appointed prefect, but when he tried to take up his functions, the office clerks, sole masters of the place, refused to recognize him, and forced him to retreat. All in all he was a good fellow, harmless and helpful, and with incomparable ardor had set about organizing the defense of the town. He had arranged for holes to be dug in the plains, had chopped down all the young trees in the neighboring forests, pitted the roads with traps, and, at the approach of the enemy, satisfied with his preparations, he had rapidly withdrawn to the town. Now he thought he could make himself more useful in Le Havre, where new entrenchments would be necessary.

The woman, one of those referred to as "loose," was famous for her premature fatness which had earned her the nickname "Ball of Lard." She was small, completely round, bulging with fat, her swollen fingers strangled at the joints, like strings of short sausages. With shiny, stretched skin, and an enormous bust which thrust against her dress, she nevertheless remained tempting and was much courted, because her freshness was such a feast for the eyes. Her face was a red apple, a peony bud on the point of flowering; and within it there opened at the top two splendid brown eyes, shaded by long thick lashes that cast a shadow in them; below, a charming mouth, narrow and moist for kisses, furnished with gleaming, microscopic teeth.

It was said, moreover, that she was full of priceless qualities.

As soon as she was recognized, whispers were exchanged among the honest women, and words like "prostitute" and "public shame" were whispered so loud she raised her head. Then she ran over her neighbors a glance that was so provocative and bold that immediately there was a great silence, and everyone dropped their eyes, except for Loiseau, who peered at her with a look of arousal. But soon a conversation was struck

---

6. *fourth of September:* the date of Napoleon III's abdication in 1870.

up again among the three ladies, who had suddenly become friends, almost intimates, through the presence of this woman. It seemed to them that they should create a kind of shield with their wifely dignity in the face of that shameless woman who put herself up for sale; for legal love always takes the high ground with her free sister.

The three men, too, drawn closer by a conservative instinct at the sight of Cornudet, talked money in that tone that despises the poor. Count Hubert told of the damage the Prussians had caused him, the loss that would result from stolen cattle and spoiled crops, and all this with the assurance of a great lord who was a millionnaire ten times over, and whom these ravages would scarcely discommode for a year. M. Carré-Lamadon, an old hand in the cotton trade, had been careful to send to England a sum of six hundred thousand francs, something for a rainy day that he'd been accumulating on all possible occasions. As for Loiseau, he had arranged to sell to the French Commissariat all the ordinary wine that remained in his cellars, so that the State owed him a formidable sum that he fully expected to be able to draw on in Le Havre.

All three exchanged quick friendly glances. Although they were of different classes, they felt that money made brothers of them, united them in the great freemasonry of those who own, who can make the gold jingle when they put their hands in their trouser pockets.

The coach traveled so slowly that at ten in the morning they had covered a mere four leagues. The men got down three times to walk up the hills. They were beginning to grow worried, for the plan had been to lunch at Tôtes, and they now had no hope of reaching the town before night. Everyone was peering out in the hope of spotting an inn on the road, when the coach sunk into a pile of snow and it took two hours to free it.

Their growing hunger disturbed their thoughts; and no hostelry, no wine shop came into view, for the approach of the Prussians and the passage of the troops had scared all industry out of sight.

The gentlemen sought provisions in the farms beside the road, but they found not even a crust of bread there, since the distrustful peasant hid his reserves in the fear of being pillaged by soldiers who—not knowing where their next meal was coming from—might take by force whatever they discovered.

Toward one in the afternoon, Loiseau announced that he really felt his stomach was hollow. Everyone had been suffering as he had for a long time, and the violent need to eat—which went on growing— brought an end to conversation.

From time to time someone yawned; almost immediately someone else did so, too, and everyone in turn, according to character, knowledge of the world, and social position noisily opened their mouth or modestly put their hand quickly in front of the gaping hole from which some steam escaped.

On several occasions Ball of Lard leaned down as if she were seeking something under her skirts. She hesitated for an instant, looked at her neighbors, then sat up again calmly. Faces were pale and drawn. Loiseau swore he would pay a thousand francs for a bit of ham. His wife made a gesture as if in protest, then calmed down. She always suffered when she heard people talking about wasting money and did not even understand jokes on the subject. "The truth of the matter is that I don't feel at all well," said the count. "How can I have forgotten to bring some provisions?" Everyone reproached themselves in the same way.

Nevertheless, Cornudet had a flask of rum, which he offered around. It was coldly refused. Loiseau alone accepted a few drops and when he handed back the flask thanked him by saying, "It's good. It warms you up and it fools your appetite." The alcohol put him in a good humor, and he suggested they do as the sailors did in the little boat in the song: eat the fattest of the passengers. This allusion to Ball of Lard shocked the well-brought-up folk. They didn't answer. Cornudet alone smiled. The two nuns had stopped mumbling their rosaries and, hands deep in their broad sleeves, they sat motionless, no doubt offering to heaven the suffering that heaven had sent them.

Finally, at three o'clock, when they were in the middle of an endless plain without a single village in sight, Ball of Lard, bending down abruptly, took from beneath her bench a large basket covered with a white cloth.

First she took out a little pottery plate, a fine silver drinking cup, then a vast pan in which were two complete chickens, cut up, and set in their jelly; and you could also see in the basket other good things wrapped up, pâtés, fruit, sweetmeats, provisions for a journey lasting three days, to avoid eating in the inns. The mouths of four bottles thrust up through the packages of food. She took the wing of a chicken and delicately set about eating it with one of those rolls that are called "Regen cies" in Normandy.

All eyes were on her. Then the smell wafted around, stretching nostrils, bringing to their mouths an abundant amount of saliva together with a painful contraction of the jaws below the ears. The scorn the ladies felt for the prostitute became ferocious, as though they wanted to kill her or throw her out of the coach, into the snow, together with her cup, her basket, and her provisions.

But Loiseau was devouring the pot of chicken with his eyes. He said, "Well, well, well. Madame had more foresight than we had. Some people manage to think of everything." She raised her head to him, "Would you like some, Monsieur? It's hard to fast all day." He bowed, "Frankly, Madame, I won't refuse, I can't bear it any longer. You've got to take the rough with the smooth, don't you, Madame!" And casting a glance around he added, "In moments like these it's a pleasure to meet obliging folk." He had a newspaper which he unfolded to avoid staining his trousers, and with the tip of a knife he always kept in his pocket, he removed a thigh varnished all over with jelly, tore it apart with his teeth, and chewed it with such obvious satisfaction that the coach resounded with a great sigh of distress.

But Ball of Lard, in a humble and gentle voice, invited the good sisters to share her meal. They both accepted immediately, and without raising their eyes they began to eat very fast after having stammered a few words of thanks. Cornudet didn't refuse his neighbor's offers either, and together with the nuns they made a kind of table by unfolding newspapers on their knees.

Their mouths opened and shut ceaselessly, fiercely swallowing, chewing, and bolting it down. Loiseau in his corner was hard at work and softly urged his wife to follow his lead. For a long time she resisted, then, after a contraction had run through her entrails, she yielded. Then her husband, in flowery phrases, asked their "charming companion" if she would allow him to offer a small morsel to Mme Loiseau. She said, "But of course, indeed, Monsieur," with a friendly smile, and passed the pan to him.

There was a moment of embarrassment when they uncorked the first bottle of claret, for there was only one cup. They each passed it on, after wiping it. Cornudet alone, no doubt through gallantry, put his lips on the place that was still damp from his neighbor's lips.

Then, surrounded by people who were eating, suffocated by the smell of food, the Count and Countess de Bréville, like M. and Mme Carré-Lamadon, experienced that horrible torture which has kept the name of Tantalus.[7] Suddenly the manufacturer's young wife sighed loudly enough to turn all heads; she was as white as the snow outside; her eyes closed, her brow dropped; she had lost consciousness. Her husband, terrified, begged everyone to help him. Everyone was panicking, when the elder of the nuns, supporting the ill woman's head, slipped between her lips Ball of Lard's cup and made her swallow a few drops of wine. The pretty woman stirred, opened her eyes, smiled, and announced in a faint voice that she felt very well now. But, to prevent its happening again, the nun forced her to drink a full glass of claret and added, "It's hunger, nothing else."

Then Ball of Lard, blushing and embarrassed, stammered as she looked at the four passengers who had not been eating, "Goodness, if

---

7. *Tantalus:* In Greek mythology, a son of Zeus who divulged to mortals secrets of the gods and was punished by being plunged up to the chin in a river of Hades with a cluster of berries hanging from a tree just above his head. Both the water and the fruit eluded his attempts to drink and to eat.

I could make so bold as to offer these ladies and gentlemen . . . " She
fell silent, afraid that she had insulted them, but Loiseau butted in,
"Good Lord, yes, in cases like these we're all brothers and ought to help
each other out. Come on, ladies, don't stand on ceremony, say yes, devil
take it! Do we even know if we'll be able to find a house where we can
spend the night? With the speed we're making we won't get to Tôtes
before tomorrow at noon." There was a moment's hesitation, as no one
assumed the responsibility for saying "yes."

But the count settled the question. He turned toward the fat, intimidated prostitute and with his grandest, most noble air said to her, "We
accept with gratitude, Madame."

It was only the first step that was hard to take. Once the Rubicon
had been crossed, they went at it hammer and tongs. The basket was
emptied out. There was still some pâté de foie gras, a bit of smoked
tongue, some Crassane pears, a block of Pont-l'Evêque cheese, and a
container full of gherkins and onions in vinegar, for Ball of Lard, like
all women, adored pickles.

You couldn't eat her provisions and not talk to her. So, they chatted
at first reservedly, then, as she behaved extremely correctly, they loosened up. Mmes de Bréville and Carré-Lamadon, who had excellent
manners, were delicately gracious. The countess above all revealed that
friendly condescension of very high-born women whom no contact can
sully, and she was quite charming. But fat Mme Loiseau, who had the
soul of a policeman, remained cantankerous, speaking little and eating
a lot.

They talked about the war, naturally enough. They recounted tales of
the dreadful deeds of the Prussians, and examples of French courage,
and all these people who were fleeing paid homage to the bravery of
other people. Soon it was the turn of personal stories and Ball of Lard
recounted, with real emotion and that warmth in the voice that prostitutes sometimes achieve in expressing their natural transports, how
she had left Rouen: "At first I thought I could stay. My house was full
of provisions, and I preferred to feed soldiers than to leave my country
and go and live goodness knows where. But when I saw those Prussians,
it was too much for me! It curdled my blood with rage! And I wept
with shame for a whole day. Oh, if I were a man it would be different!
I looked at them from my window, those fat pigs with their pointed
helmets, and my maid had to hold my hands to stop me throwing my
furniture down on their backs. Then some came to lodge with me, and
I leaped at the first one's throat! They're no more difficult to strangle
than anyone else. And I'd have finished that one off if I hadn't been
dragged away by the hair. After that I had to hide. And then when the
chance came, I left and here I am."

The others applauded her warmly. She grew in her companions' esteem, for they hadn't shown such pluck. Listening to her, Cornudet

maintained the approving and benevolent smile of an apostle. He was just like a priest listening to a believer praise God, for long-bearded democrats have a monopoly on patriotism, just as the men in cassocks have a monopoly on religion. He spoke in turn in a doctrinaire tone with a grandiloquence learned from the proclamations that had been pasted on the walls every day, and he concluded with a flourish of eloquence in which he soundly thrashed that "scoundrel Badinguet."[8]

But Ball of Lard instantly grew angry, for she was a Bonapartist. She went redder than a tomato and stuttering in indignation she said, "I'd really like to have seen you lot in his place! That would have been a sight! You're the ones who betrayed him. There'd be nothing else but to leave France if we were ruled by rascals like you!" Cornudet remained unmoved, keeping a disdainful and superior smile on his lips, but it was clear that curses weren't far off when the count interposed and, with some difficulty, calmed the exasperated prostitute down by proclaiming in tones of authority that all sincere opinions were worthy of respect. Meanwhile the countess and the manufacturer's wife, whose souls were full of the irrational hatred felt by well-brought-up people for the Republic, and of that instinctive tenderness that all women nourish for flamboyant and despotic governments, felt themselves drawn, against their wills, toward this prostitute who was full of dignity and whose emotions resembled their own so closely.

The basket was empty. The ten of them had emptied it with ease, regretting only that it wasn't larger. The conversation continued for some time, though a little less genially now that they had finished eating.

Night fell. Little by little the darkness became profound, and the cold which they felt more now they were digesting made Ball of Lard shiver despite her fat. Then Mme de Bréville offered her her little heater, whose coal had been renewed several times since morning, and the other accepted instantly, for she felt that her feet were frozen. Mmes Carré-Lamadon and Loiseau gave theirs to the nuns.

The coach driver had lit his lanterns. They shed a bright light over a cloud of mist above the sweating rumps of the leading horses and on each side of the road the snow seemed to stream past under the moving reflection of the lamps.

Inside the coach nothing could be seen anymore, but suddenly there was a movement between Ball of Lard and Cornudet. Loiseau, peering through the gloom, thought he saw the big-bearded man move swiftly away, as if he had received a good blow landed without a sound.

Small points of light appeared ahead of them on the road. It was Tôtes. They had traveled for eleven hours, and together with two hours

---

8. *Badinguet:* The left wing's nickname for Napoleon III. It is said to be the name of the worker whose clothes he wore as a disguise to escape from the fortress of Ham in 1846; he had been incarcerated there since 1840.

of rest taken on the four occasions when the horses had been given a break to get their breath back and eat their oats, they had spent some fourteen hours on the road. They entered the town and stopped in front of the Hôtel du Commerce.

The gate opened. A well known sound made all the passengers tremble. It was the sound of sabre scabbards against the ground. Immediately a German voice called out some command.

Although the coach had stopped no one got out, as if they were expecting to be massacred when they did so. Then the driver appeared, holding one of his lanterns, which shed a sudden light into the depths of the coach with its two rows of terrified heads, mouths gaping and eyes wide in surprise and horror.

Beside the coach driver there stood, the light full on him, a German officer, a tall young man who was extremely slender and blond, as tightly bound in his uniform as a girl in her corset, and wearing on his shoulder his flat, waxed cap, which made him look like the bellboy of an English hotel. His enormous mustache with its long straight whiskers imperceptibly thinning out on each side and ending with a single blond hair, so thin one couldn't make out the end, seemed to hang over the edges of his mouth and, by pulling his cheek down it made his lips droop.

Using Alsacian French he invited the passengers to get out, saying abruptly, "Vould you get out, laties and gentlemen?"

The two nuns were the first to obey, showing that docility common to holy women used to all forms of submission, the count and the countess appeared next, followed by the manufacturer and his wife, then Loiseau pushing in front of him his large better half. As he stepped onto the ground he said to the officer, "Good day, Monsieur," moved more by prudence than politeness. The officer with the insolence common to the all-powerful, looked at him without answering.

Ball of Lard and Cornudet, although nearest the door, got out last, grave and contemptuous before the enemy. The fat prostitute tried to control herself and force herself to be calm: the Red tormented his long reddish beard with a tragic and slightly trembling hand. They wanted to maintain their dignity, for they realized that in such meetings everyone more or less represents their own country. Each was equally revolted by the servility shown by their companions, so that *she* tried to appear more proud than her neighbors, the honest women, while *he*, realizing full well that he should set an example, maintained his attitude of resistance which had begun with the destruction of the roads.

They went into the inn's vast kitchen and the German, having demanded to see the departure pass, signed by the commander-in-chief and mentioning all their names, and giving descriptions and the profession of each passenger, examined all these people lengthily, comparing the faces with the written information.

Then he said abruptly, "All in order," and disappeared.

Then they drew breath. They were hungry again; supper was ordered. It took a half an hour to prepare it, and while two servants appeared to be busying themselves with it, they went to see what the rooms were like. All were situated in a long corridor that ended with a glass door bearing a significant number.

At last they were about to sit down to dinner when the innkeeper himself appeared. He was a former horse-dealer, a fat, asthmatic man with the phlegm singing in his larynx. His father had handed down to him the name of Follenvie.[9]

He asked for Mlle Elisabeth Rousset. Ball of Lard trembled and said, "That's me."

"Mademoiselle, the Prussian officer wants to talk to you straight away." "Me?"

"Yes, if you are indeed Mlle Elisabeth Rousset." She looked disturbed, reflected for a moment, and then said straightforwardly, "So he may, but I'm not going."

There was a movement around her. Everyone was talking, trying to guess the reason behind this order. The count came up, "You are making a mistake, Madame, for your refusal could cause considerable difficulties, not just for you but also for your companions. One should never resist those stronger than oneself. This request can certainly not present any danger—it's surely just for some formality that has been overlooked."

Everyone lent their voices to his argument, they begged her, urged her, lectured her, and they ended by convincing her, for all of them feared the complications that could ensue from such a whim.

At last she said, "I'm doing it for you, of course."

The countess took her by the hand, "And we're grateful to you for it."

She went out. They waited for her before sitting down to the meal.

Everyone regretted that it wasn't they who had been asked for instead of this violent and irascible woman, and mentally prepared platitudes just in case they themselves were sent for. But ten minutes later she returned, puffing, red to bursting point, enraged. She stammered, "Oh, those scoundrels! Those scoundrels!"

All rushed to discover what had happened, but she said nothing. And as the count insisted, she replied with great dignity, "No, it has nothing to do with you. I cannot speak of it."

Then they sat around a tall soup tureen from which arose the smell of cabbages. Despite this upset, the supper passed gaily by. The cider was so good that the Loiseau couple and the nuns took some as an economy measure. The others ordered wine; Cornudet demanded beer. He had a special way of uncorking the bottle, making the liquid foam

---

9. "Mad desire."

up, a way of looking at it, as he held the glass at an angle before lifting it between the lamp and his eye to appreciate the color fully. When he drank, his great beard, which had taken on the shade of the drink he loved seemed to tremble with tenderness; his eyes squinted so as not to lose sight of his beer, and he seemed to be fulfilling the sole function for which he had been born. You'd have said that he was mentally drawing a parallel and a kind of affinity between the two great passions that occupied his entire life: Pale Ale and the Revolution. Certainly he could never taste one without thinking of the other.

M. and Mme Follenvie dined at the far end of the table. The husband, gasping like a broken-down locomotive, had to pull too hard on his chest to converse as he ate, but his wife never stopped talking. She told them about all her impressions on the arrival of the Prussians, what they did, what they said, hating them, first because they cost her money and then because she had two sons in the army. She addressed her remarks above all to the countess, flattered at the chance to talk to a lady of quality.

Then she dropped her voice to talk of delicate matters, and her husband from time to time would interrupt her, "You'd be better off holding your tongue, Mme Follenvie."

But she took not the slightest notice and went on, "Yes, Madame, those people eat only potatoes and pork, and then pork and potatoes. And don't you believe that they're clean, oh no! They leave their droppings everywhere, if you'll pardon the expression. And if you were to see them exercising for hours and hours and days and days; they're all there in a field: they march forward, then they march back, they turn this way, they turn that way. If they were at least plowing the land, or working on the roads in their own country, it might be different! But no, Madame, these soldiers, they don't bring anyone any profit. Why should the poor have to nourish them just so they can learn to massacre folk! I'm only an old woman without any education, that's true, but when you see them exhausting themselves tramping up and down from morning to evening you say to yourself, "When there are people who make so many discoveries to make themselves useful, do we really need others who do themselves such damage just to be harmful? Really, isn't it an abomination to kill people, whether they're Prussians or English or Polish or French? If you take revenge on someone who's done something evil to you, that's bad, must be, because they condemn you for it; but when they exterminate our lads like game with rifles, we're supposed to think it's good, seeing that they hand out decorations to those who kill the highest number? No, don't you see, I'll never understand that!"

Cornudet raised his voice, "War is an act of barbarism when you attack a peaceful neighbor, but it's a sacred duty when you defend your fatherland."

The old woman lowered her head, "Yes, when you defend yourself, it's a different matter. But wouldn't it be better to kill all the kings who do that just for fun?"

Cornudet's eyes lit up. "Bravo, Citizen!" he said.

M. Carré-Lamadon was lost in thought. Although he was a fanatical supporter of famous captains, this peasant woman's good sense had made him dream of the opulence that so many idle and therefore ruinously expensive hands could bring to a country, all that strength that is kept from being productive. Think how it would be if one employed them in the great industrial constructions that it was going to take years to complete.

But Loiseau, leaving his seat, went to talk quietly with the innkeeper. The fat man laughed, coughed, and spat: his enormous stomach leaped with joy at his neighbor's jokes, and he bought six quarter-casks of claret from him, to be delivered in spring, when the Prussians had left.

Supper had barely ended when all of them, crushed with exhaustion, went to bed.

But Loiseau, who'd kept an eye on things, put his wife to bed, and then went to put first his ear, then his eye, to the key hole to try to discover what he called the "mysteries of the corridor."

After about an hour, he heard a soft sound, looked quickly and saw Ball of Lard who seemed even larger than ever in a blue cashmere peignoir with a border of white lace. She held a candle in her hand and was heading for the large number at the far end of the corridor. But a side door opened a crack, and when she returned a few minutes later, Cornudet, in his braces, was following her. They spoke softly and then stopped. Ball of Lard seemed to be energetically denying him entrance to her room. Loiseau unfortunately couldn't hear what they were saying, but at last when they raised their voices, he could catch the odd word. Cornudet was insisting determinedly. He was saying, "Look, don't be silly, what does it matter to you?"

She looked indignant and said, "No, my dear, there are times when such things are not done, and besides, here it would be shameful!"

Doubtless he didn't understand and asked why. Then she lost her temper and raised her voice even more, "Why? Can't you understand why? When there are Prussians in the house, perhaps even in the next room?"

He fell silent. This patriotic prudery of a whore, who wouldn't let herself be caressed near the enemy, must have awakened in his heart his weakening dignity, for having done nothing more than kiss her, he tiptoed back to his own door.

Loiseau, greatly aroused, left the keyhole, clapped his heels together in the middle of the room, put on his night shirt, lifted the sheet under which reposed the hard carcass of his spouse, whom he awoke with a kiss as he murmured, "Do you love me, sweetheart?"

Then the whole house fell silent. But soon there arose from some room or other in a direction that was hard to establish and could just as easily have been the cellars as the attic, a powerful snoring, monotonous, regular, a soft, prolonged noise with the vibration of a boiler under pressure. M. Follenvie was sleeping.

As they had decided to leave at eight the next morning, everyone met in the kitchen, but the coach, whose canvas top wore a cap of snow, arose in solitary splendor in the middle of the courtyard, without horses or driver. It was in vain that they looked for the driver in the stables, in the hay, in the store rooms. Then all the men decided to search in the surrounding countryside, and they set out. They found themselves on the square with the church opposite them and on either side low houses in which could be seen Prussian soldiers. The first they saw was peeling potatoes. The second, further off, was washing out a barber's shop. Another, bearded to the eyes, was hugging a kid who was crying, and rocking him on his knees to try to calm him down; and the plump peasant women whose men were off in the army showed through signs what tasks they required from their obedient victors: chopping wood, preparing the soup, grinding the coffee; one of them even washed his hostess's linen, since she was a completely crippled old granny.

The count, astonished by such behavior, questioned the beadle who was just coming out of the presbytery. That old church mouse answered, "Oh! They aren't particularly evil. They're not Prussians, so people say. They're from further off. I don't really know where they come from. They've all left a wife and children in their own country. They don't enjoy war, believe you me! I'm sure that over in their country, the women weep for their men just as much as they do here. And it's going to cause terrible suffering there just as it will here. Here we're not too badly off yet because they aren't doing us any harm, and they're working as if they were at home. You see, Monsieur, poor people have got to help each other out . . . It's the great who make wars."

Cornudet, indignant at the cordial understanding that had grown up between victors and vanquished, went off, preferring to lock himself away in the inn. Loiseau produced a joke: "They're repopulating." M. Carré-Lamadon produced a serious comment: "They're making reparations." But the coach driver couldn't be found. At last they unearthed him in the village café, sitting down at table in brotherly fashion with the officer's aide-de-camp. The count summoned him: "Didn't you receive our orders to harness up for eight o'clock?"

"Well, yes, but I was given other orders later."

"What orders?"

"Not to harness up at all."

"Who gave you those orders?"

"Well, the Prussian commander."

"Why?"

"I don't know anything about it. Go and ask him! When I'm forbidden to harness up, I don't harness up, that's all there is to it."

"Did he give you the order himself?"

"No, Monsieur, it was the innkeeper who gave me the order on his behalf."

"When was that?"

"Yesterday evening, when I was going to bed."

The three men returned, deeply worried.

They asked for M. Follenvie, but the waitress said that Monsieur, because of his asthma, never got up before ten o'clock. He had even given strict orders not to be wakened earlier except in the case of fire.

They wanted to see the officer, but that was quite out of the question, although his lodgings were in the inn. M. Follenvie alone was authorized to talk to him about civilian matters. So they waited. The women returned to their rooms and occupied themselves with trivial matters.

Cornudet settled himself under the high chimney in the kitchen, where a fine fire was blazing. He got them to bring him one of the little tables from the café, ordered a beer, and drew out a pipe which, among democrats, enjoyed a reputation almost equal to his own, as if it had served the Republic in serving Cornudet. It was a superb meerschaum pipe, admirably seasoned, as black as its master's teeth, but scented, curved, gleaming, sitting familiarly in his hand, and completing the outline of his face. And he remained motionless, his eyes fixed now on the flames from the fire, now on the foam crowning his glass; and each time he drank, he ran his long thin fingers through his long gray hair with an air of satisfaction while he breathed in the odor of his mustache fringed with foam.

Loiseau, using the excuse that he wanted to stretch his legs, went and arranged to sell various parcels of wine to the local merchants. The count and the manufacturer settled down to a discussion of politics. They predicted what future awaited France. One believed in the Orléans branch of the royal family, the other in an unknown savior, a hero who would appear when all hope seemed lost, a Du Guesclin,[10] a Joan of Arc, perhaps, or another Napoleon I. Oh, if only the Crown Prince were not so young! Cornudet, listening to them, smiled the smile of a man who knows what fate really has in store. His pipe filled the kitchen with its aroma.

On the stroke of ten, M. Follenvie appeared. They rushed to ask him what was happening, but all he could do was repeat the following statement several times, without changing a single word: "The officer just said to me, 'Monsieur Follenvie, you are to give orders that the travelers'

---

10. Bertrand du Guesclin (1310/1320–1380) was a central figure in driving the English from France.

coach is not to be harnessed up tomorrow. I do not want them to leave until I give the order. You understand? That is all.' "

Then they tried to see the officer. The count sent him a card on which M. Carré-Lamadon added his name and all his titles. The Prussian sent word that he would admit these two men to talk to him when he had had his lunch, around one o'clock.

The ladies reappeared, and they all ate a little, despite their anxiety. Ball of Lard seemed ill and horribly concerned. They were finishing their coffee when the aide de camp came to fetch the two gentlemen.

Loiseau joined them; as they tried to drag Cornudet along to add more solemnity to their representation, he proudly announced that he had no intention of having any dealings with Germans, and he settled himself back in the chimney, ordering another beer.

The three men went upstairs and were introduced into the inn's finest room, where the officer received them, sprawled in a chair, his feet on the chimneypiece, smoking a long porcelain pipe and wrapped in a flamboyant dressing gown, stolen no doubt from the home of some middle-class citizen of bad taste. He did not get up, did not greet them, didn't look at them. He presented a splendid sample of the bad manners natural to victorious soldiers.

At last, after a few minutes, he said: "Vot do you vant?"

The count spoke for them: "We wish to leave, sir."

"No."

"May I take the liberty of asking why you refuse?"

"Because I don't vish it."

"May I respectfully point out to you, Monsieur, that your commanding general granted us the permission to leave in order to reach Dieppe; and I do not believe we have done anything to justify your harsh treatment of us."

"I do not vish it, that is all. You can go back downstairs now."

All three bowed and withdrew.

That afternoon was dismal. They couldn't understand this German officer's whim at all. The strangest of ideas worried them. Everyone gathered in the kitchen and they discussed it endlessly, imagining the most unlikely causes. Perhaps they were to be kept as hostages—but to what end? Or to make them prisoners? Or, more likely, demand from them a considerable ransom? This thought really put them into a mad panic. The richer they were the more horrified they were, already seeing themselves forced to ransom their lives by pouring bags full of gold into the hands of that insolent soldier. They racked their brains to dig up acceptable lies, to find ways of concealing their wealth, to pass themselves off as poor, very poor. Loiseau took off his gold watchchain and hid it in his pocket. Nightfall increased their fears. The lamp was lit, and as there were still two hours before dinner, Mme Loiseau suggested a game of thirty-one. It would take their minds off things. They accepted. Cornudet himself took part, after putting out his pipe as a gesture of politeness.

The count shuffled, dealt, and immediately Ball of Lard had thirty-one. Soon the interest of the game dulled the fear that haunted their minds. But Cornudet cottoned on to the fact that the Loiseaus were in cahoots to cheat the others.

As they were about to go to dinner, M. Follenvie reappeared, and in his phlegm-laden voice he announced, "The Prussian officer asks Mlle Elisabeth Rousset whether she has changed her mind yet."

Ball of Lard stood there, very pale. Then she suddenly turned crimson and was so suffocated with rage that she could no longer talk. At last she burst out, "Tell that scoundrel, that bastard, that dirty swine of a Prussian, that I will never be willing. Do you understand me: never, never, never."

The fat innkeeper went out. Then Ball of Lard was surrounded, questioned, begged by everyone to reveal the mystery behind this visit. At first she resisted, but soon exasperation ran away with her: "What does he want? You want to know what he wants? He wants to sleep with me!" she shouted. No one was shocked by her expression, so lively was their indignation. Cornudet broke his glass by banging it violently down on the table. There was an outcry of castigation directed at this ignoble soldier, a blast of anger, everyone was united in resistance as if each of them had been ordered to pay their part in the sacrifice demanded of her. The count declared in tones of disgust that those folk carried on just like the barbarians of old. The women especially commiserated with Ball of Lard, energetically covering her with caresses. The nuns, who appeared only at the meal, had lowered their heads and didn't say a word.

Nevertheless, they dined once the first rage had passed, but they spoke little: they were thinking.

The ladies withdrew early, and the men, as they smoked, organized a game of écarté in which M. Follenvie was invited to take part. They'd planned to question him cunningly on what means they could use to overcome the officer's resistance. But he kept his mind on his cards, listened to nothing, answered nothing. And he repeatedly said, "Think of the game, gentlemen, the game."

He was concentrating so intensely on the game that he forgot to spit, which sometimes meant that his chest roared like an organ. His whistling lungs offered the whole gamut of asthma, from the deep bass notes to the sharp huskiness of young cocks trying to crow.

He even refused to go upstairs when his wife, who was so tired she could hardly stand, came to fetch him. So she went off on her own, for she was a morning person, always up before the sun, whereas her husband was a night owl, always ready to spend the night with his friends.

He called out to her, "Put my egg flip in front of the fire," and returned to the game. When it became clear that they would get nothing out of him, they said it was time to call it a day, and everyone went to bed.

They got up fairly early the next morning, again with a vague hope, a growing desire to be off, a feeling of terror at spending another day in this horrible little inn.

Alas, the horses remained in the stable, the coachman stayed out of sight. Having nothing better to do, they cooled their heels around the coach.

Lunch was a grim affair; and their relationships toward Ball of Lard had cooled, for night brings counsel, and had somewhat altered their conclusions. They were close to bearing the prostitute a grudge now, for not having secretly gone in search of the Prussian in order to procure her companions a pleasant surprise when they woke up. What could be simpler? Who would have known, moreover? She could have saved face by telling the officer she pitied the distress of the other passengers. It meant so little for a woman like her!

But no one confessed to such thoughts.

In the afternoon, as they were deadly bored, the count suggested they stroll around the village. Everyone wrapped up well and the little group set out, with the exception of Cornudet, who preferred sitting by the fire, and the nuns, who spent their days in the church or with the local priest.

The cold, which grew daily more intense, stung their noses and ears cruelly; their feet hurt so much that each step was torture; and when the countryside came into view, it struck them as so terribly mournful under that endless whiteness that everyone immediately turned round, their souls frozen and their hearts wrung.

The four women took the lead, the three men a little behind them. Loiseau, who understood the situation, suddenly asked if that "bitch there" was going to make them spend much more time in such a spot. The count, invariably polite, said that one could not demand so painful a sacrifice from a woman, and that the offer should come from her. M. Carré-Lamadon observed that if, as was rumored, the French were launching a counterattack through Dieppe, the two armies could meet only at Tôtes. This reflection made the others uneasy. "What if we escaped on foot?" asked Loiseau. The count shrugged his shoulders. "You're not serious! In this snow? With our wives? And what's more, we'd be pursued immediately, caught in ten minutes, and brought back as prisoners at the mercy of the soldiers." It was true. They fell silent.

The ladies were discussing clothes, but a certain constraint seemed to come between them.

Suddenly, at the end of the street, the officer appeared. Against the snow that bounded the horizon they could see his tall, uniformed shape, with its wasp-like slimness, and he walked along with his knees apart, in that movement which is peculiar to soldiers who are striving not to dirty boots they have carefully waxed.

He bowed as he walked past the ladies, and cast a disdainful glance at the men who, moreover, were dignified enough not to take their hats off, although Loiseau did begin the gesture of removing his.

Ball of Lard had blushed to the tips of her ears. And the three married women felt deeply humiliated at having been met thus by this soldier in the company of the prostitute he had treated in so cavalier a fashion.

Then they talked about him, his bearing, his face. Mme Carré-Lamadon, who had known many officers and judged them as a connoisseur, considered this one not at all bad; she even regretted that he wasn't French, because he'd make a very attractive hussar and would surely drive all the women wild.

Once they'd returned to the inn, they had no idea what to do. Bitter words were exchanged even about trivial matters. Dinner was silent and short, and everyone went upstairs to bed, hoping they would sleep to kill time. They came down the next morning with weariness on their faces and irritation in their hearts. The women barely spoke to Ball of Lard.

A bell rang. It was to announce a baptism. The fat prostitute had a child being brought up by peasants at Yvetot. She saw it only once a year and never gave it a thought; but the image of the child who was to be baptized filled her heart with a sudden and violent tenderness for her own child, and she was determined to attend the ceremony.

As soon as she had left, everyone exchanged glances then drew their chairs together, for they felt only too clearly that a decision had to be reached. Loiseau had a sudden inspiration. He suggested they propose to the officer that he keep Ball of Lard on her own and let the rest leave.

M. Follenvie undertook to carry the message, but he came back downstairs almost immediately. The German, knowing human nature, had ejected him. He insisted on retaining everyone until his desire was satisfied.

Then Mme Loiseau's low-born temperament burst out: "But we're not going to die of old age here. Since it's that trollop's profession, to do that with all men, it's my view she hasn't the right to refuse one rather than another. Just think, she took everything she could lay her hands on in Rouen, even coach drivers! Yes, Madame, the coach driver from the prefecture! I know that for a fact, because he buys his wine from us. And now that it's a question of getting us out of a scrape, she pretends to be fussy, the tramp! . . . So if you ask my opinion, this officer is behaving perfectly well. He may have been deprived for a long time; and there are three of us whom he could have preferred. But no, he's happy to take the woman everyone has had. He respects married women. Just think, he's the master. All he had to say was *I want*, and he could take us by force with his soldiers."

The two women shuddered slightly. Pretty Mme Carré-Lamadon's eyes gleamed and she went a little pale, as if she already felt herself forcibly seized by the officer.

The men, who were discussing matters together, drew closer. Loiseau, enraged, wanted to hand that "wretch" over to the enemy, bound hands and feet. But the count, who was descended from three generations of ambassadors, and was blessed with a diplomat's physiognomy, preferred cunning: "We'll have to convince her," he said.

Then they plotted.

The women drew closer together, they dropped their voices, and the discussion became general, everyone giving their opinion. It was all very decent, moreover. The ladies in particular found delicate euphemisms, charming subtleties of expression, to express the most juicy matters. A foreigner would have understood nothing, so carefully were the linguistic precautions observed. But the thin layer of prudery that covers every woman of the world is only skin deep, and they blossomed in this smutty adventure, in truth delighted in it, feeling they were in their element, pawing love with the sensuality of a greedy cook preparing someone else's supper.

Gaiety returned of its own accord, for by the end the story struck them as very funny. The count considered the jokes a shade improper, but so well told that they brought a smile to the lips. In his turn Loiseau let fall a few off-color jokes which were rather more explicit, but which offended no one; and the thought his wife had brutally expressed dominated everyone's thoughts: "Because it's that prostitute's job, why should she refuse this man more than any other man?" Nice Mme Carré Lamadon even seemed to think that in her place she would be less likely to refuse that man than anyone else.

They prepared the siege at length, as if for a defended fortress. Each of them agreed on the role they were to play, on the arguments they'd use, on the maneuvers they'd carry out. They drew up a plan of attack, worked out what tricks to employ, what surprises they'd use for the assault, in order to force this living citadel to let the enemy enter its walls.

Cornudet remained to one side, however, a complete outsider in the whole matter.

They were so absorbed that they did not hear Ball of Lard return. But the count whispered a soft "Hush," which made them all raise their eyes. She was there. They stopped talking abruptly, and a degree of embarrassment at first prevented them from talking to her. The countess, whose familiarity with the duplicity of salons had made her more supple than the others, asked her, "Did you enjoy yourself at the baptism?"

The fat prostitute, still in an emotional state, told them all about it, and described the faces, the attitudes, and even the church itself. And she added, "It's so nice to pray now and again."

In the interval up to lunch time, the ladies contented themselves with being friendly toward her, to build up her confidence and make her more malleable in accepting their advice.

As soon as they had sat down for lunch, they began their sorties. At first there was a vague conversation on self-sacrifice. Examples from antiquity were cited: Judith and Holophernes,[11] then, for no reason at all, Lucretia and Sextus,[12] Cleopatra, who made all the enemy generals share her couch and reduced them to slavish servility. Then someone told an imaginary story that had blossomed in the minds of those ignorant millionaires, in which the women of Rome had gone to Capua to rock Hannibal to sleep in their arms, and with him, his lieutenants and the phalanxes of mercenary soldiers. They mentioned all the women who had stopped conquerors, made their bodies into battle fields—a means of mastering the army—and had vanquished hideous and hated beings through their heroic caresses, and sacrificed their chastity in an act of revenge and devotion.

They even discussed, in veiled terms, that highborn Englishwoman who had allowed herself to catch a horrible and contagious illness in order to transmit it to Bonaparte, who had been saved in miraculous fashion by a sudden weakness at the time of the fatal rendez-vous.

The whole tale was narrated in perfectly acceptable, moderate terms, with an occasional burst of enthusiasm considered likely to inspire emulation.

By the time they'd finished you might have thought it was woman's sole role here on earth to perform a perpetual sacrifice of her person, to abandon herself constantly to the whims of the army.

The two nuns appeared not to hear, lost in deep thought as they were, and Ball of Lard said nothing.

Through the entire afternoon, they left her to her reflections. But instead of calling her "Madame" as they had done hitherto, they simply called her "Mademoiselle," without anyone really knowing why, as if they had wanted to make her drop one step down in the esteem that she had scaled, to make her feel how shameful her situation was.

At the moment when the soup was being served, M. Follenvie reappeared, repeating the question he had asked the previous night: "The Prussian officer wishes to know if Mlle Elisabeth Rousset has changed her mind."

---

11. *Judith and Holophernes:* Judith was a Jewish heroine who saved her city by seducing Holophernes, the enemy general, and cutting off his head while he slept.

12. *Lucretia:* Roman lady who killed herself after being raped by Sextus, the son of Tarquin the Proud.

Ball of Lard answered coldly, "No, Monsieur."

But at dinner the coalition weakened. Loiseau came out with three unfortunate sentences. Everyone was struggling to find new examples and couldn't think of any, when the countess—perhaps without thinking it over first—felt a vague need to pay homage to religion and questioned the elder of the nuns about the great facts in the lives of the saints. Well, many of them had committed acts that in our eyes would be crimes, but the Church has no difficulty in absolving such misdeeds when they're carried out for the glory of God or for the good of one's neighbor. This was a powerful argument: the countess turned it to advantage. Then, either through those tacit agreements, those moments of veiled complacency in which all those who wear an ecclesiastical gown excel, or simply through a fortunate stupidity, a helpful inanity, the old nun gave the plotters considerable assistance. They thought she was shy, but she revealed herself to be bold, verbose, and violent. She wasn't one to be troubled by the tentative explorations of casuistry. Her doctrine seemed to be an iron bar, her faith never hesitated, her conscience had no scruples. She found Abraham's sacrifice perfectly simple, for she herself would have killed her mother and father forthwith on an order from above and, in her opinion, nothing could displease the Lord when one's intentions were praiseworthy. The countess, profiting from the holy authority of her unexpected accomplice, made her provide a kind of edifying paraphrase of this moral axiom, "The end justifies the means."

She asked her, "Well, Sister, do you think that God accepts all means, and forgives the deed when the motive is pure?"

"Who could doubt it, Madame? An action which is blameworthy in itself often becomes meritorious through the thought that inspires it."

And so they went on, revealing the will of God, seeing in advance what His decisions would be, making Him take an interest in things which in truth barely concerned Him at all.

All this was carefully wrapped up, discreetly and cleverly conveyed. But every word spoken by the holy woman in the coif made a breech in the indignant resistance of the harlot. Then, changing the conversation a little, the woman with the dangling rosary talked about the houses in her order, of her mother superior, of herself and her sweet little neighbor, dear Sister Saint Nicéphore. They had been summoned to Le Havre to care for hundreds of soldiers struck down with smallpox in the hospitals. She described them, these poor sufferers, explaining their illness in detail. And while they were held up en route by this Prussian's whims, a great number of French men could die, men that they may well have saved! It was her own specialty, caring for soldiers. She'd been in the Crimea, in Italy, in Austria, and, as she talked about her campaigns, she suddenly showed herself to be one of those drum-and-bugle nuns who seem created to follow the camps, pick up the wounded in the swirl of battle, and know better than a general how to cow those great undisciplined troops with a single word; a real Sister Boom-Boom-Boom whose ravaged face, pitted with countless holes, seemed to be the very image of the devastation of war.

No one said anything after her, so good was the effect she seemed to have created.

Immediately after the meal had ended, they quickly went upstairs and did not come back down the following day until fairly late in the morning.

Lunch was calm. They were giving the sown grain time to germinate and to bear seed.

The countess suggested a stroll in the afternoon; then the count, as had been agreed, took Ball of Lard's arm and remained behind the others, with her.

He spoke to her, paternally and a little disdainfully, in familiar tones such as men of the world use when talking to prostitutes, calling her "my dear child," talking down to her from his high social position, and claiming that her honor was above question. He went instantly to the heart of the matter: "So, you prefer to make us stay here, exposed as you yourself are to all the violence that would follow if the Prussian troops were defeated, rather than consent to an act of accommodation of the sort you've often had to perform in your life?"

Ball of Lard made no answer.

He attacked her through gentleness, through reason, through sentiment. He was able to remain "monsieur le comte" while staying gallant when it was necessary to be so, complimenting her and even being amiable. He exalted the service she would be paying them, spoke of their gratitude, then suddenly, cheerfully addressing her informally, he added, "You know, my dear, he'd be justified in boasting that he'd enjoyed a pretty girl of the sort he'll rarely find in his own land."

Ball of Lard said nothing and joined the others.

As soon as they got back she went upstairs and did not appear again. Their anxiety was extreme. What was she going to do? What a mess it would be if she resisted!

The hour for dinner came; they waited for her in vain. M. Follenvie came in and announced that Mlle Rousset felt unwell and that the others should start eating. They all pricked up their ears. The count went up to the innkeeper and whispered to him: "Has it worked?" "Yes." Through a sense of decency, he said nothing to his companions, but merely nodded his head to them slightly. Immediately a great sigh of relief escaped from all those breasts, and their faces were lit with joy. Loiseau shouted, "Hang it! I'll buy some champagne if you've got any!" and Mme Loiseau felt a pang of anguish when the innkeeper returned with four bottles in his hands. Suddenly everyone had become communicative and noisy.

Their hearts were filled with ribald joy. The count appeared to notice that Mme Carré-Lamadon was a charming woman; the manufacturer paid the countess compliments. The conversation was lively, amusing, witty.

Suddenly, Loiseau, his expression worried and his hand cupped around his ear, shouted, "Quiet!" Everyone fell silent, surprised and almost frightened already. Then he listened intently, gesturing at them to be quiet, lifted his eyes to the ceiling, listened again, and then went on in his normal voice: "It's all right, everything's going well."

At first reluctant to understand, they soon smiled.

Fifteen minutes later he began the same farce again and renewed it often during the course of the evening. He would pretend to call someone on the upper story, giving advice in a series of double entendres drawn from his traveling salesman mentality. From time to time he adopted a set expression and sighed, "Poor girl!"; or he would grit his teeth and mutter with an air of fury, "You scoundrel of a Prussian!" Sometimes, just when no one was thinking about it any more, he would shout in ringing tones, "That's enough!" and added, as if talking to himself, "I just hope we see her again and that he doesn't do her to death, the wretch!"

Although these jokes were in terribly bad taste, they amused everyone and no one was offended, for indignation like other things depends on the circumstances, and the atmosphere that had slowly grown around them was heavy with lewd thoughts.

At dessert, the women themselves made witty and discreet allusions to what was happening. Their eyes gleamed: they had drunk a great deal. The count, who, even in his indiscretions, maintained his lofty appearance of gravity, made a much-appreciated comparison concerning the end of winter at the pole and the joy of icebound sailors when they see a route to the south open up.

Loiseau, steamed up, rose, holding a glass of champagne in his hand: "A toast to our deliverance!" Everyone stood up and applauded him. Even the two nuns, invited by the ladies, consented to dip their lips in the foaming wine they had never tasted. They proclaimed that it tasted like fizzy lemonade but that it was nevertheless rather more delicate.

Loiseau summed matters up. "What a pity we don't have a piano! We could have picked out a quadrille."

Cornudet hadn't said a word or made a gesture. He even seemed plunged in very serious thoughts and occasionally pulled at his great beard with a furious gesture that seemed to want to make it even longer. Finally, near midnight, as the party was about to break up, Loiseau, who was staggering about, suddenly struck him on his paunch and said to him thickly, "You're not enjoying yourself this evening. Haven't you got something to say, Citizen?" But Cornudet lifted his head abruptly and, sending a gleaming and terrible glance around the group, he said, "I tell the lot of you that you've just committed an infamous deed!" He got up, reached the door, repeated again, "Infamous!" and disappeared.

At first, this poured cold water on things. Loiseau, taken aback, remained dumbfounded. But he soon regained his aplomb, then suddenly shook with laughter and repeated, "Sour grapes, old man, sour grapes." Since no one understood, he told them about the "mysteries of the corridor." Then everyone was wildly amused once again. The ladies were enjoying themselves hugely. The count and M. Carré-Lamadon laughed until the tears poured down their cheeks. They could not believe it.

"What? You're sure, he wanted to . . . "

"I tell you I saw it."

"And she knocked him back?"

"Because the Prussian was in the room next door."

"You're kidding!"

"I swear it's true."

The count was suffocating with laughter. The captain of industry clutched his stomach with both hands. Loiseau went on, "And you can see why this evening he doesn't find it funny, not at all."

That set all three off again, sick and breathless with laughter. On that note they separated. But Mme Loiseau, who belonged to the stinging-nettle family, pointed out to her husband as they went to bed that "that prude," little Mme Carré-Lamadon had only pretended to laugh the whole evening through: "You know, with women when they go for a uniform, it doesn't matter a hoot to them if it's French or Prussian. It's a crying shame, Lord knows!"

All night through, there ran down the dark corridor what can only be described as rustling sounds, light noises that could barely be heard, like sighs, the padding of bare feet, imperceptible creaking sounds. And it was certainly the case that sleep came very late, for rays of light slipped from under the doors for a very long time. Champagne has such effects: it's said to disturb sleep. The next day, a bright winter sun made the snow glitter. The coach, at last harnessed up, waited before the gateway, while an army of white pigeons, puffed up in their thick feathers, with pink eyes spotted in the middle with a black mark, wandered gravely between the six horses' legs, and tried to sustain themselves from the smoking droppings they scattered about.

The coach driver, wrapped in his sheepskin, was smoking a pipe as he sat waiting, and all the radiant passengers swiftly had provisions wrapped up for the rest of the journey.

All they were waiting for was Ball of Lard. She appeared. She seemed a bit disturbed, ashamed, and she moved shyly to join her companions, who all in an identical movement turned away as if they had not seen her. The count took his wife's arm in a dignified way and removed her from this tainted contact.

The fat prostitute stopped dead, stupefied. Then, gathering her courage together, she went up to the manufacturer's wife and said, "Good morning, Madame," in a humble murmur. The other merely gave a little, impertinent nod of greeting, which she accompanied with a glance of outraged virtue. Everyone seemed very busy, and they kept away from her as if she were carrying some infection in her skirts. Then they rushed to the coach, which she reached last of all, alone, and resumed in silence the seat she'd occupied during the first part of their journey.

They seemed not to see her, not to know her. But Mme Loiseau, indignantly considering her from a distance, said half under her breath to her husband, "Luckily I'm not sitting next to her."

The heavy coach set off, and the journey began again.

At first no one spoke. Ball of Lard did not dare raise her eyes. She felt simultaneously indignant at all her neighbors and humiliated that she had yielded, sullied by the kisses of that Prussian into whose arms they had hypocritically thrown her. But the countess, turning to Mme Carré-Lamadon soon interrupted this painful silence.

"I believe you know Mme d'Etrelles?"

"Yes, she's a friend of mine."

"What a charming woman!"

"Ravishing! A truly lofty nature, very well educated moreover, an artist to her fingertips. She sings delightfully and draws perfectly."

The manufacturer was chatting with the count, and in the midst of the din of the windows a word occasionally could be heard: "Coupon—due date—premium—settlement."

Loiseau, who had filched from the inn the old pack of cards, greasy from five years of rubbing against poorly cleaned tables, launched into a hand of bezique with his wife.

The nuns took their long rosaries from their belts, both made the sign of the cross and suddenly their lips began moving swiftly, rushing through their vague murmur more and more quickly, as if they were in a prayer race and from time to time they would kiss a medallion, cross themselves again, then launch once more into their swift and continuous mutterings.

Motionless, Cornudet meditated.

After they had been traveling for three hours, Loiseau picked up the cards and said, "I'm hungry."

Then his wife took a package tied up in string from which she extracted a piece of cold veal. She cut it neatly into thin firm slices and both began to eat.

"What if we did the same?" said the countess. It was agreed and she unpacked the provisions prepared for the two couples. In one of those long pots whose lid has a porcelain hare on it, to indicate that under-neath lies hare pâté, was a succulent preparation in which white rivers of lard ran through the brown flesh mingled with other meats which had been finely cut up. A fine square of gruyère cheese, wrapped in a sheet of newspaper, bore the words "news items" on its creamy skin.

The two nuns brought out a round of sausage that smelled of garlic, and Cornudet thrusting both hands simultaneously into the vast pock-ets of his overcoat sack, from one withdrew four hard-boiled eggs and from the other, a crust of bread. He would break off a shell, throw it under his feet in the straw, and begin to bite straight into the egg, drop-ping onto his vast beard little flakes of light yellow that looked like stars in its darkness.

Ball of Lard, in the haste and flurry of getting up, had not given any thought to food. Exasperated, choking with fury, she watched all these people who were calmly eating. A tumultuous anger contorted her at first and she opened her mouth to scream out what she thought of them in a flood of insults that leaped to her lips, but rage strangled her so much that she couldn't speak.

No one looked at her or thought about her. She felt she was drown-ing in the scorn of these honest rogues who had first sacrificed her, then rejected her, like something unclean and useless. Then she thought of her big basket full of good things that they had greedily devoured, her two chickens gleaming in their jelly, her pâtés, her pears, her four bottles of claret; and as her fury suddenly collapsed like an elastic band that has been stretched to breaking point, she felt herself close to tears. She made a desperate effort, whipped up her courage, swallowed back her sobs as children do, but the tears rose, gleaming on the edges of her eyelids, and soon two fat tears dropped from her eyes and rolled slowly down her cheeks. Others followed more rapidly, flowing like drops of water that filter through a cliff and falling regularly on the swollen curve of her breast. She remained upright, eyes straight ahead, her face stiff and pale, hoping no one would see.

But the countess noticed and showed her husband with a sign. He shrugged his shoulders as if to say, "Well, what can I do, it's no fault of mine." Mme Loiseau laughed silently in triumph and murmured, "She's crying because she's ashamed."

The two nuns had gone back to their prayers, having wrapped the remains of their sausage in paper.

Then Cornudet, who was digesting his eggs, stretched out his long legs under the opposite bench, lent back, crossed his arms, smiled like a man who has just discovered a good joke, and began to whistle the Marseillaise.

All the faces started to scowl. The popular song certainly did not please his neighbors. They grew nervous, irritated, and looked as if they were close to howling like dogs that hear a hurdy-gurdy. He realized what was happening, but he didn't stop. From time to time he even sang the words: "Sacred love of our country, guide, support our avenging arms. Freedom, beloved freedom, fight with your defenders!"

They moved more swiftly, the snow being harder, and all the way to Dieppe, during the long dull hours of traveling, through the jolts along the way, through the falling night, then in the deep darkness of the coach, he continued his ferocious stubbornness, his vengeful monotonous whistling, forcing the weary and exasperated spirits to follow the song from beginning to end, to remember every word and apply them to each beat.

And Ball of Lard wept on; and sometimes a sob that she had been unable to suppress burst out between two stanzas in the darkness.

◆

In this tale, Maupassant reveals his mastery of the fantastic, his ability to chill and disturb the reader with the most economical of details and in the most straightforward of styles. The device of setting the tale in a framework is typical of Maupassant, at once an acknowledgment of a long tradition that goes back to Chaucer and Boccaccio and an invitation to see the situation of storytelling as profoundly familiar. It is against the familiarity of the situation that the apparently equally familiar situation of brushing someone's hair takes on its particularly eerie quality.

APPARITION (1891)

The conversation had turned to illegal restraint, a subject that had arisen as a result of a recent trial. It was at the end of an intimate gathering, at the Rue de Grenelle, in a former hotel, and everyone had his or her own story, a story each teller swore was true.

Then the old Marquis de la Tour-Samuel, who was eighty-two years old, stood up and came to lean against the mantelpiece. He said in his slightly trembling voice, "I, too, know something strange, so strange that it has been the obsession of my life. Fifty-six years have now gone by since this happened to me, and not a month passes without my seeing it again in my dreams. That day left its mark on me, a scar of fear, do you see what I mean? Yes, I suffered horrible fear for the space of ten minutes, with the result that since that moment a kind of constant terror has remained in my soul. Unexpected noises make me shudder to my very heart; objects I can barely distinguish in the evening shadows fill me with a wild desire to run away. And at night, I'm afraid.

Oh! I wouldn't have admitted that before reaching my present age. I can say everything now. You're allowed not to be brave in the face of imaginary dangers when you're eighty-two years old. In the face of real danger, Mesdames, I have never retreated.

This incident shook me so profoundly, filled me with such deep anxiety, an anxiety so mysterious and so horrible, that I have never told it. I kept it in the depths of my being, in those depths where one hides shameful secrets, painful secrets, all those weaknesses we have in our existence and that we dare not confess to.

I shall tell you the story as it happened to me, without trying to explain it. Of course there surely is an explanation, unless I simply went mad for an hour. But no, I wasn't mad, and I'll prove to you that I wasn't. You can think what you want to about it. Here are the simple facts of the matter.

It was in 1827, in July. I was in my garrison at Rouen.

One day, as I was strolling down the quay, I met a man I thought I recognized, although I couldn't remember exactly who he was. Instinctively I made as if to stop. The stranger saw my gesture, looked at me, and fell into my arms.

It was a friend of my youth whom I had greatly loved. In the five years since I had last seen him he seemed to have aged half a century. His hair was completely white; he walked bent over, as if exhausted. He understood my surprise and told me his life story. A terrible sorrow had broken him.

He had fallen madly in love with a young girl and married her in a kind of ecstasy of happiness. After a year of superhuman bliss and undulled ardor, she had suddenly died from a heart disease, killed by love itself, no doubt.

He left his chateau the very day of the funeral, and had gone to live in his house in Rouen. He lived there, alone and in despair, devoured by grief, so unhappy he thought only of suicide.

"Since I've found you again," he said to me, "I'll ask you to do me a great service. I'd like you to go to my bedroom at home, our bedroom, and take from my desk a few papers I urgently need. I can't entrust this task to a subaltern or an agent, for I need unbreachable discretion and complete silence. As for me, nothing in the world could induce me to return to that house.

"I'll give you the key to my room, which I closed myself when I left, and the key to my desk. Moreover, you'll have a letter from me to give my gardener, and he'll open the chateau for you.

"But come and dine with me tomorrow, and we'll talk about it."

I promised him I'd do this small service for him. For me, moreover, it was nothing more than an outing, his domain lying some five leagues from Rouen. It would take me about an hour on horseback.

At ten the next morning I was at his place. We lunched alone together. But he barely spoke a word. He begged me to forgive him. The thought of the visit I was going to make to that room, where his happiness lay, had distressed him, he told me. Indeed, he struck me as strangely disturbed, preoccupied, as if a mysterious conflict were taking place in his soul.

At last he told me exactly what it was that I had to do. It was very simple. I had to take two packets of letters and a bundle of papers that were shut away in the first drawer on the right of the desk whose key I had been given. He added, "I don't need to beg you not to look at them."

I was almost hurt by this statement, and told him so, somewhat sharply. He stammered, "Forgive me, I'm suffering too deeply."

And he began to cry. I left him around one o'clock to carry out my task.

It was a glorious day, and I went at a smart trot through the meadows, listening to the songs of the larks and the rhythmical noise of my saber against my boot.

Then I went into the forest and drew my horse back to a walk. The branches caressed my face, and from time to time I caught a leaf with my teeth and chewed it avidly, in one of those enthusiasms for life that fill you, heaven knows why, with a kind of tumultuous and intangible happiness, a kind of intoxication of strength.

As I approached the chateau, I searched in my pocket for the letter I had for the gardener and realized to my astonishment that it was sealed. I was so surprised and annoyed that I almost turned back without carrying out my task. Then I thought that if I did that, I'd be showing a touchiness that was not in the best of taste. Besides, my friend could easily have sealed the message without thinking about it, he was in such distress at the time.

The manor looked as if it had been abandoned for some twenty years. The rotted gate hung open, barely upright. The avenues were full of weeds, and you could no longer tell where the gardens ended and the lawn began.

At the sound I made kicking at a shutter, an old man came out of a side door and seemed thunderstruck to see me. I leapt down and handed him the letter. He read it, reread it, turned it over, looked up at me, put the letter in his pocket and said, "Well, what do you want?"

I answered brusquely: "Surely you know that, since you've just received your master's orders in that letter. I want to go into the chateau."

He seemed flabbergasted. He said, "So . . . you're going into his bedroom?"

I began to grow impatient. "For heaven's sake! You're not going to interrogate me, are you?"

He stammered, "No . . . sir . . . it's just that . . . it hasn't been opened since . . . since . . . the death. If you'll wait five minutes I'll go and see if . . . if. . . . "

I interrupted him angrily: "Oh cut it out! What impertinence is this? You can't go in there, since I have the key here."

He was at a loss for words. "Very well, sir. Let me show you the way."

"Show me the staircase and then leave me alone. I can find it quite well without you."

"But . . . sir . . . nevertheless. . . . "

At that, I really flew into a rage: "Now hold your tongue, hear me? Or you'll really have to deal with me." I pushed him violently aside and went into the house. First I went through the kitchen, then two small rooms that the caretaker lived in, together with his wife. I then entered a vast hallway, and I climbed the stairs until I reached the door I recognized from my friend's description. I opened it without difficulty and went in.

The suite was so dark that at first I could make nothing out. I stopped, arrested by that damp, stale smell that comes from uninhabited, closed rooms, the rooms of the dead. Then, little by little, my eyes grew accustomed to the darkness, and I could see fairly clearly a large, untidy room, a bed without sheets, but with the mattress and pillows still in place, one of the pillows deeply indented with the mark of an elbow or a head, as if someone had just leaned on it.

The chairs seemed to be in a state of turmoil. I noticed that a door, no doubt belonging to a wardrobe, had remained half-open.

First of all, I went to the window to get some light, planning to fling it open; but the ironwork fixtures on the shutters were so badly rusted that I could not make them budge.

I even tried to break them with my saber, but in vain. As I grew angry with these useless efforts, and as my eyes had at last grown perfectly accustomed to the darkness, I abandoned all hope of seeing clearly, and went to the desk.

I sat down in the arm chair, pulled out the sliding shelf, and opened the relevant drawer. It was completely full. All I needed was three packets, which I knew how to identify, and I set about searching for them.

I was staring at the labels, trying to decipher them, when I thought I heard, or rather felt, a soft sound behind me. I paid no attention to it, thinking that a draft had set some material in motion. But, after a minute, another movement, almost indistinct, sent a strange, unpleasant little shudder over my skin. It was so stupid to be alarmed, even slightly alarmed, that I was unwilling to turn around, for fear of shaming myself in my own eyes. I had just discovered the second of the bundles I needed; and it was just when I came across the third that a deep and painful sigh which I felt on my shoulder made me leap wildly to a point two yards off. In my flight I had spun around, my hand on the hilt of my saber, and I can assure you that if I had not felt it at my side I would have taken to my heels like a coward.

A tall woman clad in white was looking at me, standing behind the armchair in which a second earlier I had been sitting.

My limbs shook so much that I almost fell over backward! Oh! no one can understand, without having experienced them personally, these horrible and stupid terrors. Your soul turns to jelly; you no longer feel your heart; your entire body becomes as soft as a sponge; you have the impression that your entire substance is collapsing.

I do not believe in ghosts. And yet my strength gave way under the hideous fear of the dead. And I suffered, oh! I suffered in a few moments more than in all the rest of my life, in the irresistible anguish of supernatural dread.

If she hadn't spoken, I may well have died! But she spoke; she spoke in a soft and painful voice that set my nerves trembling. I would not dare to say that I regained control of myself and that I found my reason once more. No. I was so shaken that I didn't know what I was doing; but that kind of intimate pride in myself, and to some extent the pride associated with my profession, too, made me preserve an honorable expression almost in spite of myself. I put on an appearance for myself and no doubt for her, too, whoever she might be, woman or specter. I realized all this much later, for I can assure you that, in the moment when she appeared before me, I didn't think of anything. I was afraid.

She said, "Oh, sir! You could perform such a great service for me!"

I wanted to reply, but I was incapable of pronouncing a single word. A vague noise came out of my throat. She went on: "Would you be so kind? You can save me, you can cure me. I'm suffering awfully. I'm suffering, oh, how I'm suffering!"

And she sat down gently in the chair. She looked at me. "Would you help me?"

I nodded, for my voice was still paralyzed. Then she handed me a tortoise-shell comb and murmured, "Oh, comb my hair! Please comb my hair? That would make me better. I must get my hair combed. Look at my head . . . I'm suffering so much, and my hair really hurts me!"

Her unbound hair, very long and very black, so it seemed to me, hung over the back of the chair and touched the floor.

Why did I do it? Why did I take the comb with a shiver, and why did I take up in my hands her long hair, which gave my skin a sensation of terrible cold, as if I were playing with snakes? I don't know.

That feeling has never left my fingers, and I tremble whenever I think of it. I combed her hair. Somehow or other I handled that icy hair. I twisted it around my hand, I tied it up again, I untied it. I braided it as one braids a horse's mane. She sighed, her head to one side, and she seemed happy.

Suddenly she said, "Thank you," snatched the comb from my grasp, and fled through the open door that I'd previously noticed.

Left alone, I felt, for a few seconds, that bewildered agitation that comes when you wake up after a nightmare. Then at last I came to my senses again; I dashed to the window and broke the shutters into a furious cloud of dust.

Light flooded in. I hurled myself at the door through which this being had just left. I found it immovably shut. Then I was seized with a feverish need to leave, a panic, the true panic of the battlefield. I abruptly seized the three packets of letters on the open desk, ran through the suite, leapt down the stairs four at a time, and found myself somehow or other outside. I caught sight of my horse ten strides away, leapt onto it, and set off at a gallop.

I didn't stop until I reached Rouen and was in front of my lodgings. Having thrown the reins to my orderly, I dashed into the bedroom, where I locked myself in so I could think things over.

Then for an hour or so I wondered anxiously whether I had been the victim of a hallucination. It was undeniable that I had suffered from one of those incomprehensible nervous shocks, one of those mental panics that give birth to miracles and to which the Supernatural owes all its power. I was on the point of believing I had seen a mirage, an error of my senses, when I went over to the window. My eyes, as chance would have it, fell on my breast. My cloak was covered with long, feminine hairs that had twisted around my buttons!

I seized them one by one and hurled them outside with trembling fingers.

Then I summoned my orderly. I felt too emotional, too disturbed, to go to my friend's place that very day. Besides, I wanted to give careful consideration to what I should say to him.

I had his letters taken to him, and he gave the soldier a receipt for them. He asked a great many questions about me. He was told that I was unwell, that I had a touch of sunstroke, I don't quite know what they said. He seemed worried.

I went to visit him the following day, as soon as it was light, determined to tell him the truth. He had gone out the previous evening and had not returned.

I came back in the course of the day, but he had not been seen again. I waited a week. He did not reappear. Then I informed the police. They sought him everywhere, but no trace was found of which way he had gone or where he had gone to.

A meticulous search of the abandoned chateau turned up nothing suspicious.

There was no indication that a woman had been hiding there. The inquiry reached no conclusions and the search was abandoned. And for fifty-six years, I've learned nothing about it. That's all I know."

◆

In this final example of Maupassant's skill as a prose stylist, he turns his attention to contemporary sexual mores, setting up a powerful and disturbing series of parallels between the flowing river and the mobility of human relationships, between fish and men, between the beauty of the natural setting and the squalor of sexual behavior. By focusing on external details, Maupassant is able to enter deeply into the personalities of his high-class hero and his sexually ambivalent lover. As is so often the case in Maupassant's writing, what is perhaps most remarkable is the economy and lack of emotion with which so much is so powerfully suggested.

PAUL'S GIRL (1882)

Grillon's restaurant, that phalanstery[13] of oarsmen, was slowly emptying. Just outside could be heard a tumult of shouts and cries as great strapping lads in white bathing trunks gesticulated at each other, their oars on their shoulders.

The women, in light spring dresses, carefully stepped into their yawls and sat at the rudder, tucking their skirts under them while the master of the establishment, a large lad with a red beard, famous for his energy, held out his hand to the pretty little lasses while simultaneously holding their fragile boats steady.

The rowers, in their turn, took their places, their arms bare and their chests bulging, posing for the gallery, a gallery composed of middle-class people in Sunday best, workers, and soldiers leaning on the balustrade of the bridge, all watching the spectacle closely.

One by one the boats moved away from the pontoon. The rowers leaned forward then back, in regular rhythm; and under the impulsion of the long curved oars the swift yawls slid away along the river, growing smaller and smaller until at last they disappeared under another bridge, the railroad bridge, on their way down to La Grenouillère.[14]

Only one couple remained. The young man, almost beardless still, thin, pale-faced, held his arm around his mistress's waist. She was a thin

---

13. *phalanstery:* The socialist thinker Charles Fourier (1772–1837) coined this term for the communities into which he urged society should be divided.

14. *La Grenouillère:* Literally, the froggery. This bar was painted by various impressionist painters.

little brown-haired woman with the movements of a grasshopper; and from time to time they would gaze deep into each other's eyes.

The innkeeper shouted, "Come on, Mr. Paul, get a move on there!" And they went over to him.

Of all the clients of the house, M. Paul was the most loved and the best respected. He paid well, and regularly, whereas with the others you often had to drag it slowly out of them, or else they simply disappeared without paying at all. And he was also a sort of living advertisement for the inn, since his father was a senator. And when a stranger asked, "Who's that young man over there, then, who's so attached to his girl?" one of the regulars would answer in a whisper with an air of importance and mystery, "It's Paul Baron. You know, the senator's son." And, invariably, the other couldn't refrain from saying, "The poor devil! He's caught and caught for good!"

Old Mother Grillon, an admirable woman who knew the trade very well, called the young man and his companion "her two turtledoves" and seemed completely bowled over by this love affair that bought such custom to her house.

The couple slowly walked away. The yawl *Madeleine* was ready, but at the moment when they were stepping into her, they kissed each other, to the laughter of the crowd on the bridge. And M. Paul, taking up the oars, set off for the Grenouillère like the others.

When they arrived, it was almost three o'clock. The great floating café was packed with people. The vast raft, covered with a tarred roof supported by wooden columns, is moored to the charming island of Croissy by two gangways, one of which leads into the center of this aquatic inn while the other links the far end with a minuscule island. On the island there's a tree, so they've nicknamed it the Flower Pot. From there the gangway continues on to land near the bathing area.

M. Paul tied his boat up beside the inn, clambered over the café balustrade, then, seizing his mistress's hands, he lifted her up, and the two of them sat down at the end of a table, facing each other.

On the tow path on the other side of the river stretched a long line of vehicles. Cabs alternated with the fine carriages of the rich: some were heavy, their enormous bellies crushing the springs, harnessed to a nag with a sagging neck and broken knees; some were elegant, riding high on their thin wheels, with horses whose legs were slender and taut, who held their necks high, the bit white with foam, while the coach driver, stiff as starch in his livery, head erect on his thick neck, sat motionless, back unmoving and carrying the whip over his knee.

The bank was covered with people who had come in family parties, or in groups, or two by two, or on their own. They tore up tall grass, went down to the water's edge, mounted the path again, and, when they'd all reached the same point, they stopped, waiting for the ferryman. The loaded ferry went ceaselessly from one bank to the other, unloading its passengers on the island.

The arm of the river (which is called the dead arm) over which this drink-serving pontoon looks, seemed to sleep, so weak was the current. Flotillas of yawls, skiffs, canoes, small pedal-powered boats, gigs, boats of all shapes and kinds, skimmed along on the motionless water, passing each other, mingling together, approaching each other, suddenly stopping with a wild shake of the arms to set off again under an abrupt tensing of muscles and glide swiftly along like long yellow or red fish.

New ones were constantly arriving. Some came from Chatou, upstream; others from Bougival, downstream; laughter wafted over the water from one boat to another, there were people calling, shouting, or swearing. The rowers exposed to the burning rays of the sun the tanned and bulging skin of their biceps; and, like strange flowers, if one can imagine swimming flowers, the silk parasols in red, yellow, green, or blue carried by the girls at the rudder bloomed at the back of the boats.

A July sun flamed in the middle of the sky; the air seemed full of burning gaiety; no shiver of wind moved the leaves on willows and poplars.

Over there, on the opposite bank, the inescapable Mont Valérien displayed its fortified slopes in the harsh sunlight, while on the right, the adorable hill of Louveciennes, turning with the river, rose up in a half circle, here and there revealing through the exuberant, dark greenery of the great gardens the white walls of country houses.

In the area around La Grenouillère a crowd of strollers promenaded under the giant trees that make this part of the island the world's most delightful park. Women and girls with golden hair, breasts bulging inordinately, buttocks exaggerated, complexions plastered with powder, eyes darkened with kohl, lips blood red, laced and corseted into extravagant dresses, dragged over the fresh lawns the screaming bad taste of their outfits while beside them young men put on airs, clad in the kinds of clothes you find in fashion journals, wearing light-colored gloves and highly polished boots, carrying canes the size of a thread and sporting monocles that emphasized the stupidity of their smiles.

The island is narrow as far as the Grenouillère, and on the other bank, where a ferry also operates ceaselessly to bring people from Croissy, the fast arm, full of whirlpools, currents, and foam, roars past with torrential speed. A detachment of pontooneers, wearing the uniform of artillerymen, is camped on this bank, and the soldiers, sitting in a line on a long beam, watch the water flowing past.

The floating inn was full of sound and fury. The wooden tables, where drinks that had been spilled left thin, sticky rivulets, were covered with half-full glasses and surrounded by half-drunk people. The entire crowd was shouting, singing, bellowing. The men, hats tilted back on their heads, their faces red, with the glittering eyes of drunkards, were swaying and yelling through a need for uproar natural to animals. The women, on the lookout for a prey for the evening, had drinks bought for them while they waited. The open spaces between the tables were thronged with the inn's normal customers, a battalion of rowdy oarsmen with their girls in short flannel skirts.

One of them was going mad at the piano, and seemed to be playing with feet and hands; four couples leapt about in a quadrille; and young men looked on—elegant, correct young men who would have seemed quite the thing, had the taint not been apparent in spite of it all.

For what you smell there, and it's a smell that fills your nostrils, is all the scum of the world, all the distinguished scoundrels, all the mold of Parisian society, a mixture of counter-jumpers, play-actors, pen-pushers, gentlemen whose affairs are carefully controlled by a third party, shady speculators, tainted revelers, elderly pleasure-seekers, rotten through and through. It's a dubious cohort of all the suspicious types, half-known, half-lost, half-greeted, half-dishonored, crooks, scoundrels, pro-curers of women, knights of industry who look worthy enough, and yet who have the appearance of bullfighters who seem to say, "The first of you who treats me as a rogue will get it in the guts."

It's a place that oozes stupidity, that stinks of roguery and the kind of gallantry you see in a bazaar. Males and females are equal here. An odor of love floats over all this, and people fight over trifles, to uphold worm-eaten reputations that sword blows and bullets merely poke fur-ther holes in.

A few of the locals pass through it out of curiosity, every Sunday; a few young men, very young men, turn up every year, to learn about life. Strollers, promenading by, display themselves; a few ingenus lose their way here.

They're right to call it La Grenouillère. Next to the covered raft where people drink, right by the Flower Pot, people swim. Those women who are sufficiently well-padded come here to show their equipment naked, and to pick up business. Others, full of disdain, al-though they themselves are amplified by cotton, supported by springs, lifted here, modified there, scornfully watch their sisters paddling about.

On a small platform, swimmers jostle each other to be able to dive head-first. As long as spindles and as plump as pumpkins, knotted like olive branches, bent over forwards or backwards by the amplitude of their bellies, and invariably ugly, they leap into the water, sending it splashing up as far as the drinkers in the café.

Despite the immense trees that lean over the floating inn, and despite the proximity of the water, the place is full of a suffocating heat. The smells of spilled drinks mingle with the odors of bodies and the violent perfumes the love-merchants rub deep into their skins and that evapo-rate in the furnace-like heat. But running under all these different scents was a slight aroma of rice powder that sometimes fades away, returns, and is always to be found again, as if a hidden hand were shaking it into the air from some invisible powder puff.

The real show was on the river, with the ceaseless coming and going of boats. The boats-women sprawled in their seats opposite their strong-wristed males, and cast contemptuous glances at those women who prowled up and down the island in search of a free dinner.

Sometimes, when a team in full flight went past at top speed, friends who had already disembarked would shout out, and the entire audience, suddenly seized with a fit of madness, would begin to howl.

At the bend of the river toward Chatou, new boats could be seen in an endless stream. They came closer, growing larger as they did so, and as faces gradually became recognizable, yet more shouts would be set off.

A boat covered with a tent and carrying four women slowly came down with the current. The woman who was rowing was small, thin, faded, wearing a cabin boy's costume and with her hair held up under a waxed hat. Opposite her, a plump blond woman dressed as a man, with a waistcoat of white flannel, lay on her back in the bottom of the boat, her legs in the air on a bench, one on each side of the rower, and she smoked a cigarette while at each movement of the oars her breasts and belly shook, jolted by the shock. At the far end, under the cover, two attractive girls, tall and slender, one a brunette and the other a blonde, sat with their arms around each other's waists, keeping a constant eye on their companions.

A shout rose up from La Grenouillère: " 'Ere's Lesbos!" and suddenly there was a furious uproar. A terrifying hurly-burly took place. Glasses fell over. People leapt up on tables. In the pandemonium everyone was bellowing, "Lesbos! Lesbos! Lesbos!" The shout rolled around, became indistinct, became nothing more than a kind of terrible howling, then, suddenly, it seemed to leap up again, climbing up through space, covering the plane, filling the heavy foliage of the great trees, spreading out to the distant hillsides, reaching the sun itself.

The rower, faced with this ovation, had stopped tranquilly. The fat blonde spread out in the depths of the boat turned her head nonchalantly, lifting herself up on her elbows, and the two pretty girls, in the back, begin to laugh and greeted the crowd.

Then the shouts redoubled, sending tremors through the floating inn. The men lifted their hats, the women waved their handkerchiefs, and all the voices, deep and high, shouted together, "Lesbos!" You felt that this race, this collection of the corrupt of the earth, were greeting a chief. It was for all the world just like the cannon fired by squadrons when an admiral passes before them.

The large flotilla of boats also acclaimed the women's craft, as it set off again at its sleepy speed to come to shore somewhat further down.

M. Paul, unlike the others, took a key from his pocket, and whistled with all his strength.[15] His girl, nervous and even paler, grasped his arm to make him stop, and this time when she looked at him, it was with rage in her eyes. But he seemed infuriated, as if stirred by some male jealousy, a deep, instinctive, disorderly fury. He stammered, his lips trembling with indignation, "Shameful! They ought to be drowned like dogs with a stone tied around their necks."

But Madeleine suddenly flew into a rage. Her high little voice be-came a whistle, and she spoke garrulously as if she were pleading her own cause: "What's it to do with you? Aren't they free to do as they please, since they don't owe anything to anybody? Just let us off for a bit, you and your manners, and don't stick your nose into what doesn't concern you . . . "

But he interrupted her: "It's the police that ought to be concerned! I'll get them thrown into Saint-Lazare, see if I don't!"

She made a sudden start. "You?"

"Yes, me! And in the meanwhile I forbid you to talk to them. Hear me? I forbid it."

Then she shrugged her shoulders and, suddenly calm again, said, "My sweet, I'll do what I like. If you don't like it, then you can take yourself off straightaway. I'm not your wife, am I? So just shut up."

He didn't answer, and they stayed staring at each other, mouths set and breathing fast.

At the far end of the big wooden café, the four women came in. The two dressed as men came first: one was thin, looking like a little boy grown old, with yellowish tints on her forehead; the other, her fat filling her white flannel clothes, her backside bulging in her broad trousers, waddled like a plump goose, with her vast thighs and her sunken knees. Their two friends followed them, and the crowd of oarsmen surged for-ward to shake their hands.

The four of them had rented a little chalet by the water, and they lived there as two married couples might live.

Their vice was public, official, obvious. People talked about it as something quite natural, something that made them almost likeable, and there were whispers of strange tales, dramas set in train by wild, female jealousy, and secret visits by well-known women, actresses who came to visit the little house by the water.

A neighbor, revolted by these scandalous rumors, had alerted the po-lice, and the brigadier, followed by one of his men, had gone to make an enquiry. Their's had been a delicate mission. After all, you couldn't actually accuse these women of anything, since they didn't go in for prostitution. The brigadier, very puzzled, not even knowing exactly what were the crimes of which they were suspected, had asked ques-

---

15. In France, whistling is a sign of an audience's disapproval.

tions at random, and made a monumental report concluding that they were innocent.

That had raised a laugh all the way to Saint Germain.

Like queens, they sauntered slowly through La Grenouillère, apparently proud of their fame, happy to be stared at, rising above this crowd, this rabble, these plebs.

Madeleine and her lover watched them come, and in the girl's eye a flame burst into fire.

When the first two were at the end of the table, Madeleine called out, "Pauline!" The fat girl turned round, stopped, still grasping the arm of her female cabin boy.

"Gosh! It's Madeleine . . . Come and talk to me, darling."

Paul gripped his fingers around his girl's wrist, but she said to him, "You know, laddy, you can just take yourself off," with such expression that he fell silent and stayed on his own.

Then all three of them stood together, chatting softly. Happy moments of merriment passed along their lips as they spoke rapidly, and Pauline, from time to time, stole a glance at Paul with a bantering and ill-intentioned smile.

Finally he could stand it no longer, he leaped abruptly to his feet, and was at her side in a bound, trembling in all his limbs. He seized Madeleine by the shoulders. "Come on, I insist," he said. "I forbade you to talk to these tramps."

But Pauline raised her voice and began to abuse him in her fishwife's repertory. Around them people were laughing. Others came closer. Some stood on tiptoes to get a better view while Paul stood in astonishment under this rain of muddy insults. He had the impression that the words coming out of that mouth and falling on him soiled him like dung. Faced with the growing scandal, he retreated, turned on his heels, and leaned on his elbows on the balustrade facing the river, turning his back on the three victorious women.

He stayed there, watching the water and sometimes, with a rapid gesture, as if it had been torn from him, he removed with a shaking finger a tear that had formed in the corner of his eye.

The thing was that he was wildly in love, without knowing why, despite all his delicate instincts, despite what reason and even will might say. He had fallen into that love as one falls into a muddy hole. Tender and fine by nature, he had dreamed of exquisite relationships, love affairs that were ideal and passionate, and the fact was that this little cricket of a woman, as stupid as prostitutes always are, exasperatingly stupid, not even pretty, thin and quick-tempered, had caught him, captivated him, possessed him from head to toe, body and soul. He was experiencing that female sorcery in all its mystery and omnipotence, that unknown force, that prodigious domination, that comes goodness knows from where, the sway held by the demon of the flesh, that throws the most sensible man at the feet of a worthless prostitute who has nothing to explain her fatal and supreme power.

And there, behind his back, he could sense that something infamous was being cooked up. Their laughter pierced his heart. What should he do? He knew perfectly well, but he couldn't bring himself to do it. He stared unblinkingly at a fisherman who stood on the opposite bank, his line motionless.

Suddenly the fisherman snatched from the river a little silver fish that wiggled on the end of the line. Then he tried to pull out the hook, twisted it, turned it, but in vain, then, seized with impatience, he began to pull, and the animal's entire bleeding throat came out, together with the entrails. And Paul trembled, torn to the heart himself. He felt as if the hook were his love and that if he had to pull it out, everything he had in his breast would come out in exactly the same way, at the end of an iron hook, plunged deep into his entrails, while Madeleine held the line.

A hand fell on his shoulder. He leapt and spun around; his girl stood beside him. They did not speak. Both of them leaned on the balustrade, staring at the river.

He tried to think of something to say to her, and could find nothing. He couldn't even succeed in working out what was going on in his mind; all he felt was a sense of joy that she should be there next to him, that she had come back, and a shameful cowardice, a need to be all-forgiving, a longing to let her do anything at all, provided she didn't leave him.

At last after a few minutes he asked her very gently, "Shall we go? It'd be more comfortable in the boat."

She answered, "Yes, honey."

He helped her down to the boat, supporting her, squeezing her hands, full of tenderness, a few tears still in his eyes. Then she looked at him with a smile, and they kissed again.

They went back upstream slowly, following the bank with its willows, a bank covered in grasses, tranquilly bathed in the afternoon warmth.

When they returned to Grillon's restaurant it was barely six, so, leaving the boat, they set off on foot along the island toward Bezons, through the meadows, beside the tall poplars that border the river.

The grain stood high, ready to be harvested, and full of flowers. The sun, moving lower in the sky, spread over it a sheet of reddish light, and in the soft warmth of the closing day the wafting odors of the grass mingled with the damp smells of the river, impregnating the air with a tender languor, a gentle happiness, a kind of vapor of well-being.

Hearts felt a soft weakness and a form of communion with that calm evening splendor, that vague and mysterious trembling of life, with that penetrating, melancholy poetry that seemed to emanate from the plants, to form objects, and to bloom, revealing itself to the senses in that soft and contemplative hour.

He, for his part, felt all this; but the woman didn't. They walked side by side. Suddenly, tired of being silent, she sang. She sang in her sharp, tuneless voice some popular air, something to be found in everyone's memory, that abruptly tore asunder the deep and serene harmony of the evening.

Then he looked at her, and felt an uncrossable abyss between them. She swiped at the grass with her umbrella, her head slightly lowered, watching her feet and singing, threading notes together, trying out roulades, even daring to try the odd trill.

Her narrow little forehead, which he loved so much, must be empty, then, completely empty! Inside there was nothing but this organ-grinder's song and the thoughts that accidentally formed there were like that music. She didn't understand anything about him. They were further apart than if they didn't live together. So, did her kisses go no further than her lips?

Then she raised her eyes to him and smiled again. He was moved to the very marrow of his bones, and opened his arms in a redoubling of love. He embraced her passionately.

Because he was crushing her dress, she eventually broke free from him, murmuring to make up for it, "There, there, I love you, honey."

But he grasped her by the waist and, seized with madness, carried her off at a run and kissed her on the cheek, on the temple, on the neck, leaping in happiness as he did so. They collapsed, gasping for breath, at the foot of a bush set ablaze by the rays of the setting sun, and before they'd got their breath back, their bodies fused, while she still could not understand his exaltation.

They were walking back slowly, holding both hands, when suddenly, through the trees, they saw on the river the boat with the four women. Plump Pauline saw them, too, for she sat up, blowing kisses to Madeleine. Then she shouted, "See you this evening!"

Madeleine answered, "See you then."

Paul felt as if his heart had suddenly been wrapped in ice.

And they went back to have dinner.

They settled under one of the arbors by the water and began to eat in silence. When night had fallen, someone brought a candle, covered with a glass chimney, which lit them with a feeble, trembling light, and all the time they could hear the explosions of shouts from other oarsmen in the great first-floor dining room.

Toward dessert, Paul, taking Madeleine's hand tenderly in his own, said, "I feel very tired, sweetheart. Let's go to bed early tonight."

But she saw through his ploy and threw him an enigmatic glance, that perfidious glance that appears so quickly in the depths of a woman's eye. Then, after thinking it over, she said, "You go to bed if you want, but I've promised to go to the ball at the Grenouillère."

He gave a pathetic smile, one of those smiles you use to cloak the most horrible of sufferings, but he answered with a caressing, distressed voice, "If you were kind, we'd both stay home." She shook her head without opening her mouth. He insisted, "Please, honey lamb!" Then she broke roughly away from him. "You know what I told you. If you're not happy, the door's open. No one's holding you. As for me, I've given my word, and I'll go."

He put his elbows on the table, hid his head in his hands, and stayed there, lost in painful reverie.

The oarsmen came down again, still shouting. They set off in their craft for the ball at the Grenouillère. Madeleine said to Paul, "If you're not coming, say so, and I'll ask one of these gentlemen to take me."

Paul got up, "Let's go!" he murmured.

And off they went. It was dark now, a night full of stars, penetrated with a fiery blast, a heavy sigh, ardent, full of ferment and living seeds that mingled with the breeze to weigh it down. A warm caress passed over faces, making people breathe more quickly, gasp a little, so thick and heavy did it seem.

The craft set out, each bearing on its prow a Venetian lantern. You couldn't see the boats themselves, only these little, colored lights, dancing swiftly by like delirious fireflies. And on all sides voices could be heard in the shadows.

The boat belonging to the young couple slipped softly along. Sometimes, when a speeding boat went close by them, they would suddenly catch a glimpse of the oarsman's white back lit by his lamp.

When they had turned the bend in the river, they could see the Grenouillère in the distance. The inn was bedecked with chandeliers, with garlands of colored lights, with clusters of lamps. On the Seine could be seen moving slowly a few large wherries representing domes, pyramids, complicated monuments in flames of all kinds of shades. Flaming festoons hung down to the water's edge and sometimes a red or blue lamp at the end of an immense and invisible fishing rod, looked like a great star hanging there.

All this illumination shed a glare of light around the café, lighting from top to bottom the great trees on the bank, whose trunks stood out in a pale gray and whose leaves were a milky green against the deep blackness of the sky and the fields.

The orchestra, which consisted of five local musicians, hammered out its dance-hall music, a thin bouncy sort of music that set Madeleine singing again.

She wanted to go in right away. Paul would have liked to walk around the island first, but he had to give in.

The crowd was less mixed now. The oarsmen were almost the only ones there, with a handful of bourgeois scattered here and there, and a few lads with their girls. The director and organizer of this ball, majestic in a tired black suit, could be seen everywhere, his ravaged face recalling that of an old merchant of cheap public pleasures.

Plump Pauline and her companions weren't there. Paul breathed again.

They danced. Couples facing each other leapt and bounded madly, throwing their legs so high in the air that they reached the nose of the person standing opposite them.

The women, thighs spread wide apart, sprang about under their enveloping skirts, showing what was underneath. Their feet went up over their heads with surprising ease, and they shook their bellies, waggled their backsides, wiggled their breasts, unleashing around them an energetic smell of sweating women.

The males squatted like toads with obscene gestures, contorting their bodies, grimacing and hideous, turning cartwheels on their hands, or in an effort to be funny, aping good manners with ridiculous grace.

A fat maid and two servants brought the drinks.

This café-boat was covered only with a roof, and had no walls separating it from the outside world, such that the wild dance was displayed to the peaceful night and the firmament with its dusting of stars.

Suddenly, Mont Valérien, opposite them, seemed to light up as if a fire had been set behind it. The light extended, increased, invading the sky little by little, describing a great circle of pale, white light. Then something red appeared and swelled, blazing red like iron on an anvil. It grew slowly into a circle, seeming to issue from the earth, and the moon, detaching itself from the horizon, soon mounted calmly into space. As it rose, its crimson tinge grew softer, turned yellow, a clear, gleaming yellow. And it seemed to grow small as it floated away.

Paul watched it for a long time, lost in this contemplation, forgetting his mistress. When he turned round, she had disappeared.

He went looking for her, but could not find her. He ran an anxious eye over the tables, moving ceaselessly back and forth, asking here and there if she'd been seen. No one had seen her.

He was wandering around like this, tortured by worry, when one of the waiters said to him, "You're looking for Madeleine? She left just now with Madame Pauline." At that very moment, Paul saw, standing at the far end of the café, the cabin boy and the two pretty girls, all three with their arms around each other's waists, spying on him and whispering. He realized what had happened and dashed like a madman onto the island.

At first he ran toward Chatou, but, faced with the plain, he doubled back. Then he began to search through the thick shrub, wandering wildly, stopping occasionally to listen.

The toads, all round the horizon, were making their short, metallic cry.

In the direction of Bougival an unknown bird modulated a few sounds that reached him, muted by distance. On the broad lawns the moon shed its pale light like a sprinkling of cotton wool. It penetrated the foliage, so that its light flowed down the silvered bark of the poplars, its brilliant rain pierced holes in the trembling summits of the great trees. The intoxicating poetry of that summer's night penetrated Paul in spite of himself, pierced his mad anguish, stirred his heart with ferocious irony, increasing to the point of blind fury in his gentle and meditative soul his need for ideal tenderness, his longing to pour out his heart passionately into the bosom of an adored and faithful woman.

He was forced to stop, strangled by sobs that rushed through him and tore him apart.

The crisis passed, and he set off again.

Suddenly he received a shock like a knife blow. A couple were kissing, over there, behind the bush. He ran over; two lovers were there, their silhouettes stretching sharply out toward him, locked in each other's arms, joined in an endless kiss.

He dared not call, knowing full well that She would not answer. And he was also terribly frightened of discovering them suddenly.

The repeated phrases of the quadrilles with the heart-rending solos of the cornet, the false laughter of the flute, the sharp rage of the violin tore his heart in two, increasing his suffering. The wild music ran limping under the trees, now soft, now louder in a brief breath of wind.

Suddenly he thought that she might have come back. Yes! She would have come back! Why not? He had lost his head for no reason at all, stupidly carried away by his terror, by disorderly suspicions that had been invading him for some time now.

Seized by one of those strange calms that sometimes pass through the deepest despair, he went back to the ball.

He glanced round the room. She wasn't there. He walked round the tables and suddenly found himself once more face-to-face with the three women. He must have looked strange and desperate, for all three burst into a simultaneous gale of laughter.

He took to his heels, set off along the island once more, hurled himself through the undergrowth, gasping for breath. Then he listened again. He listened for a long time, for his ears were buzzing. But at last he thought he heard, not far away, a little piercing laugh he knew very well; he moved softly forward, crawling, parting the branches—his breast so shaken by the pounding of his heart that he was unable to breathe.

Two voices were murmuring words he couldn't yet hear. Then they fell silent.

Then he had an immense desire to run away, not to see, not to know, to escape forever, to go far from that wild passion that was tearing him apart. He would return to Chatou, take the train and never return, never see her again. But the image of her suddenly invaded him, and he saw her in his mind's eye when she awoke in the morning in their warm bed and rubbed herself tenderly against him, throwing her arms around his neck, her hair hanging loose, slightly bunched on her forehead, her eyes still closed and her lips open for the first kiss; and the sudden memory of that morning caress filled him with wild regrets and mad desire.

They were talking again; and he went closer, bent double. Then a light cry ran under the branches close by him. A cry! One of those cries of love that he had learned to recognize in the hours of their joyful lovemaking. He came closer still, yet closer, as if in spite of himself, drawn irresistibly without realizing anything . . . and he saw them.

Oh! if it had been a man, that other lover! But this! This! He felt himself enchained by their very infamy. And he stayed there, crushed, overwhelmed, as if he had suddenly discovered a beloved body mutilated, a monstrous crime against nature, a disgusting profanation.

Then in a flash of involuntary thought, he remembered the little fish whose entrails he had seen torn out . . . But Madeleine was murmuring, "Pauline!" in the same impassioned tone she'd used to say "Paul!" and he was filled with such pain that he fled as fast as he could.

He collided with trees, fell over a root, set off again, and found himself suddenly before the river, facing the fast stream lit by the moon. The swift current created great whirlpools filled with moonlight. The high bank dominated the water like a cliff, leaving at its foot a large dark band where the whirlpools extended into the shadows.

On the other bank, the country houses of Croissy spread out, fully visible.

Paul saw all that as if in a dream or through a memory. He thought of nothing, he understood nothing, and all these things, his very existence even, seemed to him vague, far off, forgotten, finished.

The river was there. Did he understand what he was doing? He was mad. Nevertheless, he turned back toward the island, toward Her. And into the calm night air in which still danced the weak and obstinate refrains of the dance, he let out, in a desperate, high-pitched superhuman voice, the terrible cry: "Madeleine!"

His heart-rending cry crossed the broad silence of the sky and ran round the horizon.

Then with a formidable leap, the leap of an animal, he jumped into the river. The water splashed up, closed over him, and at the point where he had disappeared a succession of circles appeared, spreading out right to the other bank in their gleaming undulations.

The two women had heard. Madeleine sat up. "It's Paul." A suspicion leapt up in her soul. "He's drowned himself." She leapt toward the river where plump Pauline joined her.

A heavy wherry with two men on board turned back and forth on the same spot. One of the boatmen rowed, the other drove a great stick into the water and seemed to be looking for something. Pauline shouted: "What are you doing? What's happened?" An unknown voice answered, "Someone's just drowned himself."

The two women, clinging to each other, haggard, followed the movement of the boat. The music of the Grenouillère still frolicked in the distance and seemed to accompany with its rhythms the movements of the somber fishermen and the river, which now hid a corpse, turned and whirled along, bathed in light.

The search went on. Waiting was so horrible that Madeleine couldn't stop trembling. At last, after at least half an hour, one of the men said: "Got it!" He lifted his pole slowly, very carefully. Then something large appeared at the surface of the water. The other boatman left his oars, and both of them, combining their strength, pulling on the inert mass, flung it into the boat.

Then they reached the bank, looking for a low and well-lit spot. At the moment they reached the bank the women arrived, too.

As soon as she saw it, Madeleine recoiled in horror. Under the light of the moon, he already seemed green, with his mouth, his eyes, his nose, his clothes full of mud. His closed and stiffened fingers were frightful. A kind of blackish, liquid plaster coated his entire body. The face seemed swollen and dirty water ceaselessly trickled from his hair, which was plastered with mud. The two men examined him.

"You know him?" asked one of them.

The other, a ferryman from Croissy, hesitated. "Yes, I do think I've seen that face before, but you know, looking like that, it's not easy to recognize." Then suddenly he added, "Why, it's M. Paul!"

"Who's he?"

The other man went on. "He's Paul Baron, the senator's son, the lad who was so much in love."

The other added philosophically, "Well, he's certainly stopped messing about now. But what a waste!"

Madeleine had fallen to the ground and was sobbing. Pauline went over to the body and asked, "Is he really dead? Completely dead?"

The men shrugged their shoulders. "Oh, after all that time! Not a doubt of it."

One of them asked, "Was he staying at Grillon's?" "Yes," replied the other. "Better take him back there, they'll pay a wad to get him back."

They returned to their boat and set off again, moving slowly away because of the swiftly flowing current. Long after they were lost from sight from the place where the two women had remained, the sound of their regular oar strokes falling in the water could be heard.

Then Pauline took poor, tear-stained Madeleine in her arms, caressed her, embraced her for a long time, consoled her. "Look, it isn't your fault, is it? There's no way you can stop men doing stupid things. He wanted to do it, and, after all, it's his own decision!" Then, lifting her up, she said, "Come on, sweetheart, come and sleep at our place. You can't go back to Grillon's tonight." She hugged her again. "Come on, we'll make you better," she said.

Madeleine got up, still weeping, but less violently, her head resting on Pauline's shoulder, as if she had taken refuge in a more intimate and safer tenderness, a love that was more familiar and more trustworthy, and she slowly walked away.

PROSE POETRY

Bertrand

◆
―――――――――

Aloysius Bertrand (1807–1841) was one of the first French poets to explore the area of prose poetry, and his Gaspard de la nuit, *subtitled "Fantasies in the Style of Rembrandt and Callot," was described by Baudelaire as an influential source for his own prose poetry. Bertrand lived and worked in Dijon, a city he captures in his writing and which he transforms into a wonderfully evocative and highly imaginative Gothic stage set. Remote both physically and intellectually from the Romantic figures who dominated Paris, his work strikes a modern reader as profoundly original, its medievalism less part of a current vogue than something deeply felt, and its nightmare quality no mere nod to literary convention but intrinsic to the writer's fantasy world. His prose poems suggest a somewhat morbid and gothic sensibility, with strong erotic overtones, but, unlike the massive novels of gothic masters such as Pétrus Borel, they reveal a delight in cryptic formulae and epigrammatic brevity. Some of his prose poems inspired compositions by Maurice Ravel.* Gaspard de la nuit *was first published after the poet's death by his friend, the critic Sainte-Beuve.*

TEXT USED: *Gaspard de la nuit*, ed. C. Asselineau (Brussels: Muquardt, 1868).

THREE POEMS FROM GASPARD OF THE NIGHT
(1868)

THE SERENADE

At night, all cats are gray.

Folk proverb

A lute, a guitar, an oboe. Discordant and ridiculous symphony. Mme Laure on her balcony, behind a venetian blind. No lanterns in the street, no lights in the windows. A horned moon.

*

"Is that you, d'Espignac?"

"Alas, no."

"So it's you, is it, my little Almond Flower?"

"Neither the first nor the second."

"What! It's not you again, M. de la Tournelle? Be off with you! Always getting the wrong end of the stick!"

The musicians whispering to one another:

"All the councillor will get for his troubles is a cold."

"But isn't the suitor afraid of the husband?"

"Of course not! The husband's off in the West Indies."

Meanwhile, what are they whispering together?

"A hundred louis a month."

"Charming!"

"A carriage with two liveried lackeys."

"Superb!"

"A house in the princes' quarter."

"Magnificent!"

"And my heart full of love."

"Oh, what a lovely little slipper that would be for my foot!"

The musicians continue to mutter under their breath:

"I can hear Mme Laure laughing."

"The cruel one's coming round."

"Yes indeed! Orpheus with his lyre could charm tigers in the days of antiquity."

Mme Laure: "Come closer, my sweet, and let me slip my key to you on the end of a ribbon."

And the councillor's wig grew moist from a dew not distilled by the stars. "Hey there, Gueudespin," shouted the evil female, as she closed the balcony, "quick, take a whip and rub the gentleman dry for me."

SCARBO

> Lord, grant me, at the hour of my death,
> the prayers of a priest, a linen shroud, a
> pine coffin and a dry place.
>
> *The Paternosters of M. le Maréchal*

"Whether you die absolved or damned," Scarbo muttered in my ear tonight, "you'll have for your shroud a spider's web, and I'll bury the spider with you!"

"Oh! Let me at least have for a shroud," I said to him, my eyes red from weeping so much, "the leaf of a poplar in which the breath of the lake can rock me."

"No!" sneered the mocking dwarf, "you would be food for the evening dung beetle as it hunts blinded by the setting sun!"

"So would you rather," I replied, still sobbing, "would you rather see me sucked dry by a tarantula with an elephant's trunk?"

"Well," he said, "here's consolation for you! You'll have for your shroud the gold-spotted bands of a snake skin, in which I shall bind you as if you were an Egyptian mummy."

"And from the shadowy crypt of Saint-Benignus, in which I shall prop you up against the wall, you will have all the time in the world to hear the little children sobbing in limbo."

ONDINE

> I thought I heard a vague harmony en-
> chant my sleep and next to me spread out
> a murmuring like broken songs, sung in a
> sad and tender voice.
>
> CH. BRUGNOT, *The Two Genii*

"Listen, listen! It's me, Ondine, touching with these drops of water the sonorous diamonds of your window lit by the pale rays of the moon. And here in her watered silk dress, the lady of the castle, who contemplates from her balcony the beautiful starry night and the fine sleeping lake.

"Each wave is a water sprite who swims in the current, each current is a path that winds its way to my castle, and my castle is a liquid structure in the depths of the lake, in the triangle of fire, earth, and air.

"Listen, listen! My father beats the croaking water with a branch of green alder, and my sisters' foamy arms caress the fresh islands of grasses, water lilies, and irises, or play tricks on the leafless, bearded willow that fishes with his rod!"

*

When she had murmured her song, she begged me to receive her ring on my finger so that I would be Ondine's husband, and visit her castle with her so that I could be the king of the lakes.

And since I replied that I loved a mortal woman, sulky and scornful, she shed a few tears, burst out laughing, and disappeared in a sudden shower that dripped whitely along my blue window panes.

Baudelaire

◆

Although he acknowledged the influence of Bertrand, Baudelaire sought to forge the genre of the prose poem into something new and different, uniquely capable of conveying the complexities and bizarre juxtapositions of modern city life. Refusing the lyricism of earlier prose poets and abandoning the balladic echoes still found in Bertrand, he succeeded in creating what he termed "a poetic prose, musical but without rhythm and rhyme, both supple and staccato enough to adapt itself to the lyrical movements of our souls, the undulating movements of our reveries, and the convulsive movements of our consciences."

TEXT USED: *Petits Poèms en prose* (Paris: Michel Lévy, 1869).

THREE SHORT PROSE POEMS (1869)

THE CROWDS

Not everyone has a gift for taking a plunge into the multitude: there is an art to enjoying the crowd, and they alone can draw from the human race a feast of vitality on whom a fairy has bestowed, while they were still in their cradles, a taste for disguise and masks, a hatred of home life, and a passion for travel.

Multitude and solitude: equal and interchangeable terms for the poet who is active and productive. Those who are not able to people their solitude are equally unable to be alone in a busy crowd.

The poet benefits from an incomparable privilege which allows him to be, at will, himself and others. Like those wandering souls in search of a body, he enters, when he so desires, into the character of each individual. For him alone, everything is vacant; and if certain places appear to be closed to him, that is because in his eyes they are not worth the bother of visiting.

The solitary and pensive stroller finds this universal communion extraordinarily intoxicating. He who finds it easy to espouse the crowd knows feverish pleasures which will be eternally denied to the selfish man, who is as tightly sealed as a strong box, or the lazy man, who is as self-contained as a mollusc. He makes all the professions his own, all the joys and all the sufferings that chance presents to him.

What men call love is very small, very restricted, and very weak compared with this ineffable orgy, this holy prostitution of the soul which gives itself entirely, poetry and charity, to the unforeseen which reveals itself, to the unknown which chances by.

It is good from time to time to teach the fortunate of this world, if only to humiliate, momentarily, their stupid pride, that their are joys superior to their own, joys which are more immense and more delicate. Founders of colonies, pastors of peoples, missionary priests living in exile in the world's farthest corners, have doubtless known something of this mysterious intoxication; and in the bosom of the vast family their genius has created for itself, they must sometimes laugh at those who pity them for a fate so troubled and an existence so chaste.

LOSS OF A HALO

"Good gracious! You here, my dear? You, in a den of iniquity? You, the drinker of quintessences! You, the eater of ambrosia! Truly, it's enough to surprise me."

"My dear, you know how terrified I am of horses and vehicles. A moment ago, as I was crossing the boulevard, in great haste, and hopping across the mud, through that moving chaos where death arrives at a gallop from all directions at once, my halo, in a sudden movement, slipped from my head and fell into the mire of the tarmac. I didn't have the courage to pick it up. I thought it would be less disagreeable to lose my insignia than to break my bones. And then, I said to myself, it's an ill wind that blows nobody any good. Now I can stroll about incognito, perform despicable acts, indulge in the pleasures of the scum, like ordinary mortals. And here I am, just like yourself, as you see!"

"You should at least advertise the loss of your halo or ask the police to get it back for you again."

"Good Lord, no! I feel perfectly happy here. You're the only one who recognized me. Moreover, dignity bores me. And what's more, it's a delight to think that some bad poet will pick it up and impudently stick it on his head. What pleasure it would give me to make someone happy! And especially if that someone also made me laugh! Just think of X or Z! Hey? Wouldn't that be a joke!"

THE GENEROUS GAMBLER

Yesterday, amid the crowds on the boulevard, I felt myself brushed against by a mysterious Being whom I had always longed to know and whom I recognized immediately, although I had never seen him. He no doubt nurtured a similar desire where I was concerned, for as he passed by he gave me a meaningful wink which I hastened to obey. I followed him attentively, and before long he led me down into a dazzling underground dwelling, which glittered with a degree of luxury that none of the better Parisian abodes could come anywhere near equaling. It struck me as strange that I could so frequently have passed by this prestigious retreat without even suspecting the entrance to it. In that dwelling there reigned an exquisite, though heady, atmosphere, in which one forgot almost instantaneously all the tiresome horrors of life; there one breathed in a somber beatitude, like that which the lotus-eaters must have experienced when setting foot on an enchanted island, lit by the glow of an eternal afternoon, they felt arise within them, to the soothing sounds of melodious cascades, the longing to see no more their homes, their wives, their children, and never to return again to the sea's soaring breakers.[1]

There you could see strange faces of men and women marked by a fatal beauty which I felt I had seen already, at times and in countries which I was incapable of recalling exactly and which inspired within me more a fraternal sympathy than that fear that usually arises from the sight of the unknown. Were I to try to find some way of defining the singular expression of their gaze, I would say that I had never seen eyes gleaming more energetically with the horror of boredom and the undying desire to feel themselves alive.

By the time we sat down, my host and I were already old and perfect friends. We ate, and we drank exorbitantly all manner of extraordinary wines, and, what is no less extraordinary, it seemed to me, after several hours, that I was no more drunk than he was. Meanwhile, gambling, that superhuman pleasure, had from time to time interrupted our frequent libations, and I have to confess that I had gambled on my soul and lost it with heroic insouciance and lightness of heart. The soul is so impalpable, and so often useless, and sometimes such a nuisance, that I felt no more emotion on losing it, than if, on a stroll, I had mislaid my visiting card.

We spent a long time smoking a few cigars whose incomparable savor and perfume left in our hearts a sense of nostalgia for countries and joys we had not known, and, intoxicated with all these delights, I seized a brimming goblet and dared to shout, in an outburst of familiarity which

---

1. *lotus-eaters . . . breakers:* This passage is a reference to Tennyson's poem "The Opium Eaters."

did not seem to displease him, "To your immortal health, Old Cloven Hoof!"

We also chatted about the universe, its creation and its future destruction; about the great idea of the age, by which I mean progress and perfectibility, and in general of all forms of human infatuation. On that subject, his Highness poured out an unending flow of light-hearted and irrefutable jokes, and expressed himself with a smoothness of diction and a tranquil drollery that I have never found in the most celebrated human conversationalists. He explained to me the absurdity of the different philosophies which have, until now, taken hold of the human mind and even deigned to confide in me a few fundamental principles, the benefits and ownership of which it would not be fitting for me to share with anyone at all. He made no complaint whatsoever about the bad reputation he had attracted throughout the world, assured me that he himself was the person most concerned by the destruction of *superstition* and admitted to me that as far as his own power was concerned he had been afraid on only one occasion, which was when he had heard a preacher, more subtle than his colleagues, shout out from the pulpit: "Dearly beloved, never forget, when you hear anyone vaunt the progress of enlightenment, that the Devil's finest trick is to persuade you that he does not exist!"

The memory of that famous orator led us naturally to the subject of academies, and my strange host assured me that in many cases he didn't disdain to inspire the pen, the page, and the conscience of teachers, and that he almost always attended in person, although invisible, all academic gatherings.

Encouraged by so much kindness, I asked him if he had any news of God, and if he'd seen him recently. He replied, with a carelessness tinged with a certain sadness, "We bow to each other when we meet, like two old noblemen, in whom an innate politeness cannot completely stifle the memory of former resentment."

It is doubtful whether His Highness has ever given so long an audience to a simple mortal, and I was afraid I might be abusing his good will. Finally, as shivering dawn whitened the window panes, this famous person, sung by so many poets and served by so many philosophers who work for his glory unawares, said to me, "I want you to have good memories of me, and I'd like to prove to you that I, of whom so much ill is spoken, am sometimes a *good old* devil, to use one of your everyday expressions. To make up for the irremediable loss of your soul, I'll give you the prize you would have gained if fate had been on your side, that is, the ability to soothe and defeat throughout your entire life that strange disease of Boredom, which is the source of all your illnesses and all your wretched progress. Never will you form a desire without my helping you to achieve it; you will reign over your common fellow men; you will be provided with flattery and even adoration; silver, gold, dia-

monds, and fairy-tale palaces will come to seek you and beg you to accept them without your having to make any effort to win them; you
will change country as often as your fancy decrees; you will grow drunk
on pleasure and never weary of it, in charming lands where the weather
is always warm and where the women smell as sweet as flowers, —et
cetera, et cetera . . . ," he added, rising and dismissing me with a kind
smile.

Had I not been afraid to humiliate myself before so great a gathering,
I would willingly have fallen at the feet of this generous gambler, to
thank him for such unheard-of munificence. But little by little, after I'd
left him, my incurable distrust returned to me; I no longer dared to
believe in such prodigious good fortune and, as I went to bed, saying
my prayers through a remnant of imbecilic habit, I repeated half-asleep,
"My God! Lord, my God, make the devil keep his promise to me!"

Rimbaud

◆

Arthur Rimbaud (1854–1891), perhaps the nineteenth century's most extraordinary poetic genius, producing most of his highly original and frequently enigmatic poetry between the ages of fifteen and nineteen, seized on the freedoms and contrasts of prose poetry, taking it well beyond the point it had reached with Baudelaire. His determination to capture the unknown, his exploitation of all the senses, his delight in the unexpected image and his exploration and juxtaposition of lexicons not usually employed in poetry all lead to a remarkably muscular, innovative, and disturbing recreation of prose. Critics have used many paradigms in an attempt to explain his poetry, from the esoteric to the erotic, from the political to the intensely private, but attempts to reduce its possibilities to one single reading invariably fail to contain all its suggestions or accommodate its power.

FURTHER READING: *A Season in Hell*, tr. Norman Cameron (London: Anvil Press Poetry, 1994).
BIOGRAPHY: Enid Starkie, *Arthur Rimbaud* (New York: W. W. Norton, 1947).
TEXT USED: *Illuminations* (Paris: Mercure de France, 1914).

THREE ILLUMINATIONS (1874)

AFTER THE FLOOD

As soon as the idea of the Flood had been calmed,
A hare stopped in the sainfoins and the moving bellflowers and said its prayer to the rainbow through the spider's web.
Oh the precious stones that hid themselves away—the flowers that were already looking.
In the dirty high street the stalls were set up, and barks were dragged toward the sea which rose up over there in tiers, as in the engravings.

Blood flowed, at Blue Beard's—in the abattoirs—in the circuses, where God's seal whitened the windows. Blood and milk flowed.

The beavers were building. The "mazagrans"[1] steamed in the public houses.

In the great house of windows, still steaming, the children in mourning looked at the wonderful images.

A door slammed, and on the village square, the child wheeled his arms, understood by the weather vanes and the steeplecocks everywhere, under the dazzling hailstorm.

Madame xxx set up a piano in the Alps. The mass and first communions were celebrated at the hundred thousand altars of the cathedral.

Caravans set out. And the Splendid Hotel was built in the chaos of ice and darkness at the Pole.

From that time, the Moon has heard jackals howling through the deserts of thyme, —and eclogues in clogs groaning in the orchard. Then, in the violet thicket, full of buds, Eucharis told me that it was springtime.

Well up, pond, —foam, roll across the bridge and over the woods—black fabric and organs, thunder and lightning, rise and roll, —water and sorrow, rise and raise up the Floods.

For since they have faded, —oh the precious stones burying themselves away, and the open flowers! —how dull! and the Queen, the Witch, who lights her fire in the earthenware pot, will never tell us what she knows and what we do not know.

DAWN

I have embraced the summer dawn.

Nothing yet moved on the brows of the palaces. The water was dead. The encampments of shadows had not yet left the track through the wood. I walked, awakening vigorous warm breaths, and the stones that looked, and the wings that rose without a sound.

The first project was on the path which was already filled with cool pale light, a flower that told me her name.

I laughed at the blond waterfall unraveling through the pines: on the silvered summit I recognized the goddess.

Then I lifted her veils, one by one. In the avenue I waved my arms. On the plain, where I denounced her to the cock. In the town she fled through the bell towers and domes, and running like a beggar on the marble quays, I hunted her.

Above the road, near a laurel wood, I enfolded her with all her veils,

---

1. *mazagrans:* coffee liqueur.

and I felt something of her immense body. Dawn and the child fell to the bottom of the wood.

On my awakening, it was midday.

COMMON NOCTURNE

A sigh opens the operadic[2] breaches in the walls, —blurs the revolving of the eroding roofs, —disperses the limits of hearths, —eclipses the casements.— Down the vine, for I had leaned my foot on a gargoyle, I went, into the carriage whose epoch is indicated pretty clearly by its convex mirrors, the bulging panes and the curved sofas. Hearse of my sleep, isolated, caravan of my foolishness, the vehicle turns on the grace of the obliterated highway: and in a flaw at the top of the right-hand window turned pale, lunar figures, leaves, breasts;— A very dark green and blue invade the picture. Unharnessing around a gravel stain.

"Here will whistle up the storm, and Sodoms—and Solymes[3]—and wild beasts and armies, —(will postilions and dream animals they reappear under the most suffocating plantation of tall trees, to thrust me down to my eyes in the silk spring?)—and will send us whipped across the lapping waters and the widespread bushes to roll along to the barking of mastiffs . . . "

—A sigh disperses the limits of the hearth.

---

2. *operadic:* An erudite word, such as Rimbaud loved to use.
3. *Solymes:* Used here for Jerusalem.

Mallarmé

◆

Stéphane Mallarmé (1842–1898), best known for his finely wrought, beautiful, and very demanding poetry, also produced translations, journalism, and prose poetry. His subtle, enigmatic style derives in part from his refusal of cliché, his rejection of any form of banality, and his determination to give his readers the joy of discovering little by little the meaning of what he wrote. His prose poems are frequently self-reflective meditations on the function and possibilities of writing, but they also show him striving to create a blend of creative and critical writing that would elevate the prose of the daily papers to the level of imaginative writing.

TEXT USED: *Pages* (Brussels: Edmond Deman, 1891).

TWO PROSE POEMS (1891)

THE DEMON OF ANALOGY

Have unknown words ever sung on your lips, accursed shreds of an absurd sentence?

I went out from my apartment feeling exactly as if a wing had slid over the strings of an instrument, slow and light, only to be replaced by a voice pronouncing these words in a falling tone: "The Penultimate is dead," in such a way that "the penultimate" ended the line, and "is dead" broke free from that fatal suspension all the more pointlessly because it was bereft of meaning. I strolled down the street and recognized in the sound "nul" the taut string of a forgotten musical instrument, an instrument whose glorious memory must surely just have visited me with her wing or a palm, and, my finger on the key to the mystery, I smiled, begging, intellectual that I am, for a different conjecture. The phrase returned, full of promise, set free by an earlier fall of a feather or a branch, heard henceforth through the voice, until at last it spoke on its own, alive with its own personality. I was strolling on (no longer content with a single insight) reading it as the end of a line, and, once, as an experiment, adapting it to my own way of speaking; soon I began pronouncing it with a silence after "Penultimate" in which I found a painful pleasure: "The Penultimate," then the string of the instrument, so taut in oblivion on the sound *nul* no doubt, would snap, and I would add by way of a prayer, "Is dead." I did not cease trying to return to favorite thoughts, alleging, to calm myself down, that certainly *penultimate* is the lexical term meaning the last syllable but one in a word, and its manifestation was merely the ill-recanted remains of a linguistic task which daily forces a tearful interruption of my noble poetic faculty: the very sonority and the mendacious aspect assumed by the rapidity of this facile affirmation were a cause of torment. Harassed, I resolved to let words of so sad a nature wander of their own accord over my mouth, and I strolled on, murmuring in tones suitable for condolences, "The Penultimate is dead, she is dead, truly dead, the despairing Penultimate," believing that in doing so I was satisfying my disquiet, and not without the secret hope of burying it away in elaborating the psalm, when, oh horrors!, through a magic easily deduced, a magic caused by nervousness, I felt I possessed, as my hand reflected by a store window sketched the gesture of a caress that falls on something, the voice itself (the first voice, which had indubitably been the only one).

But the moment when I felt completely convinced that there could only be a supernatural explanation, the moment that marked the onset of that anguish in which my formerly lordly spirit now dies, was the moment when I raised my eyes and saw, in the street of antique dealers that I had instinctively followed, that I was standing before the shop of a lute-maker who sold old instruments that were hanging on the wall, and, on the floor, yellow palms and wings buried in the shadow, wings of ancient birds. I fled, bizarre, probably condemned to bear forever the bereavement of the inexplicable Penultimate.

AN INTERRUPTED SPECTACLE

How far civilization is from procuring the pleasures one might attribute to such a state! It astonishes me, for instance, that in every great town there does not exist a guild of those dreamers who dwell there, to support a newspaper which would comment on the day's events from the perspective appropriate to dream. *Reality* is an artifice, useful in that it fixes the average intelligence between the mirages of a fact. But through that very fact reality reposes on some universal understanding: it would, therefore, be worth seeing if the ideal possesses a necessary, evident, simple aspect that serves as an archetype. I want, simply for my own satisfaction, to write about how my poet's eye was stuck by a certain Anecdote, before the reporters distribute it to the crowd trained to assign to everything its common characteristics.

The small Prodigalities Theater combines a show revealing the living cousin of Atta Troll[1] or Bruin with its classic fairy tale "The Bear and the Genie." In recognition of the invitation made with a pair of tickets that had been left with me yesterday, I had placed my hat in the empty stall beside me, the absence of a friend bearing witness to the general taste for avoiding this naive show. What took place before me? Nothing, except this: from elusive muslin parlors taking refuge on twenty pedestals in an architecture reminiscent of Baghdad there escaped a smile and arms open to the heavy grief of the bear. Meanwhile a hero, the one who summoned forth these *sylphides* and kept watch over them, a clown, in his high silver nakedness, teased the animal with all humanity's superiority. How restful to delight, like the crowd, in the myth with all its banality and, as I had no neighbors with whom I could share my thoughts, how restful to see the ordinary and splendid vigil revealed on the stage by my quest, upheld by imagination and symbols. Unlike many reminiscences of similar evenings, the newest of accidents! aroused my attention: one of the numerous salvos of applause aroused according to the degree of enthusiasm by the illustration on stage of the authentic privilege of man, had just, interrupted by what? stopped abruptly, with a fixed outburst of glory at its height, unable to express itself. Having been all ears, we now had to be all eyes. From the mime's gesture, a taut palm in the air opening five fingers, I understood that he had ingeniously won his audience's sympathy by appearing to catch something as it flew by him, an image (no more than that) of the ease with which anyone can seize an idea. At that, moved in the light wind, the bear, rising rhythmically and gently pondering this exploit, placed a paw on the ribbons of the human shoulder. There was no one in the audience who was not gasping, for the situation was fraught with serious consequences for the honor of the race: what would happen? The other paw dropped down, supple, on an arm that rested by the bathing suit. And we could see, in this couple brought together by a secret proximity, what appeared to be an inferior man, short-set and good, standing on the apex of two hairy legs, his skull with its black muzzle only reaching halfway up the other, yet grasping, in order to understand the strategies of a genius, the body of his brilliant and supernatural brother. But he, for his part, his mouth made mad by the indefinite, raised a terrible head, moved by a visible thread, denying, horrified, a fly of paper and gold. The spectacle was clear, vaster than the stage itself, for it had the gift, which is that of art, of lasting for a long time. To make

---

1. *Atta Troll:* The German poet and prose writer Heinrich Heine (1797–1856) wrote the satirical mock epic *Atta Troll*, in which the central character is a bear.

it perfect, I let burst silently from me, without offending the attitude, which was probably fatal, assumed by the mime who held within him all our pride, the words forbidden to the scion of Arctic sites: "Be kind (this was the sense of my speech) and rather than lack charity, tell me the power of this atmosphere of splendor, dust, and voices, in which you taught me to move. My request is urgent and just. Do not appear, in an anguish which is mere pretense, to answer that you do not know, you, my subtle elder who have been rocketed up into the realm of knowledge, do not, to gain your liberty, give such an answer to me, who am still clad in the shapeless dwelling of the caves in which I plunge my latent strength anew, in the night of humble epoques. Let us authenticate through this close embrace, before the multitude waiting for such a conclusion, the pact of our reconciliation." The absence of any breath, linked with the sense of space, for I was living in a place of absolutes, one of the dramas of astral history which had chosen to play itself out in this modest theater. The crowd faded completely from sight, as an image of its spiritual situation magnifying the stage: alone, that modern dispenser of ecstasy, the gas, high up in the auditorium, with the impartiality of something elementary, continued its luminous noise of expectation.

The spell was broken. A scrap of flesh, naked, brutal, crossed my gaze as I stared at the interval between sets, a few seconds in advance of the, normally mysterious, reward that follows these performances. A bleeding scrap had been substituted beside the bear, which, his instincts rediscovered before a higher curiosity with which the theatrical glow had endowed it, dropped back on all fours and, as if taking Silence with it, went off with the silent walk of its species, to sniff and sink its teeth into its prey. A sigh, almost free of disappointment, incomprehensibly relieved the audience, whose lorgnettes, from row to row, sought out, lighting up the clarity of their glasses, the performance of the magnificent imbecile who had evaporated in its fear. But what they saw was an abject meal preferred, perhaps, by the animal to that very thing which he would have had first to form *in our image*, if he were to enjoy it. The curtain, hesitating until then to increase the danger or the emotion, suddenly dropped its list of prices and clichés. Like everyone else I got up, to get a breath of air outdoors, astonished at not having felt, yet again, the same kind of impression as my fellow men, but remaining serene: for my way of seeing things, after all, had been superior and may well have been the right one.

IMAGES OF
CHILDHOOD

George Sand

◆

George Sand (1804–1876) wrote numerous novels, plays, and essays. In novels like Lélia *and* Indiana *she explores the position of women in contemporary society, while* Consuelo *charts the development and sufferings of the artistic spirit.* The Master Pipers, *written in the aftermath of the 1848 revolution, blends the themes of romantic love, ideal (and idealized) marriage, and the mind and fate of the artist, with a detailed and anguished exploration of the nature of violence and the possibility of nonviolent social change. Intensely involved in much of the social, artistic, and political life of her time, she left a detailed and illuminating autobiography that is one of the first to explore in close detail the effect that personal and national history experienced in childhood can exert on the adult. Her evocation of childhood, which is far removed from that of the happy innocent enshrined in certain early Romantic texts, also explores the long-term effects of many contemporary educational practices.*

FURTHER READING: *Flaubert–Sand Correspondence,* tr. Francis Steegmuller and Barbara Bray (New York: Knopf, 1993), *Lélia,* tr. Maria Espinosa (Bloomington: Indiana University Press, 1978), *The Master Pipers,* tr. Rosemary Lloyd (Oxford: Oxford University Press, 1994), *Winter in Majorca,* tr. Robert Graves (Chicago: Chicago Academy, 1978).
BIOGRAPHY: Donna Dickenson, *George Sand* (Oxford: Berg, 1988); Renee Winegarten, *The Double Life of George Sand* (New York: Basic Books, 1978).
TEXT USED: *Histoire de ma vie* (Paris: Victor Lecou, 1854–1855).

DESCHARTRES

FROM *THE STORY OF MY LIFE* (1854–1855)

It was when I was about seven that I begin to experience the teaching of Deschartres. For a fairly long time I had no cause for complaint, for, in the first years he was as calm and patient with me as he was rough and brutal with Hippolyte.[1] That was why I made rapid progress with him, for he explained things clearly and concisely when he was calm, but once he started to lose his temper, he became less precise, his explanations were confused, and anger, which made him stutter, rendered him completely incomprehensible. He mistreated and bullied poor Hippolyte, and yet the boy was quick to learn and had an excellent memory. He refused to take into consideration the fact that a robust nature needed some activity and grew exasperated by lessons that lasted too long. I'll willingly admit, despite the friendship I felt for my brother, that he was an unbearable child. His sole thought was for breaking things, destroying them, teasing people, and playing bad tricks on all and sundry.

One day he threw some flaming logs into the chimney, under the pretext that he was *sacrificing to the gods of the underworld*, and he set fire to the house. Another day, he put some powder in a big log so that it would explode in the hearth and hurl the stew into the middle of the kitchen. He claimed that he was studying the theory of volcanos. Then he tied pans to dogs' tails and delighted in watching them flee in terror, howling, across the garden. He put clogs on the cats, by which I mean that he glued their four feet in coconut shells and threw them onto ice or parquet floors, to watch them as they slid, falling over hundreds of times with horrifying snarls. Other times, he proclaimed that he was Calchas, the great priest of the Greeks, and, under the pretext of sacrificing Iphigenia on the kitchen table, he would take the knife destined for less illustrious victims, and wildly striking left and right would wound others or himself.

It's true that from time to time I would join in this bad behavior, as far as my nature urged me to, for I was less fiery than he. One day when we'd seen a pig killed in the farmyard, Hippolyte dreamed up the game of treating the garden cucumbers in the same fashion. He pushed a little wooden stick into the end that he claimed represented the animal's neck, then, stamping on the poor vegetables with his feet, he squeezed out all the juice. Ursula collected it in an old flower pot, to make pudding, and I gravely lit a fictional fire next to it, to grill the pork, that's to say, the cucumber, as we had seen the butcher do. This game delighted us so much that we passed from one cucumber to the other, at first choosing the fattest ones and finishing with the less plump and thus swiftly devastated one bed on which the gardener had lavished his care. I leave you to imagine his grief when he saw this scene of carnage. Hippolyte, in the midst of these corpses, looked like Ajax immolating the troops of the Greek army in his delirium. The gardener complained and we were punished, but that didn't bring the cucumbers back to life, and none were eaten that particular season.

---

1. *Hippolyte:* George Sand's half-brother.

Another of our unpleasant joys was to make what the children of our village used to call *dog-deceivers*. These are holes that you fill with light soil, soaked in water. You cover it over with little sticks on which you put tiles and a light layer of earth or dry leaves, and when you've set your trap in the middle of a path or a walkway in the garden, you spy out passers-by and hide in the bushes to watch them cover themselves with mud, and hear them shout at the abominable hoodlums who *invent* such tricks. If the hole is deep enough, your victims can break their legs, but ours never offered that danger, for they were fairly wide. What was funny was to see the gardener's terror when he felt the earth disappear below his feet in the finest spots of his well-raked gardens, and realize it would take him an hour to repair the damage. One fine day we caught Deschartres. He always wore handsome ribbed stockings, very white, with short trousers and pretty Nanking gaiters, for he was vain about his feet and legs. He was always extremely clean and very selective in his choice of shoes. In addition, like all pedants (this is a characteristic sign that lets you recognize them with certainty, even when they are not earning a living as teachers), he always walked with his legs held stiff and his feet turned out. We were walking behind him, to get a better view. Suddenly the ground gave way beneath him, and there he was up to his knees in a yellow mud which had been admirably prepared to stain his stockings. Hippolyte feigned astonishment, and all Deschartres's rage had to fall on Ursula and me, but we were not at all afraid of him, we were well away from him before he had time to fish his shoes out again.

As Deschartres used to beat my poor brother cruelly, while merely saying silly things to us little girls, Ursula, Hippolyte, and I had made a pact that we two would take the blame for all sorts of things. We had even dreamed up a little comedy to make this deception seem more likely, and for a while it was quite successful. Hippolyte used to take the initiative: "Look at those two little fools!" he used to shout, whenever he broke a chair or made a dog howl too near Deschartres's ear, "they never do anything right! Would you just stop that, girls!" And he would take to his heels while Deschartres, peering out the window, would be amazed to find no little girls in sight.

One day when Deschartres had gone to sell some animals at the fair, for his first duties were connected with agriculture and the management of our farms, Hippolyte was supposed to be studying his lesson in the *great man's* room, and took it into his head to play the great man in all seriousness. He put on his great hunting coat, which fell down to his ankles, put on the hat with the tassel, and strolled up and down the room, feet sticking out, hands clasped behind his back just like the teacher. Then he set about imitating his language, went up to the blackboard, drew some pictures with chalk, began a demonstration, grew angry, stuttered, shouted that his pupil was a *dirty ignoramus* and a *thick-*

head; and then, satisfied with his talent for imitation, he stood at the window and lectured the gardener on the way he was shaping the trees. He criticized him, reprimanded him, swore at him, and threatened him, all in the style of Deschartres, and with his usual shouts. Either because the imitation was pretty good, or because he was so far away, the gardener, who in any case was a simple and credulous lad, was taken in and began to answer back and mutter. But you can imagine his stupor when he saw the real Deschartres a few strides away from him, watching this scene and not losing a single gesture or word from his little Sir Echo! Deschartres ought to have laughed at it, but he couldn't bear anyone to cast aspersions on his personality, and unfortunately Hippolyte didn't see him, for Deschartres was hidden by the trees. The tutor, who had returned from the fair earlier than expected, climbed silently up to his room and abruptly opened the door, at the moment when the mischievous boy was saying in a loud voice to an imagined Hippolyte, "You don't work, you write like a cat, and you spell like a thief! Bang, bang, that's for your ears, you animal!"

At that point the scene was doubled and while the false Deschartres boxed the ears of an imaginary Hippolyte, the true Deschartres boxed the ears of the true Hippolyte.

Banville

◆

Théodore de Banville (1823–1891) was a virtuoso poet, known for his extraordinary skill in manipulating rhyme and rhythm. Yet he was also a master of prose style, writing short stories, a travelogue, and a delicately nostalgic autobiography. While his autobiography focuses primarily on the writers and artists he had known through his lifetime, he does devote several witty, bittersweet chapters to his early childhood. The limpidity and sensitivity of his prose style confers on what might otherwise be banal incidents a symbolic dimension of timeless power.

TEXT USED: *Mes Souvenirs* (Paris: Fasquelle, 1910).

SERVICEBERRIES
FROM *MY CHILDHOOD* (1882)

My grandfather's system of education, a system he handed on to me, and the one I have followed faithfully, consisted in letting children do everything they wanted to do and in giving them everything their hearts desired, preventing them only from ever hearing anything untrue or stupid. Thus his little Zélie[1] was divinely good, because everyone around her had always been good. She was intelligent and intuitive because no one had ever taught her not to be. Her mother was a homebody and enjoyed remaining at home, but her father took her on long walks and, through games, taught her botany and entomology without all the horrible fuss of notepads and textbooks.

As they wandered through the countryside, they often went into an attractive vineyard, where they were made very welcome. Little Zélie

---
1. *Zélie:* Banville's mother.

simply adored those pretty fruits that are called serviceberries, and the owner, out of the goodness of his heart, or the wine grower if the owner was away, used to give her as many as would fit into her pockets and her little hands, for in the vineyard there was a giant service tree, which was more than a hundred years old and could have provided the whole of Moulins[2] with serviceberries. One day as they were passing along the road that ran near the vineyard, Grandfather noticed his daughter looking in its direction and sighing, but she said nothing, not wanting to be indiscreet.

"Ah!" said the father, reading her thoughts, "wouldn't it be fun to visit our friend in the vineyard and ask him for some serviceberries?"

"Oh, yes! said the little girl, sighing all the more.

"The only thing is, perhaps he'll think we ask for them too often. But, after all, there is a way of fixing everything up, and that would be to buy the service tree, because then we could go and get berries whenever we wanted to."

"Oh!"

"Yes," Grandfather went on, "but perhaps those people might not like us to go into their place at any time of the day to go to our service tree. I think the simplest thing would be to buy the vineyard as well!"

No sooner said than done. The owner happened to be there, Grandfather went in with his little daughter and straightaway he bought the property just as he had said he would. This was that Font-Georges[3] which so enchanted my childhood that later I celebrated it, none too poorly, according to Sainte-Beuve.[4] The vines, together with peach trees and other fruit trees, were planted on a small hill, and the terrain dropped down to a large stream which ran past the master's little house. In this lower part of the property, there were cultivated fields, meadows, and fine trees, including the tall service tree, and further on there was a lofty chapel of poplars, and most important of all a clear, limpid, cold fountain fed by springs, which poured its water into a pool shaded by willows. The peasants would come and wash their linen here. From time immemorial, the peasants had brought coins to the fountain to repay, as far as their circumstances would permit them, the benevolent spirits of the springs, and in exchange for this naive offering, they drank there, or took home the salutary waters, which immediately cured them and their families of illnesses and fevers, or so they claimed.

On that score, I do not know what to believe, but what is truly certain is that at night, in the moonlight, Fairies came to dance and sing near

---

2. *Moulins:* The town in central France where Banville spent his childhood.

3. *Font-Georges:* Farm including the spring in Moulins, celebrated by Banville in a poem with that title, included in his collection *Le Sang de la coupe* (1857).

4. Charles-Auguste Sainte-Beuve (1804–1869), French critic, novelist, and poet. His system of closely interrelating a writer's life and works became highly influential in the second half of the nineteenth century.

the murmuring waters, and as I myself have often slept in the grass there, it's probably at such times that they kissed my childish lips and passed on to me the divine and incurable fever of poetry.

In buying his little girl an entire vineyard so that she could have serviceberries, Grandfather had shown yet again how wise he was, for he was wise to the point of genius and beyond all expression. He knew that all unhappiness is the result of a misunderstanding or of a commission that has been carried out poorly. That's why he took all his messages himself, and would leave the most important tasks to go and mail his letters personally. He taught his granddaughter, who later taught me in her turn, that if you have a piece of cake and a piece of bread, you should always begin by eating the cake, because you never know if you'll live long enough to eat the bread as well.

Judith Gautier

◆

Judith Gautier (1845–1917) was the daughter of the writer Théophile Gautier and the actress Ernesta Grisi. She played a central role in building Richard Wagner's reputation in France, wrote many novels based in an exotic and largely imaginary Orient, and produced a fascinating, if romanticized, autobiography, the first volume of which throws harsh light on the fate of a child torn between two very different parents and their even more different families, at a time when adults rarely thought it worth explaining to children why they were taking certain actions on their behalf. In the passage translated here, Judith Gautier attempts to re-enter the linguistic and imaginary world of childhood to recreate the sense of being sent, without explanation, to live in a convent school.

BIOGRAPHY: Joanna Richardson, *Judith Gautier, A biography* (New York: F. Watts, 1987).
TEXT USED: *Le Collier des jours* (Paris: F. Juven, 1902).

CARLOTTA GRISI
FROM *THE NECKLACE OF DAYS* (1902)

The fairy, the radiant diva shimmering in sequins and light, the godmother whom I had not yet seen and who was to overwhelm me with wonderful presents, suddenly decided to take an interest in me.[1] And she showed her solicitude in a way that was not at all what anyone could have imagined.

---

1. *The fairy:* Carlotta Grisi (1819–1899), Judith Gautier's aunt on her mother's side, was a leading ballerina. It was for her that the poet Théophile Gautier, Judith's father, wrote the story of the ballet *Giselle*.

My free and easy outdoor life, my tomboy ways as I climbed trees and played in the streets, really couldn't be seen as suitable for the niece and goddaughter of a person of such importance as a dancer at the Opera . . . If the family wanted her to take an interest in me and shed her protection over me, all that would have to change, as quickly as possible.

The completely acceptable thing for a well-bred young lady to do was to go into a convent in order to be brought up and instructed there according to all the rules.

This project certainly cannot have pleased my father, but he had to give in to my mother, who could not see that anyone could make serious objections to anything her sister had decided.

This time, I was taken by treachery. I had not the slightest indication of what was going to happen to me, not an inkling, except for a little sadness in those I frequented, a few enigmatic and threatening words spoken by the aunts, and a complete indulgence. If I expressed surprise at no longer going to Mlle Lavenue's,[2] Aunt Lili[3] would mutter through her teeth, "Enjoy what you have left."

It was Aunt Zoé who took me, one day in the fall. As we took no packets with us, there was nothing to stop me thinking it was a simple stroll. On our way, she explained to me, in embarrassed tones, that I was going to see people I didn't know yet, but who belonged to the other side of my family, the Italian side.

"It doesn't matter what they do, you are a real Gautier," she said. "We'll see if they succeed in winning you over to their side. In the meanwhile, they're taking you by force."

Between my father's family, who were strict and conservative middle-class people, and my mother's family, who were mainly show people, enjoying a noisy celebrity, there could exist little sympathy. Indeed, I would have to confess that among the women there was an open aversion which, moreover, they never abandoned.

At the end of our walk, the Pantheon appeared. To me it seemed colossal, and in order to look at it longer I walked along almost backward, my aunt pulling me by the hand, as we walked around the square to reach the steep, narrow street that runs up la Montagne-Sainte-Geneviève.

Some old buildings, ugly and gray, a dark-green gate with an arch above it and a spyhole: we had arrived.

There was a chain with a handpull; when you pulled it, you heard the nearby sound of a cracked bell. First the spyhole slid open, although we couldn't see who was looking at us, then a little door inside the big

---

2. *Mlle Lavenue:* Judith's teacher up to this point.

3. *Aunt Lili:* The two aunts mentioned here, Lili and Zoé, are Judith's paternal aunts, sisters of the poet Théophile Gautier.

door swung half open, with a grating sound of bolts and keys, and a young nun in a white veil, smiling all over her face, greeted us and invited us to come in.

"I don't want to go in!" I shouted, pulling Aunt Zoé away.

But she clung to me and pushed me in front of her.

"You don't want to! . . . Are you forgetting the policemen? . . . " she said. "You can't do just what you want to in life."

The door had closed behind us, soundlessly, and I had the impression that I was going down into a cave. We were in a narrow paved space covered with a ceiling and leading to another massive door, which was jealously closed and can't have opened very often, for an accumulation of dust filled all its crevices. On the right, near that door, bulged a kind of turret in oak, whose function I didn't understand. On the left, along the wall that bordered the street, ran a corridor, and it was in this direction that the nun led us. This corridor led to a series of cells, each of whose doors bore a number. One of them was partly opened, and from it we could hear the sound of many voices. Three ladies, seated, filled the narrow space, into which the nun led us, with the silky folds of their dresses. The back of the cell was closed from chest level right to the ceiling by a grill in black wood, which formed little squares, behind which moved a veiled shadow.

But the three ladies seized me, all speaking at the same time in Italian with very sonorous voices, and I stared at them with considerable astonishment.

One of the unknown ladies struck me as a character from a fairy tale, the queen of the "once upon a times," or the fairy godmother who changes pumpkins into carriages, and rats into powdered servants. She was tall, very stout, most majestic, highly colored, and wore a striking outfit, covered in white laces and jewels, with amazing feathers on her hat. She was a noble Spanish lady, the Marchioness of Guadalcazar, and I later learned that the gloomy nun I had vaguely glimpsed was the daughter of this sumptuous person.

The second lady, who was no longer young, was richly dressed, short, stocky, with a crotchety and grumpy appearance, and she filled me from the outset with a deep antipathy. She was my maternal grandmother.

Giselle[4] was there, too, the least striking of these three ladies, the least remarkable, in her sober and discreet elegance, so she was the one I noticed least, fascinated and dumbstruck as I was by the marchioness, whose laughter and tumultuous speech dominated everything.

Aunt Zoé had refused to sit down; simultaneously embarrassed and hostile, she remained upright in her thin black dress, her lips pressed tight, maintaining her distance and keeping at arm's length this worldly group who somehow shocked her principles and her narrow bourgeois

---

4. *Giselle:* That is, Carlotta Grisi (*see note 1*).

ideas, while at the same time striking her as somehow enviable. Humiliated that she had come, and distressed at being obliged to abandon me to others, she immediately signaled her protest through her attitude and her desire now that her mission had been accomplished.

"This is the young lady," she said, when she was able to get a word in, "I'm putting her into your hands, and now I'll take my leave."

"Not without me!" I shouted, running toward her.

"My poor child, I am not your mother, I have no authority over you; it has been decided that you're to remain here, and there's not a thing I can do about it."

She kissed me, obviously close to tears, and went rapidly away, while Carlotta picked me up in her arms, saying to me, "Every one gets a turn, I'm as much your aunt as she is, and you know perfectly well we don't want to kill you."

With a light step she carried me down the corridor, with everyone following her, to the oak turret, which swung around and revealed a kind of hollow niche. This was the "tour," which alone provided access into the convent. My aunt stepped in with me, laughing at the way it worked, in an attempt to make me laugh, too. The marchioness came next, filling the entire niche with her corpulence and her frills; then came the grandmother, groaning and grimacing at this bizarre system.

The tower sister, veiled in black, received us in a kind of vast lodge, very bright and gleaming, and soon there arrived, stepping quickly and setting her chaplets clicking, the nun we had glimpsed behind the grill in the parlor. She threw herself into the marchioness's arms and also embraced Carlotta, who said to her, "Dear Sister Sainte-Madeleine, this is my goddaughter. She won't be in your class, but you will be a little mother to her all the same, won't you?"

I wasn't surprised at that point by the strangeness of my entry into the convent, in the arms of an Opera ballerina and accompanied by such an astounding marchioness.

Other nuns had joined our group and took us to see the pupils' playground, enclosed by dull buildings, then we went into the sisters' private garden. There, paths covered with gravel, long flower beds bordered with box, fruit trees, espaliers, and as a special ornament a trellis which stretched down an entire side and formed a gallery of greenery.

Wrapped in myself, I didn't answer a single word to the questions I was asked, or to all the kindnesses with which I was overwhelmed, in an attempt to remove my resentment. I was like a captive animal that doesn't think it worth struggling and whose captors believe they have conquered. But I measured at a glance the height of the walls, I examined the nature of the stones and the placing of the branches; the espaliers struck me as providing steps that could help me climb out; the broken bottles along the tops of the walls didn't worry me at all, for I thought I'd be able to avoid them, and the tops of trees suggested the presence of neighboring gardens and showed me the path to freedom. But if I were to take it, I realized I would need to use patience and ruses.

I was already forming a plan in my head: if I could hide, I'd wait until the following morning, and then I would escape.

To make them relax their guard a little, I pretended to take an interest in the flowers, and feigned a desire to run about. This appearance of tameness was immediately rewarded.

"Off you go, run about and enjoy the garden," they told me. At first I went ahead of the group, then I lingered behind as they went on walking, and I set about preparing myself a furtive exit which would spare me the farewells. I watched them go back through the garden gate, which one of the sisters locked with a key.

Quickly I glanced around me. I was entirely alone, but the garden offered no corners in which I could hide, the fruit trees were spindly, and only the interwoven stems of the vines and their leaves offered a thick network.

I had no difficulty climbing up the outside of the trellis, but would the flat part that formed the top be capable of supporting me? Wouldn't it be likely to collapse under my weight? I sought out a spot well provided with leaves and branches, and slipped in cautiously. There were a few cracks, but nothing broke. Then, stretched out on my stomach, completely buried, I stayed utterly motionless.

I soon heard the sound of the gate opening again and the clacking of sandals. At first the sisters looked calmly for me, then they began to call me.

"Now, little girl, don't hide, there's no point, for we can see each other perfectly well!"

"What liars!" I said to myself. "They can't see me at all. I'm the one that can see them."

After walking around the garden several times in vain, they must have imagined that I'd slipped behind them when they went out, without being seen, for they left the garden.

The sky was covered with clouds, and night was falling rapidly. A bell began to ring very loudly and for a very long time. Then I heard from the courtyard on the other side of the wall the sound of feet and voices, sounds I couldn't explain at that stage; this was the pupils crossing the courtyard to go to the refectory.

This unknown place grew gloomier and gloomier in the growing dark. My heart was full and could certainly have cried, for there was no one to see me—but I didn't want to. If I happened to cry too loudly, I would be heard and discovered. More sisters came back in larger numbers, very worried, this time. There were some in white veils, who ran everywhere, then they went away again, and more time passed. I heard the bell again, and soon a great silence fell over everything.

It was utterly black, and a thin rain began to fall, softly wetting everything without making a sound. The leaves sheltered me a little, but the drips fell down my neck, and I felt completely stiff from staying still so long. I stuck it out, however, and I was so sad that I no longer thought about being frightened, despite the shivering of the wind in the branch, the muffled sounds of the city, and the unknown darkness around me.

Suddenly an animal galloped past me, swearing and screaming, almost running over me. No doubt it was cats chasing each other, but I thought it was a wolf, the wolf I'd forgotten all about! In a few leaps I clambered down the trellis, trembling with fear.

Lanterns appeared at the end of the path. It was two sisters who were returning yet again, sheltered by umbrellas.

This time I let them catch me, piteously. Sister Sainte-Madeleine kept me with her all night long, warmed me up, and tried to make me eat. All I could swallow was a little sweetened wine in which she must have mixed a tranquilizer, and I must have fallen asleep, for I remember no more.

Loti

◆

Pierre Loti is the pseudonym of Julien Viaud (1850–1923). He was a prolific novelist, drawing on his experiences as a sailor to evoke the exotic in a simple yet sensuous prose. Although much of his work has fallen out of favor, he was greatly admired during his lifetime for the exoticism of his works and for the pure simplicity of his prose style. Works such as Iceland Fisherman *and* Madame Chrysanthème *led to his election to the French Academy in 1891, defeating Emile Zola. His evocation of childhood,* A Child's Story, *is a strikingly rich, nostalgic, and sensitive account of a rather lonely and deeply imaginative boy, set in a landscape that symbolizes the child's own sense of self.*

FURTHER READING: *Japan: Madame Chrysanthemum*, tr. Laura Ensor (London: KPI, 1985), *The Desert*, tr. Jay Paul Minn (Salt Lake City: University of Utah Press, 1993).
BIOGRAPHY: Lesley Blanch, *Pierre Loti: Portrait of an Escapist* (London: Collins, 1983).
TEXT USED: *Le Roman d'un enfant* (Paris: Calmann-Lévy, 1924).

A DREAM
FROM *A CHILD'S STORY* (1890)

This is a dream dating from my fourteenth month of May. It came to me on one of those warm soft nights that follow long, delicious dusks.

In the bedroom I had had since childhood, I had fallen asleep to the far-off sounds of the airs for round dances that sailors and little girls sing around the May bouquets, in the streets. Right until the moment when I fell profoundly asleep, I had listened to those very old refrains of France that the working classes in our region repeat loudly and freely, and that reached me muffled, faded, poeticized, through the tranquil silence. I had been rocked somewhat strangely by those sounds of people enjoying life, those overwhelming joys, the sort experienced in their very brief youth, by those beings who are more simple than we are, and less conscious of death.

In my dream, there reigned a kind of half-light, which wasn't gloomy but, on the contrary, as mild as the real May night outside, mild, warm, and full of the lovely scents of spring. I was in our back yard, and there was nothing misshapen or strange about it. Along the walls covered with flowering jasmine, honeysuckle, and roses, I wandered with no fixed purpose, and with a sense of unease, seeking I know not what, aware that someone was expecting me and that I deeply longed to see that person, or perhaps something unknown was about to happen and was filling me with delight even before it happened . . .

At the point where a very vigorous rosebush grows, planted by one of our ancestors and kept out of respect, although it scarcely produces a single rose every two or three years, I saw a girl, standing motionless and smiling mysteriously.

The darkness grew heavy, making me feel listless.

All around me it grew darker and darker, and yet, she alone was clad in a kind of vague light, as if shed by a reflector and outlining her silhouette clearly with a narrow line of shadow.

I guessed that she must be extremely pretty and youthful, but her brow and her eyes remained lost under a veil of night. The only thing I could see well was her mouth, which partly opened to smile in the delightful oval of the lower part of her face. She stood right next to the old flowerless rosebush, almost in its branches. The night grew thicker and thicker. She seemed to be perfectly at home, wherever she had come from, and although no door had opened to let her in. She seemed to find it perfectly natural to be there, just as I for my part found it natural for her to be there.

I went right up to her to see her eyes, which intrigued me, and then suddenly I saw them perfectly well, despite the darkness which grew thicker and thicker and heavier and heavier. Like her mouth, they were smiling, and they weren't just any old eyes—as they might have been if she'd represented an impersonal statue of youth, for instance. No, on the contrary, they were very remarkable. They were *someone's* eyes. The more I looked, the more they reminded me of a gaze I had already loved and that I was finding again, with wave on wave of tenderness. . . .

I woke with a start and tried to retain the phantom as it fled away, taking flight, becoming less and less touchable and more and more unreal as my mind grew ever more awake in its effort to remember. Could it be possible, however, that she was not and had never been anything but a lifeless void, who had now plunged back again into the abyss of imaginary things, things that have faded from view . . . I wanted to go back to sleep, to see her again; the thought that it was over, that it was finished, that it was merely a dream, filled me with disappointment and almost despair.

It took me a long time to forget her. I loved her, I loved her tenderly. As soon as I thought of her again, I felt an inner shock, at once sweet and painful. Everything that was not her seemed to me for the moment devoid of color and substance. This was indeed love, true love, with its immense melancholy and its immense mystery, with its supreme sad charm, which it left behind like a perfume on everything it had touched. The corner of the yard where she had appeared to me, and that old flowerless rosebush which had surrounded her with its branches, retained in my eyes something painful and delightful that came from her.

Vallès

◆

Jules Vallès (1832–1885) is remembered above all, perhaps, for his revolutionary journalistic articles and his uncompromising role in the Paris Commune of 1870–1871. He was imprisoned in 1853 for his revolutionary thinking, and exiled for his part in the Commune, but was allowed to return to France in 1880. A committed socialist, he constantly used his journalism to attack the hypocrisy of the bourgeoisie. His newspaper, Le Cri du Peuple, *was a vocal opponent to the complacent, self-seeking politicians of the age. Devoid of self-pity, highly intelligent, and often searingly ironic, his was a profoundly uncomfortable view of the Second Empire and the Third Republic. Little of his writing has been translated in English: his focus on contemporary issues and his idiosyncratic style, with its puns and onomatopoeias make his work particularly resistant to translation. His semi-autobiographical trilogy,* Jacques Vingtras, *is characteristic of his thematic and stylistic innovations. It opens with a searing depiction of the alienation of childhood, with its suffering and its loneliness. The rage with which Vallès rejects the Romantic image of childhood happiness, purity, and innocence is intensified by his acerbic humor and his attempts to recreate the verbal world of the child through a constant experimentation with language.*

FURTHER READING: *The Insurrectionist* (Englewood Cliffs, N.J.: Prentice Hall, 1971). Apart from this, little of Vallès has been satisfactorily translated into English. For an entertaining and sympathetic study, see Walter Redfern, *Jules Vallès: Feet First* (Glasgow: University of Glasgow French and German Publications, 1992).
TEXT USED: *L'Enfant* (Paris: Grund, 1950).

TWO SCENES FROM CHILDHOOD (1881)

Was it my mother who fed me? Was it a peasant woman who gave me her milk? I have no idea. Whatever breast it was that I bit, I cannot recall a single caress from the days when I was very small; I was not coddled, tickled, or cuddled. But I was thoroughly whipped.

My mother says, "Spare the rod and spoil the child," and she whips me every morning; when she doesn't have time in the morning, she puts it off for noon, but rarely after four o'clock.

Mlle Balandreau puts tallow on it.

She's a dear old spinster in her fifties. She lives above us. At first she was pleased; as she didn't have a clock, it let her know what the time was. "Bing! Bang! Slap! Bang! Ah, there they are, beating little thinga-majig; it's time to make my breakfast coffee."

But one day when I lifted the back of my pants, because it was smart-ing too much, and was getting some fresh air between two doors, she saw me—my behind filled her with pity.

At first, she wanted to show it to everyone, rouse the neighbors; but then she thought that this was no way to save me, and she dreamed up something different.

Whenever she heard my mother say to me, "Jacques, I'm going to whip you!" she'd say, "Madame Vingtras, don't bother, I'll do it for you."

"Oh, my dear lady, you're really too kind."

Mlle Balandreau takes me off with her; but instead of whipping me, she claps her hands together and I bellow. Each evening my mother thanks her *locum tenens*.

"Any time," says the good woman, as she secretly slips me a candy.

My first memory, then, dates from a spanking. My second is full of astonishment and tears.

We're sitting beside a fire of faggots, under the mantel of an old chimney. My mother is knitting in one corner, and one of my cousins, who acts as a maid in this pauper's house, is stacking—on worm-eaten planks—a few plates of coarse crockery decorated with roosters whose combs are red and whose tails are blue.

My father has a knife in his hand, and he's carving a piece of pine; the shavings drop down as yellow and silky as scraps of ribbon. He's making me a chariot with strips of fresh wood. The wheels have already been made. They're slices of potato with their brown skin imitating the iron rim . . . The chariot is nearly completed. I'm waiting, very excited and my eyes wide open, when my father cries out and lifts his hand, full of blood. He's jabbed the knife into his finger. I turn pale and hurry to him. A violent blow stops me in my tracks. It comes from my mother, who is foaming at the lips and whose hands are curled into fists. "It's all your fault that your father's hurt himself!"

She drives me out onto the dark stairwell, banging my head on the door as she does so.

I cry, I beg for forgiveness, I call out for my father. With the terror of a child's vision, I see his hand dangling, cut completely to shreds. And it's all my fault! Why won't they let me in to see what's happening? They can whip me afterwards if they want to. I cry, but there's no answer. I can hear them moving jugs about and opening drawers: they're applying compresses.

"It's nothing," my cousin comes and tells me, as she folds a strip of linen streaked with red.

I sob and choke. My mother reappears and pushes me in the little room I sleep in, the little room where every night I'm afraid.

I must be about five, and I believe I'm a parricide.

And yet it wasn't my fault!

Did I force my father to make that chariot? Wouldn't I have preferred to lose my own blood rather than make him suffer any pain?

Yes, and I scratch my hands so that I'm in pain, too.

It's because my mother loves my father so much. That's why she flew into a rage.

They teach me to read in a book where it says, in big letters, that you have to obey your father and mother. My mother is quite right to beat me.

*

One day at school I was punished. I think it's because I was pushed by one of the big boys and fell over, rolling under the legs of one of the monitors who was passing by and who in turn fell head over heels! It gave him a dreadful bump, and he broke a bottle he was carrying in his pocket; it was a flask of brandy he used to drink in hiding, little by little, rolling his eyes as he did so. We used to see him do it. It looked as if he were praying, and he would rub his stomach in ecstasy. It's my fault that the flask is broken and that he has such a lump. The monitor flew into a rage.

He put me in detention; —he himself locked me into an empty study, turned the key, and there I was alone, surrounded by the dirty walls, in front of a geography map suffering from jaundice and a big blackboard adorned with white circles and the discipline master's ugly mug.

I wander from desk to desk. They're empty—the room is going to be cleaned, and the pupils have moved out.

Nothing, apart from a ruler, some rusty pens, a bit of string, a little drafts game, a dead lizard, a lost agate.

In a cranny, a book. I can see the spine and tear my nails as I try to pull it out. At last, using the ruler and breaking a desk in the process, I manage to do it. I hold the volume and look at the title:

ROBINSON CRUSOE

It's night.

I suddenly realize that it's dark. How many hours have I spent in that book? What's the time?

I don't know. But let's see if I can still read. I rub my eyes, I stretch my gaze, the letters fade away, the lines mingle together, I can still seize the edge of a word, but then nothing more.

My neck's stiff, my shoulders ache, my chest feels hollow. I have been crouched over, reading chapter after chapter without raising my head, without hearing anything, devoured by curiosity, glued to Robinson's side, seized by an immense emotion, shaken to the very depths of my brain and to the bottom of my heart. And in the moment when the moon showed the tip of its curve, I was sending across the sky all the birds of the island, and I saw before my eyes the long head of a poplar tree looking just like the mast of Crusoe's ship! I filled the empty space with my thoughts just as he filled the horizon with his fears. Standing before the window I dreamed of that eternal solitude and wondered how I would grow bread . . .

Suddenly I feel hungry, very hungry.

Am I going to be reduced to eating those rats I can hear in the keel of the school room? How can I light a fire? I'm thirsty, too. No bananas! He was lucky, he had fresh limes! And I just love lime juice!

Click clack, someone's turning the key. Is it Friday? Is it savages?

It's the little monitor who remembered, as he got up, that he'd forgotten me, and who's coming to see whether I've been eaten by the rats, or if I'm the one who's doing the eating . . .

Rosemary Lloyd *is Professor of French and Chair of the Department of French and Italian at Indiana University. She is the author of several books, including* Land of Lost Content: Children and Childhood in Nineteenth-Century French Literature *and* Closer and Closer Apart: Jealousy in Literature. *Her translations include* Selected Letters of Charles Baudelaire, Selected Letters of Stéphane Mallarmé, *Baudelaire's* Short Prose Poems *and* La Fanfarlo, *and George Sand's* The Master Pipers.